T0202960

Lecture Notes in Computer Science 12259

More information about this series at http://www.springer.com/series/7409

Max van Duijn · Mike Preuss ·
Viktoria Spaiser · Frank Takes ·
Suzan Verberne (Eds.)

Disinformation in
Open Online Media

Second Multidisciplinary International Symposium, MISDOOM 2020
Leiden, The Netherlands, October 26–27, 2020
Proceedings

 Springer

Editors
Max van Duijn (iD)
Leiden Institute of Advanced
Computer Science
Leiden University
Leiden, The Netherlands

Mike Preuss (iD)
Leiden Institute of Advanced
Computer Science
Leiden University
Leiden, The Netherlands

Viktoria Spaiser (iD)
School of Politics and International Studies
University of Leeds
Leeds, UK

Frank Takes (iD)
Leiden Institute of Advanced
Computer Science
Leiden University
Leiden, The Netherlands

Suzan Verberne (iD)
Leiden Institute of Advanced
Computer Science
Leiden University
Leiden, The Netherlands

ISSN 0302-9743   ISSN 1611-3349   (electronic)
Lecture Notes in Computer Science
ISBN 978-3-030-61840-7   ISBN 978-3-030-61841-4   (eBook)
https://doi.org/10.1007/978-3-030-61841-4

LNCS Sublibrary: SL3 – Information Systems and Applications, incl. Internet/Web, and HCI

This Springer imprint is published by the registered company Springer Nature Switzerland AG
The registered company address is: Gewerbestrasse 11, 6330 Cham, Switzerland

Preface

Fake news, social bots, and disinformation are prevalent phenomena in online media. The potential impact on people's opinion and perception of the truth is substantial. Hence, the automated detection and combat of misinformation is an extremely worthwhile task. Modern techniques from machine learning, text mining, and social network analysis have proven successful in this regard. But not only computer scientists show a keen interest in studying misinformation in online media. Nowadays, a bulk of human-generated content is at the fingertips of those with perhaps the strongest interest in human behavior: social scientists. Misinformation is an exciting topic for researchers in communication sciences, political sciences, and sociology.

Whereas computer scientists and social scientists have found each other in an interdisciplinary field named computational social science, the topic of misinformation in online content appeals to an even broader audience. News content is the object of study of academics in media studies and therefore also gauges the interest of researchers in the humanities. Moreover, practitioners and journalists themselves often have extremely useful and hands-on experience with the matter.

The Multidisciplinary International Symposium on Disinformation in Open Online Media (MISDOOM) seeks to bring together the abovementioned communities. This volume contains the papers accepted at the second edition of the symposium, organized in 2020. In light of the COVID-19 pandemic, the symposium did not take place on the intended dates of April 20–22, 2020, in Leiden, The Netherlands, but was postponed to October 26–27, in a fully virtual format.

In total there were 80 submissions: 57 extended abstracts and 23 full papers. The Organizing Committee decided to accept 18 full paper submissions for publication in

Fig. 1. Topics of MISDOOM 2020. Size is proportional to frequency of the word in the titles of the submissions accepted to the symposium.

this LNCS volume. In addition, 52 extended abstracts were accepted for presentation at the symposium. Figure 1 gives an impression of the topics of all contributions to the symposium.

We want to express our gratitude towards all those who contributed to organizing and running this symposium. This includes the Program Committee, the local organizers, Leiden University, the Leiden Institute of Advanced Computer Science (LIACS), the European Research Center for Information Systems (ERCIS), and the H2020 RISE-SMA Social Media Analytics project.

We hope that participants of all communities taking part in this multidisciplinary endeavor had a nice symposium and found some new insights and personal connections, especially between communities that usually do not meet so often in a symposium setting.

September 2020

Max van Duijn
Mike Preuss
Viktoria Spaiser
Frank Takes
Suzan Verberne

Organization

Program Committee

Kelechi Amakoh	Aarhus University, Denmark
Dennis Assenmacher	University of Münster, Germany
Ebrahim Bagheri	Ryerson University, Canada
Antonio Barata	Leiden University, The Netherlands
Giulio Barbero	Leiden University, The Netherlands
Alessio Maria Braccini	University of Tuscia, Italy
Jonathan Bright	University of Oxford, UK
Jens Brunk	University of Münster, Germany
André Calero Valdez	RWTH Aachen University, Germany
Chico Camargo	University of Oxford, UK
Travis Coan	University of Exeter, UK
Stefano Cresci	IIT-CNR, Italy
Eric Fernandes de Mello Araujo	Vrije Universiteit Amsterdam, The Netherlands
Natalie Fitch	Georgia Institute of Technology, USA
Lena Frischlich	University of Münster, Germany
Marcello A. Gómez-Maureira	Leiden University, The Netherlands
Jan Homburg	HAW Hamburg, Germany
Laszlo Horvath	University of Exeter, UK
Lorien Jasny	University of Exeter, UK
Kanishk Karan	Atlantic Council, India
Neta Kligler Vilenchik	The Hebrew University of Jerusalem, Israel
Mehwish Nasim	CSIRO Data61, Australia
Marco Niemann	European Research Center for Information Systems, Germany
Myrto Pantazi	Oxford Internet Institute, UK
Mike Preuss	Leiden University, The Netherlands
Thorsten Quandt	University of Münster, Germany
Dennis M. Riehle	University of Münster, Germany
Jan Schacht	HAW Hamburg, Germany
Tim Schatto-Eckrodt	University of Münster, Germany
Hyunjin Song	University of Vienna, Austria
Viktoria Spaiser	University of Leeds, UK
Stefan Stieglitz	University of Duisburg-Essen, Germany
Frank Takes	Leiden University and University of Amsterdam, The Netherlands
Ross Towns	Leiden University, The Netherlands

Heike Trautmann	University of Münster, Germany
Milos Ulman	Czech University of Life Sciences, Czech Republic
Peter van der Putten	Leiden University and Pegasystems, The Netherlands
Max van Duijn	Leiden University, The Netherlands
Suzan Verberne	Leiden University, The Netherlands
Martin Wettstein	University of Zurich, Switzerland
Florian Wintterlin	University of Münster, Germany
Taha Yasseri	University of Oxford, UK

Additional Reviewers

Belavadi, Poornima
Burbach, Laura
Hlbach, Patrick
Hosseini, Hawre
Mahdavimoghaddam, Jalehsadat
Nakayama, Johannes
Paydar, Samad
Sabou, John
Sela, Alon
Vo, Duc-Thuan

Contents

Checkworthiness in Automatic Claim Detection Models: Definitions and Analysis of Datasets

Liesbeth Allein$^{(\boxtimes)}$ ⓘ and Marie-Francine Moens$^{(\boxtimes)}$ ⓘ

KU Leuven, Leuven, Belgium
{liesbeth.allein,sien.moens}@kuleuven.be

Abstract. Public, professional and academic interest in automated fact-checking has drastically increased over the past decade, with many aiming to automate one of the first steps in a fact-check procedure: the selection of so-called checkworthy claims. However, there is little agreement on the definition and characteristics of checkworthiness among fact-checkers, which is consequently reflected in the datasets used for training and testing checkworthy claim detection models. After elaborate analysis of checkworthy claim selection procedures in fact-check organisations and analysis of state-of-the-art claim detection datasets, checkworthiness is defined as the concept of having a spatiotemporal and context-dependent worth and need to have the correctness of the objectivity it conveys verified. This is irrespective of the claim's perceived veracity judgement by an individual based on prior knowledge and beliefs. Concerning the characteristics of current datasets, it is argued that the data is not only highly imbalanced and noisy, but also too limited in scope and language. Furthermore, we believe that the subjective concept of checkworthiness might not be a suitable filter for claim detection.

Keywords: Checkworthiness · Checkworthy claim detection · Automated fact-checking

1   Introduction

Fact-checking coverage has been diffusing rapidly in U.S. political media over the past few years, with media emphasizing a journalist's supposed professional role and status as 'truth-seeker' to the public [18]. Not only has fact-checking seen an increase in news media, but also the number and spread of independent fact-check organisations and organisations linked to news papers around the world has drastically risen and expanded over the past few years. The number has nearly quintupled from 44 active fact-checkers primarily in the U.S. and Europe in 2014 [5] to around 210 active fact-check organisations in 68 countries all over the world in 2019 [33]. Research, more specifically computational journalism and computer science, has joined this growing trend and has been exploring the automation of fact-check processes. Several international workshops have

© Springer Nature Switzerland AG 2020
M. van Duijn et al. (Eds.): MISDOOM 2020, LNCS 12259, pp. 1–17, 2020.
https://doi.org/10.1007/978-3-030-61841-4_1

been organised to tackle computational fact-check models. In the Workshop on Fact Extraction and VERification (FEVER), for example, participants are challenged to create classifiers that can predict whether information retrieved from Wikipedia pages supports or refutes human-written factoid claims [34]. For the CheckThat! Lab at the Conference and Labs of the Evaluation Forum (CLEF), several research groups have built verification models that rank given web pages based on their usefulness for fact-checking a given claim, classify those pages, identify useful passages in the texts and, eventually, predict the claim's factuality based on those retrieved passages [22]. In order to automatically decide which information needs to be fact-checked, researchers have been attempting to develop computational models that extract so-called *checkworthy* claims from given texts. The checkworthiness of claims indicates that checkworthy claims are somehow distinguishable from other, non-checkworthy claims and that a claim's veracity can and should be recovered based on evidence extracted from other sources. However, the concept of *checkworthiness* lacks a generally accepted and shared definition among fact-check organisations with many of them applying their own delineation to their fact-checking pipeline. The disagreement on the definition of checkworthiness and the difference between checkworthy and non-checkworthy claims, subsequently, permeates the datasets which are used to train and test checkworthy claim detection models, resulting in inconsistent and less reliable datasets. In this paper, we discuss the definition of checkworthiness in journalism, fact-check organisations and, more elaborately, computational claim detection models for fact-checking. Furthermore, we delve into the characteristics of several datasets and how these influence model performance.

2   Checkworthiness

In this section, we aim at providing a more elaborate characterization of checkworthiness by looking at how it is defined in dictionaries, journalism, fact-check organizations and, consequently, claim detection models. Furthermore, we discuss the shortcomings of these characteristics in several datasets.

2.1   General Definition

Checkworthiness is not explicitly mentioned or defined in any of the large English dictionaries (Cambridge, Oxford, Collins, Merriam-Webster and Macmillan). Therefore, we split the concept and attempt to define it using the definitions of *check*, *worthiness* and *worthy*. By checking a claim, a person - or in this case, a system - quickly verifies its correctness [1]. Worthiness can be defined as the quality of deserving to be treated in a specified manner or deserving attention, on the one hand, and as the worth, value and suitability of something, on the other [3,4]. A checkworthy claim thus deserves to be treated in a specified manner - in this case, it should be checked - and attention should be paid to it. Moreover, a worthy claim has a certain worth, value and suitability which is relative in respect to its importance, usefulness and merit [2]. In all, checkworthiness can be defined as the characteristic of entailing a certain worth, value, suitability and, especially, need to have the correctness of what it conveys verified. That definition of checkworthiness, however, is still rather abstract. Due to a lacking generally accepted definition of checkworthiness, researchers resort to their own interpretation and delineation and/or on those specified by journalists and fact-checkers.

2.2 Datasets and Computational Models

The divergent interpretations of checkworthiness are reflected in the datasets used for training and testing checkworthy claim detection models. In this section, we discuss the characteristics of the ClaimBuster [23,24], CT-CWC-18 [28], CT19-T1 [8], CW-USPD-2016 [16] and TATHYA [29] datasets and how they define checkworthiness. Furthermore, we look at how these datasets are constructed and briefly mention some models that use these datasets. These datasets will be further analyzed in the remainder of this paper.

ClaimBuster. The team behind ClaimBuster [23,24] constructed a dataset of non-factual (NFS), unimportant factual (UFS) and checkworthy factual sentences (CFS) taken from American presidential debate transcripts [24]. The NFS category contains subjective sentences such as opinions, beliefs and questions. As for the UFS and CFS, they argue that the difference between the two is a difference in checkworthiness, with checkworthiness being rather generally defined as the present appeal of the general public to recover a claim's truthfulness. The sentences were randomly labeled by paid journalists, professors and university students with basic knowledge of U.S. politics, each of them requiring to label a number of randomly assigned screening sentences to check their labeling quality. A score between 0 and 1 is assigned to each participant based on the label agreement between them and three domain experts. Participants with high labeling agreement were named top-quality participants. In total, presidential debate transcripts from 2016, 2012, 2008 and 2004 were labeled, with each sentence labeled by at least two participants. Only sentences with an agreed label by two top-quality participants were used in the training and evaluation set, resulting in a dataset of 1,571 sentences (882 NFS, 252 UFS, 437 CFS) in 2015 [24] and 20,617 sentences (13,671 NFS, 2097 UFS, 4849 CFS) in 2017 [23].

Feature-based models such as Support Vector Machine (SVM), Naive Bayes Classifier and Random Forest Classifier were implemented for the classification task, with the models trained on the larger dataset [23] outperforming those trained on the smaller dataset [24]. SVM obtained the highest results for both datasets. Jiminez and Li [25] took a neural approach and computed a CNN + BiLSTM model and trained the model on a hand-labeled dataset of 8,231 sentences with NFS, UFS and CFS labels. They looked at the difference in model performance when the model needs to predict three classes and two classes (where NFS and UFS are concatenated in one class). It appears that, in this case, model performance is higher for all three classes when the claim detection task is approached as a three-class classification problem (Table 1).

Table 1. Overview of model performance using the ClaimBuster dataset

Model	Precision CFS	Recall CFS	F1-score CFS	Dataset size: number of sentences
SVM [24]	0.69	0.65	0.67	1571
SVM [23]	0.72	0.67	0.70	20,617
CNN + BiLSTM [25]				8231
Three classes (NFS, UFS, CFS)	0.68	0.65	0.61	
Two classes (NFS + UFS, CFS)	0.60	0.59	0.59	

CT-CWC-18. For the first CLEF CheckThat! Lab in 2018, the CT-CWC-18 was constructed and contains U.S. presidential debate transcripts and, additionally, Donald Trump speeches [7,28]. Instead of manually labeling non-factual, unimportant factual and checkworthy factual sentences, they approached it as a binary classification task and automatically assigned two labels - checkworthy and non-checkworthy - to the dataset. The gold standard labels were automatically derived from the analysis carried out by FactCheck.org. If a claim was fact-checked, it was labeled as checkworthy. However, the FactCheck annotations did not consistently cover whole sentences or sometimes exceeded sentence boundaries. In order to have sentence-level annotations, the authors gave the label of an annotated sentence part to the entire sentence and to all the sentences containing a part of the annotation. In total, the dataset contains 8,946 sentences of which 282 are labeled checkworthy. They also created an equivalent Arabic dataset by translating the English dataset.

Two models that outperformed both baselines (random permutation of the input sentences and n-gram based classifier) are a multilayer perceptron with feature-rich representation [37] and a recurrent neural network [21]. Zuo, Karakas and Banerjee [37] took a hybrid approach and combined simple heuristics for assigning a checkworthiness score to each sentence with SVMs, multilayer perceptrons and an ensemble model combining the two supervised machine learning techniques. The claim detection model of Hansen et al. [21] transforms the input claims to sentence embeddings learnt by a Recurrent Neural Network, which are subsequently sent to a Recurrent Neural Network with GRU memory units. The official evaluation measures were, among others, Mean Average Precision (MAP), Mean Reciprocal Rank (MRR) and Mean R-Precision (MR-P). Results of the two models are given in Table 2.

CT19-T1. For the 2019 edition of the CheckThat! Lab, the CT-CWC-18 was extended with three press-conferences, six public speeches, six debates and one post, all annotated by factcheck organisation FactCheck.org. The extended dataset was named CT19-T1 [8]. However, instead of determining whether or not a sentence is checkworthy, the claim detection models are expected to rank sentences in terms of checkworthiness, with a higher rank indicating a higher level of checkworthiness. The models thus output a score between 0 (certainly

Table 2. Overview of model performance in the CLEF CheckThat! Lab using CT-CWC-18 and CT19-T1 datasets

Model	MAP	MRR	MR-P	Dataset
Multilayer perceptron [37]	0.1332	0.4965	0.1352	CT-CWC-18
RNN + GRU [21]	0.1152	0.3159	0.1100	CT-CWC-18
LSTM [20]	0.1660	0.4176	0.1387	CT19-T1
Feedforward NN [13]	0.1597	0.1953	0.2052	CT19-T1

non-checkworthy) and 1 (certainly checkworthy). Checkworthy sentences in the train set are, again, automatically identified based on the transcript analyses from FactCheck.org.

Hansen et al. [20] have built further upon their RNN model [21] in the 2018 workshop. Sentences are transformed to dual sentence representations capturing both semantics (Word2Vec word embeddings) and syntactic sentence structure (syntactic dependencies for each word) which are then fed to a LSTM neural network with an attention layer on top. Favano, Carman and Lanzi [13] built a feedforward neural network that takes Universal Sentence Encoder embeddings as input. They, additionally, experimented with various training data modifications. The performance of these results are shown in Table 2.

CW-USPD-2016. For the CW-USPD-2016 dataset [16], a similar dataset and labeling method as in CT-CWC-18 and CT19-T1 are used, but the number of annotated transcripts is limited to one vice-presidential and three presidential debates. Gold standard labels are retrieved from nine reputable fact-check sources instead of one, resulting in 5,415 labeled sentences. Their feedforward neural network has a MAP of 0.427.

TATHYA. As all the datasets discussed above, the TATHYA dataset [29] collected transcripts of multiple political debates: seven Republican primary debates, eight Democratic primary debates, three presidential debates and one vice-presidential debate. They also included Donald Trump's Presidential Announcement Speech. The period in which these debates occurred is not specified, however we can infer that they took place during the 2016 presidential campaign. A statement is labeled checkworthy if it is fact-checked by at least one of eight fact-check websites (Washington Post, factcheck.org, Politifact, PBS, CNN, NY Times, Fox News, USA Today). The dataset consists of 15,735 sentences of which 967 are checkworthy. Their SVM model obtains 0.227 precision, 0.194 recall and 0.209 F1-score on the held-out test set of the presidential debates. Their clustering multi-classifier system has 0.188 precision, 0.248 recall and 0.214 F1-score on the same test set.

2.3   Fact-Check Organisations

The fact-check organisation that is regularly used as label reference in the above-mentioned datasets is FactCheck.org [12]. When fact-checkers at FactCheck.org perform fact-checking, they look for statements that are based on facts. Once they suspect that a factual, objective statement could contain disinformation, misinformation, deceit or inaccuracy, they contact the person or organisation who uttered the statement and ask for clarification and evidence to support the claim. If the given evidence is insufficient or inaccurate, they conduct their fact-check procedure. As a result, the claims for which sufficient, truthful evidence is provided are not explicitly marked on their website; only claims that underwent the full fact-check procedure are indicated. Moreover, the checked topics and persons/organisations slightly depend on the election cycle, with a focus on presidential candidates, Senate candidates and members of Congress during presidential elections, midterm elections and off-election years, respectively. In all, it can be said that FactCheck.org selects checkworthy claims based on their objectivity, their suspected falsity and the election cycle at the time of fact-checking. Politifact, on the other hand, states on their website that they choose a statement to fact-check based on its verifiability, possibly misleading character, significance, transferability and truthfulness that could be questioned by common people. Furthermore, they claim to select statements about topics that are currently in the news, attempt to balance fact-check coverage on Democrats and Republicans, and focus on the political party currently in power and people who are prone at making attention-drawing and/or misleading statements [11]. Contrary to choosing claims that are currently in the news, Snopes take a more reader-oriented stance and states that they write about topics that are in high demand or interest among their readers. They recover readers' interests by querying their search engine, reader submissions, comments and questions on their social media accounts and trending topics on Google and social media. They claim to avoid making personal judgements about a claim's importance, controversy, obviousness or depth [32]. Full Fact states that it fact-checks claims about topics of national interest - such as economy, crime, health, immigration, education, law and Europe - for which reference sources exist and for which they have in-house expertise [15]. They do not discuss how they evaluate a claim's checkworthiness in more detail. Some fact-check organisations such as Truthor-Fiction [35] do not elaborate on how they choose the statements they fact-check, thus not providing any definition of checkworthiness.

The organisations highly differ in how they define checkworthiness characteristics and how they approach the choice of checkworthy claims. The authors of the TATHYA dataset conducted an empirical analysis of the dataset and found that fact-check organisations differ in the number and choice of claims that they fact-check [29]. In the CW-USPD-2016, the authors also analysed annotation agreement between fact-check organisations and stated that agreement is low: only one out of 880 sentence is labeled as checkworthy by all nine sources, twelve sentences by seven sources and 97 sentences by four sources [16]. Fact-checkers seem to primarily focus on claims with questionable veracity, leading to initial veracity judgements and/or fact-check procedures that are not explicitly reported. This is particularly the case with FactCheck.org where factcheckers do not indicate which questioned, checkworthy claims appeared to have sufficient supporting evidence after contacting the person or organisation uttering the claim. Consequently, gold standard checkworthiness labels extracted from FactCheck.org (such as in CT-CWC-18 and CT19-T1) do not cover all checkworthy claims, but merely indicate checkworthy sentences that were not well and correctly corroborated by the speaker/writer afterwards. For example, the labeling choices of the following sequence of sentences, in which checkworthy sentences are in italics, call into question the difference between checkworthy and non-checkworthy, whereas some sentences are arguably comparable:

"I think the fact that – that under this past administration was of which Hillary Clinton was a part, we've almost doubled the national debt is atrocious. I mean, I'm very proud of the fact that – I come from a state that works. *The state of Indiana has balanced budgets. We cut taxes, we've made record investments in education and in infrastructure, and I still finish my term with $2 billion in the bank.* That's a little bit different than when Senator Kaine was governor here in Virginia. He actually – he actually tried to raise taxes by about $4 billion. He left his state about $2 billion in the hole. *In the state of Indiana, we've cut unemployment in half; unemployment doubled when he was governor.*" - Mike Pence, Vice-Presidential debate in the 2016 US campaign, labeled by FactCheck.org [28]

The checkworthiness of a claim also seems to entail temporarily popular topics and speakers. The popularity of a topic is characterized by its prevalence in the news at that moment and/or its demand and interest among the general public/readership. During the first labeling run of the ClaimBuster dataset, the authors observed that claims by more recent presidential candidates were more often labeled as checkworthy than earlier candidates [23], suggesting that checkworthiness indeed has a temporal dimension.

In sum, fact-check organisations appear to differ in their approach to select checkworthy claims. Many base their selection on the perceived falsity of the conveyed information in a claim and on the popularity of topics in the news and/or public interest at the time of speaking/writing. As a result, checkworthiness has a strong temporal character and is dependent on how an individual perceives and estimates the veracity of a claim.

2.4   Empirical Analysis of Checkworthiness

In the previous section, we analysed the definitions of checkworthiness and checkworthy claim selection as mentioned on the website of several fact-check organisations, and briefly discussed how these are reflected in the datasets. In this section, we examine the characteristics of checkworthiness as defined by Graves [17] in the datasets. Graves [17] observed political fact-checkers and elaborated on how fact-checkers at 'elite' fact-check organisations (FullFact.org, PolitiFact and The Washington Post's Fact Checker) choose which claims they are going to fact-check. He states that these organisations focus on objective claims uttered by political figures and organisations that have scientific validity and questionable veracity. We analyse if and how these characteristics are reflected in the datasets.

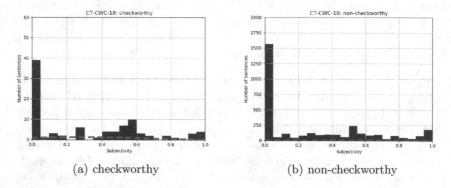

(a) checkworthy   (b) non-checkworthy

Fig. 1. Histogram of subjectivity scores of checkworthy (a) and non-checkworthy sentences (b) in CT-CWC-18

A Checkworthy Claim is Always an Objective Statement. It is never a subjective statement such as opinions and speculations [17]. Hassan et al. [23] ran a subjectivity classifier over a section of the ClaimBuster dataset. The results show that factual claims (UFS and CFS) are not exclusively classified as objective, and non-factual sentences (NFS) are more often classified as objective than subjective. They argue that a classification model basing it predictions solely on subjectivity and objectivity ratings cannot be used to separate non-factual sentences from factual, optionally checkworthy sentences. We examine whether similar observations can be made for the CT-CWC-18 and CT19-T1 datasets and run a subjectivity classifier over the two datasets. Each sentence in the dataset is assigned a subjectivity score using the sentiment library of the TextBlob package built on NLTK: a score of 0.0 denotes a highly objective sentence and a score of 1.0 a highly subjective sentence. Results are shown in Fig. 1 and Fig. 2. About 45.65% and 41.99% of all checkworthy claims in, respectively, CT-CWC-18 and CT19-T1 have a subjectivity score of 0.1 or lower, while this is the case for 51.97% and 51.67% of all non-checkworthy claims in the respective datasets. It appears that the bulk of the sentences in both datasets is classified as objective and that there is no considerably large difference between the checkworthy and non-checkworthy class in terms of objectivity/subjectivity ratings. We, therefore, argue that most checkworthy claims are indeed objective, but that objectivity cannot be used as the only parameter to distinguish checkworthy from non-checkworthy claims. A number of checkworthy claims are labeled as (highly) subjective sentences. For example, the following two sentences, labeled as checkworthy, can be interpreted as speculations, whereas they talk about possible futures in which different tax plans would be implemented:

> *"Independent experts have looked at what I've proposed and looked at what Donald's proposed, and basically they've said this, that if his tax plan, which would blow up the debt by $5 trillion and would in some instances disadvantage middle-class families compared to the wealthy, were to go into effect, we would lose 3.5 million jobs and maybe have another recession. They've looked at my plans and they've said, OK, if we can do this, and I intend to get it done, we will have 10 million more new jobs, because we will be making investments where we can grow the economy."* - Hillary Clinton, First 2016 US Presidential Debate, labeled by FactCheck.org [28]

However, it can be checked whether independent experts indeed had made these statements.

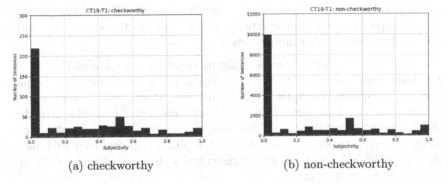

(a) checkworthy   (b) non-checkworthy

Fig. 2. Histogram of subjectivity scores of checkworthy (a) and non-checkworthy sentences (b) in CT19-T1

A Checkworthy Claim Does not Contain Information that is Common Knowledge or Self-evidently True. These statements do not often entail false information [17]. This means that people need to make a first veracity judgement for each sentence in order to reject self-evidently true or commonly known claims for fact-checking. In the field of psychology, there has been ample research on how people judge veracity and how these judgements are influenced. If a statement is ambiguous and one is uncertain about a statement's truth value, one resides to heuristic cues using attributes such as source credibility, context in which the statement is presented, the statement itself and the metacognitive experience of fluency [10]. Otherwise, the veracity judgement of a statement is mainly based on prior knowledge [10]. However, prior knowledge does not necessarily constrain the influence of source credibility, context and fluency [14], especially when previous reliance on fluency has resulted in valid judgements [31]. Types of fluency are processing fluency (i.e. the ease of processing), conceptual fluency (i.e. the ease of constructing a meaning and a more general semantic knowledge structure), perceptual fluency (i.e. the ease of perceiving) and linguistic fluency (i.e. the ease and simplicity of phonology) [6]. Fluency commonly results in a higher truth value [14]. If we want to incorporate the ability of filtering commonly known or self-evidently true claims from factoid statements into a computational checkworthy claim detection model, the model needs to have access to the context in which the claim occurs and the credibility of the source. Even though the textual context in which the claims are uttered and the speakers are provided in most datasets, much more information about the context and the speakers is necessary to make a valid judgement, such as previous debates and political persuasion of the speakers. Concerning fluency, we doubt that a general, objective veracity judgement can be based on fluency, whereas the perception of fluency differs among individuals and is, therefore, subjective. Finally, if a model wants to judge the self-evident truth of a claim based on prior knowledge, it is basically performing a first fact-check procedure where it compares a claim to the veracity of previous, comparable claims and/or to a large database of, for example, texts.

> "*In El Paso, they have close to 2,000 murders right on the other side of the wall.* And they had 23 murders. *It's a lot of murders, but it's not close to 2,000 murders right on the other side of the wall, in Mexico. So everyone knows that walls work.* And there are better examples than El Paso, frankly. You take a look. Almost everywhere. Take a look at Israel. They're building another wall. Their wall is 99.9% effective, they told me – 99.9%." - Donald Trump, National Emergency Remarks (February 2019), labeled by FactCheck.org [8]

The perceived veracity of the checkworthy claim *"So everyone knows that walls work"* can thus depend on an individual's prior knowledge and judgement on walls around the world today and in the past, their veracity judgements of the murder numbers in El Paso and/or the effectiveness of the Israeli wall, their judgement on Donald Trump's credibility, the context in which Trump declares national emergency and fluency of the claim.

During the annotation of the ClaimBuster dataset [23,24], the labeling choice of the participants was compared to that of three domain experts. Participants were then assigned a score between 0 and 1 according to their accordance with the domain experts. However, domain expertise does not necessarily mean that these experts have a more objective and correct first veracity judgments than non-experts. Moreover, it contradicts with the definition of checkworthiness given in the ClaimBuster papers, in which checkworthiness is the present appeal of the general public to recovering a claim's truthfulness. By ranking participants based on label agreement with expert domain labeling, the annotation may not reflect the general public's interest and appeal, but rather the interest and appeal of these three experts. As for the lower number of labeled checkworthy sentences in older transcripts in the ClaimBuster dataset, checkworthiness labeling may have been affected by both prior and posterior knowledge of the participants. In the CT-CWC-18 and CT19-T1 datasets, a checkworthiness label is automatically assigned to a sentence if it is fact-checked by FactCheck.org. An important shortcoming to this method has been discussed earlier in Sect. 2.3: the fact-checkers from FactCheck.org do not report their first fact-check procedure, during which they fact-check statements that may be inaccurate by contacting the person/organisation from which the statements originates. In view of veracity judgements, this means that a number of claims with initially questioned veracity are wrongly contained within the non-checkworthy class. As a result, the non-checkworthy class consists of subjective, non-factual claims and objective statements that could be common knowledge or not.

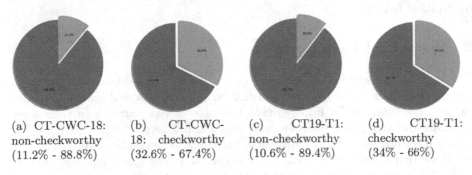

(a) CT-CWC-18: non-checkworthy (11.2% - 88.8%)

(b) CT-CWC-18: checkworthy (32.6% - 67.4%)

(c) CT19-T1: non-checkworthy (10.6% - 89.4%)

(d) CT19-T1: checkworthy (34% - 66%)

Fig. 3. Real numbers in the sentences of the CT-CWC-18 (a, b) and CT19-T1 (c, d) dataset (real numbers - no real numbers)

A Checkworthy Claim States a Fact that has Scientific Validity. The claim reflects well the reality it supposedly represents and it has supporting scientific evidence for that representation [17]. In other words, the claim is 'checkable' and a veracity verdict is based on public data sources and independent experts [17]. For example, a claim containing real numbers can be checked against objective data. Real numbers can refer to, for example, a number of people, a percentage of income or a specific date. However, these numbers are subject to change and do not necessarily remain the same throughout time and space. For the CT-CWC-18 and CT19-T1 datasets, we compared the presence of real numbers - both written in numbers and words - in the checkworthy and non-checkworthy class (Fig. 3). In CT-CWC-18, approximately one out of ten non-checkworthy sentences contains a cardinal number, with 1.4 numbers per sentence on average, while nearly one out of three checkworthy sentences have at least one cardinal number, with 1.9 numbers per sentence on average. Similar results are found in CT19-T1. Those results may indicate that checkworthy claims contain cardinal numbers more often than non-checkworthy claims and that the average number of cardinals is higher. Other checkable information such as place names, personal names and time indications might be more prominent in checkworthy sentences than in non-checkworthy sentences, but we leave this to further research.

Professional Fact-Checkers and Journalists Pay Attention to the Individual or Group/organisation Uttering the Statement. Especially statements from political figures are verified, while political news and statements of political persuasion are prone to deceiving and false information in order to persuade citizens of their convictions [17]. Apart from politicians, statements from labor unions and trade associations should be commonly fact-checked as well [17]. In this paper, however, we cannot check whether fact-checkers pay more attention to political figures and organisations, whereas the datasets predominantly consist of political debate transcripts where almost all claims are made by political figures.

3   Scope and Language Use

The bulk of datasets for checkworthy claim detection consists of written transcripts of debates, speeches and/or conferences. Whereas oral language in the debates inherently differ from written language in news articles in their level of reciprocity (reciprocity between speakers and listeners vs. limited reciprocity between author and reader), discourse (primary vs. secondary), intersentence relations (paratactic vs. hypotactic) and cohesion cues (paralinguistic vs. lexical) [19], it may not be straight-forward to transfer the models trained on transcripts of spoken language to predict checkworthiness in written language. Furthermore, the general aim of political debates and speeches to persuade the audience affects rhetorics and linguistics: speakers use more nominalization, passivization, metaphores, modality, parallellism (reiteration of similar syntactical and lexical units) and unification strategies (use of 'we' and 'our') [26]. The following excerpt, in which all sentences are labeled as checkworthy, is an example of parallellism:

> *"But here, there was nothing to investigate from at least one standpoint. They didn't know the location. They didn't know the time. They didn't know the year. They didn't know anything."* - Donald Trump, UN press conference (September 2018), labeled by FactCheck.org [8]

Several researchers constructing checkworthy claim detection models touch on the linguistic and rhetorical characteristics of debates and speeches, as well. Zuo, Karakas and Banerjee [37], who trained and tested their model on the CT-CWC-18 dataset, argue that the rhetorical and conversational features of debates, such as schesis onomation (= the repetition of synonymous expressions - predominantly nouns and adjectives - to emphasize and reinforce ideas), cause issues for the classification of checkworthy sentences. They also claim that the checkworthiness of many short sentences strongly depends on prior sentences and mention that interruptions by interlocutors or surroundings cause ill-formed or partly-formed sentences and discontinuous trains of thought. According to Hansen et al. [20], the higher number of raised topics in debates and the unbalanced representation of speakers cause their full neural checkworthiness model to perform worse on debates (0.0538 MAP) than on speeches (0.2502 MAP) in the CT19-T1 datasets. Not only the linguistic and rhetorical dynamics of debates and speeches, but also unbalanced speaker representation, low number of check-worthy claims and noisy data might explain those low MAP results. The next section elaborates on the latter, potential causes. All things considered, there need to be datasets containing diverse types of written and (transcribed) spoken language from different domains if a computational model is to detect checkworthy claims in various settings such as debates, speeches, news articles and blog posts.

4   Imbalance and Noise

The datasets are highly imbalanced in terms of checkworthy sentences, non-checkworthy sentences and speaker representation. Figure 4 displays the balance between checkworthy and non-checkworthy sentences in the five datasets. Overall, the majority of sentences is non-checkworthy and only a small share of the sentences is checkworthy, especially in the CT-CWC-18, CT19-T1 and TATHYA datasets. Consequently, classification models may have too few observations of the checkworthy class in order to accurately and precisely learn checkworthiness characteristics. Not only is there imbalance between the checkworthy and non-checkworthy class, but also the non-checkworthy class is highly noisy. This noise has several causes. Firstly, there is low label agreement due to diverging checkworthiness definitions. Secondly, a notable number of checkworthy claims are present in the non-checkworthy class whereas these are considered commonly know and/or self-evidently true or appear to be truthful after corroboration by the speaker - the latter is the case in the CT-CWC-18 and CT19-T1 datasets. Although a claim's checkworthiness is dependent on prior and, possibly, posterior sentences, annotators are asked to judge and label the checkworthiness of a claim of which the context is omitted by default. That is, especially, the case in the ClaimBuster dataset. Thirdly, labeling entire sentences as checkworthy leads to inclusion of non-checkworthy information in the checkworthy class.

As for speaker representation, imbalance in the dataset can affect bias towards or against speakers and, thus, overall model performance. Speakers may differ in lexicon, syntax, rhetorics, points-of-view and topics of interest. Table 3 and 4 display the speaker distributions in CT-CWC-18 and CT19-T1, respectively. The audience and moderators are left out, whereas the fact-checkers at FactCheck.org mainly focused on the politicians participating in the debates. It appears that Trump is strongly represented in both datasets: 34.52% and 44.10% of all sentences in, respectively, CT-CWC-18 and CT19-T1 are uttered by Trump. This is due to the presence of his speeches in both datasets. It might be beneficial for model performance to include speeches by other politicians, especially from those representing other political stances.

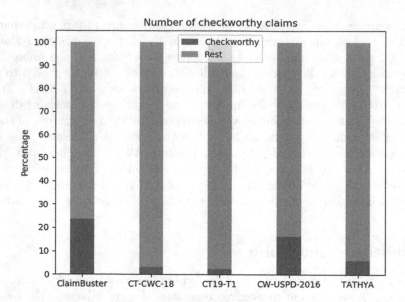

Fig. 4. Imbalance

Table 3. Speaker representation in CT-CWC-18

Speaker	# Sentences	Share in dataset	# Checkworthy	Share in dataset	CW/tot. sent.
Trump	1403	34.52%	49	52.13%	3.49%
Clinton	790	19.46%	15	15.96%	1.90%
Kaine	600	14.76%	19	20.21%	3.17%
Pence	524	12.89%	9	9.57%	1.72%

Table 4. Speaker representation in CT19-T1

Speaker	# Sentences	Share in dataset	# Checkworthy	Share in dataset	CW/tot. sent.
Trump	10363	44.10%	398	69.10%	3.84%
Clinton	2485	10.57%	60	10.42%	2.41%
Sanders	1202	5.11%	23	3.99%	1.91%
Rubio	823	3.50%	22	3.82%	2.67%
Cruz	690	2.94%	21	3.65%	3.04%
Kasich	643	2.74%	4	0.69%	0.62%
Kaine	600	2.55%	19	3.30%	3.17%
Pence	524	2.23%	9	1.56%	1.72%
O'Malley	230	0.98%	5	0.87	2.17%
Carson	177	0.75%	0	0%	0%
Bush	144	0.61%	0	0%	0%
Christie	127	0.54%	0	0%	0%
Paul	116	0.49%	0	0%	0%
Pelosi	97	0.41%	1	0.17%	1.03%
Schumer	66	0.28%	1	0.17%	1.52%

5   Conclusion

It can be argued that there are several shortcomings in automated checkworthy claim detection research. Firstly, there is insufficient agreement on the definition and characteristics of checkworthiness and how a checkworthy claim can be differentiated from a non-checkworthy claim. Drawing from dictionary entries on *check, worthiness* and *worthy*, we provided a preliminary, rather abstract delineation of checkworthiness, where we defined it as a the concept of having a certain worth, value, suitability and need to have the correctness of what it portrays or entails verified. Given the definitions applied by several fact-check organisations in combination with computational journalism research and psychology, we specify checkworthiness as follows: checkworthiness is the concept of having a time-dependent, space-dependent and context-dependent worth, value, suitability, ability and need to have the correctness of the objectivity it conveys verified, irrespective of its perceived veracity judgement by an individual based on prior knowledge and beliefs. Aside from the diverging definitions of checkworthiness, we come to the conclusion that current datasets are too limited in scope and language, and that the classes are too noisy. Therefore, we do not only deem current datasets used for training and testing the models insufficient for the task, but we also argue that the checkworthiness detection task itself is too subjective and can thus not be objectively approached by computational models. However, it would be too computationally demanding to check every objective, factual claim in each text. We, therefore, suggest that it might be better to apply other filtering methods instead of a checkworthiness filter, such as speculation detection [9,30], rumour detection [36] and/or topic-dependent claim detection [27].

References

1. Check: Cambridge Dictionary. Cambridge University Press (2019). https://dictionary.cambridge.org/dictionary/english/check. Accessed 23 Dec 2019
2. Worth: Oxford English Dictionary. Oxford University Press (2019). http://www.oed.com/view/Entry/230376. Accessed 6 Dec 2019
3. Worthiness: Oxford English Dictionary. Oxford University Press (2019). http://www.oed.com/view/Entry/230389. Accessed 6 Dec 2019
4. Worthiness: Cambridge Dictionary. Cambridge University Press (2019). https://dictionary.cambridge.org/dictionary/english/worthiness. Accessed 6 Dec 2019
5. Adair, B.: Duke study finds fact-checking growing around the world. Duke University Reporter's Lab (April 2014). https://reporterslab.org/duke-study-finds-fact-checking-growing-around-the-world/
6. Alter, A.L., Oppenheimer, D.M.: Uniting the tribes of fluency to form a metacognitive nation. Pers. Soc. Psychol. Rev. **13**(3), 219–235 (2009)
7. Atanasova, P., et al.: Overview of the CLEF-2018 CheckThat! Lab on automatic identification and verification of political claims. Task 1: check-worthiness. In: CEUR Workshop Proceedings, Avignon, France (2018)

8. Atanasova, P., Nakov, P., Karadzhov, G., Mohtarami, M., Da San Martino, G.: Overview of the CLEF-2019 CheckThat! Lab on automatic identification and verification of claims. Task 1: check-worthiness. In: CEUR Workshop Proceedings, Lugano, Switzerland (2019)

9. Cruz, N.P., Taboada, M., Mitkov, R.: A machine-learning approach to negation and speculation detection for sentiment analysis. J. Assoc. Inf. Sci. Technol. **67**(9), 2118–2136 (2016)

10. Dechêne, A., Stahl, C., Hansen, J., Wänke, M.: The truth about the truth: a meta-analytic review of the truth effect. Pers. Soc. Psychol. Rev. **14**(2), 238–257 (2010)

11. Dobric Holan, A.: The principles of the truth-o-meter: politifact's methodology for independent fact-checking (2018). https://www.politifact.com/truth-o-meter/article/2018/feb/12/principles-truth-o-meter-politifacts-methodology-i/#How %20we%20choose%20claims

12. FactCheck.org: Our process (2019). https://www.factcheck.org/our-process/. Accessed 16 Dec 2019

13. Favano, L., Carman, M., Lanzi, P.: TheEarthIsFlat's submission to CLEF'19 CheckThat! challenge. In: CLEF 2019 Working Notes, Working Notes of CLEF 2019 Conference and Labs of the Evaluation Forum (2019)

14. Fazio, L.K., Brashier, N.M., Payne, B.K., Marsh, E.J.: Knowledge does not protect against illusory truth. J. Exp. Psychol.: Gen. **144**(5), 993 (2015)

15. Fullfact.org: Effectiveness - full fact (2019). https://fullfact.org/about/effectiveness/. Accessed 6 Dec 2019

16. Gencheva, P., Nakov, P., Màrquez, L., Barrón-Cedeño, A., Koychev, I.: A context-aware approach for detecting worth-checking claims in political debates. In: Proceedings of the International Conference Recent Advances in Natural Language Processing, RANLP 2017, pp. 267–276 (2017)

17. Graves, L.: Deciding what's true: fact-checking journalism and the new ecology of news. Ph.D. thesis, Columbia University (2013)

18. Graves, L., Nyhan, B., Reifler, J.: Why do journalists fact-check (2016). https://www.dartmouth.edu/~nyhan/journalist-fact-checking.pdf

19. Halliday, M.A., Horowitz, R., Samuels, S.J.: Comprehending Oral and Written Language. Emeral Group, Bingley (1987)

20. Hansen, C., Hansen, C., Simonsen, J., Lioma, C.: Neural weakly supervised fact check-worthiness detection with contrastive sampling-based ranking loss. In: 20th Working Notes of CLEF Conference and Labs of the Evaluation Forum, CLEF 2019 Conference and Labs of the Evaluation Forum, vol. 2380 (2019)

21. Hansen, C., Hansen, C., Simonsen, J.G., Lioma, C.: The Copenhagen team participation in the check-worthiness task of the competition of automatic identification and verification of claims in political debates of the CLEF-2018 CheckThat! Lab. In: CLEF (Working Notes) (2018)

22. Hasanain, M., Suwaileh, R., Elsayed, T., Barrón-Cedeno, A., Nakov, P.: Overview of the CLEF-2019 CheckThat! Lab on automatic identification and verification of claims. Task 2: evidence and factuality. In: CEUR Workshop Proceedings, Lugano, Switzerland (2019)

23. Hassan, N., Arslan, F., Li, C., Tremayne, M.: Toward automated fact-checking: detecting check-worthy factual claims by ClaimBuster. In: Proceedings of the 23rd ACM SIGKDD International Conference on Knowledge Discovery and Data Mining, pp. 1803–1812. ACM (2017)

24. Hassan, N., Li, C., Tremayne, M.: Detecting check-worthy factual claims in presidential debates. In: Proceedings of the 24th ACM International Conference on Information and Knowledge Management, pp. 1835–1838. ACM (2015)

25. Jimenez, D., Li, C.: An empirical study on identifying sentences with salient factual statements. In: 2018 International Joint Conference on Neural Networks (IJCNN), pp. 1–8. IEEE (2018)
26. Kazemian, B., Hashemi, S.: Critical discourse analysis of Barack Obama's 2012 speeches: views from systemic functional linguistics and rhetoric. Theory Pract. Lang. Stud. (TPLS) **4**(6), 1178–1187 (2014)
27. Levy, R., Bilu, Y., Hershcovich, D., Aharoni, E., Slonim, N.: Context dependent claim detection. In: Proceedings of COLING 2014, the 25th International Conference on Computational Linguistics: Technical Papers, pp. 1489–1500 (2014)
28. Nakov, P., et al.: Overview of the CLEF-2018 CheckThat! Lab on automatic identification and verification of political claims. In: Bellot, P., et al. (eds.) CLEF 2018. LNCS, vol. 11018, pp. 372–387. Springer, Cham (2018). https://doi.org/10.1007/978-3-319-98932-7_32
29. Patwari, A., Goldwasser, D., Bagchi, S.: Tathya: A multi-classifier system for detecting check-worthy statements in political debates. In: Proceedings of the 2017 ACM Conference on Information and Knowledge Management, pp. 2259–2262. ACM (2017)
30. Qian, Z., Li, P., Zhu, Q., Zhou, G., Luo, Z., Luo, W.: Speculation and negation scope detection via convolutional neural networks. In: Proceedings of the 2016 Conference on Empirical Methods in Natural Language Processing, pp. 815–825 (2016)
31. Scholl, S.G., Greifeneder, R., Bless, H.: When fluency signals truth: prior successful reliance on fluency moderates the impact of fluency on truth judgments. J. Behav. Decis. Mak. **27**(3), 268–280 (2014)
32. Snopes.com: Transparancy (2019). https://www.snopes.com/transparency/. Accessed 6 Dec 2019
33. Stencel, M., Luther, J.: Reporter's lab fact-checking tally tops 200. Duke University Reporter's Lab (October 2019). https://reporterslab.org/category/fact-checking/#article-2551
34. Thorne, J., Vlachos, A., Cocarascu, O., Christodoulopoulos, C., Mittal, A.: The Fact Extraction and VERification (FEVER) shared task. In: Proceedings of the First Workshop on Fact Extraction and VERification (FEVER), pp. 1–9. Association for Computational Linguistics, Brussels (2018)
35. Truthorfiction.com: Our methodology and process (2019). https://www.truthorfiction.com/our-methodology-and-process/. Accessed 6 Dec 2019
36. Zubiaga, A., Aker, A., Bontcheva, K., Liakata, M., Procter, R.: Detection and resolution of rumours in social media: a survey. ACM Comput. Surv. (CSUR) **51**(2), 32 (2018)
37. Zuo, C., Karakas, A., Banerjee, R.: A hybrid recognition system for check-worthy claims using heuristics and supervised learning. In: CLEF (Working Notes) (2018)

How Fake News Affect Trust in the Output of a Machine Learning System for News Curation

Hendrik Heuer[1,2]($\boxtimes$) and Andreas Breiter[1,2]

[1] Institute for Information Management Bremen GmbH (ifib), Bremen, Germany
{hheuer,abreiter}@ifib.de
[2] Centre for Media, Communication and Information Research (ZeMKI),
University of Bremen, Bremen, Germany
{hheuer,abreiter}@uni-bremen.de

Abstract. People are increasingly consuming news curated by machine learning (ML) systems. Motivated by studies on algorithmic bias, this paper explores which recommendations of an algorithmic news curation system users trust and how this trust is affected by untrustworthy news stories like fake news. In a study with 82 vocational school students with a background in IT, we found that users are able to provide trust ratings that distinguish trustworthy recommendations of quality news stories from untrustworthy recommendations. However, a single untrustworthy news story combined with four trustworthy news stories is rated similarly as five trustworthy news stories. The results could be a first indication that untrustworthy news stories benefit from appearing in a trustworthy context. The results also show the limitations of users' abilities to rate the recommendations of a news curation system. We discuss the implications of this for the user experience of interactive machine learning systems.

Keywords: Human-centered machine learning · Algorithmic experience · Algorithmic bias · Fake news · Social media

1 Introduction

News curation is the complex activity of selecting and prioritizing information based on some criteria of relevance and in regards to limitations of time and space. While traditionally the domain of editorial offices of newspapers and other media outlets, this curation is increasingly performed by machine learning (ML) systems that rank the relevance of content [3,17]. This means that complex, intransparent ML systems influence the news consumption of billions of users. Pew Research Center found that around half of U.S. adults who use Facebook (53%) think they do not understand why certain posts are included in their news feeds [2]. This motivates us to explore how users perceive news recommendations and whether users can distinguish trustworthy from untrustworthy ML recommendations. We also examine whether untrustworthy news stories like fake news

© Springer Nature Switzerland AG 2020
M. van Duijn et al. (Eds.): MISDOOM 2020, LNCS 12259, pp. 18–36, 2020.
https://doi.org/10.1007/978-3-030-61841-4_2

benefit from a trustworthy context, for instance, when an ML system predicts five stories, where four are trustworthy news stories and one is a fake news story. We operationalized the term fake news as "fabricated information that mimics news media content in form but not in organizational process or intent" [28]. Investigating trust and fake news in the context of an algorithmic news curation is important since such algorithms are an integral part of social media platforms like Facebook, which are a key vector of fake news distribution [3]. Investigations of trust in news and people's propensity to believe in rumors has a long history [4,5].

We focus on trust in a news recommender system, which connects to O'Donovan et al. and Massa and Bhattacharjee [35,41]. Unlike them, our focus is not the trust in the individual items, but the trust in the ML system and its recommendations. The design of the study is shaped by how users interact with machine learning systems. Participants rate their trust in the recommendations of a machine learning system, i.e. they rate groups of news stories. Participants were told that they are interacting with an ML system, i.e. that they are not simply rating the content. We focus on trust because falling for fake news is not simply a mistake. Fake news are designed to mislead people by mimicking news media content. Our setting connects to human-in-the-loop and active machine learning, where users are interacting with a live system that they improve with their actions [7,26,52]. In such settings, improving a news curation algorithm by rating individual items would require a lot of time and effort from users. We, therefore, explore explicitly rating ML recommendations as a whole as a way to gather feedback.

An investigation of how ML systems and their recommendations are perceived by users is important for those who apply algorithmic news curation and those who want to enable users to detect algorithmic bias in use. This is relevant for all human-computer interaction designers who want to enable users to interact with machine learning systems. This investigation is also relevant for ML practitioners who want to collect feedback from users on the quality of their systems or practitioners who want to crowdsource the collection of training data for their machine learning models [20,53,58].

In our experiment, participants interacted with a simple algorithmic news curation system that presented them with news recommendations similar to a collaborative filtering system [22,49]. We conducted a between-subjects study with two phases. Our participants were recruited in a vocational school. They all had a technical background and were briefed on the type of errors that ML systems can make at unexpected times. In the first phase, participants rated their trust in different news stories. This generated a pool of news stories with trust ratings from our participants. Participants rated different subsets of news stories, i.e. each of the news stories in our investigation was rated by some users while others did not see it. In the second phase, the algorithmic news curation system combined unseen news stories for each user based on each news stories' median trust rating. This means that the trust rating of a story is based on the intersubjective agreement of the participants that rated it in the first phase.

This allowed us to investigate how the trust in individual stories influences the trust in groups of news stories predicted by an ML system. We vary the number of trustworthy and untrustworthy news stories in the recommendations to study their influence on the trust rating on an 11-point rating scale. Our main goal is to understand the trust ratings of ML output as a function of the trust of individual news items for a machine learning system. In summary, this paper answers the following three research questions:

- Can users provide trust ratings for news recommendations of a machine learning system (RQ1)?
- Do users distinguish trustworthy ML recommendations from untrustworthy ML recommendations (RQ2)?
- Do users distinguish trustworthy ML recommendations from recommendations that include one individual untrustworthy news story (RQ3)?

We found that users are able to give nuanced ratings of machine learning recommendations. In their trust ratings, they distinguish trustworthy from untrustworthy ML recommendations, if all stories in the output are trustworthy or if all are untrustworthy. However, participants are not able to distinguish trustworthy news recommendations from recommendations that include one fake news story. Even though they can distinguish other ML recommendations from trustworthy recommendations.

2 Related Work

The goal of news recommendation and algorithmic news curation systems is to model users' interests and to recommend relevant news stories. An early example of this is GroupLens, a collaborative filtering architecture for news [49]. The prevalence of opaque and invisible algorithms that curate and recommend news motivated a variety of investigations of user awareness of algorithmic curation [17,18,21,46]. A widely used example of such a machine learning system is Facebook's News Feed. Introduced in 2006, Facebook describes the News Feed as a "personalized, ever-changing collection of posts from the friends, family, businesses, public figures and news sources you've connected to on Facebook" [19]. By their own account, the three main signals that they use to estimate the relevance of a post are: who posted it, the type of content, and the interactions with the post. In this investigation, we primarily focus on news and fake news on social media and the impact of the machine learning system on news curation.

Alvarado and Waern coined the term algorithmic experience as an analytic framing for making the interaction with and experience of algorithms explicit [6]. Following their framework, we investigate the algorithmic experience of users of a news curation algorithm. This connects to Shou and Farkas, who investigated algorithmic news curation and the epistemological challenges of Facebook [54]. They address the role of algorithms in pre-selecting what appears as representable information, which connects to our research question whether users can detect fake news stories.

This paper extends on prior work on algorithmic bias. Eslami et al. showed that users can detect algorithmic bias during their regular usage of online hotel rating platforms and that this affects trust in the platform [18]. Our investigation is focused on trust as an important expression of users' beliefs. This connects to Rader et al., who explored how different ways of explaining the outputs of an algorithmic news curation system affects users' beliefs and judgments [45]. While explanations make people more aware of how a system works, they are less effective in helping people evaluate the correctness of a system's output.

The Oxford dictionary defines trust as the firm belief in the reliability, truth, or ability of someone or something [14]. Due to the diverse interest in trust, there are many different definitions and angles of inquiry. They range from trust as an attitude or expectation [48,50], to trust as an intention or willingness to act [36] to trust as a result of behaviour [13]. Trust was explored in a variety of different contexts, including, but not limited to intelligent systems [22,56], automation [29,38,39], organisations [36], oneself [34], and others [50]. Lee and See define trust as an attitude of an agent with a goal in a situation that is characterized by some level of uncertainty and vulnerability [29]. The sociologist Niklas Luhmann defined trust as a way to cope with risk, complexity, and a lack of system understanding [30]. For Luhmann, trust is what allows people to face the complexity of the world. Other trust definitions cite a positive expectation of behavior and reliability [39,50,51].

Our research questions connect to Cramer et al., who investigated trust in the context of spam filters, and Berkovsky et al., who investigated trust in movie recommender systems [9,12]. Cramer et al. found that trust guides reliance when the complexity of an automation makes a complete understanding impractical. Berkovsky et al. argue that system designers should consider grouping the recommended items using salient domain features to increase user trust, which supports earlier findings by Pu and Chen [44]. In the context of online behavioral advertising, Eslami et al. explored how to communicate algorithmic processes by showing users why an ad is shown to them [16]. They found that users prefer interpretable, non-creepy explanations.

Trust ratings are central to our investigation. We use them to measure whether participants distinguish trustworthy from untrustworthy machine learning recommendations and investigate the influence of outliers. A large number of publications used trust ratings as a way to assess trust [32,38,39,43]. In the context of online news, Pennycook and Rand showed that users can rate trust in news sources and that they can distinguish mainstream media outlets from hyperpartisan or fake news sources [43]. Muir et al. modeled trust in a machine based on interpersonal trust and showed that users can meaningfully rate their trust [39]. In the context of a pasteurization plant simulation, Muir and Moray showed that operators' subjective ratings of trust provide a simple, nonintrusive insight into their use of the automation [38]. Regarding the validity of such ratings, Cosley et al. showed that users of recommender system interfaces rate fairly consistently across rating scales and that they can detect systems that manipulate outputs [11].

3   Methods

To explore trust in the context of algorithmic news curation, we conducted an experiment with 82 participants from a vocational school with a focus on IT. In the first phase of the study, participants with a technical background rated individual news stories, one at a time. In the second phase of the study, participants rated ML recommendations, i.e. five news stories that were presented together as the recommendations of an algorithmic news curation system. The study was conducted in situ via a web application that presented the two phases.

We recruited a homogeneous group of participants in a German vocational school. To prevent a language barrier from adding bias, the experiment was conducted in German. In Germany, the performance of students is strongly dependent on socio-economic factors [42]. Students of a vocational school, which starts after compulsory schooling, have a similar background. This allows us to control for age, educational background, and socio-economic background. The mean age of the 82 participants was 21.40 (SD = 3.92). The school had a strong STEM focus: All of the six classes were trained in IT (but they had no formal training in machine learning). The IT focus of the vocational school introduced a gender bias: 73 participants identified as male, 5 as female, 2 chose not to disclose their gender and 2 identified as a non-binary gender. This gender bias is representative of a vocational school with a STEM focus in Germany. In the training year 2016, women only accounted for 7.9% of new IT trainees in Germany [1].

Like Muir et al. and Cramer et al., we adopt Luhmann's definition of trust as a way to cope with risk, complexity, and a lack of system understanding [12,30,39]. Our operationalization focuses on interpersonal and social trust, which can be described as the generalized expectancy that a person can rely on the words or promises of others [50]. When consuming news, a person is making herself or himself reliant on a highly complex system that involves journalists, publishers, and interviewees. When interacting with an algorithmic news curation system, a person is making herself or himself reliant on a highly complex socio-technical system, which cannot be understood entirely and which can malfunction for myriad reasons. Each part of the system poses a risk, either due to mistakes, misunderstandings, or malicious intent. A social media platform that performs algorithmic news curation includes actors like the platform provider, the advertisers, other users, and all the different news sources with different levels of trustworthiness. All add complexity and risk. Understanding and auditing how this socio-technical system works is neither possible nor practical.

Before the experiment, we explained the rating interface, provided Mitchell's definition of ML, and briefly mentioned ML applications like object detection and self-driving cars. According to Mitchell, "a computer program is said to learn from experience E with respect to some class of tasks T and performance measure P if its performance at tasks in T, as measured by P, improves with experience E" [37]. To illustrate this, we showed participants how an ML algorithm learns to recognize hand-written digits. This was meant to show how and why some digits are inevitably misclassified. Algorithmic news curation was introduced as another machine learning application. The term fake news was illustrated using examples like Pope Francis backing Trump and the German Green party banning meat.

3.1   Rating News Stories (Phase 1)

The task in the first phase was to provide trust ratings for news stories from different sources. In this phase, participants evaluated each piece of content individually. As news stories, we used two days of publicly available Facebook posts of 13 different sources. The study was conducted in May 2017, i.e. before the Cambridge Analytica scandal and before the Russian interference in the 2016 United States elections became publicly known.

We distinguish between seven quality media sources, e.g. public-service broadcasters and newspapers of record, and six biased sources, including tabloid media and fake news blogs. The quality media sources and the tabloid sources were selected based on their reach as measured by Facebook likes. Fake news sources were selected based on mentions in news articles on German fake news [8]. Tabloid newspapers are characterized by a sensationalistic writing style and limited reliability. But, unlike fake news, they are not fabricated or intentionally misleading. For our experiment, a weighted random sample of news stories was selected from all available posts. Each of the 82 participants rated 20 news stories from a weighted random sample consisting of eight quality media news stories, four tabloid news stories, and eight fake news stories. The weighted sample accounted for the focus on fake news and online misinformation. The selected stories cover a broad range of topics, including sports like soccer, social issues like homelessness and refugees, and stories on politicians from Germany, France, and the U.S.

The presentation of the news stories resembled Facebook's official visual design. For each news story, participants saw the headline, lead paragraph, lead image, the name of the source, source logo, source URL, date and time, as well as the number of likes, comments, and shares of the Facebook post. Participants were not able to click on links or read the entire article. The data was not personalized, i.e. all participants saw the same number of likes, shares, and comments that anybody without a Facebook account would have seen if s/he would have visited the Facebook Page of the news source. In the experiment, participant rated news stories on an 11-point rating scale. The question they were asked for each news story was: "Generally speaking, would you say that this news story can be trusted, or that you can't be too careful? Please tell me on a score of 0 to 10, where 0 means you can't be too careful and 10 means that this news story can be trusted". Range and phrasing of the question are modeled after the first question of the Social Trust Scale (STS) of the European Social Survey (ESS) which is aimed at interpersonal trust and connected to the risk of trusting a person respectively a news story [47]. After the experiment, the ratings of the news stories from Phase 1 were validated with media research experts. Each media researcher ranked the news sources by how trustworthy they considered the source. These rankings were compared to the median trust ratings of the news sources by the users. The experts were recruited from two German labs with a focus on media research on public communication and other cultural and social domains. All members of the two labs were contacted through internal newsletters. In a self-selection sample, nine media researcher (three male, six female) provided their ranking via e-mail (two from lab A, seven from lab B).

3.2   Rating News Recommendations (Phase 2)

In the second phase, participants rated their trust in the output of a news curation system. The task was not to identify individual fake news items. Participants rated the ML recommendations as a group selected by an ML system. In the study, the output of the ML system always consisted of five unseen news stories. We selected the unseen news stories based on their median trust ratings from Phase 1. The median is used as a robust measure of central tendency [24], which captures intersubjective agreement and which limits the influence of individual outliers. We adapted our approach from collaborative filtering systems like GroupLens [22,49]. Collaborative filtering systems identify users with similar rating patterns and use these similar users to predict unseen items. Since our sample size was limited, we couldn't train a state-of-the-art collaborative filtering system. Therefore, we used the median trust rating as a proxy.

Our goal was to understand how the presence of fake news changes the feedback users give for a machine learning system and whether trust ratings account for the presence of fake news. Our motivation was to explore how fine-grained the user feedback on a system's performance is. This is important for fields like active learning or interactive and mixed-initiative machine learning [7,23,25,55], where user feedback is used to improve the system. While the experiment brief made people believe that they were interacting with a personalized ML system, the recommendations were not actually personalized. We did this to be able to compare the ratings. Unlike in Wizard of Oz experiments, there was no experimenter in the loop. Users freely interacted with an interactive software system that learned from examples.

3.3   Types of News Recommendations

To investigate how the trust ratings of the recommendations change based on the trustworthiness of the individual news stories, we combine five news stories in random order with different levels of trustworthiness. The scale ranges from "can't be too careful (0)" to "can be trusted (10)". We refer to the trustworthiness of a news story as low (if the trust rating is between 0 and 3), medium (4 to 6), and high (7 to 10).

Figure 1 shows the four types of news recommendations that we discuss in this paper as well as the rating interface.

- a) **Medium**—ML output that consists of five news stories with median trust ratings between 4 and 6.
- b) **Medium, 1 Low**—ML output with four news stories with ratings between 4 and 6 and one with a rating between 0 and 3 (shown in Fig. 1).

Types of News Recommendations,
which combine five news stories
by their median trust rating

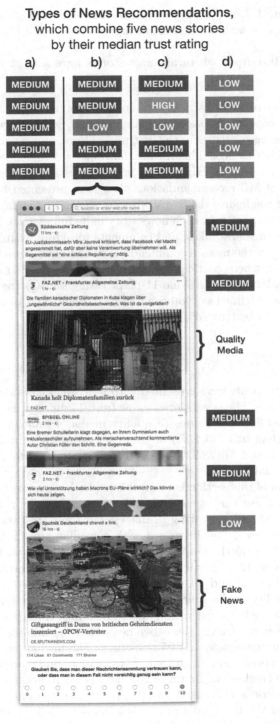

Fig. 1. For Phase 2, different types of ML recommendations were generated by combining five news stories from Phase 1 by their median trust rating. Participants rated the trustworthiness of these collections of unseen news stories with a single score on an 11-point rating scale.

- c) **Medium, 1 Low, 1 High**—ML output that consists of three medium news stories, one with a low trust rating and one with a high rating between 7 and 10.
- d) **Low**—ML output where all news stories have a trust rating between 0 and 3.

Our goal was to show as many different combinations of news recommendations to participants as possible. Unfortunately, what we were able to test depended on the news ratings in the first phase. Here, only a small subset of participants gave high ratings. This means that news recommendations like **High, 1 Low**, as well as **Low, 1 High** could not be investigated. Figure 1 shows the different types of ML recommendations that were presented to more than ten participants. In the figure, the five stories are shown in a collapsed view. In the experiment, participants saw each news story in its full size, i.e. the texts, images and the number of shares, likes, and comments were fully visible for each of the five news stories in the news recommendation. The news stories were presented in a web browser where participants were able to scroll. Participant rated the news recommendation on the same 11-point rating scale as the individual news items, where 0 was defined as "you can't be too careful" and 10 as "this collection of news stories can be trusted".

4   Results

In Phase 1, participants were presented with individual news stories, which they rated one at a time. The news stories came from 13 different news sources. Each participant rated 20 news stories (8 quality media, 4 tabloid, and 8 fake news stories). More than half (53.47%) of the trust ratings are rated as low (with a rating between 0 and 3). 28.22% are rated as medium (rated 4, 5 and 6) and 18.32% high (7 and 10).

The first goal of this section is to establish whether our method and the trust ratings are valid. For this, we grouped the news stories by source and ranked them by their median trust rating (Table 1). The most trustworthy news source is a conservative newspaper of record with a median trust rating of 6.0 (N = 256). The least trustworthy news sources is a fake news blog with a median trust rating of 1.0 (N = 129). Participants distinguish quality media (Sources A to F) from tabloid media and fake news blogs (G to M). There is one exception: Rank H is a quality media source - produced by the public-service television - which received a median trust rating of 4.0 and which is ranked between tabloid media and fake news. Unlike the other news sources, this median trust rating is only based on one article and 25 responses. The median ratings of all other news sources are based on four or more news articles and more than 100 ratings per news source (with a maximum of 258 ratings for 10 articles from source G). The fake news outlets are ranked as I (9), K (11), and M (13).

We validated the trust ratings of news items by comparing them to rankings of the news sources by nine media researchers (three male, six female), also

Table 1. Quality media sources (marked in green) are distinguished from tabloid media (yellow) and fake news sources (red) in the Participants' Ranking ($N = 82$, median trust rating) and the Media Researchers' Rankings ($N = 9$).

Rank	Trust Ratings		News Sources Ranked By Media Researchers								
1	6.0	A	H	D	D	D	C	C	D	H	H
2	6.0	B	C	H	C	B	B	H	H	D	D
3	6.0	C	D	C	B	H	H	B	C	B	C
4	5.0	D	B	B	H	C	D	D	E	C	B
5	5.0	E	A	E	A	A	E	A	B	I	A
6	4.5	F	E	F	E	E	A	F	A	A	E
7	4.5	G	F	A	F	F	F	E	F	F	F
8	4.0	H	G	G	L	G	G	G	G	K	K
9	4.0	I	L	L	G	L	L	L	L	J	I
10	3.0	J	J	I	J	I	K	J	I	E	M
11	3.0	K	K	K	K	K	I	I	K	G	G
12	2.0	L	I	J	I	J	J	M	J	M	L
13	1.0	M	M	M	M	M	M	K	M	L	J

Participants'   Media Researchers'
Ranking   Rankings

■ Quality Media Sources ■ Tabloid Media Sources ■ Fake News Sources

shown in Table 1. Unlike the vocational school students, the experts did not rate individual news stories but ranked the names of the news sources by their trustworthiness. With one exception, researchers made the same distinction between quality media and biased media (fake news and tabloid media). Like our participants, the experts did not distinguish tabloid media from fake news blogs. Overall, the comparison of the two rankings shows that the trust ratings of the participants correspond to expert opinion. This validates the results through a sample different in expertise, age, and gender. The experts have a background in media research and two-thirds of the experts were female (which counterbalanced the male bias in the participants).

4.1 Trust Ratings for Algorithmic News Curation (RQ1)

The first research question was whether users can provide trust ratings for recommendations of an algorithmic news curation system. We addressed this question with a between-subjects design where the samples are independent, i.e. different participants saw different news stories and news recommendations [31]. Participants provided their trust ratings for the news stories and the news recommendations on an 11-point rating scale. We analyzed this ordinal data using a non-parametric test, i.e. we made no assumptions about the distance between the different categories. To compare the different conditions and to see whether the trust ratings of the news recommendations differ in statistically significant ways, we applied the Mann-Whitney U test (Wilcoxon Rank test) [31,33]. Like the t-test used for continuous variables, the Mann-Whitney U test provides a

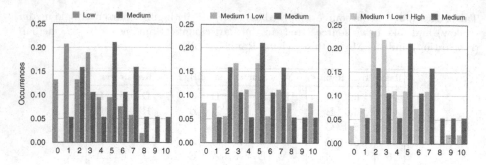

Fig. 2. Histograms comparing the trust ratings of the different recommendations of the ML system.

p-value that indicates whether statistical differences between ordinal variables exist. Participants were told to rate ML recommendations. The framing of the experiment explicitly mentioned that they are not rating an ML system, but one recommendation of an ML system that consisted of five news stories. The results show that participants can differentiate between such ML recommendations. The ranking of the ML recommendations corresponds to the news items that make up the recommendations. Of the four types of news recommendations, a) Medium recommendations, which consist of five news stories with a trust rating between 4 and 6, have a median rating of 5.0. d) Low recommendations with five news stories with a low rating (0 and 3), have a median trust rating of 3.0. The trust ratings of b) Medium, 1 Low recommendations, which combine four trustworthy stories and one untrustworthy, are rated considerably higher (4.5). ML recommendations that consist of three trustworthy news items, one untrustworthy news items (rating between 0 and 3) and one highly trustworthy news story (7 and 10), received a median trust rating of 3.0.

4.2   Trustworthy News Recommendations (RQ2)

Table 2. The Mann-Whitney U test was applied to see whether statistically significant differences between the trust ratings of different news recommendations exist (italic for $p < 0.05$, bold for $p < 0.01$).

Comparison of news recommendations		U	p
Medium	Low	258.50	**.0008**
Medium	M., 1 Low	303.50	.2491
Medium	M., 1 Low, 1 High	358.50	*.0204*
M., 1 Low	Low	619.50	*.0024*
M., 1 Low	M., 1 Low, 1 High	801.50	.0618
M., 1 L., 1 High	Low	1141.50	*.0250*

The second research question was whether users can distinguish trustworthy from untrustworthy machine learning recommendations. To answer this, we compare the trust ratings of a) Medium and d) Low recommendations. The trustworthy a) Medium recommendations have the same median rating (5.0) as the quality media sources D and E. Untrustworthy d) Low recommendations with a median rating of 3.0 have the same rating as the tabloid news source J and the fake news source K. The Mann-Whitney U test shows that participants reliably distinguish between a) Medium and d) Low recommendations ($U = 258.5$, $p = .001$). Figure 2 (left) shows the histogram of the a) Medium recommendations, which resembles a normal distribution. 5 is the most frequent trust rating, followed by 8 and 2. The histogram of d) Low is skewed towards negative ratings. Here, 1 and 3 are the most frequent trust rating. Nevertheless, a large number of participants still gave a rating of 6 or higher for d) Low recommendations. A large fraction also gave a) Medium recommendations a rating lower than 5.

4.3   Fake News Stories (RQ3)

The first two research questions showed that technically advanced participants are able to differentiate between trustworthy and untrustworthy ML recommendations in an experiment where they are primed to pay attention to individual fake news stories. The most important research question, however, was whether users distinguish trustworthy ML recommendations from recommendations that include one fake news story in their ratings. For this, we compare the trust ratings of a) Medium recommendations to those of b) 4 Medium, 1 Low recommendations, which have a median trust rating of 4.5 ($N = 36$). Compared to a) Medium at 5.0 ($N = 19$), the median is slightly lower. Compared to the news sources, b) 4 Medium, 1 Low at 4.5 is similar to quality media (Source F) and tabloid media (Source G). The Mann-Whitney U test shows that the ratings for b) Medium, 1 Low recommendations are significantly different from d) Low recommendations ($U = 619.5$, $p = .002$). However, the difference between a) Medium and b) 4 Medium, 1 Low is not statistically significant ($U = 303.5$, $p = .249$). This means that the crucial fake news case, where a recommendation consists of four trustworthy news stories and one fake news story, is not distinguished in a statistically significant way. The histogram in Fig. 2 (center) shows that a) Medium and b) Medium, 1 Low are very similar. Both resemble a normal distribution and both have strong peaks at 5, the neutral position of the 11-point rating scale. a) Medium recommendations have strong peaks at 2 and 7, b) Medium, 1 Low recommendations have peaks at 3 and 7. To see whether participants are able to distinguish the fake news case from other recommendations, we also compare b) 4 Medium, 1 Low recommendations to c) Medium, 1 Low, 1 High recommendations, which consist of three trustworthy news stories (rated between 4 and 6), one highly trustworthy story (7 and 10) and one untrustworthy news item (0 and 3). The c) 3 Medium, 1 Low, 1 High recommendations are rated as 3.0 (N = 55). This is the same as d) Low recommendations (3.0). It is also much lower than the ratings of b) Medium, 1 Low recommendations (4.5). In comparison to the median trust rating of the news sources, this places c) 3 Medium, 1 Low, 1 High between the tabloid source J and the fake news source K. According to the Mann-Whitney U test, participants are able to distinguish c) 3 Medium, 1 Low, 1 High recommendations from a) Medium (U = 358.5, p = .020) and d) Low (U = 1141.5, p = .025) recommendations. c) 3 Medium, 1 Low, 1 High recommendations are not distinguished from the fake news case of c) Medium, 1 Low recommendations (U = 801.50, p = .062). Figure 2 (right) compares the histograms of a) Medium and c) 3 Medium, 1 Low, 1 High recommendations. The largest peaks for c) recommendations are at 2 and 3, with very few high ratings of 7, 8, 9 or 10, but also few ratings of 0 and 1. The difference between the ratings of the two recommendations is clearly recognizable in the histograms.

5   Discussion

The study found that participants with a technical background can provide plausible trust ratings for individual news items as well as for groups of news items presented as the recommendations of an ML system. The ratings of the news recommendations correspond to the news stories that are part of the news recommendations. We further showed that the trust ratings for individual news items correspond to expert opinion. Vocational school students and media researchers both distinguish news stories of quality media sources from biased sources. Neither experts nor participants placed the fake news sources at the end of the rankings. These findings are highly problematic considering the nature of fake news. Following Lazer et al.'s definition of fake news as fabricated information that mimics news media content in form but not in organizational process or intent [28], fake news are more likely to emulate tabloid media in form and content than quality media.

We found that users can provide trust ratings for an algorithmic news curation system when presented with recommendations of a machine learning system. Participants were able to assign trust ratings that differentiated between news recommendations in a statistically significant way, at least when comparing trustworthy from untrustworthy machine learning recommendations. However, the crucial fake news case was not distinguished from trustworthy recommendations. This is noteworthy since the first phase of our study showed that users are able to identify individual fake news stories. When providing trust ratings for groups of news items in the second phase, the presence of fake news did not affect the trust ratings of the output as a whole. This is surprising since prior research on trust in automation reliance implies that user's assessment of a system changes when the system makes mistakes [15]. Dzindolet et al. report that the consequences of this were so severe that after encountering a system that makes mistakes, participants distrusted even reliable aids. In our study, one fake news story did not affect the trust rating in such a drastic way. An untrustworthy fake news story did not lead to a very low trust rating for the news recommendation as a whole. The simplest explanation for this would be that the task is too hard for users. Identifying a lowly trusted news story in the recommendations of an algorithmic news curation system may overstrain users. A contrary indication against this explanation is that trustworthy and untrustworthy recommendations can be distinguished from other news recommendations like the c) Medium, 1 Low, 1 High recommendations.

Our findings could, therefore, be a first indication that untrustworthy news stories benefit from appearing in a trustworthy context. Our findings are especially surprising considering that the users have an IT background and were primed to be suspicious. If users implicitly trust fake news that appear in a trustworthy context, this would have far-reaching consequences. Especially since social media is becoming the primary news sources for a large group of people [40]. The question whether untrustworthy news stories like fake news benefit from a trustworthy context is directly connected to research on algorithmic experience and the user awareness of algorithmic curation.

Our understanding of the user experience of machine learning systems is only emerging [17,18,21,46]. In the context of an online hotel rating platforms, Eslami et al. found that users can detect algorithmic bias during their regular usage of a service and that this bias affects trust in the platform [18]. The question, therefore, is why participants did not react to the fake news stories in our study in a similar way. Further research has to show what role the context of our study - machine learning and algorithmic news curation - may have played. While framing effects are known to affect trust, our expectation was that the framing would have primed users to be overly cautious [32]. This would mean that participants can distinguish them in the experiment, but not in the practice. This was not the case.

In the instructions of the controlled experiment, we define the terms fake news and machine learning. This increased algorithmic awareness and the expectation of algorithmic bias. It could also have influenced the perception and actions of the participants by making them more cautious and distrusting. We show that despite this priming and framing, participants were not able to provide ratings that reflect the presence of fake news stories in the output. If people with a technical background and a task framed like this are unable to do this, how could a layperson? Especially considering that participants were able to distinguish uniformly trustworthy from uniformly untrustworthy output. All this makes the implications of our experiment on the UX of machine learning and how feedback/training data needs to be collected especially surprising and urgent. This adds to a large body of research on algorithmic experience and algorithmic awareness [10,16,57].

6   Limitations

Studying trust in machine learning systems for news curation is challenging. We had to simplify a complex socio-technical system. Our approach connects to a large body of research that applies trust ratings to study complex phenomena [32, 38,39,43]. Since no ground truth data on the trustworthiness of different news stories was available, we designed a study that used the median trust ratings of our participants as intersubjective agreement on the perceived trustworthiness of a news story. A real-world algorithmic news curation system is more complex and judges the relevance of postings based on three factors: who posted it, the type of content, and the interactions with the post [19]. Even though we recreated the design of Facebook's News Feed, our setting was artificial. Interactions with the posts were limited, participants did not select the news sources themselves and they did not see the likes, shares, and comments of their real Facebook "friends". We focused on news stories and did not personalize the recommendations of the ML system. Further research could investigate how the different sources affect the trust perception of news stories respectively the trust perception of ML recommendations. However, not personalizing the results and focusing on news was necessary to get comparable results.

We conducted the experiment in a German vocational school with an IT focus. This limits biasing factors like age, educational background, and socio-economic background, but led to a strong male bias. We counteracted this bias by validating the trust ratings of news stories with nine media research experts - a heterogeneous group that is different in age, gender (three male, six female), and background, which confirmed our results. Prior research also implies that the findings from our sample of participants are generalizable despite the strong male bias. A German study (N = 1,011) from 2017 showed that age and gender have little influence on experience with fake news, which is similar for all people under 60, especially between 14-to-24-year olds and 25-to-44-year olds [27]. The participants in this study had a background in IT, which could have influenced the results. Prior work on algorithmically generated image captions showed that technical proficiency and education level do not influence trust ratings [32]. Moreover, even if the technical background of the participants would have helped the task, they were not able to provide nuanced ratings that accounted for untrustworthy news items, which further supports our arguments.

7   Conclusion

Our study investigated how fake news affect trust in the output of a machine learning system for news curation. Our results show that participants distinguish trustworthy from untrustworthy ML recommendations in significantly different trust ratings. Meanwhile, the crucial fake news case, where an individual fake news story appears among trustworthy news stories, is not distinguished from trustworthy ML recommendations. Since ML systems make a variety of errors that can be subtle, it is important to incorporate user feedback on the performance of the system. Our study shows that gathering such feedback is challenging. While participants are able to distinguish exclusively trustworthy from untrustworthy recommendations, they do not account for subtle but crucial differences like fake news. Our recommendations for those who want to apply machine learning is, therefore, to evaluate how well users can give feed-back before training active learning and human-in-the-loop machine learning systems. Further work in other real-world scenarios is needed, especially since news recommendation systems are constantly changing.

References

1. Fachinformatiker: IT-Berufsausbildung auf dem Arbeitsmarkt sehr gefragt - Golem.de (2017). https://www.golem.de/news/fachinformatiker-it-berufsausbild-ung-auf-dem-arbeitsmarkt-sehr-gefragt-1702-126214.html
2. Many Facebook users don't understand its news feed (2019). http://www.pewresearch.org/fact-tank/2018/09/05/many-facebook-users-dont-understand-how-the-sites-news-feed-works/
3. Allcott, H., Gentzkow, M.: Social media and fake news in the 2016 election. Tech. rep., National Bureau of Economic Research (2017)
4. Allport, F.H., Lepkin, M.: Wartime rumors of waste and special privilege: why some people believe them. J. Abnorm. Soc. Psychol. **40**(1), 3 (1945)
5. Allport, G.W., Postman, L.: The psychology of rumor (1947)
6. Alvarado, O., Waern, A.: Towards algorithmic experience: initial efforts for social media contexts. In: Proceedings of the 2018 CHI Conference on Human Factors in Computing Systems, CHI 2018, pp. 286:1–286:12. ACM, New York (2018). https://doi.org/10.1145/3173574.3173860, http://doi.acm.org/10.1145/3173574.3173860
7. Amershi, S., Cakmak, M., Knox, W.B., Kulesza, T.: Power to the people: the role of humans in interactive machine learning. AI Mag. **35**(4), 105–120 (2014)
8. Bento, Katharina Hölter, S.L.: Fake news in Deutschland: Diese Webseiten machen Stimmung gegen Merkel (2017). http://www.bento.de/today/fake-news-in-deutschland-diese-seiten-machen-stimmung-gegen-merkel-1126168/
9. Berkovsky, S., Taib, R., Conway, D.: How to recommend?: User trust factors in movie recommender systems. In: Proceedings of the 22nd International Conference on Intelligent User Interfaces, IUI 2017, pp. 287–300. ACM, New York (2017). https://doi.org/10.1145/3025171.3025209, http://doi.acm.org/10.1145/3025171.3025209
10. Binns, R., Van Kleek, M., Veale, M., Lyngs, U., Zhao, J., Shadbolt, N.: 'It's reducing a human being to a percentage': perceptions of justice in algorithmic decisions. In: Proceedings of the 2018 CHI Conference on Human Factors in Computing Systems, CHI 2018, pp. 377:1–377:14. ACM, New York (2018). https://doi.org/10.1145/3173574.3173951, http://doi.acm.org/10.1145/3173574.3173951
11. Cosley, D., Lam, S.K., Albert, I., Konstan, J.A., Riedl, J.: Is seeing believing?: How recommender system interfaces affect users' opinions. In: Proceedings of the SIGCHI Conference on Human Factors in Computing Systems, CHI 2003, pp. 585–592. ACM, New York (2003). https://doi.org/10.1145/642611.642713, http://doi.acm.org/10.1145/642611.642713
12. Cramer, H.S., Evers, V., van Someren, M.W., Wielinga, B.J.: Awareness, training and trust in interaction with adaptive spam filters. In: Proceedings of the SIGCHI Conference on Human Factors in Computing Systems, CHI 2009, pp. 909–912. ACM, New York (2009). https://doi.org/10.1145/1518701.1518839, http://doi.acm.org/10.1145/1518701.1518839
13. Deutsch, M.: Trust, trustworthiness, and the F scale. J. Abnorm. Soc. Psychol. **61**(1), 138 (1960)

14. Dictionaries, O.: Trust (2018). https://en.oxforddictionaries.com/definition/trust
15. Dzindolet, M.T., Peterson, S.A., Pomranky, R.A., Pierce, L.G., Beck, H.P.: The role of trust in automation reliance. Int. J. Hum.-Comput. Stud. **58**(6), 697–718 (2003)
16. Eslami, M., Krishna Kumaran, S.R., Sandvig, C., Karahalios, K.: Communicating algorithmic process in online behavioral advertising. In: Proceedings of the 2018 CHI Conference on Human Factors in Computing Systems, CHI 2018, pp. 432:1–432:13. ACM, New York (2018). https://doi.org/10.1145/3173574.3174006, http://doi.acm.org/10.1145/3173574.3174006
17. Eslami, M., et al.: "I always assumed that i wasn't really that close to [her]": reasoning about invisible algorithms in news feeds. In: Proceedings of the 33rd Annual ACM Conference on Human Factors in Computing Systems, CHI 2015, pp. 153–162. ACM, New York (2015). https://doi.org/10.1145/2702123.2702556, http://doi.acm.org/10.1145/2702123.2702556
18. Eslami, M., Vaccaro, K., Karahalios, K., Hamilton, K.: "Be careful; things can be worse than they appear": understanding biased algorithms and users' behavior around them in rating platforms. In: ICWSM, pp. 62–71 (2017)
19. Facebook: Facebook news feed (2018). https://newsfeed.fb.com/
20. Gulla, J.A., Zhang, L., Liu, P., Özgöbek, O., Su, X.: The Adressa dataset for news recommendation. In: Proceedings of the International Conference on Web Intelligence, WI 2017, pp. 1042–1048. ACM, New York (2017). https://doi.org/10.1145/3106426.3109436, http://doi.acm.org/10.1145/3106426.3109436
21. Hamilton, K., Karahalios, K., Sandvig, C., Eslami, M.: A path to understanding the effects of algorithm awareness. In: CHI 2014 Extended Abstracts on Human Factors in Computing Systems, CHI EA 2014, pp. 631–642. ACM, New York (2014). https://doi.org/10.1145/2559206.2578883, http://doi.acm.org/10.1145/2559206.2578883
22. Herlocker, J.L., Konstan, J.A., Riedl, J.: Explaining collaborative filtering recommendations. In: Proceedings of the 2000 ACM Conference on Computer Supported Cooperative Work, pp. 241–250. ACM (2000)
23. Horvitz, E.J.: Reflections on challenges and promises of mixed-initiative interaction. AI Mag. **28**(2), 3 (2007)
24. Lovric, M. (ed.): Robust Statistics. International Encyclopedia of Statistical Science, pp. 1248–1251. Springer, Heidelberg (2011). https://doi.org/10.1007/978-3-642-04898-2
25. Kim, B.: Interactive and interpretable machine learning models for human machine collaboration. Ph.D. thesis, Massachusetts Institute of Technology (2015)
26. Kulesza, T., Burnett, M., Wong, W.K., Stumpf, S.: Principles of explanatory debugging to personalize interactive machine learning. In: Proceedings of the 20th International Conference on Intelligent User Interfaces, IUI 2015, pp. 126–137. ACM, New York (2015). https://doi.org/10.1145/2678025.2701399, http://doi.acm.org/10.1145/2678025.2701399
27. Landesanstalt für Medien NRW (LfM): Fake news. Tech. rep., forsa (May 2017). https://bit.ly/2ya2gj0
28. Lazer, D.M., et al.: The science of fake news. Science **359**(6380), 1094–1096 (2018)
29. Lee, J.D., See, K.A.: Trust in automation: designing for appropriate reliance. Hum. Factors: J. Hum. Factors Ergon. Soc. **46**(1), 50–80 (2004)
30. Luhmann, N.: Trust and Power. Wiley, Hoboken (1979)
31. MacKenzie, I.S.: Human-computer interaction: an empirical research perspective. Morgan Kaufmann, Amsterdam (2013). http://www.sciencedirect.com/science/book/9780124058651

32. MacLeod, H., Bennett, C.L., Morris, M.R., Cutrell, E.: Understanding blind people's experiences with computer-generated captions of social media images. In: Proceedings of the 2017 CHI Conference on Human Factors in Computing Systems, CHI 2017, pp. 5988–5999. ACM, New York (2017). https://doi.org/10.1145/3025453.3025814, http://doi.acm.org/10.1145/3025453.3025814

33. Mann, H.B., Whitney, D.R.: On a test of whether one of two random variables is stochastically larger than the other. Ann. Math. Stat. **18**, 50–60 (1947)

34. Marsh, S.P.: Formalising trust as a computational concept. Ph.D. thesis (1994)

35. Massa, P., Bhattacharjee, B.: Using trust in recommender systems: an experimental analysis. In: Jensen, C., Poslad, S., Dimitrakos, T. (eds.) iTrust 2004. LNCS, vol. 2995, pp. 221–235. Springer, Heidelberg (2004). https://doi.org/10.1007/978-3-540-24747-0_17

36. Mayer, R.C., Davis, J.H., Schoorman, F.D.: An integrative model of organizational trust. Acad. Manag. Rev. **20**(3), 709–734 (1995). https://doi.org/10.2307/258792. http://www.jstor.org/stable/258792

37. Mitchell, T.M.: Machine Learning, 1st edn. McGraw-Hill Inc., New York (1997)

38. Muir, B.M., Moray, N.: Trust in automation. Part II. Experimental studies of trust and human intervention in a process control simulation. Ergonomics **39**(3), 429–460 (1996). https://doi.org/10.1080/00140139608964474

39. Muir, B.M.: Trust in automation: Part I. Theoretical issues in the study of trust and human intervention in automated systems. Ergonomics **37**(11), 1905–1922 (1994). https://doi.org/10.1080/00140139408964957, http://dx.doi.org/10.1080/00140139408964957

40. Newman, N., Fletcher, R., Kalogeropoulos, A., Levy, D.A., Nielsen, R.K.: Reuters institute digital news report 2017 (2017). https://ssrn.com/abstract=3026082

41. O'Donovan, J., Smyth, B.: Trust in recommender systems. In: Proceedings of the 10th International Conference on Intelligent User Interfaces, pp. 167–174. ACM (2005)

42. OECD: PISA 2006 (2007). https://www.oecd-ilibrary.org/content/publication/9789264040014-en

43. Pennycook, G., Rand, D.G.: Crowdsourcing judgments of news source quality (2018)

44. Pu, P., Chen, L.: Trust building with explanation interfaces. In: Proceedings of the 11th International Conference on Intelligent User Interfaces, IUI 2006, pp. 93–100. ACM, New York (2006). https://doi.org/10.1145/1111449.1111475, http://doi.acm.org/10.1145/1111449.1111475

45. Rader, E., Cotter, K., Cho, J.: Explanations as mechanisms for supporting algorithmic transparency. In: Proceedings of the 2018 CHI Conference on Human Factors in Computing Systems, CHI 2018, pp. 103:1–103:13. ACM, New York (2018). https://doi.org/10.1145/3173574.3173677, http://doi.acm.org/10.1145/3173574.3173677

46. Rader, E., Gray, R.: Understanding user beliefs about algorithmic curation in the Facebook news feed. In: Proceedings of the 33rd Annual ACM Conference on Human Factors in Computing Systems, CHI 2015, pp. 173–182. ACM, New York (2015). https://doi.org/10.1145/2702123.2702174, http://doi.acm.org/10.1145/2702123.2702174

47. Reeskens, T., Hooghe, M.: Cross-cultural measurement equivalence of generalized trust. Evidence from the European Social Survey (2002 and 2004). Soc. Indic. Res. **85**(3), 515–532 (2008). https://doi.org/10.1007/s11205-007-9100-z

48. Rempel, J.K., Holmes, J.G., Zanna, M.P.: Trust in close relationships. J. Pers. Soc. Psychol. **49**(1), 95 (1985)

49. Resnick, P., Iacovou, N., Suchak, M., Bergstrom, P., Riedl, J.: GroupLens: an open architecture for collaborative filtering of netnews. In: Proceedings of the 1994 ACM Conference on Computer Supported Cooperative Work, CSCW 1994, pp. 175–186. ACM, New York (1994). https://doi.org/10.1145/192844.192905, http://doi.acm.org/10.1145/192844.192905

50. Rotter, J.B.: A new scale for the measurement of interpersonal trust. J. Pers. **35**(4), 651–665 (1967). https://doi.org/10.1111/j.1467-6494.1967.tb01454.x. http://onlinelibrary.wiley.com/doi/10.1111/j.1467-6494.1967.tb01454.x/abstract

51. Rousseau, D.M., Sitkin, S.B., Burt, R.S., Camerer, C.: Not so different after all: a cross-discipline view of trust. Acad. Manag. Rev. **23**(3), 393–404 (1998). https://doi.org/10.5465/AMR.1998.926617. http://amr.aom.org/content/23/3/393

52. Rubens, N., Elahi, M., Sugiyama, M., Kaplan, D.: Active learning in recommender systems. In: Ricci, F., Rokach, L., Shapira, B. (eds.) Recommender Systems Handbook, pp. 809–846. Springer, Boston, MA (2015). https://doi.org/10.1007/978-1-4899-7637-6_24

53. Russakovsky, O., et al.: Imagenet large scale visual recognition challenge. Int. J. Comput. Vis. **115**(3), 211–252 (2015). https://doi.org/10.1007/s11263-015-0816-y

54. Schou, J., Farkas, J.: Algorithms, interfaces, and the circulation of information: interrogating the epistemological challenges of Facebook. KOME: Int. J. Pure Commun. Inq. **4**(1), 36–49 (2016)

55. Stumpf, S., et al.: Interacting meaningfully with machine learning systems: three experiments. Int. J. Hum.-Comput. Stud. **67**(8), 639–662 (2009). https://doi.org/10.1016/j.ijhcs.2009.03.004.   http://www.sciencedirect.com/science/article/pii/S1071581909000457

56. Tullio, J., Dey, A.K., Chalecki, J., Fogarty, J.: How it works: a field study of non-technical users interacting with an intelligent system. In: Proceedings of the SIGCHI Conference on Human Factors in Computing Systems, pp. 31–40. ACM (2007)

57. Woodruff, A., Fox, S.E., Rousso-Schindler, S., Warshaw, J.: A qualitative exploration of perceptions of algorithmic fairness. In: Proceedings of the 2018 CHI Conference on Human Factors in Computing Systems, CHI 2018, pp. 656:1–656:14. ACM, New York (2018). https://doi.org/10.1145/3173574.3174230, http://doi.acm.org/10.1145/3173574.3174230

58. Özgöbek, O., Shabib, N., Gulla, J.: Data sets and news recommendation. In: Workshops Proceedings of the 24th ACM Conference on User Modeling, Adaptation, and Personalization, vol. 1181, pp. 5–12 (January 2014)

A Dip into a Deep Well: Online Political Advertisements, Valence, and European Electoral Campaigning

Jukka Ruohonen[(✉)][iD]

Department of Future Technologies, University of Turku, Turku, Finland
juanruo@utu.fi

Abstract. Online political advertisements have become an important element in electoral campaigning throughout the world. At the same time, concepts such as disinformation and manipulation have emerged as a global concern. Although these concepts are distinct from online political ads and data-driven electoral campaigning, they tend to share a similar trait related to valence, the intrinsic attractiveness or averseness of a message. Given this background, the paper examines online political ads by using a dataset collected from Google's transparency reports. The examination is framed to the mid-2019 situation in Europe, including the European Parliament elections in particular. According to the results based on sentiment analysis of the textual ads displayed via Google's advertisement machinery, (i) most of the political ads have expressed positive sentiments, although these vary greatly between (ii) European countries as well as across (iii) European political parties. In addition to these results, the paper contributes to the timely discussion about data-driven electoral campaigning and its relation to politics and democracy.

Keywords: Online ads · Political ads · Transparency reporting · Electoral campaigning · Valence · Manipulation · Political parties · European Parliament

1 Introduction

Political communication is increasingly affect-laden; many politicians use strong words and seek big emotions for delivering their messages. The delivery, in turn, is nowadays often done rapidly through social media and micro-targeted online advertisements. Similar delivery tactics are used to also spread outright misinformation and propaganda. There is a similarity between these and the political online communication of many politicians; both seek to appeal to emotions.

In online marketing emotions are embedded to the concept of valence. Although the origins come from psychology, there is a whole academic branch devoted to the concept in marketing research. Without delving into the details of this branch, in essence, products with a positive brand sell. By implication, it is important for marketers to try to increase positive valence expressed by

© Springer Nature Switzerland AG 2020
M. van Duijn et al. (Eds.): MISDOOM 2020, LNCS 12259, pp. 37–51, 2020.
https://doi.org/10.1007/978-3-030-61841-4_3

consumers online. When money is involved, however, anything appearing online is subject to manipulation and exploitation. In fact, it has long been known that the online marketing industry also garners massive gray and black areas, ranging from shadowy business practices that evade existing consumer protection laws to downright criminal activities [19]. There is also more to the concept of valence in online marketing settings. To increase the overall attractiveness of a brand, marketers often use so-called electronic word-of-mouth techniques; the goal is to spread a positive sentiment expressed by one consumer to other consumers [30]. There are also risks involved. For instance, customers may start to also propagate negative sentiments, leading to negative spillovers through which negative online chatter about a brand affects negatively the brand's other product segments as well as rival brands [4]. In politics such risks amalgamate into strategies; to win elections, spreading negativity and misinformation may yield a good payoff.

This brief background provides the motivation for the present paper—as well as its contribution. Although there is a growing literature on online disinformation, fake news, and related topics [27,28,37], the connection of these to online marketing is seldom explicitly articulated. A further point can be made about the intermediaries through which disinformation—and marketing material—is spread. Although Facebook continues to be the platform of choice for commercial marketers, political campaigners, and miscreants alike [5,9], practically the whole Web has been captured to serve advertising. Yet, much of the research has focused on social media, and, presumably due to the availability of open data, Twitter. Paid online advertisements have seldom been examined. In fact, this paper is likely the very first to explore the online political ads displayed through the advertisement gears of Google, the world's largest advertisement company.

By following recent research [27], the paper's focus is further framed to the mid-2019 situation in Europe, including particularly the 2019 European Parliament (EP) elections in the European Union (EU). In this regard, it is worth remarking that the EU's attempts to combat disinformation and manipulation can be roughly grouped into two approaches: the General Data Protection Regulation (GDPR) on one hand and voluntary self-regulation on the other [22]. This dual approach is a little paradoxical; while also Google has released these voluntary code-of-practice reports for political ads [11], the company is at the same time under GDPR and other investigations by authorities in the EU and its member states. A paradox is present also in politics: many European politicians and political parties—including those who campaigned for the GDPR and who have advocated better privacy regulations in general—have been eager to market themselves online by using the tools and techniques supplied by the advertisement industry. Divines do not always practice what they preach.[1]

In order to present a few sensible and testable hypotheses for the forthcoming empirical exploration of textual ads displayed through Google, Sect. 2 continues the discussion about the relation between online marketing and electoral cam-

---

[1] A Cyclopedia of the Best Thoughts of Charles Dickens, Compiled and Alphabetically Arranged by F.G. De Fontaine, New York, Hale & Son publishers, 1872, p. 267.

paigning. The dataset and the methods used are elaborated in the subsequent Sect. 3. Results and conclusions follow in Sects. 4 and 5, respectively.

2   Hypotheses and Related Work

Data-driven campaigning was one of the keywords in the 2010s politics. Throughout the decade and throughout the world, politicians and party officials were enthusiastically experimenting with new techniques for targeting electorates and influencing their opinions online [1,16,29]. The tools and techniques used were exactly the same as the ones used for commercial online marketing [6,7]. However, things changed dramatically in the late 2010s; the 2016 presidential election in the United States and the later Cambridge Analytica scandal in 2018 were the watershed moments for the change. No longer was data-driven campaigning uncritically seen in positive light by electorates and political establishments. Manipulation, disinformation, and related concepts entered into the global political discourse. This entry was nothing unexpected from a computer science perspective; academic privacy research had pinpointed many of the risks well before these gained mainstream traction [18]. Later on, social media and technology companies sought to answer to the public uproar by traditional means of corporate social responsibility: by producing voluntary transparency reports on political ads. The reports released by Google supply the data for the present work.

If full corporate social responsibility is taken for granted, these reports cover most of the political ads shown through the Google's vast online advertisement empire. These are paid advertisements for which a record is kept about the advertisers. Therefore, the paper's topic covers manipulation but excludes blatant disinformation, which, at least presently, unlikely occurs extensively through paid online ads. Yet, there is still a notable parallel between these ads and the genuine disinformation that is being primarily spread on—or via—social media.

Whether it is plain propaganda, indirect distractions, smear campaigns, peppering of political polarization, or suppressing participation through harassment, the tactics used tend to emphasize emotions or valence, the attractiveness or unattractiveness of a political message [5]. The same emotional emphasis has long been a part of online marketing [8]. Furthermore, valance provides a clear connection to political science within which negative electoral campaigning is a classical research topic. Although definitions vary, a directional definition is often used; these campaigns involve attacks against and confrontation with competing political actors [33]. Such campaigns have become common also in Europe through populist parties who seek to appeal to people and their emotions with criticism about establishments and the exclusion of others [31,32]. While populism thus involves both the directional definition and the aspect of valence, there exists also an alternative definition of negative campaigning often cherished by politicians, campaigners, and consultants: because confrontations belong to politics, negative campaigning, according to the definition, is more about negative political messages that involve untruthful or deceptive claims [36]. By loosely following this alternative, non-directional definition, the present work concentrates on the potential valance-rooted negativity present in online political ads.

Such negativity is neither a fully social nor an entirely political phenomenon; it contains also visible socio-technical traits. Although the so-called echo chambers would be a good example, the evidence regarding such chambers is mixed [23]. Therefore, it is more sensible to generally assert that incivility breeds further incivility, and online platforms are not neutral actors in this breeding [37]. On the technical side of this nurturing, a good example would be the 2012 experiment by Facebook to manipulate users' news feeds to determine whether emotionally positive or negative reactions could be invoked algorithmically [7]. Although such proactive manipulation of masses is beyond the reach of academic research, related negativity propagation topics have been examined also in marketing [4] and computer science [26]. Propagation provides a powerful tool also in politics.

On the social and political side, data-driven campaigning has presumably sought to conduct many similar experiments, as testified by the Cambridge Analytica scandal. Though, the actual power and control of politicians, campaigners, and data mining companies may still be somewhat illusory; they are dependent on the existing online advertisement machinery, which, in turn, is often based on vague datasets supplied by shady data brokers, questionable machine learning, and even plain pseudo-science. Furthermore, by nature, politics are always volatile, non-deterministic, and ambivalent—by implication, it is extremely difficult to predict which particular topics become the focal topics in a given election. The 2019 EP elections are a good example in this regard: although immigration, populism, and euroskepticism were all well-anticipated topics [27], the emergence of climate change as a topic was hardly well-predicted. The results from these European elections also polarized around these topics; populist euroskeptic parties won, but so did pro-Europe and green parties. Given this background, the first hypothesis examined in the forthcoming empirical analysis can be stated as:

H_1 *Reflecting the current political polarization and the particular themes in the 2019 EP elections, the online political ads that were shown in Europe around mid-2019 tended to exhibit negative sentiments and negativity in general.*

The literature on negative campaigning allows to refine this Hypothesis H_1 into a couple of additional, inferential hypotheses. In particular, it has been observed that party systems and characteristics of political systems in general affect negative campaigning and its prevalence [10,36]. In essence, two-party systems have often been seen as more prone to negative campaigning than the multi-party systems and coalition governments that are typical to most European countries. Therefore, it seems justified to also posit the following hypothesis:

H_2 *The sentiments—whether positive or negative—expressed in the political online ads around the 2019 EP elections varied across the EU member states.*

A corollary Hypothesis H_3 logically follows:

H_3 *The sentiments expressed in the mid-2019 European online political ads varied not only across the EU member states but also across political parties.*

As party systems vary across Europe, so do parties, contextual factors, campaigning strategies, and political cultures. Besides this truism, Hypothesis H_3 can be justified with existing observations that different parties tend to use online campaigning techniques differently [1,16,29]. Finally, it should be noted that neither H_2 nor H_3 are logically dependent on the answer for Hypothesis H_1.

3   Materials and Methods

3.1   Data

The dataset is based on Google's [12] transparency reporting on the political advertising in the European Union. The following seven important points should be enumerated about the dataset and its pre-processing for obtaining the sample:

1. The EU itself is only used by Google to distinguish the geographic origins of the authors of the political ads. By implication, the data does not separate advertisements exclusively *about* the EU and its elections—nor does it distinguish advertisements potentially placed *by* the EU and its institutions. However, information is available about elections targeted by an advertiser. Given this information, the sampling of observations was restricted to those advertisers who had announced having advertised in the 2019 EP elections.
2. Only textual advertisements were included in the sample. As can be seen from Fig. 1, most of the political ads placed through Google were in fact videos and images. The textual advertisements are those typically seen as so-called paid banners in the company's search engine results, while the political video advertisements typically appear in YouTube, and so forth.
3. All textual advertisements in the sample were further translated to English by using Google's online translation engine. By and large, this automatic translation is necessary because contemporary text mining frameworks remain limited in their coverage of the multiple languages spoken in Europe.
4. Duplicate textual advertisements were excluded. This exclusion was done with simple string matching before and after the translation: if two ads contained the exact same text, only one of these was included in the sample.
5. Given the lexicon-based sentiment analysis techniques soon described, only minimal pre-processing was applied to the translated ads. Namely: the strings "no.", "No.", and "NO." were excluded because the sentiment techniques tend to equate these to negations, although in the present context these refer to campaigning with a candidate's number in a particular election.
6. No data was available for some advertisements due to third-party hosting of the advertisements and violations of Google's policies [11] for political ads. Given the ongoing debate about online political ads in general, the quite a few policy violations are particularly interesting, but, unfortunately, no details are provided by Google regarding the reasons behind these violations.
7. The data is very limited and coarse with respect to targeting and profiling [6].

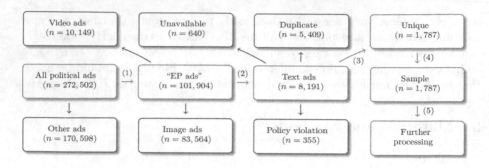

Fig. 1. The Construction of the Sample

The last point requires a brief further comment. Although hosting and technical traceability have recently been under regulatory scrutiny [13], the micro-targeting, mass-profiling, and manipulation aspects have received most of the general political attention [6,7,9]. In this respect, Google seems to have aligned itself more toward Facebook than toward Twitter and Spotify, both of which have banned all political ads in their platforms. In fact, a spokesperson from Google recently assured that the company has *"never offered granular micro-targeting of election ads"*, but, nevertheless, since the beginning of 2020, it now only allows targeting of political advertisements according to age, gender, and postal code [34]. Some data about age and gender targeting is also available in the transparency reports. In theory, this data could be useful for continuing the work on Google's demographic profiling [35], but, in practice, the data is of little practical use. For instance: from all advertisement campaigns in the raw dataset ($n = 46,880$), which group multiple ads, about 80% have not specified gender-based targeting. The second largest group (18%) is something labeled as "male, female, unknown gender", which, more than anything, foretells about (perhaps intentional) construct validity problems affecting the transparency reporting.

An additional point should be made about the longitudinal scope of the sample. The sample covers a period of about five months. The earliest and latest advertisements in the dataset are from 20 May 2019 and 6 October 2019, respectively. The starting date is constrained by data availability; in general, Google does not provide earlier data. The ending date, in turn, is framed with the date of obtaining the raw dataset (9 October 2019). Given the varying lengths of electoral campaigns, the 2019 European Parliament elections (23–26 May) are thus only partially covered. Even though the coverage captures only the few late days in the campaigning for the EP elections, it seems fair to assume that these were also the dates of particularly intense campaigning. The point is important especially in the online context, which does not require lengthy upfront planning. In other words, online political ads are easy to place even for last-minute probes.

However, even with the noted restriction of the sample to those advertisers who had advertised in the EP elections, also other elections and referendums are potentially covered because these advertisers may have advertised also in other occasions. Given the longitudinal scope, these occasions include: the Irish referendum on divorce (24 May) and the Romanian referendum on corruption (26 May), the federal election in Belgium (26 May), the second round in the Lithuanian presidential election (26 May), the Danish and Greek parliamentary elections (5 June and 7 July, respectively), the lower house election in Austria (29 September), and the Portuguese parliamentary election (6 October). In addition, the Brexit saga is visible also in the sample analyzed. Furthermore, politicians, party officials, interest groups, and individuals may also place online ads for general advocacy and publicity reasons without a clear electoral target [9]. All this said, qualitative observations and a few keyword-based searches indicate that many of the ads sampled explicitly or implicitly refer to the 2019 EP elections.

3.2   Methods

Sentiment analysis refers to a group of computational methods to identify subjective information and affective states. In the text mining context these methods can be roughly grouped into machine learning and lexicon-based approaches. Two simple lexicon-based methods are used in the present work: the algorithms of Liu et al. [21] and Nielsen [24], as implemented in an R package [15]. Both rank the sentiment of a document according to the number of times manually labeled negative and positive words appear in the document. In addition, the slightly more sophisticated method of Hutto and Gilbert [14] is used, as implemented in a Python package [25]. This method augments the lexicon-based approach with a few (deterministic) rules on the grammar and style used in a document. Based on a subjective evaluation, no normalization is used for the lexicon-based algorithms, while the algorithm of Hutto and Gilbert is scaled to the unit interval. All three methods are tailored for text mining of social media data. Therefore, the methods seem also suitable for analyzing the textual political advertisements delivered through Google. Akin to messages in Twitter, these ads are short and up to a point; the mean character count of the sample is only 118 characters.

The first Hypothesis H_1 is examined with descriptive statistics. Regression analysis is used for examining H_2 and H_3. To examine the two hypotheses in a single linear model, the following random effects (or multi-level) model is used:

$$y_{ij} = \alpha_j + \mathbf{x}'_{ij}\beta + \varepsilon_{ij}, \quad i = 1,\ldots,1787, \quad j = 1,\ldots,63, \tag{1}$$

where y_{ij} is a sentiment score from a given algorithm for the i:th ad, α_j is a random effect for the j:th political party, $\mathbf{x}'_{ij}$ is a row vector of non-random (fixed) independent variables, β is a regression coefficient vector, ε_{ij} is the error,

$$\alpha_j \sim N(0, \sigma_\alpha^2) \quad \text{and} \quad \varepsilon_{ij} \sim N(0, \sigma_\varepsilon^2), \tag{2}$$

where $N(\cdot)$ denotes the normal distribution with a mean of zero and variance σ^2.

Thus, the effects for the political parties are treated as random variables, which are both mutually independent and independent from the errors ε_{ij}. In contrast, the country effects are embedded to $\mathbf{x}'_{ij}$ together with other control variables enumerated in Table 1. This model is generally necessary because the country and party effects cannot be both included as normal (fixed) independent variables due to multicollinearity. Furthermore, the countries cannot be easily modeled as random effects because some ads have been shown in many countries.

Although further variability could be examined by allowing also the slope coefficients in β to vary across the parties, the model specified is enough to answer to the two hypotheses. It is fitted for the results from all three sentiment algorithms using well-known and well-documented R packages [2,3,20]. If the answers to both H_2 and H_3 are positive, in essence, $\hat{\sigma}_\alpha^2 \not\approx 0$ and some of the estimated coefficients in $\hat{\beta}$ for the countries are non-zero and statistically significant. In addition, the packages used provide a function to test the random effect terms $\hat{\alpha}_j$ with a likelihood ratio test. Likewise, Akaike's information criterion (AIC) is used to compare the full (unrestricted) model to a restricted model without the country effects. The simple random effects model and the basic statistical checks outlined are sufficient because the goal is not prediction, which might entail model validation with bootstrapping, cross-validation, or related techniques.

Table 1. Independent (fixed) variables

Mnemonic	Description
DAYS	A continuous variable measuring the number of days an ad was shown
IMPR	Three dummy variables for the number of Google-defined "impressions" an ad got; the reference variable is less than ten thousand impressions
EURO	Three dummy variables for the upper bound of the cost of an ad; the reference variable is 50€ (the maximum dummy variable denotes 60,000€)
AGET	A dummy variable that takes the value one in case any of the campaigns to which an ad belonged had specified any kind of age-based targeting
GENT	Defined analogously to AGET, but for gender-based targeting
MULT	A dummy variable scoring 1 if an ad was displayed in multiple countries
CNTR	Twenty-five dummy variables for the countries in which an ad was shown

A further point should be made about the identification of political parties. This identification was done manually. For unclear cases, open source intelligence (a.k.a. Google and Wikipedia) was used to check whether the name of an advertiser referred to an European political party. On the one hand, the mapping includes cases whereby a local or a regional chapter of a clearly identifiable party had placed the given political ad; on the other, electoral alliances had to be excluded from the identification. Although about 72% of all political ads could be mapped to parties, it should be emphasized that many of the political ads were placed by different support associations, marketing companies, and even individuals on behalf of some particular politicians and candidates. National election laws also differ between the EU member states with respect to the general rules on electoral campaigning. Currently, only eleven member states have specific legislations in place regarding mandatory transparency of online political ads [22]. Needless to say, these judicial aspects are an important element in the debate about political online ads—and the sample also contains some cases in which a vague support association in one country had advertised in another country.

4 Results

All three sentiment algorithms indicate pronouncedly non-negative valence. As can be seen from Fig. 2, only less than 10% of the ads have a negative sentiment polarity according. Depending on an algorithm, zero-valued sentiments account for about 33–46% of all political ads in the sample. For the two lexicon-based algorithms, these "neutral" (zero-valued) scores imply that no word in an ad was tagged as positive or negative, or that an equal number of words were tagged as positive and negative. Thus, the dataset and the algorithms do not support H_1.

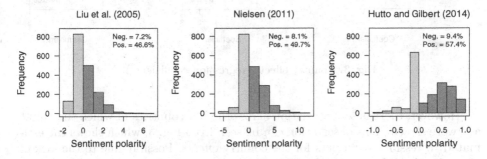

Fig. 2. Sentiment polarity according to three algorithms

Table 2. AIC values from unrestricted and restricted models

	Liu et al. (2005)	Nielsen (2011)	Hutto and Gilbert (2014)
Restricted	5316	7570	1389
Unrestricted	5271	7520	1326

Table 3. Variances of the random effects

	Liu et al. (2005)	Nielsen (2011)	Hutto and Gilbert (2014)
$\hat{\sigma}_\alpha^2$	0.168	0.697	0.035
$\hat{\sigma}_\varepsilon^2$	1.054	3.698	0.114

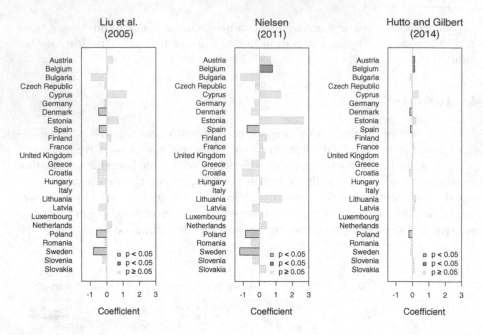

Fig. 3. Country effects (regression coefficients)

However, there is some variation across the EU countries in which the online ads were shown. This observation can be seen from Fig. 3, which shows the estimated regression coefficients for the country effects. Possibly due to the lack of normalization, there is interesting variation across the three algorithms; in particular, the coefficients are much smaller in magnitude for the sentiments computed with the algorithm of Hutto and Gilbert. Only the negative coefficients for Poland and Spain are statistically significant for all three algorithms. While the statistically significant coefficients are not substantial in magnitude for any of the algorithms, the AIC values in Table 2 still indicate small improvements. In other words, the country effects are worth retaining; there is weak support for H_2. As for the other control variables in Table 1, only one of the dummy variables for EURO is significant across all three algorithms. As seen from Table 3, the variances of the random party effects are also non-zero. The `ranova` function [20] further indicates statistical significance of the random effects for all three sentiment algorithms. Thus, also Hypothesis H_3 can be accepted.

Indeed, a substantial variation exists both in terms of the ads placed and the sentiments expressed by the manually identified political parties (see Fig. 4). However, it is difficult to say anything specific about the potential explanations behind this variation. For instance, many of the euroskeptic parties—including Alternative für Deutschland (Germany), Dansk Folkeparti (Denmark), Sloboda a Solidarita (Slovakia), or Fratelli d'Italia and Salvini's Lega in Italy—rank clearly below the average sentiment polarity scores. While this observation is expected, some other euroskeptic parties, such as Freiheitliche Partei Österreich (Austria)

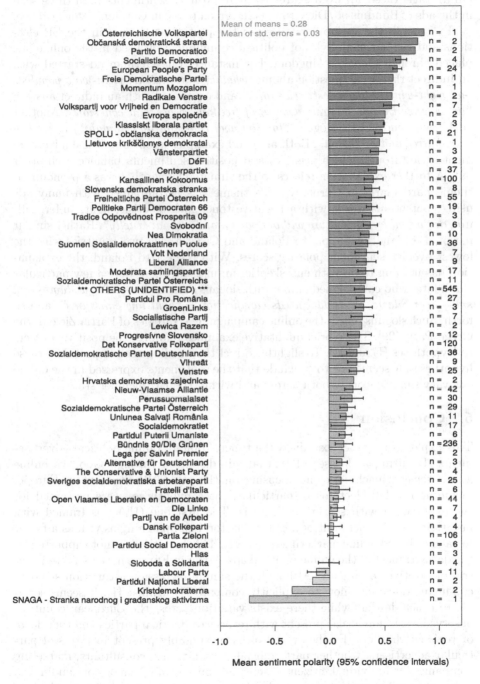

Fig. 4. Average sentiment polarity across political parties

and Svobodní (Czech Republic), have placed ads with clearly positive sentiments. On average, these ads even expressed more positive sentiments than those seen in the ads of Bündnis 90/Die Grünen (the green party in Germany), for instance.

In general, the variability traces to the particular themes in the EP elections and the national styles of political communication used in the online ads placed through Google's kingdom. For instance, one German ad started with an indirect rhetorical question about *"whether nationalists, right-wing populists and right-wing radicals destroy Europe"*, and continued with an indirect answer: *"or whether Europe remains a place of freedom, peace and cohesion"*. Another ad likewise ended to a slogan: *"for courage, cohesion and humanity instead of fear, hatred and exclusion"*. Both are good examples about a political advertisement style through which negative and positive sentiments balance each other out. A further explanation relates to the climate change that was a pronounced theme particularly in Germany. This theme was accompanied with many ads using contentious words with a negative tone, such as crisis, fight, suffer, failure, or *"a healthy agriculture without poison and animal cruelty"*. Rather similar national explanations apply to Poland and Croatia, the two countries with the lowest average sentiment polarity scores. With respect to Poland, the explanation has nothing to do with euroskepticism; instead, there were a few particular candidates who campaigned online with slogans such as *"more illegal dumps and smog over Silesia"*, *"scandal needs clarification"*, *"fight low emissions"*, and so forth. Such slogans reflect the online campaigning strategies of Partia Zieloni, the Green Party [29]. These brief qualitative examples reinforce the positive answers to Hypotheses H_2 and H_3. To slightly correct the wording used to postulate these hypotheses, it seems fair to conclude that the sentiments expressed in the online ads vary simultaneously both across and within the EU member states.

5   Conclusion

This exploratory paper examined the timely topic of online political advertisements. By using a dataset of textual ads displayed through Google's online advertisement machinery and focusing on the mid-2019 situation in Europe, including the EP elections in particular, three hypotheses were presented for the exploration with sentiment analysis. The first one (H_1) was framed with negativity—a distinct trait of negative electoral campaigning as well as a factor in valence-based online marketing in general. This hypothesis is not supported by the dataset: most of the online political ads shown in Europe have exhibited neutral or positive sentiments. Although the simple regression estimation strategy conducted does not allow to explicitly compare H_2 against H_3, it seems sensible to conclude that while there exists variation across the European countries observed, variation is also present with respect to political parties and their local or regional chapters. Further variation is presumably present in terms of particular advertisers, whether party officials, associations, consultants, marketing companies, or individual citizens placing ads on behalf of parties or candidates.

Three limitations can be noted. First, the machine-translation used likely causes inaccuracies—after all, a language's small nuances are often important particularly in political communication. The second limitation directly follows: only three simple sentiment algorithms were examined, and all of these were limited to English. Third, the empirical exploration was explicitly limited to textual ads, which, however, constitute only a minority of the political ads placed through Google's platforms (see Fig. 1). Patching these limitations offer good opportunities for further work in computer science. While multi-language sentiment algorithms are generally needed, so are specific lexicons tailored for online political communication. However, a satisfactory solution likely necessitates collaboration between computer and political scientists. For both scientists, a whole new realm also opens with a question of how to analyze disinformation, political manipulation, and sentiments expressed in these with image and video datasets.

But there are also many questions to which computers cannot answer—and with which computers should not be perhaps allowed to even interfere. Democracy and politics are among these. While the transparency of algorithms is often touted as a path forward [17], many of the problems are located deeper within the platforms. Thus, even with the limitations discussed, there are some lessons to be learned in this regard. Although H_1 was rejected and neutral sentiments have been common, all three algorithms still indicate a large amount of positive sentiments in the political ads. This observation can be used to argue that valence-based campaigning is widely practiced. Like with online marketing, such campaigning is partially explained by the technical constraints imposed by the advertising platforms. Short taglines with catchy sentimental words—whether positive or negative—are also what the platforms are imposing upon campaigners and political advertisers. As a consequence, the room for argumentation, discussion, debate, and "evidence-based politics" arguably shrinks even further.

A final point can be made about regulation. In the EU elections are regulated by national laws, and there are no cues that the EU itself would be willing to intervene. At the same time, according to a recent voluntary transparency report [11], Google detected 16,690 EU-based accounts that violated the company's misrepresentation policies between the first of May 2019 and 26 May 2019. The sample examined aligns with this number; about 12% of the EP-related textual ads were unavailable either due to policy violations or due to third-party hosting. These numbers hint that also Google has a problem with its self-regulation of political ads. But politics are always about power, and platforms provide one way to achieve and maintain power. In other words, regulating online political ads is difficult not only because of rights, freedoms, and legal hurdles [28], but also because divines do not always practice what they preach.

Acknowledgements. This research was supported by the Academy of Finland (grant number 327391).

References

1. Anstead, N.: Data-driven campaigning in the 2015 United Kingdom general election. Int. J. Press/Polit. **22**(3), 294–313 (2017)

2. Baayen, R.H., Davidson, D.J., Bates, D.M.: Mixed-effects modeling with crossed random effects for subjects and items. J. Mem. Lang. **59**(4), 390–412 (2008)
3. Bates, D., Mächler, M., Bolker, B., Walker, S.: Fitting linear mixed-effects models using lme4. J. Stat. Softw. **67**(1), 1–48 (2015)
4. Borah, A., Tellis, G.J.: Halo (spillover) effects in social media: do product recalls of one brand hurt or help rival brands? J. Mark. Res. **53**(2), 143–160 (2016)
5. Bradshaw, S., Howard, P.N.: The global disinformation order: 2019 global inventory of organised social media manipulation (2019), Working Paper 2019, Computational Propaganda Research Project, Oxford Internet Institute, University of Oxford (January 2020). https://comprop.oii.ox.ac.uk/wp-content/uploads/sites/93/2019/09/CyberTroop-Report19.pdf
6. Chester, J., Montgomery, K.C.: The digital commercialisation of US politics - 2020 and beyond. Internet Policy Rev. **8**(4), 1–23 (2019)
7. Christl, W.: How companies use personal data against people: automated disadvantage, personalized persuasion, and the societal ramifications of the commercial use of personal information (2017). Working Paper by Cracked Labs (January 2020). https://crackedlabs.org/dl/CrackedLabs_Christl_DataAgainstPeople.pdf
8. Colicev, A., Kumar, A., O'Connor, P.: Modeling the relationship between firm and user generated content and the stages of the marketing funnel. Int. J. Res. Mark. **36**(1), 100–116 (2019)
9. Dommett, K., Power, S.: The political economy of Facebook advertising: election spending, regulation and targeting online. Polit. Q. **90**(2), 257–265 (2019)
10. Elmelund-Præstekær, C., Svensson, H.M.: Ebbs and Flows of negative campaigning: a longitudinal study of the influence of contextual factors on Danish campaign rhetoric. Eur. J. Commun. **29**(2), 230–239 (2013)
11. Google Inc.: EC action plan on disinformation: Google May 2019 Report (2019). https://ec.europa.eu/newsroom/dae/document.cfm?doc_id=60042. Accessed Jan 2020
12. Google Inc.: Political advertising in the European Union (2019). https://storage.googleapis.com/transparencyreport/google-political-ads-transparency-bundle.zip. Accessed 9 Oct 2019
13. Haenschen, K., Wolf, J.: Disclaiming responsibility: how platforms deadlocked the federal election commission's efforts to regulate digital political advertising. Telecommun. Policy **43**(8), 101824 (2019)
14. Hutto, C.J., Gilbert, E.: VADER: a parsimonious rule-based model for sentiment analysis of social media text. In: Proceedings of the Eighth International AAAI Conference on Weblogs and Social Media, pp. 216–225. AAAI, Ann Arbor (2014)
15. Jockers, M.L.: Syuzhet: extract sentiment and plot arcs from text (2015). R package version 1.0.4
16. Jungherr, A.: Four functions of digital tools in election campaigns: the German case. Int. J. Press/Polit. **21**(3), 358–377 (2016)
17. Kirkpatrick, K.: Deceiving the masses on social media. Commun. ACM **63**(5), 33–35 (2020)
18. Korolova, A.: Privacy violations using microtargeted ads: a case study. In: Proceedings of the IEEE International Conference on Data Mining Workshops (ICDMW 2010), pp. 474–482. IEEE, Sydney (2010)
19. Kshetri, N.: The economics of click fraud. IEEE Secur. Priv. **8**(3), 45–53 (2010)
20. Kuznetsova, A., Brockhoff, P.B., Christensen, R.H.B.: lmerTest package: tests in linear mixed effects models. J. Stat. Softw. **82**(13), 1–26 (2017)

21. Liu, B., Hu, M., Cheng, J.: Opinion observer: analyzing and comparing opinions on the web. In: Proceedings of the 14th International Conference on World Wide Web (WWW 2005), pp. 342–351. ACM, Chiba (2005)
22. Nenadić, I.: Unpacking the "European approach" to tackling challenges of disinformation and political manipulation. Internet Policy Rev. **8**(4), 1–22 (2019)
23. Nguyen, A., Vu, H.T.: Testing popular news discourse on the "echo chamber" effect: does political polarisation occur among those relying on social media as their primary politics news source? First Monday **24**, 6 (2019)
24. Nielsen, F.: A new ANEW: evaluation of a word list for sentiment analysis in microblogs (2011). https://arxiv.org/abs/1103.2903. Accessed Jan 2020
25. The Natural Language Toolkit (NLTK): Version 3.4.5 (2019). http://www.nltk.org. Accessed Jan 2020
26. Ozer, M., Yildirim, M., Davulcu, H.: Negative link prediction and its applications in online political networks. In: Proceedings of the 28th ACM Conference on Hypertext and Social Media (HT 2017), pp. 125–134. ACM, Prague (2017)
27. Pierri, F., Artoni, A., Ceri, S.: Investigating Italian disinformation spreading on Twitter in the context of 2019 European elections. PLOS ONE **15**(1), e0227821 (2020)
28. Pollicino, O., Bietti, E.: Truth and deception across the Atlantic: a roadmap of disinformation in the US and Europe. Ital. J. Public Law **11**(1), 43–85 (2019)
29. Rafałowski, W.: Parties' issue emphasis strategies on Facebook. East Eur. Polit. Soc.: Cult. **34**(1), 96–123 (2019)
30. Ruohonen, J., Hyrynsalmi, S.: Evaluating the use of Internet search volumes for time series modeling of sales in the video game industry. Electron. Mark. **27**(4), 351–370 (2017)
31. Sakki, I., Hakoköngäs, E., Pettersson, K.: Past and present nationalist political rhetoric in Finland: changes and continuities. J. Lang. Soc. Psychol. **37**(2), 160–180 (2017)
32. Schmidt, F.: Drivers of populism: a four-country comparison of party communication in the run-up to the 2014 European parliament elections. Polit. Stud. **66**(2), 459–479 (2017)
33. Song, H., Nyhuis, D., Boomgaarden, H.: A network model of negative campaigning: the structure and determinants of negative campaigning in multiparty systems. Commun. Res. **46**(2), 273–294 (2019)
34. Spencer, S.: An update on our political ads policy (2019). Google Blog. https://blog.google/technology/ads/update-our-political-ads-policy
35. Tschantz, M.C., Egelman, S., Choi, J., Weaver, N., Friedland, G.: The accuracy of the demographic inferences shown on Google's ad settings. In: Proceedings of the 17th Workshop on Privacy in the Electronic Society (WPES 2018), pp. 33–41. ACM, Toronto (2018)
36. Walter, A.S.: Negative campaigning in western Europe: similar or different? Polit. Stud. **62**(S1), 42–60 (2014)
37. Wright, J.: 'Many people are saying...': applying the lessons of Naïve skepticism to the fight against fake news and other 'total bullshit'. Postdigital Sci. Educ. **2**, 113–131 (2020)

Misinformation from Web-based News Media? Computational Analysis of Metabolic Disease Burden for Chinese

Angela Chang(✉) 🆔

University of Macau, Macau SAR, China
wychang@um.edu.mo

Abstract. Raising the question of what and how metabolic syndrome is covered through the renowned online press, hence, this study attempted to determine the ways in which the newspapers selects chronic diseases and how the syndrome informs the public of causation and adverse outcome. Web-based news platforms from four leading newspapers in mainland China were sampled for machine computational analysis. Two prominent metabolic diseases, its causation and causal inference were identified in a total of 16,005 articles in the past 10 years. Descriptive statistics is reported while a word cloud displays the entire news content as a graphical representation of word frequency with recurring expressions. A dendograms was summarized to provide a richer context to interpret association between metabolic syndrome and causal inference to verify if misinformation was spread through the renowned online press. Results indicate that news stories tend to provide equivocal descriptions of metabolic disease burden while implying explicitly that alcohol, tobacco, or genes might be the main cause of adverse outcomes for metabolic syndrome. This study emphasized the importance of taxonomy of coding, causal assessments of news stories to inform debates on addressing causal inferences, message design, and unique frames in the media content. It concludes with limitation of datamining and directions for future research.

Keywords: Diabetes · Alcohol overconsumption · Causal inference · Misinformation type

1 Introduction

An important topic in population health studies has been metabolic disease since the major cause of death and the risk factors for metabolic syndrome affect disability-adjusted life span, especially for women in Mainland China [1]. The most common form of metabolic disease is type 2 diabetes, which accounts for 95% of diabetes cases in adults aged 18–99 years old. In China, 120 million adults have been diagnosed with diabetes as of 2017 [2]. The rate of metabolic disease continues to escalate, which calls into question the media's role in covering and promoting knowledge about metabolic syndrome for treatment and prevention (e.g., [3]). Hence, more news coverage about metabolic syndrome is assumed to raise awareness of the disease, while promoting knowledge of causation and causal inference for metabolic disease to the general public.

© Springer Nature Switzerland AG 2020
M. van Duijn et al. (Eds.): MISDOOM 2020, LNCS 12259, pp. 52–62, 2020.
https://doi.org/10.1007/978-3-030-61841-4_4

1.1 Misinformation Analysis

The problem of population health could be worsened by health-related misinformation from news media. The concept of misinformation refers broadly to honest mistakes, bias, unknown inaccuracies, uncertainties, and ignorance as distinct from disinformation [4]. Prior studies surveyed misinformation in which it was implied that something or someone might be the cause of an adverse outcome but less emphasis in these studies was placed on the function of explicitly or implicitly stating the likely cause of an outcome [5]. Hence, this study proposes to examine what is being published in web-based news media by studying the way a likely cause of an outcome is explicitly or implicitly presented. The aim of the present study was to provide reliable and up-to-date information on the prevalence and associated factors of metabolic syndrome. It allows the researchers to examine how different news outlets discuss the diseases, its cause, and the causal inferences that typically accompany it. The computational analysis improves empirical study for rendering news selection in a more efficient and better-understood process. In addition, it established a preliminary understanding of the dominated news values and the relevant risks for potentially leading news audiences to incorrect assumptions about how metabolic disease develops.

Computational analysis of misinformation has been popular in computational communication studies. Examples of text analysis applications include the examination of news stories from CNN and BBC by computer-assisted software to study the section prominence of the SARS crisis [6]. A more recent study examines how social media became a channel to terminate rumours in China by influencing the perceived credibility of health information, in contrast to the popular impression that social media degenerates into a rumour mill [7]. A similar approach adopted the concept of infodemiology for studying the science of information distribution and determinants of information in an electronic medium, with the goal of informing public health and policy [8].

Recently developed computer-aided analysis for identifying health issues has become more sophisticated in ascertaining metadata collection, media effects, particularly by integrating data engineering and machine learning [9–11]. Earlier studies argue that several news values dominate not just in the popular press laymen can understand but also in quality newspapers [12]. Based on all above mentioned concerns by employing computer-aided text processing and automatic content analysis to examine metabolic syndrome and its burden for potential impact on perception, three research questions (RQ) were formulated:

The first RQ focused on how much coverage was devoted to metabolic syndrome in mainland China press for the past 10 years? To be specific, what is the trend of the metabolic diseases with causes and casual inference covered in Chinese newspapers?

The second RQ explored how the metabolic diseases covered by considering the extent to which news selections may be misinforming?

The third RQ examined how the causal inference of metabolic syndromes and causal effect were employed to inform the public for outcome? Did the coverage provide misinformation to interpret association between metabolic syndrome and causal inference?

2 Methodology

In line with the research objectives, the platform of DiVoMiner is deployed and proves ideal at answering research questions concerning changes in the quantity of coverage over time and across newspapers. The platform is equipped with a powerful keyword retrieval function in both English and Chinese from which researchers can easily develop and identify text units containing one keyword or a combination of phrases. With optional filtering of articles, the tailored task powered by DiVoMiner is coming with a web browser extension through which news articles can be categorized. DiVoMiner is operated by the Boyi Data technology company[1] and has been considered as a powerful machine computational tool in big data collection and analysis in real time. Moreover, the embedded software in DiVoMiner provides automated content analysis while validation and reliability check are also functional. Thus, machine computational method contributes valuable clues for examining news selection in a more efficient, effective, and transparent process.

2.1 Sampling

Four Chinese newspapers that publish an electronic version on their websites with free access from January 1, 2010 to December 31, 2019 were selected for this study: *People's Daily News* (PD) (人民日报), *Beijing Evening News* (BE) (北京晚报), *Southern Metropolis Daily News* (SMD) (南方都市报), and *Guangzhou Daily News* (GD) (廣州日報). A communist party-owned outlet, PD has provided direct information from the central government since 1948 and boasts the second largest circulation of any Chinese newspaper, with 2.52 million copies sold daily [13, 14]. A state-run tabloid outlet, BE from Beijing, was founded in 1958 and has the largest-circulation of any newspaper in the capital [14]. In comparison, SMD has been a market-driven newspaper since 1995 and circulates in the Pearl River Delta with 1.40 million readers; SMD has gained extensive attention for daring to challenge institutional restrictions [15]. The official newspaper of the Guangzhou municipal party, GD was established in 1952, with the highest circulation in the metropolitan area with approximately 1.85 million copies sold daily [14].

2.2 Computational Taxonomy

DiVoMiner assisted in the implementation of the coding taxonomy to measure the concept of misinformation. The process involves pilot coding, subsequent modification of the coding scheme, and double coding adapted from earlier studies [9, 10, 16]. Special emphasis is placed on the assumptions of all emerging epidemic of metabolic syndrome that underlies all causation, casual inferences, and the news languages used in formulating these assumptions. An exploratory test was run several times by computer-aided automatic scanning and human manual assessment to ensure accuracy and relevance of the test data.

One of the main tasks is to capture both explicit and implicit assertions of casual linkages. To be specific, an explicit link is given when the assertion is that X causes, triggers, leads to, or generates Y, or that Y originates from or is attributed to X. The explicit

---

[1] BoYiData Homepage, https://www.boyidata.cn, last accessed 2020/01/01.

association between two elements is formulated using concepts or terms that signify causation, causal inferences, or causal language and effects. Additionally, implicit causal inferences do not use such specific terms but still suggest or insinuate causation. Thus, analogical reasoning on linguistic regularities for developing a more comprehensive and reliable coding which was behind a dictionary-approach to measure the concept of misinformation was considered. Moreover, corresponding to previous studies in conceptualizing mediated associations was also taken into consideration. Eventually, the code taxonomy started with the 3 types of metabolic diseases, 14 independent factors of causation contribute to metabolic diseases, and 11 types of causal inference [9, 17]. Codes are typically data-driven and consistency is less of an issue.

Our 6 keywords and 14 phrases resulted from several pilot tests that created a logical phrase the machine can assist in analyzing news data. This process involved searching for diseases names, multiple terms, phrases, concepts, and alternative terms for more precise and reliable results [9, 18]. It is worth to note that Chinese words and phrases into the meaning group have a unique morphological system than English. It is required to select different settings on semi-prefixes or semi-suffixes for computational analysis [9, 10, 17, 18]. For instance, the term of diseases frequently employed in describing metabolic syndrome were: 代謝病 (metabolic disease), 糖尿病 (diabetes), 肥胖 (obesity), 慢性腎臟病 (chronic kidney disease), 肝衰竭 (liver failure), 痛風 (gout); multiple terms of metabolic syndrome in Chinese appeared in the news stories included the following examples: 代謝性疾病, 代謝病, 代謝疾病, 新陳代謝失調症, 代謝缺陷, 代謝失調, 代谢障碍, 代謝紊亂, 代謝異常, 代謝旺盛; to some extent, these Chinese terms were often synonymous with four English phrases of metabolic disorder, metabolic defect, metabolic abnormality, or metabolism.

3 Results

The tailored platform creates researcher-defined codes entered manually and norm files are generated based on frequency analysis of keywords, phrases and content categories. The development over time of metabolic disease coverage shows a clear trend of increasing attention from journalistic decisions. Overall speaking, the highest surge of metabolic related coverage in China is observed in 2019 and 2018, but it shows a big decrease of coverage in 2014 and 2010. *People's Daily* has the least coverage on the metabolic disease with causes and casual inference which illustrated a particular discourse strategy from their editorial strategy. In comparison, *Guangzhou Daily News* starts its increased report of metabolic disease with causes and casual inference in 2017. While *Southern Metropolis Daily News* shows a sharp decline in the number of coverage in 2014, *Beijing Evening News* also has a big decrease in 2016 but no coverage data found in 2010. Figure 1 shows an overview of the development of metabolic diseases coverage in four newspapers in Mainland China for the past 10 years.

A total of 16,005 articles that covered metabolic diseases in conjunction with causation and causal inference were identified, corresponding to an average of 1,601 stories ever year., with an annual low of 906 to a high of 2,244 stories. *Southern Metropolis Daily News* and *Guangzhou Daily News* mirrored this overall development, while *Beijing Evening News* and *People's Daily* provided comparatively less coverage, below the

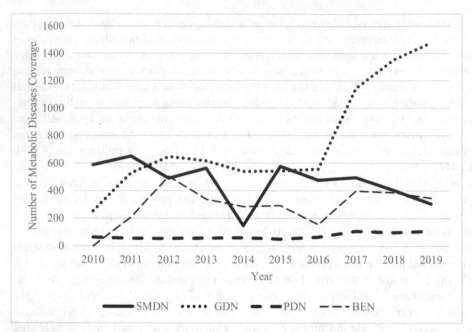

Fig. 1. Development of metabolic diseases coverage in four newspapers in Mainland China from 2010–2019. Note: SMDM stands for Southern Metropolis Daily News; GDN stands for Guangzhou Daily News, PDN stands for People's Daily News, and BEN stands for Beijing Evening News.

average of 400 stories per year. The development of metabolic diseases coverage in Chinese newspapers shows a clear trend of increasing attention over time ($x^2 = 1895.59$, df = 40, p < .001). Turning to individual newspapers, one of the nationwide newspapers, *People's Daily*, had the least coverage, while *Guangzhou Daily News* had the highest coverage of metabolic diseases and burden. Table 1 displays the distribution of metabolic diseases related articles in news media in China from 2010-2019.

For casual inference of metabolic diseases, burdens are presented in four newspapers with statistically significant difference ($x^2 = 149.08$, df = 20, p < .001). Overall, the consequence of loss of wealth outnumbered the other attributions in all newspapers. Employer cost was emphasized in the *Southern Metropolis Daily,* besides the main consequence of individual's wealth loss. As links of consequences at the environmental level, the frame was prominent in displaying societal costs explicitly in news media. Table 2 displays the casual inference of metabolic diseases covered in four newspapers in mainland China spanning 10 years, from 2010 to 2019.

A word cloud is composed of single words that denote a graphical representation of word frequency [10]. The attention of news coverage was given to metabolic syndrome constitutes 158 words from all press stories. Two of the most prominent terms highlighted are "diabetes" and "obesity and overweight", followed by "alcohol", "government", and "mental stress & burden"; next to the above-mentioned terms, the three most frequently used terms are: "smoking", "economic loss & wealth reduction", and "genes". Figure 2

Table 1. Number of metabolic diseases related articles in four Chinese web-based news media from 2010–2019

	SMDN 4697 (%)	GDN 7662 (%)	PDN 727 (%)	BEN 2919 (%)	All 16005 (%)
2010	588 (12.5)	254 (3.3)	64 (8.8)	0 (0.0)	906 (5.7)
2011	651 (13.9)	529 (6.9)	56 (7.7)	209 (7.2)	1445 (9.0)
2012	491 (10.5)	648 (8.5)	56 (7.7)	505 (17.3)	1700 (10.6)
2013	563 (12.0)	616 (8.0)	58 (8.0)	339 (11.6)	1576 (9.8)
2014	148 (3.2)	539 (7.0)	61 (8.4)	286 (9.8)	1034 (6.5)
2015	576 (12.3)	542 (7.1)	51 (7.0)	293 (10.0)	1462 (9.1)
2016	476 (10.1)	556 (7.3)	65 (8.9)	155 (5.3)	1252 (7.8)
2017	495 (10.5)	1145 (14.9)	108 (14.9)	398 (13.6)	2146 (13.4)
2018	404 (8.6)	1354 (17.7)	99 (13.6)	387 (13.3)	2244 (14.0)
2019	305 (6.5)	1479 (19.3)	109 (15.0)	347 (11.9)	2240 (14.0)

Note. SMDM for Southern Metropolis Daily News; GD stands for Guangzhou Daily News, PD stands for People's Daily News, BE for Beijing Evening News

Table 2. Casual inference of metabolic diseases related articles in four Chinese web-based news media from 2010–2019

	SMDN 1625 (%)	GDN 1994 (%)	PDN 303 (%)	BEN 753 (%)	All 4675 (%)
Loss of wealth	684 (42.1)	899 (45.1)	103 (34.0)	313 (41.6)	1999 (42.8)
Loss quality life	233 (14.3)	459 (23.0)	71 (23.4)	221 (29.3)	984 (21.0)
Employer cost	302 (18.6)	273 (13.7)	53 (17.5)	91 (12.1)	719 (15.4)
Societal cost	209 (12.9)	209 (10.5)	37 (12.2)	71 (9.4)	526 (11.3)
Unemployment	181 (11.1)	115 (5.8)	32 (10.6)	41 (5.4)	369 (7.9)
Premature death	16 (1.0)	39 (2.0)	7 (2.3)	16 (2.1)	78 (1.7)

Note. SMDM stands for Southern Metropolis Daily News; GD stands for Guangzhou Daily News, PD stands for People's Daily News, BE stands for Beijing Evening News.

displays a word cloud visualization of metabolic disease with the most frequently used causation and causal inferences.

An deductive textual analysis revealed that the coverage of metabolic diseases included diabetes mellitus (50.4%, $n = 8,906$), followed by overweight/obesity (43.3%, $n = 7,662$), and chronic kidney diseases (4.2%, $n = 738$). Frequency ranking and cluster analysis were further conducted for graphical representation of the hierarchical tree in order to verify if misinformation was spread through the renowned online press. The causations and casual inferences of metabolic diseases were grouped into three clusters

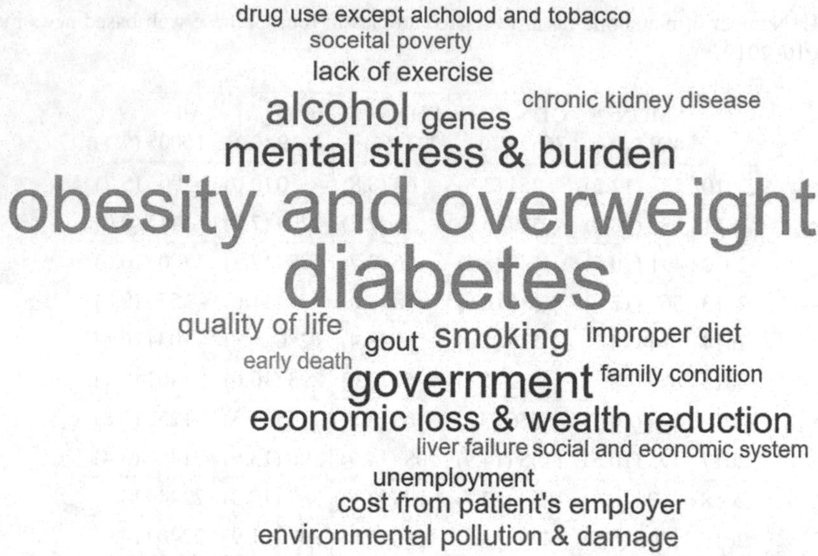

drug use except alcholod and tobacco
soceital poverty
lack of exercise
alcohol genes   chronic kidney disease
mental stress & burden
obesity and overweight
diabetes
quality of life   gout smoking   improper diet
early death
government   family condition
economic loss & wealth reduction
liver failure social and economic system
unemployment
cost from patient's employer
environmental pollution & damage

Fig. 2. Lexical groupings of overall metabolic disease covered in four leading Chinese web-based newspapers, 2010–2019

by integrating news languages used. Specifically, one cluster integrated six variables performing better than the others; the news expression included six themes of news information: governmental management, mental status, alcohol consumption, genetic concern, smoking tobacco, and economic loss. To illustrate, a dendrogram shows the hierarchical relationship between objects employed. It is most commonly created as an output from hierarchical clustering analysis to allocate causes and causal inferences by showing items are similar.

The result of the hierarchical relationship is illustrated in Fig. 3 dendograms in which there are five clusters. One cluster (A) combines three causation and two causal inferences (family condition, drugs except alcohol and tobacco, economic loss, social & economic system, and premature death); a second cluster (B) combines two causation and one causal inference (lack of exercise, wrong diet, and loss of quality life); a third cluster (C) groups one causation and three causal inferences (societal cost, unemployment, environmental pollution, and cost from patients' employer); a fourth cluster (D) combines two causes and one causal inferences (smoking, wealth reduction, and genes); and a fifth cluster (E) shows three causes are very similar (alcohol, mental stress, and government). In the dendrogram, the width of the dendrogram indicates the order in which the clusters were joined. A more informative dendrogram was also created to show where the widths reflect the distance between the clusters B and C, or D and E is close, as is shown in Fig. 3. In the findings, the dendrogram displays that a big difference is between cluster A versus that of cluster E. Overall, a dendograms provides a richer context of misinformation in interpreting associations between causation and causal inference of metabolic syndrome.

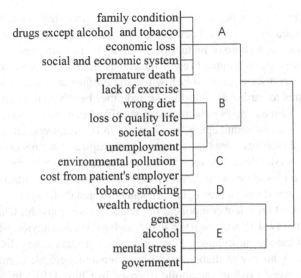

family condition
drugs except alcohol and tobacco
economic loss
social and economic system
premature death
lack of exercise
wrong diet
loss of quality life
societal cost
unemployment
environmental pollution
cost from patient's employer
tobacco smoking
wealth reduction
genes
alcohol
mental stress
government

A

B

C

D

E

Fig. 3. Dendograms of clustering causation and causal inference of metabolic syndrome from Chinese web-based news media

4 Discussion

News decisions were influential in awareness or knowledge of the public might be informed and misinformed. The trend of coverage for the past ten years indicates that efforts to enhance awareness of metabolic diseases were mainly implemented by the web-based SMD periodical, followed by GD. In comparison, the story of metabolic disease seems to not be newsworthy enough for PD and BE, although both newspapers provide direct information on relevant policies from central government in Beijing. The trends observed over the past ten years could be part of a larger cycle from individual's press and may be persist into the future coverage of metabolic diseases. Even our forecasts appear to be increasing coverage of metabolic diseases from regional newspapers, it should be cautious about forecasts that are more than ten years of time periods. Because trends can be volatile, researchers should usually only forecast 2 periods into the future pattern for Chinese readers.

A word cloud of the entire content allows researchers to identify recurring expressions. The most frequently used phrases for causal inference expression emphasized an individual's economic loss and wealth reduction, while the recurring causation phrases focused on four diverse expressions regarding an individual's condition (i.e., alcohol consumption, mental stress and burden, genetic disposition, and tobacco smoking). For additional insight into this finding, that "alcohol" is the most popular term highlighted reflects a concerted effort by journalists as well as China's government to address alcohol overconsumption as a health issue. We wonder whether alcohol is really such a large problem in China, or whether this is a preferred discourse strategy relative to discussion of diabetes.

The causal inference of type 2 diabetes can increase risk of heart disease and stroke and cause major health complications, particularly in the smallest blood vessels in the body, which nourish the kidneys, nerves, and eyes [2]. In comparison, the equivocal information provided by the general news media tends to imply that alcohol, tobacco or genes might be the main cause of metabolic disease. As a result of news selection and salience, some facts are highlighted (e.g., diabetes is linked to adverse outcomes like kidney failure, heart disease, and stroke), while some other facts are overlooked (e.g., diabetes contributes to cardiovascular disease and other health complications).

In this study, Chinese news's mentions of specific keywords – such as childhood obesity in connection with adult aging, incidence of fatty liver, hypertension, hyperlipidaemia, and type 2 diabetes – are limited to one paragraph and not necessarily linked to what follows or precedes them. The selection of ignorance in the news content also lacked details of gender issues in covering causal inference of metabolic syndrome. For example, hypertension was the most prevalent component of metabolic syndrome in Chinese males, while the most prevalent component of metabolic syndrome for Chinese females was central obesity [17, 19]. Although the scientific-based and behavioral-focused study has indicated that the age, urolithiasis, hyperuricemia, coronary artery disease, thiazide drugs intake, family history of diabetes, and hypertension were all significantly associated with an increased risk of metabolic diseases in China [19]. Unfortunately, the casual links of metabolic diseases in the scientific-based information were not reflected sufficiently in overall web-based news media. The published news pieces provides fragmented casual information, rather covering a comprehensive explanation of likely causes of an outcome of metabolic disease burden. This type of misinformation existed, particularly in state-owned news media which demonstrated its journalistic decisions on health news selection. In cluster analysis, another misinformation was evidenced in which news pieces frequently lack explicit explanation of causal inferences; instead, the news stories provided equivocal and uncertainty descriptions of metabolic syndrome for potentially leading news readers to generate incorrectly assumptions about how metabolic diseases were developed and treated.

4.1 Limitations

Several limitations are noteworthy in computational process and news data analysis. First, the result does not show absolute frequency, but relative frequency due to confined data crawling. It can be used for longitudinal comparisons of obtained frequencies to previous saved files. Secondly, there is no clear-cut criteria for the coding taxonomy developed to distinguish misinformation from proper journalism. Yet, the current coding schemes are still insufficient to recognize and filter content about metabolic syndrome circulated online. Last but not least, a word cloud is typically used to depict keyword metadata to visualize text but the analysis of word cloud lack of context in visual representation. Hence, one way to enrich the analysis of coverage bias would be to compare the news coverage with the actual metabolic disease prevalence in those locales to see whether coverage reflects the severity of the problem on the ground. Similarly, the casual inference could be compared to the ranking of causes as well as potential adverse outcomes of metabolic syndrome by epidemiologists.

5 Conclusion

The present work is about the news talking about the syndrome of metabolic diseases, but not about the syndrome itself. This paper aims at investigating the web-based news selection of metabolic syndrome, particularly on diabetes type 2 as a possible example of misinformation. Therefore, this present work explored a data set of Chinese news concerning metabolic disease information in investigating the information in order to verify if misinformation was spread through the renowned online press in China. One of the contributions was to provide reliable and up-to-date information on the prevalence and associated factors of metabolic syndrome.

The method of analysis is based on data mining by examining how machines and algorithmic systems are increasingly utilized to make complex judgements regarding unstructured data. In today's digital landscape, content such as texts, images, and recorded sounds are increasingly subjected to automatic or even semi-automatic processes of classification. When put to action, automatic content analysis methodology is improving validity and reliability in separating biased/unbiased forms of communication and is used to secure the value, authenticity, origin, and ownership of content. Although the limitations and analysis are still quite broad, the study can be a good example of a source of misinformation and possible impacts on society. Just as this study put taxonomy of news value by applying computational collection and analysis, the result explores the extent to which researchers would revisit list of news values by given the challenges faced by the emergence of web-based media today.

Acknowledgements. The views and opinions expressed in this article are from the individual author and not from sponsor organization. This study was funded by the University of Macau grant MYRG2018-0062-FSS & Higher Education Bureau of Macao grant (HSS-UMAC-2020-09). The author would like to thank Professor Peter J. Schulz, Professor Angus W. H. Cheong and anonymous reviewers for their valuable comments.

Conflicts of Interest. The authors declare no conflict of interest. The founding sponsor had no role in the design of the study; in the collection, analyses, or interpretation of data; in the writing of the manuscript, and in the decision to publish the results.

References

1. Forouzanfar, M.H., et al.: Global, regional, and national comparative risk assessment of 79 behavioural, environmental and occupational, and metabolic risks or clusters of risks, 1990–2015: a systematic analysis for the global burden of disease study 2015. The Lancet **338**(10053), 1659–1724 (2016)
2. CDS Homepage. https://www.idf.org/our-network/regions-members/western-pacific/dia betes-in-wp.html. Accessed 25 May 2019
3. Dan, V., Raupp, J.: A systematic review of frames in news reporting of health risks: characteristics, construct consistency vs. name diversity, and the relationship of frames to framing functions. Health Risk Soc. **20**(5-6), 203–226 (2018)
4. Søe, S.O.: Algorithmic detection of misinformation and disinformation: Gricean perspectives. J. Documentation **74**(2), 309–332 (2018)

5. Rich, P.R., Zaragoza, M.S.: The continued influence of implied and explicitly stated misinformation in news reports. J. Exp. Psychol. Learn. Mem. Cogn. **42**(1), 62–74 (2016)
6. Yan, T., Stewart, C.M.: Framing the SARS crisis: a computer-assisted text analysis of CNN and BBC online news reports of SARS. Asian J. Commun. **15**(3), 289–301 (2005)
7. Zhao, L., Yin, J., Song, Y.: An exploration of rumor combating behavior on social media in the context of social crises. Comput. Hum. Behav. **58**, 25–36 (2016)
8. Eysenbach, G.: Infodemiology and infoveillance: framework for an emerging set of public health informatics methods to analyze search, communication and publication behavior on the internet. J. Med. Internet Res. **11**(1), e11 (2009)
9. Chang, A.: Digitalized news on non-communicable diseases coverage-what are the unhealthy features of media content induced for Chinese? In: Staab, S., Koltsova, O., Ignatov, D.I. (eds.) Social Informatics: Lecture Note Series in Computer Science, vol. 11186, pp. 29–39. Springer Nature, Switzerland (2018)
10. Chang, A., Hu, J.Y., Liu, Y.C., Liu, M.: Data mining approach to Chinese food analysis for diet-related cardiometabolic diseases. In: 2019 IEEE 35th International Conference on Data Engineering Workshops (ICDEW), IEEE Xplore digital library. https://doi.org/10.1109/icdew.2019.00-29
11. Dutta, M.J.: Content effects: personal and public health. In: Rössler, P., Hoffner, C.A., Zoonen, L.V. (eds.) The International Encyclopedia of Media Effects. John Wiley & Sons, New Jersey (2017)
12. Harcup, T., O'neill, D.: What is news? news values revisited (again). Journalism Stud. **18**(12), 1470–1488 (2017)
13. Hu, S., Zhang, Z.: The discursive construction of party identification of Chinese party-owned media by means of social media—Setting "xiake_island" as an example. Commun. Soc. **48**, 57–91 (2019)
14. Velker, M.: Top 10 daily newspapers in China. http://www.china.org.cn. Accessed 05 May 2019
15. Zhang, W.: Online UGC, public power conflicting issues and media publicity: a study of the routinely use of online UGC in China's market-driven newspaper. Commun. Soc. **48**, 131–162 (2019)
16. Kaefer, F., Roper, J., Sinha, P.: A software-assisted qualitative content analysis of news articles: example and reflections. In: Forum Qualitative Sozialforschung/Forum: Qualitative Social Research, vol. 16, no. (2), pp. 1–55 (2015)
17. Li, R., et al.: Prevalence of metabolic syndrome in mainland China: a meta-analysis of published studies. BMC Public Health **16**, 296–305 (2016). https://doi.org/10.1186/s12889-016-2870-y
18. Boumans, J.W., Damian, T.: Taking stock of the toolkit: an overview of relevant automated content analysis approaches and techniques for digital journalism scholars. Digit. Journalism **4**(1), 8–23 (2016)
19. Lan, Y., et al.: Prevalence of metabolic syndrome in China: an up-dated cross-sectional study. PLoS ONE **13**(4), e0196012 (2018)

Students Assessing Digital News and Misinformation

Thomas Nygren$^{(\boxtimes)}$ (iD), Jenny Wiksten Folkeryd (iD), Caroline Liberg (iD),
and Mona Guath (iD)

Department of Education, Uppsala University, Uppsala, Sweden
thomas.nygren@edu.uu.se

Abstract. Previous research has highlighted how young people struggle to distinguish news from misinformation. In this study, we investigate how ca. 400 students determine the trustworthiness of false, biased and credible news. We find that students use different strategies depending on what they evaluate. For example, students who fail to debunk a manipulated image often rely on what they see in the image in contrast to students who determine credibility upon what is not in the image. Students finding junk news credible may have special problems separating different kinds of sources. We identify potentials and pitfalls among students important for further investigation, research and a focus on education.

Keywords: Media and Information Literacy · Digital literacy · Fake news · Critical thinking

1 Introduction

The digitization of society means that news today can be spread quickly and easily, even when it is manipulative and false. The challenge of fake news means that international organizations now increasingly emphasize the importance of digital source criticism. International organizations uphold UNESCO's so-called Media and Information Literacy (MIL) as an important defense against misinformation[1] [1]. Media researchers such as Koltay [2] and Carlsson [1] describe MIL as an umbrella term covering other knowledge, skills and attitudes necessary if we are to use new media wisely [1–3]. The ability of people to manage new media can also be described as digital literacy with subgroups such as photo-visual literacy and information literacy [4]. Eshet [4] identifies the ability to read and evaluate digital information (information literacy) as a "survival skill" for

---

[1] In this article, we define misinformation as inaccurate, manipulative or false information, including disinformation, which is deliberately designed to mislead people.

The original version of this chapter was revised: the chapter was changed to open access retrospectively under a CC BY 4.0 license and the presentation of Table 3 and the positioning of Tables 5-8 have been corrected. The correction to this chapter is available at
https://doi.org/10.1007/978-3-030-61841-4_19

M. van Duijn et al. (Eds.): MISDOOM 2020, LNCS 12259, pp. 63–79, 2020.
https://doi.org/10.1007/978-3-030-61841-4_5

citizens in a digital world. Similarly, McGrew et al. [5] emphasize the importance of "civic online reasoning" and "the ability to effectively search for, evaluate, and verify social and political information online". Even though digitization in society include new aspects, literacy researchers note that the human ability to interact with different forms of artifacts has a very long history [6]. However, the digital dimension involves new potentials and challenges when people search for, access, review, analyze and create information [7–9]. Theories about information literacy that focus primarily on printed text have therefore been expanded also to include multimodal aspects [10].

When it comes to critical and constructive information management, theoretical and empirical investigations have drawn attention to the value of noting who is behind the information, the context of the source, the information in respect of what it alleges, how the information is presented, and why it was created based on underlying purposes [11–14]. Previous research has shown that students have problems with evaluating digital news [5, 15, 16] but have not studied what this is based on more closely.

The purpose of this study is to investigate the way students assess the credibility of digital news and misinformation with regard to whether, and if so how, they express themselves about the source (who), the content (what), the presentation (how) and the underlying purpose (why). In other words, how do they justify their assessments when they in various ways determine the credibility of factual, biased or false information in text and images? Which assessments appear to be more or less successful?.

2 Previous Research

Internationally, the poor ability of young people to assess credibility was observed in quantitative studies in the USA [5, 15] and in the latest PISA study [17]. Previous Swedish research has shown that young people have difficulty navigating digital environments [16, 18, 19]. Certain young people may use digital information reflexively, while others easily go astray, maybe due to non-constructive assessments. Studies have shown that people use different cues and heuristics to judge credibility, which can lead to errors. Examples of this include search engine reputation, website design and functionality, previous experiences from websites, and perceived authenticity and expertise in the digital environment [20–23]. The value of reading between the lines and considering different sources are considered to be constructive methods [14, 24]. Studies by professional fact-checkers show that it is crucial to note and evaluate who is behind the information, when and where it was created, the text's objectivity and bias, underlying objectives and to compare the information with other independent sources [14]. In line with this research, students are recommended to get better at assessing various types of digital news [13, 16, 25]. However, the question is what they base their assessment on.

3 Material and Method

This study addresses four tasks used in previous research for evaluating the ability of teenagers to determine the credibility of digital news [16]. Each task contains questions with both fixed response options and open response questions where the students must justify their choice of fixed response options. It is these open text responses that we have analyzed to better understand how the students reason when they assess the credibility of digital news. A total of 483 upper secondary students, age 16-19, took part in the program with a focus on social science (48%), aesthetics (23%), science (16%) and economics (9%). The participants in the study were recruited through their teachers and do not constitute a representative sample. All students agreed to participate anonymously in this study in line with ethical guidelines. Participating students come from different high school programs and they have different backgrounds, but the study's representativeness is limited to theoretical programs.[2] The number of students who responded by indicating a fixed response option and those who justified their responses are shown in the result section below.

In line with previous research, the four tasks were designed and found useful for testing the ability of students to identify the source, evaluate evidence and corroborate news [5, 16]. The first task investigated the ability of the students to distinguish news written by journalists to objectively inform from advertising created to manipulate the reader into purchasing something. The second, the ability of the students to assess the validity of the evidence in a task with a manipulated image. In this case, the manipulated image of a smoker's cheek and mouth was not proof that smoking damages the heart and blood vessels. In the third task, the students had to compare two news reports from a press conference held by the government. A straightforward, objective report from a public service had to be compared with a more biased report from a right-wing populist magazine. Comparing and assessing argumentation was also included in the fourth task where a plastic surgeon's statements concerning weight reduction were compared to current research into weight reduction. This task investigated the ability of the students to compare different statements about an important health issue where independent research was placed in relation to statements by a plastic surgeon at a company that sells gastric surgery and other forms of plastic surgery.

Our analysis is based on a mixed methods approach where we combine both qualitative and quantitative considerations. The analysis of the student justifications was based on the above-mentioned four dimensions deemed crucial when it comes to critical and constructive digital information management: *who* is behind the information, *what* is the information alleged to contain, *how* the information is designed and *why* it was created on the basis of underlying purposes. Three of the participating researchers in an iterative, multi-step process, carried out the analysis. The researchers switched between analyzing parts of the material (approx. 10% of the student responses in each task) individually and verifying their respective analyses with each other. When a reliable inter-rater consensus was reached (minimum 80%), the researchers analyzed the remaining responses in the tasks based on the established coding schedule (see Appendix A).

In order to evaluate whether the coded categories reflected performance on the respective items we made logistic regressions with fixed response questions as depended variables and the respective coding categories as independent variables for each item. An answer that was included in a category was coded as 1 and otherwise 0. The coefficients for logistic regressions denote the log odds for going from an incorrect to a correct

---

[2] In Sweden, 2017, approx 30% studied social science, 11% aesthetic, 22% science and 20% economics (SiRiS). Our study does not include students in vocational training. One third (34%) of the students stated that they speak a different language at home. Of the respondents, 60% described themselves as girls, 35% as boys, 3% as other identity and 2% chose not to present their gender.

answer on the dependent variable. A negative coefficient denotes a smaller log odds for a correct answer, whereas a positive coefficient represents a larger log odds for a correct answer. We report coefficients and p-values for the significant effects in the text, for a full specification of the models we refer to Table 5, 6, 7 and 8 in Appendix B.

4 Results

4.1 Aftonbladet - Distinguishing News from Advertising

This task investigated how students are able to distinguish editorial material from advertising material in an authentic front page from Aftonbladet. The task was formulated as follows: "This is Aftonbladet's website. The page contains news and advertising. Using the arrows 1 to 5, mark the articles below which you believe to be news. Explain why you think they are news". The page students had to assess was a screen shot directly from www.aftonbladet.se.

Of the 483 students who answered the question, only 116 (24%) distinguished between news and advertising by identifying the only two alternatives that were news. The remaining students interpreted the other alternatives also as news. Of the 483 students who answered the question, 395 also justified their answers (see Table 1.) Only a few (13 students) considered who the source was.

Table 1. Student justifications for their assessments of what is news or advertising

	Answers with comments		Main type of justification							
	N	%	WHO? Source		WHAT? Contents		HOW? Structure		WHY? Function	
Correct	91	23	6	7%	39	43%	45	49%	21	23%
Incorrect	304	77	7	2%	173	57%	138	45%	58	19%
TOT.	*395*	*100*	*13*	*9%*	*212*	*100%*	*183*	*95%*	*79*	*42%*

Note: Often, student justifications include combinations of these four main inputs. Accordingly, the total number of justifications exceeds the number of participating students.

Students noting how the page was designed, with for instance labels telling readers what is advertising, were significantly better at separating advertising from news than other students $[b = 3.410, p < .001]$.[3] They note the design of the texts as a justification for their assessments. This concerns markings of advertising and news and include considerations of headlines, color or position on the page, for instance "one article is clearly placed beneath the heading 'News'" and "it says news in red and not advertising or weight club". However, how a page appears may also trick students into believing that everything in the right side column is advertising.

---

[3] The same result was obtained if number of correct items was regressed on the categories: there was a larger log count $[b = 0.331, p < .001]$ for those whose comment was categorized as "how". Mean number of correct was 4.008 $(SD = 1.254)$.

Students who correctly distinguished between news and advertising made comments about how news should be about things that have happened, have a basis in actual circumstances and be based on reviewed information. Some examples from students include "Because this 'news' is either proven or can be proved by others" and "Because they inform about facts such as…". Some students also emphasized that ads can be seen as click baits and an attempt to attract purchases as in the text about the weight club, which is not marked as advertising. Thus in these cases, the content assessed as a combination with its purpose. Another purpose students criticize is that news is written to inform, which a number of students compare to the advertisement's sales interest: "Because its purpose is information" and "It is information rather than an attempt to sell something".

Among the 304 students who incorrectly identified news as advertising and vice a versa, we find good arguments, but they lead to incorrect conclusions nevertheless. For example, one student describes how an advertisement for a dietary supplement labeled as advertising, "has nothing to do with advertising" while another student explains in his justification that an advertisement for an energy company is news "because it's something that concerns us as humans and how we live, and is as such essential". The contents of advertisements can thus seduce students into believing that it is news, even though it is labeled advertisement. Other students perceive, wrongly, that the advertisements "have nothing to do with products". Among the students, we also find others who are very critically regard news to be more biased than the advertising. Just under half of these 304 students also seem to have problems identifying which heading or content a highlight on the website refers to. With the argument "it says news where there's news" and "it says news above news, not advertising" the students failed to identify news, despite its being marked as such. Layouts with "news on the left side" as one student puts it, is also used. One fifth of the students display problems with their ability to see through the purpose of various texts. They express this as e.g. "None of this seems to be trying to sell us anything, but is just a straightforward heading with information" and "because it's just news and they're not trying to sell anything".

4.2 Smoking – Evaluating Evidence

In this task, a manipulated image was used deceptively to show severely injured blood vessels in the cheek of a smoker. [4] The task given to students was formulated as follows: "Smoking may not only cause cancer but also serious damage to the cardiovascular system with an impact on blood vessels and the heart. Can the above picture of Kai Bastard be seen as evidence that such injuries can occur through smoking? Please justify your response"

406 students answered the question. Of them, 307 (76%) noted that the image could not be seen as evidence for injury occurring through smoking, while 99 students (24%) stated that the image could be seen as evidence for the harmful effects of smoking. Of the 406 students, 361 justified their answers (see Table 2).

Few students addressed the issue of the source (who), while many spoke about content (what) and design (how) and around one sixth also raised the purpose of the image (why). Students noting how the design looked manipulated were significantly

---

[4] Image source: https://www.vice.com/en_uk/article/yp54bw/kai-bastard-photo-manipulations

Table 2. Student justifications for assessments of the manipulated image as evidence for the harmful effects of smoking

	Answers with comments		Main type of justification								
	N	%	WHO? Source		WHAT? In the image		WHAT? Outside the image		HOW? Structure		WHY? Function	
No	280	78	10	4%	13	5%	149	53%	154	55%	43	15%
Yes	81	22	1	1%	61	75%	12	15%	12	15%	12	15%
TOT.	*361*	*100*	*11*	*5%*	*74*	*80%*	*161*	*68%*	*166*	*70%*	*55*	*30%*

Note: Often, student justifications include combinations of these five main inputs. Accordingly, the total number of justifications exceeds the number of participating students.

better than other students were at identifying the image as poor evidence [$b = 1.930$, p $< .001$]. Of the students who assessed the image as inadequate evidence of the harmful effects of smoking, only ten justified this by the lack of information about the source and the lack of references to other sources.

Just over half of the students mentioned the content, and most of them compared the content of the image with their own knowledge (what; outside the image) and they were significantly better at identifying the image as poor evidence [$b = 1.736$, p $< .001$]. They wrote such things as "smoking cannot do that. My grandfather smoked almost all his life and had no dark veins in the mouth" and "I have never seen that effect from smoking before". Several students who assessed the image as poor evidence combined what, how and sometimes also why in their assessments with justifications such as "It's not an authentic picture; it's probably been photoshopped because veins in the face never get black through smoking as in the picture" and "it's been photo shopped; we see people who smoke and they don't look like this, the image is intended to frighten". In other words, they placed great importance on how the design of the image seemed to be faked or manipulated in some way. In the assessment concerning how the image appears faked, they also referred to their own digital capabilities in editing images, e.g. "The image can be edited, retouched, photoshopped, counterfeited and so forth" and "because part of my course includes learning Photoshop, I know how easy it is to manipulate a picture". The students who also assess the purpose saw the image more as a way of frightening people based on a false or exaggerated example.

In contrast students with a focus on what was in the image showed a significant inability to identify the image as manipulated [$b = -2.892$, p $< .001$]. For example, students noted that "we can see how the blood vessels are black, and because the person in the image is smoking we clearly see that this is the cause" and "we see how the poison that gets into the body spreads throughout the rest of the body". Also, 12 students identified the image as true and the purpose of it as an attempt to warn people about the actual harmful effects of smoking, e.g. "the image shows how things can look if you smoke too much, which frightens smokers and leads to their cutting down on smoking".

4.3 New Legislation Against Hate Crimes – Comparing News Without Source Information

The task presented the students with two texts reporting on a government press conference about new legislation against hate crimes. One item (Article A), was a text published the day after the press conference in a right-wing populist newspaper classified as a purveyor of junk news [26]. The other text (Article B) was a direct report from the press conference made by Swedish Radio, a Swedish public service broadcaster. In order to investigate how the students compare and assess texts on the basis of aspects other than the source's credibility, we removed source information about where the text was published. The task asked the students to indicate which of the articles they "believed to be most credible" and to justify their responses. The response alternatives were (1) Article A, (2) Article B and (3) Neither – they appear to be equally credible.

399 students answered the question. Of these, 86 (22%) pointed to the right-wing populist copy (A) as being most credible, 171 (43%) indicated the copy from Swedish Radio (B) as the most credible, and 146 (36%) assessed the texts as equally credible. Of the above, 275 students justified their answers (see Table 3).

Table 3. Student assessments of credibility in news copy about new legislation against hate crimes

	Answers with comments		Main type of justification												
	N	%	WHO? Source		WHO? Primary source		WHO? Secondary source		WHO? Proximity in time		WHAT Contents		HOW? Trends		WHY? Function	
Right-wing populist (A)	67	24	25	37%	4	6%	30	45%	5	7%	4	6%	8	12%	1	1%
Public service (B)	144	52	5	3%	96	67%	4	3%	15	10%	14	10%	41	28%	13	9%
Equally credible	64	23	14	22%	19	30%	22	34%	9	14%	15	23%	11	17%	1	2%
TOT.	275	100	44	63%	119	102%	56	82%	29	32%	33	39%	60	58%	15	12%

Note: Often, student justifications include combinations of these four main inputs. Accordingly, the total number of justifications exceeds the number of participating students.

In contrast to the two previous tasks, there were many students who assessed credibility by attempting to identify who was behind the information (who). The task was designed such that the students were able to do this in four different ways: (1) which source published the text; (2) whether it was based on first-hand information, or (3) was a rendering of second-hand information, and (4) the writer's proximity in time in relation to the event.

Because the right-wing populist text referred to Swedish Radio as the source for its biased rendering of the press conference, many students incorrectly identified the source as Swedish Radio and therefore significantly more often considered the text to be credible [$b = -2.80, p < .001$]. For example: "It's Swedish Radio; the other text doesn't show the source or say who wrote it". However, five students who assessed text B as the most credible, incorrectly identified the source in A as Swedish Radio. But three of the students balanced their misunderstanding with other considerations, one example of this being "On one hand, Article A is from Swedish Radio, which boosts credibility, but this is easy to fake. Article A seems to be too radical, while B seems calm and collected, which feels more reasonable in a newspaper format when they comment on a new reform". In addition, among the students who assessed the texts as being equally credible, relatively many incorrectly interpreted the source of Article A to be Swedish Radio.

A significant number of students [$b = 2.886, p < .001$] mentioned that reproducing an interview with the minister responsible as the primary source was an important reason for assessing the text from the public service (B) as more credible than the text from the right-wing populist newspaper (A); see Table 4. For example: "It is what the Minister of the Interior said, and they even have a quote of what he said about this, so this article is more credible than the one above". General references to sources were significantly more common among students who saw the right-wing populist text or both texts as equally credible than those who assessed the public service text as more credible [$b = -2.743, p < .001$].

Table 4. Student assessments of credibility in articles about weight loss

	Answers with comments		Main type of justification							
	N	%	WHO? Source		WHAT? Contents		HOW? Structure		WHY? Function	
Research	196	52	138	70%	150	77%	18	9%	27	14%
Surgeon	181	48	160	88%	93	51%	36	20%	9	5%
TOT.	*377*	*100*	*298*	*159%*	*243*	*128%*	*54*	*29%*	*36*	*19%*

Note: Often, student justifications include combinations of these four main inputs. Accordingly, the total number of justifications exceeds the number of participating students.

The fact that the texts were written the same day or the day after the press conference was also given as the reason for an assessment of credibility. One student, who saw text B as the most credible noted that "Article A is dependent on information in Article B as it was published one day later" in contrast to another student who noted that "the date and time make A more credible as there was more time to gather information".

In addition, students also noted biases in the use of language in the texts. A significant number of students assessed the public service texts as more credible based upon how the texts were balanced or biased [$b = 1.402, p < .001$]. Focusing on the function of the texts, one student gave the example "Article A has completely spun the news to make it appear as if the government will punish those critical of immigration". Another student found that "A uses language that tries to downplay racism ("racism") and hate crimes" with reference to the populist text's use of quotation marks in connection with the word racism. A focus on the purposes behind the information also a significant amount of students identify Article B as more credible [$b = 2.232, p = .00868$]. Here we find a few students noting Article B as propaganda or a simple attempt to "getting you to react".

Among the students who identify text A as more credible, there was also the comment "A is a little more honest about how authoritarian the government is, and it does not try to dress up the oppression of differing opinions with fine words". Other students perceived text A as more credible as it was "impersonal" and "looks more professional". Of the students who assessed the sources as equally credible, some saw both texts as equally biased while others saw both texts as equally objective. For example, one student thought that "the people who published the articles just want to create drama" while another felt that "neither seemed biased".

4.4 Weight Loss - Comparing Complex Articles on Health

In this task, information about ways to lose weight were compared with each other. Statements from a surgeon who performed weight loss procedures published in a morning newspaper (Article A), were compared to a recent study from a publicly funded, top ranking university published by a weekly paper with a section that focused on health issues (Article B). The task was worded as follows "Is Article A or B more credible as a source of information about weight loss? Please justify your choice of A or B. Why is this article more credible?"

Of the 420 students who answered the question, 222 (53%) saw the research-based article as more credible, while 198 (47%) judged the other article to be more credible. Of the 420 students, 377 justified their answers (see Table 4).

In contrast to the three previous tasks, a different pattern can be seen here with most justifications relating to who and what. The students who assessed the article that presented recent research as most credible pointed significantly more at the content (what?) [$b = 0.809$, p $< .001$] and the purpose (why?) behind the information [$b = 1.107$, p $= .008$]. They point out that the article contains research in the form of a study carried out at the university and also includes statistical data. The justifications they provide regarding this are e.g. "it sounds reasonable and has a lot of figures and studies which make me think that it's the more credible" and "because it's a fact that exercise reduces weight and going on a diet helps weight loss, but diet alone doesn't work". Some of the students also compare the two articles as in "A is only about a person's thoughts while B has a carried out a study that supports it (even if it is a small study) and explains why things are the way they are instead of just saying it is what it is". Students commenting the purpose of the articles finds that the interview with the doctor is not credible "because he wants more people to have procedures so he can earn more money", i.e. he wants to advertise his procedures. Not many of the students raise the design of Article B as credible. The comments made by those who do, point out that the article about research has more links to sources, is more nuanced, looks more professional and is thus more credible.

In contrast, those who assessed the article based on the surgeon's statements as being more credible did so in most cases based on an assessment of the source (who?). The fact that the information was published in an established morning newspaper was given by a significant number students as the main reason for assessing the article as credible [$b = -1.073, p < .001$]. In addition, a significant number of the students [$b = -0.806$,

$p = .0131$] also based this judgement upon the credible design (how?) of the morning newspaper, for instance in comparison to how "the other article reads more like a blog".

5   Conclusions

This study shows that youths often find it difficult to determine credibility when faced with different types of digital news and misinformation. The results suggest that different strategies are necessary for navigating credible, biased or false news.

Several previous studies have noted that students find it difficult to distinguish news from advertising [5, 15, 16, 25]. Our findings in this study show that this may depend on a number of factors. In comparison with other students, those who succeed best are able more often to identify how advertising is labeled and they are able to navigate the design of the page. However, it is also difficult for many students to know how to interpret advertising labels. Labeling above an advertisement, aimed at helping the reader see that something is an advertisement, may be interpreted as applying to the text above rather than the ad. Students can also be tricked by the location of the news on the web page. Items placed to the right or left are easily interpreted as advertisements, probably due to the experience of ads following customers in the margins on various web pages.

Examinations carried out by students of a manipulated image purporting to be evidence of the harm caused by smoking show other assessment patterns. In this case, many students make relevant assessments based not on what is presented in the image but on their own experience and knowledge and how easy it is to manipulate images using e.g. Photoshop. On the other hand, students can be misled by a focus on the strong content in the image. The students who arrive at inaccurate assessments are often convinced of the image's authenticity and they regards its symbolic content as facts. The students' previous knowledge and familiarity with handling manipulated images is thus at the heart of their ability to assess this type of task.

When it comes to student assessment of more objective news versus biased news regarding new legislation against hate crimes, it is primarily the ability to distinguish first-hand information from second-hand information that would appear to be key. In this task, critical aspects that focus on different types of sources, primary and secondary, appear to lead in the right direction. Students who consider *how* the information can be biased through the use of language and identified the underlying purpose of the right-wing populist news also found the text from public service to be more credible.

What made students assess the right-wing populist news as more credible was often incorrect identification of who the source was, their problematic interpretation of proximity in time and their treatment of sources in a non-specific manner. Students who referred to sources without distinguishing between them often gave equal credibility to both texts or greater credibility to the right-wing populist text. Thus, *who* was behind the first-hand information and *how* texts can be biased were key in managing this task.

When comparing the texts regarding weight loss, it was mainly students who considered the content (what) and the text's function and potential underlying purpose (why) that determined the researched-based article to be the most credible. Those who assessed the text on the premise of the plastic surgeon's statements did so to a greater extent based on how the article looked and the fact that it was published in an established morning newspaper (who).

6   Concluding Discussion

There seems to be a number of reasons why it is difficult for young people to distinguish news from advertising. It may in part be due to a lack of experience in reading the newspaper we used in the study, despite the fact that previous research found it to be a popular source of news among many young people in Sweden [27]. That so many missed or misunderstood advertising labels may be due to a lack of experience or attention. It was apparent in the student assessments that labeling, color and location may not only act as an aid, but can also easily be misunderstood. The fact that information in the margins can be interpreted as advertising indicates a heuristic approach that can easily lead to errors. Important information can be missed and new techniques for inserting advertisements in a more central location in digital environments may lead to misunderstandings. The example of this website also shows the real issues with the blurred line between news and advertising. In journalism, it is crucial to distinguish between content produced with and without the influence of direct market interests [28]. But it is obviously difficult for the reader in digital environments to distinguish between them, especially when the material is written by journalists and in a form that is very similar to news produced to inform and not to manipulate [29]. It is clear that many young people need to be better at distinguishing news from advertising. It remains to be seen how teaching can help here as previous attempts at teaching students in this matter has had very limited effect [25]. The fact that many students do not explicitly note the source would seem to be a problem, even if it was not a significant factor in our study. Perhaps this is the reason why so few students succeed in distinguishing news. Thus, the design of teaching methods that help more students reflect over who a source is may be worth exploring in future research. Our findings indicate that it could be constructive for teachers to show and discuss the design of news pages, since many students have difficulty understanding labeling and layout. A lack of practice and experience in handling news and advertising may need to be weighed up in teaching.

The task with the manipulated image of the smoker highlights the importance of possessing good subject knowledge. Those who compared the content of the image with information outside the image were able to determine its credibility on this basis. Other students were caught up in the deceptive design of the image. This may also depend on emotional aspects where strong visual messages can be misleading. With regard to evaluating the manipulated image, personal experience from having worked with image manipulation also appears to be an advantage much in line with previous research [30]. As regards education, this not only shows the importance of schools teaching about actual factual circumstances, but also allowing students to test new image manipulation technologies.

Students who found the right-wing populist text to be more credible than the text from Swedish Radio were in many cases mistaken about who the source was. The students who incorrectly believed that text A came from Swedish Radio often chose to name it as being more credible. Thus, the main reason for choosing the right-wing populist text was the students' misinterpretation of who was behind the text. This demonstrates the importance of the ability to correctly identify the source. It can be difficult, especially in digital environments to determine who is behind the information when fake accounts are created to disseminate misleading information. The false account phenomenon has been noted as a serious threat to democracy [31], especially as disinformation can be used to reinforce divisions in society and spread discontent and suspicion.

This especially highlights the importance of the ability to distinguish between primary sources and secondary sources. Those who understood the value of information on the basis of a primary source found success, while others who were more careless and considered different sources as equivalent, failed. Thus not being fooled by references to more credible sources puts students on the right track. The fact that external websites with misleading information pages refer to other sources with high credibility has already been identified as a manipulative strategy that can even mislead highly educated people [14]. Another problem identified is where students feel that indirect reports can be seen as better. Thus, source-critical knowledge about proximity in time and space is important and must be reinforced.

Our findings also shows that it can be constructive to consider how texts can be written to inform objectively or to manipulate. Students who focused on the underlying purpose about why a text was written also succeeded in navigating the text in a critical, constructive manner. The fact that there were relatively few students who based their assessments on how and why the texts were created is a challenge for future research and teaching. Seeing and interpreting trends does not seem to form a natural part of the assessments of many students. The study also shows that there is a risk that texts are interpreted as equally factual or biased, despite their possessing distinct differences. There is clearly a need for more training in calling the author into question and the ability to recognize what is worth trusting.

The difficulty in choosing between conflicting information was also clear in the fourth task. Previous research has underscored the importance of source credibility [32] and students identifying the morning paper as credible missed the fact that the primary source in the article was not as credible as research from a university. Self-assured statements from a doctor in an established morning newspaper were deemed by many to be more credible than less overconfident research outcomes from a recent minor study published in a paper with less credibility. Thus, layers of source credibility made it hard for students to navigate this task. In spite of this problem, the majority of students in this case assessed the article with references to research as the most credible. Students who named the article about research as being the most credible focused on the more objective content of the article, which put across what the complex facts about weight loss the research had arrived at, and the underlying purpose of a plastic surgeon in private practice. This task also showed the need to get more students to consider why the information was created and communicated in the manner chosen. In the case of issues about health advice, there are obvious challenges as advertisements for dietary supplements are interpreted as news, while research can be regarded as less credible than plastic surgeons. Dietary and health advice is evidently difficult to assess. In a digital world with many affluent stakeholders [33], young people need guidance about e.g. food and cosmetic surgery. They need the ability to evaluate available information. We need to study how this can be done in critical, constructive ways in more detail in future research.

What is clear from this study is that the issues raised as crucial in terms of information handling – who, what, how and why – are useful for assessing digital news. However, it is evident that different types of news and misinformation require different types of assessments. In education, we need to find ways to support multiple ways of assessing credibility, while also understanding the risk that focusing on the right thing may still lead to the wrong conclusion.

7 Limitations

Questionnaires and tests were completed in a classroom environment, and student vigilance regarding manipulations may therefore have been higher than otherwise when encountering credible, biased and fake news on the Internet. We did not ask students about their habits and experiences of smoking and diets, which may have affected their motivated reasoning.

Acknowledgements. We are truly grateful to all the students accepting to participate in this study and teachers distributing the survey. We would also like to direct a very special thanks to Ebba Elwin, Kerstin Ekholm and Maria Lindberg and the anonymous reviewers of Misdoom for valuable input.

Appendix A Coding Schedule

Aftonbladet

1. Who? – source – identifies who is behind the information.
2. What? – content – describe what the information is about.
3. How? – structure – describes design.
4. Why? – function – the purpose is to sell something or to objectively inform.

Smoking

1. Who? – source – identifies who is behind the information,
2a What? – content – describes the knowledge present in the image.
2b What? – content – compares the image to knowledge outside the image.
3. How? – structure – describes design e.g. Fake, manipulated, metaphorical image, symbolic
4. Why? – function – the purpose is to objectively inform or manipulate.

Hate crimes

1a Who? – source – identifies (incorrectly) Swedish radio as the source in article A.
1b Who? – source – identifies the source in B as first-hand (primary source).
1c Who? – source – refers to a more general source or secondhand information.
1d Who? – source – identifies the articles as having different publishing dates.
2. What? – content – describes what the information is about.
3. How? – structure – neutral or biased use of language.
4. Why? – function – purpose is to objectively inform or manipulate.

Table 5. *Estimates of Best Fitting Logistic Regression Model for Correct/Incorrect Answer on Hate crime, with Coefficients Denoting the Log Odds of Answering Correct when Classified in or Not in one of the Coding Categories Who 1, Who 2, Who 3, Who 4, What, How and, Why.*

Coefficent	Estimate	Std. error	z value	Pr(>|z|)
(Intercept)	−1.005	.184	−5.450	<.001
Hate crime who 1	−2.680	.579	−4.633	<.001
Hate crime who 2	2.886	.338	8.544	<.001
Hate crime who 3	−2.743	.633	−4.331	<.001
Hate crime who 4	0.121	.521	0.233	.816
Hate crime what	0.642	.432	1.486	.137
Hate crime how	1.402	.384	3.649	<.001
Hate crime why	2.232	.851	2.624	0.00868

Note: Residual deviance: 349 on 391° of freedom. AIC = 365

Weight loss

1. Who? – source – identifies who is behind the information.
2. What? – content – describes what the information is about.
3. How? – structure – describes design.
4. Why? – function – the purpose is either to sell something or to objectively inform

Appendix B

Table 6. *Estimates of Best Fitting Logistic Regression Model for Correct/Incorrect Answer Aftonbladet with Coefficients Denoting the Log Odds of Answering Correct when Classified or Not in one of the Coding Categories Who, What, Why and, How*

Coefficent	Estimate	Std. Error	z value	Pr(>|z|)
(Intercept)	−4.159	0.621	−6.698	<.001
Aftonbladet who	−0.548	1.126	−0.487	.627
Aftonbladet what	−0.809	0.452	−1.790	0.0735
Aftonbladet why	−0.104	0.602	−0.173	0.863
Aftonbladet how	3.410	0.622	5.484	<.001***

Note: Residual deviance: 249 on 478° of freedom. AIC = 259

Table 7. *Estimates of Best Fitting Logistic Regression Model for Correct/Incorrect Answer on Weight Loss, with Coefficients Denoting the Log Odds of Answering Correct when Classified or Not in one of the Coding Categories Who, What, How and, Why.*

Coefficient	Estimate	Std. error	z value	Pr($>$|z|)
(Intercept)	0.431	.232	1.862	0.0626
Weight loss who	−1.073	.240	−4.478	<.001
Weight loss what	0.809	.215	3.765	<.001
Weight loss how	−0.806	.325	−2.480	0.0131
Weight loss why	1.107	.417	2.654	0.00797

Note: Residual deviance: 527 on 414° of freedom. AIC= 537

Table 8. *Estimates of Best Fitting Logistic Regression Model for Correct/Incorrect Answer on Smoking, with Coefficients Denoting the Log Odds of Answering Correct when Classified or Not in one of the Coding Categories Who, What 1, What 2, How and, Why.*

Coefficient	Estimate	Std. error	z value	Pr($>$|z|)
(Intercept)	0.667	0.270	2.469	.0135
Smoking who	2.529	1.291	1.959	.0501
Smoking what 1	−2.892	0.393	−7.367	<.001
Smoking what 2	1.736	0.392	4.426	<.001
Smoking how	1.930	0.398	4.854	<.001
Smoking why	0.357	0.484	0.738	0.461

Note: Residual deviance: 254 on 397° of freedom. AIC = 266

References

1. Carlsson, U. (ed.): Understanding Media and Information literacy (MIL) in the Digital Age: A Question of Democracy. Department of Journalism. Media and Communication (JMG), Gothenburg (2019)
2. Koltay, T.: The media and the literacies: media literacy, information literacy, digital literacy. Media Cult. Soc. **33**, 211–221 (2011)
3. Koltay, T.: New media and literacies: amateurs vs. professionals. First Monday **16** (2011)
4. Eshet, Y.: Digital literacy: a conceptual framework for survival skills in the digital era. J. Educ. Multimedia Hypermedia **13**, 93–106 (2004)
5. McGrew, S., Ortega, T., Smith, M., Wineburg, S.: Can students evaluate online sources? learning from assessments of civic online reasoning. Theor. Res. Soc. Educ. **46**, 1–29 (2018)
6. Säljö, R.: Literacy, digital literacy and epistemic practices: the co-evolution of hybrid minds and external memory systems. Nord. J. Digit. Literacy **7**, 5–19 (2012)
7. Aufderheide, P.: Media Literacy. A Report of the National Leadership Conference on Media Literacy. ERIC, Washington, D.C. (1993)

8. Hobbs, R.: Digital and Media Literacy: A Plan of Action. A White Paper on the Digital and Media Literacy Recommendations of the Knight Commission on the Information Needs of Communities in a Democracy. ERIC, Washington, D.C. (2010)
9. Livingstone, S.: Media literacy and the challenge of new information and communication technologies. Commun. Rev. **7**, 3–14 (2004)
10. Kress, G.: Literacy in the New Media Age. Routledge, New York (2003)
11. Breivik, P.S., Gee, E.G.: Information Literacies for the Twenty First Century. MacMillan, New York (1989)
12. Metzger, M.J.: Making sense of credibility on the web: models for evaluating online information and recommendations for future research. J. Am. Soc. Inf. Sci. Technol. **58**, 2078–2091 (2007)
13. McGrew, S., Ortega, T., Breakstone, J., Wineburg, S.: The challenge that's bigger than fake news: civic reasoning in a social media environment. Am. Educ. **41**, 4–9 (2017)
14. Wineburg, S., McGrew, S.: Lateral reading and the nature of expertise: reading less and learning more when evaluating digital information. Teachers College Record **121**(11) (2019). https://www.tcrecord.org/Content.asp?ContentId=22806. Article 2
15. Breakstone, J.M., et al.: Students' civic online reasoning: a national portrait (2019)
16. Nygren, T., Guath, M.: Swedish teenagers' difficulties and abilities to determine digital news credibility. Nordicom Rev. **40**, 23–42 (2019)
17. OECD: PISA 2018 Results. OECD Publishing, Paris (2019)
18. Enochsson, A.-B.: Teenage pupils' searching for information on the Internet. In: Information Research (2019)
19. Solli, A.: Handling Socio-Scientific Controversy: Students' Reasoning Through Digital Inquiry. Gothenburg University, Gothenburg (2019)
20. Metzger, M.J., Flanagin, A.J., Medders, R.B.: Social and heuristic approaches to credibility evaluation online. J. Commun. **60**, 413–439 (2010)
21. Francke, H., Sundin, O., Limberg, L.: Debating credibility: the shaping of information literacies in upper secondary school. J. Documentation **67**, 675–694 (2011)
22. Pan, B., Hembrooke, H., Joachims, T., Lorigo, L., Gay, G., Granka, L.: In google we trust: users' decisions on rank, position, and relevance. J. Comput. Mediated Commun. **12**, 801–823 (2007)
23. Mason, L., Junyent, A.A., Tornatora, M.C.: Epistemic evaluation and comprehension of web-source information on controversial science-related topics: effects of a short-term instructional intervention. Comput. Educ. **76**, 143–157 (2014)
24. Flanagin, A.J., Winter, S., Metzger, M.J.: Making sense of credibility in complex information environments: the role of message sidedness, information source, and thinking styles in credibility evaluation online. Inf. Commun. Soc. 1–19 (2018)
25. McGrew, S.: Learning to evaluate: an intervention in civic online reasoning. Comput. Educ. **145**, 103711 (2019)
26. Hedman, F., Sivnert, F., Kollanyi, B., Narayanan, V., Neudert, L., Howard, P.N.: News and political information consumption in Sweden: mapping the 2018 Swedish general election on twitter. In: Data Memo 2018.3. Oxford, UK (2018)
27. Nygren, T., Brounéus, F., Svensson, G.: Diversity and credibility in young people's news feeds: a foundation for teaching and learning citizenship ina digital era. J. Soc. Sci. Educ. **18**, 87–109 (2019)
28. Christians, C.G., Glasser, T., McQuail, D., Nordenstreng, K., White, R.A.: Normative Theories of the Media: Journalism in Democratic Societies. Routledge, Urbana (2010)
29. Schauster, E.E., Ferrucci, P., Neill, M.S.: Native advertising is the new journalism: how deception affects social responsibility. Am. Behav. Sci. **60**, 1408–1424 (2016)

30. Shen, C., Kasra, M., Pan, W., Bassett, G.A., Malloch, Y., O'Brien, J.F.: Fake images: the effects of source, intermediary, and digital media literacy on contextual assessment of image credibility online. New Media Soc. **21**, 438–463 (2019)
31. EU: Action Plan against Disinformation. Joint communication to the European parliament, the European council, the council, the European economic and social committee and the committee of the regions (2018)
32. Sundar, S.S., Knobloch-Westerwick, S., Hastall, M.R.: News cues: information scent and cognitive heuristics. J. Am. Soc. Inf. Sci. Technol. **58**, 366–378 (2007)
33. Nestle, M.: Unsavory Truth: How Food Companies Skew the Science of What We Eat. Basic Books, New York (2018)

Defend Your Enemy. A Qualitative Study on Defending Political Opponents Against Hate Speech Online

Lilian Kojan[1], Hava Melike Osmanbeyoglu[2], Laura Burbach[1], Martina Ziefle[1], and André Calero Valdez[1]([✉])

[1] Human-Computer Interaction Center, RWTH Aachen University, Campus Boulevard 57, 52074 Aachen, Germany
{kojan,burbach,ziefle,calero-valdez}@comm.rwth-aachen.de
[2] RWTH Aachen University, Templergraben 44, 52052 Aachen, Germany
melike.osmanbeyoglu@rwth-aachen.de

Abstract. Both hate speech and disinformation negatively influence the internet's potential for public deliberation and lead to polarization between political groups. In this paper, we examine the potential of counter speech to bolster public deliberation and reduce polarization. In two focus groups, we interview participants on what motivates them to engage in counter speech in general as well as counter speech favoring political adversaries. Firstly, we find a sharp distinction between participants who avoid engaging with hate speech and participants who actively engage with hate speech in order to combat it. Thus, the most important predictor for counter speech favoring adversaries is an individual's propensity for counter speech in general. In turn, motivations for counter speech in general are a strong sense of morality, a perception of the internet as an important space for public deliberation, and a sense of responsibility to enforce rules for a fair debate. Many of those participants view their online activitiy as a form of activism. Additionally, individuals engaging in counter speech hope to positively influence not necessarily the hater, but the broader audience.

Keywords: Hate speech · Counter speech · Social media · Political deliberation

1 Deliberation in Digital Media

Since the commercialization of the Internet, the relationship between digital media and political life has grown ever stronger [8]. Apart from election campaigns, one important facet is the Internet's potential to strengthen democratic society by facilitating public deliberation [14,39]. At the same time, several limitations for online public deliberation have emerged. For one, offline power imbalances are often mirrored in the online world through an overrepresentation of groups in power, e.g., well-educated white men [21]. In addition, online groups

M. van Duijn et al. (Eds.): MISDOOM 2020, LNCS 12259, pp. 80–94, 2020.
https://doi.org/10.1007/978-3-030-61841-4_6

tend to be very homogenous meaning that users are seldomly exposed to cross-cutting opinions or differing viewpoints [16]. And when differing opinions do collide, incivility and even hate speech can occur [15, 38, 40].

1.1 Hate Speech and Misinformation

Although hate speech has been extensively discussed by the public at large as well as studied in academia, finding a universally valid definition is challenging [22]. Legal institutions and social networks alike tend to provide broad definitions that allow for judgement and possible sanctions on a case-by-case basis [22].

From a communication science perspective, Erjavec and Kovačič [20] define hate speech as an expression that is in itself harmful or possibly harm-inciting and targets members of a group determined by characteristics like race or sexual orientation. Similar characteristics can be found in other definitions that consider the purpose and the effects of hate speech. Waldron [44] characterizes speech as hateful when it serves one or both of two functions: Firstly, to dehumanize a target group and diminish its members and secondly, to reinforce a sense of in-group with other like-minded individuals. Similarly, Susan Benesch has coined the term *dangerous speech* which she defines as "[a]ny form of expression (e.g. speech, text, or images) that can increase the risk that its audience will condone or commit violence against members of another group". [5] Often, the groups targeted are marginalized social groups [1]. But especially in common parlance, hate speech can also describe speech directed at groups like politicians that are arguably powerful [22]. In summary, hate speech both reenforces the boundaries between groups and is harmful to members of the other group, either in itself or in its effects.

Hate speech is inextricably linked to disinformation. For one, online hate often takes the form of over-generalization, exaggeration or even outright deceit about the targeted group. E.g., Awan [3] stresses the use of false stories to exacerbate islamophobic hate. For another, disinformation like fake news often serve the same purpose as hate speech: Polarization, radicalization and othering of the out-group [6].

There is ample evidence for the damaging effects of hate speech, not only on the victim of the hate speech but also on the broader audience. Constant exposition shapes the user's worldview and influences their decision-making [19, 27]. Reading hateful and uncivil content increases attitude polarization [7, 29]. And by inducing negative emotions, it can also discourage people from engaging in discourse [25, 26, 29, 35]. Thereby, it actively impedes on the Internet's potential for public deliberation.

One possible way to counter hate speech is counter speech. Counter speech can be defined as a dissenting response to hate speech [48]. Although it is sometimes used in a way that also encompasses actions like flagging hateful content, our study focusses on counter speech in the form of content, e.g., comments in answer to the hateful content itself.

1.2   Effectiveness of Counter Speech

Counter speaking is encouraged in many anti-hate speech programs [22]. Furthermore, Chen [14] argues that countering online incivility is necessary to realize the potential of online spaces as a place for political deliberation. In spite of that, only a few studies have actually evaluated the effectiveness of counter speech. Buerger and Wright [11] have reviewed the studies available in November 2019. They differentiate between the effects of counter speech on the hateful speaker and the effects on the wider audience.

The results concerning the effects of counter speech on the hateful speaker are inconclusive [11]. However, there is some evidence that counter speech by users that are perceived as more influential, can curb hate speech at least temporarily (e.g., [36]). Findings on the effects of counter speech on the wider audience are less ambiguous. They all find evidence for something that Buerger and Wright [11] call the "contagion effect", i.e., the presence of hateful comments increases the probability of a user also making a hateful comment. On the opposite hand, civil comments also lead to more civil comments. Moreover, meta-comments urging people to be civil promote further meta-comments about discussion quality [35].

So while further research on the effects of counter speech is desirable, the existing indications for its success prompt us to ask what predicts users engaging in counter speech.

1.3   Predictors for Counter Speech

There already exist several studies examining willingness to intervene against hate speech and incivility in general and even more studies from the field of cyber-bystander research. As bystander intervention in cyber-bullying is similar to counter speech, predictors from a review on cyber-bystanding studies by Lambe et al. [30] are included as well.

The following predictors refer to intervention intention, with intervention ranging from more distanced behavior like using the reporting function (e.g., [47]) to deeply involved behavior like verbally confronting the individual engaging in hate speech (e.g., [18]).

The factors we summarize as *individual factors* concern properties of a would-be counter speaker that make intervention more likely. The predictors found are female gender [30,46], high prosociality and empathy [30], high self-efficacy [30], a negative attitude towards passive bystanding [30], an expectation that defending will help [30], and a high importance of morality, including low moral disengagement, high moral identity scores and individualizing moral foundation [30,46]. Additionally, there are situation-dependent factors like the would-be counter speaker feeling negative affect [14,17,18] and them perceiving social pressure and responsibility to intervene [17,18,47].

Other factors relate to the *properties of the victim* of the hate speech or bullying. Users are more likely to intervene if the victim is an individual person as a victim rather than an abstract social group [37], if the victim is more popular

[30], if they have a friendship or positive relationship with the victim [30] and if they exhibit a low level of prejudice towards the victim's social group [17].

Concerning *situational factors*, users were more likely to intervene if the situation was more deviant [17,18,37], if there was more than one perpetrator [28] and if more steps of the bystander intervention model were met (situation is noticed, fewer number of bystanders, information on how to confront is provided) [30,37].

To summarize, the existing research on hate speech intervention mainly considers the properties of the would-be counter speaker. For this study, we wanted to further the research on hate speech intervention by focussing in on the relationships between the would-be counter speaker and the victim. To be precise, with hate speech as an instrument for social division and polarization, can counter speech bridge the gap between in- and out-group? Therefore, our research question is:

In social media discussions, what are predictors for users to engage in counter speech in support of political adversaries?

2 Method

As laid out in Sect. 1.3, there is some research on predictors for counter speech in general as well as a breadth of studies in the field of cyber-bystander research. To our knowledge, however, there have not been any studies on out-group favoring counter speech. Therefore, an exploratory study design was chosen. Data was gathered in two focus groups. Afterwards, the data was transcribed and analysed to find the most pertinent predictors. The full transcriptions and the full analysis as well as the questionnaire, the slides and the guide used to collect our data can be found in our github repository for this project.[1]

2.1 Focus Groups

We conducted two focus groups, asking participants about their experiences with online hate speech in general and their own reactions to hate speech in particular, i.e., if they engaged in in counter speech at all. Special emphasis was placed on counter speech on behalf of political adversaries, that is, people the participants considered to be their opponents in an online discussion.

Guide and Structure. The focus groups were conducted using a guide which was pre-tested in advance. The sequence was structured into four sections, each concerned with one main topic:

1. Own experiences with hate speech.
2. Engagement in counter speech.
3. Conditions for counter speech for political adversaries.

---

[1] The repo can be found here: (github.com/digitalemuendigkeit/misdoom2020).

4. Motivations for counter speech for political adversaries.

In this context, conditions referred to predictors for counter speech in specific situations (i.e, when will you engage in counter speech) and motivations to general predictors (i.e., why do you engage in counter speech).

Stimuli. During the focus groups, we used screenshots of pertinent online interactions as stimuli, see e.g., Fig. 1. As the research question aimed at counter speech on behalf of one's political adversary, we aimed to select stimuli in a way that different political affiliations were accounted for. Therefore, we chose online interactions and tweets involving Alice Weidel, a member of the German right-wing party AfD, as well as posts aimed at one politician of the Greens, Claudia Roth. Not only can the Greens and the AfD be described as being representative of two ends of the political spectrum [24,31,33]. Also, both the AfD and the Greens, especially Claudia Roth, could be considered highly polarizing in November and December of 2018 when the focus groups were conducted [23,43].

Fig. 1. Stimulus B (insulting replies to one of German politician's Alice Weidel's tweets)

Recording and Transcription. Each focus group was recorded on audio. We then transcribed the recordings using MAXQDA, employing a modified version of GAT 2 as the transcription system [42].

2.2   Participants

The participants were recruited through convenience sampling. Based on preliminary questioning, they were sorted into two homogenous groups, the *moderately active* group and the *very active* group, in order to obtain more detailed results [41]. Potential participants who reported only passive social media use or none at all were excluded. The *moderately active* group (n = 5) included participants who mostly consumed social media but only seldomly posted or commented. Participants who not only used but also commented and posted in social media became part of the *very active group* (n = 6).

Before starting the focus group, each participant was surveyed on demographic details as well as the frequency of their social media use in general, the frequency of them posting and commenting online, and their political left-right self-placement [10]. The results are displayed in table 1.

Table 1. Focus group participants

	Moderately active group (n = 5)	Very active group (n = 6)
Gender	Female: 2, Male: 3	Female: 3, Male: 3
Age	M = 26.6, SD = 4	M = 32.3, SD = 7
Highest Level of Education	Abitur[a]: 1, University Degree: 4	Abitur[a]: 2, University Degree: 4
Occupation	Student: 3, Full-Time Employed: 2	Student: 1, Full-Time Employed: 5
Frequency of Social Media Use[bc]	M = 3.5, SD = 0.5	M = 4.2, SD = 0.4
Frequency of Posting and Commenting Online[b]	M = 2.2, SD = 0.8	M = 5.5, SD = 0.8
Political Left-Right Self-Placement[d]	M = 4, SD = 1.2	M = 3.5, SD = 1.6

[a] General Higher Education Entrance Qualification;
[b] 1 = never, 2 = very rarely, 3 = several times a month, 4 = several times a week, 5 = daily, 6 = several times a day;
[c] averaged over 6 types of platforms (social networking sites, video platforms, blogs, online newspapers, infotainment, social news);
[d] 1 = left, 10 = right

The participants from the *very active* group score somewhat higher on average social media use frequency and much higher on the posting and commenting frequency. Therefore, the classification based on the preliminary questioning was proven valid.

2.3   Content Analysis

We conducted a qualitative content analysis as described by Mayring [34] using MAXQDA. After we first developed a categorization, we tested for intercoder reliability by calculating coefficient kappa using the approach of Brennan and Prediger [9] (minimum coding overlap = 60%). Overall, a kappa of 0.26 was calculated. This proposes unsatisfactory reliability which is, however, not out of the ordinary for the first iteration of intercoder reliability examination. [13,32] To resolve the discrepancies between the different coders, we employed the Intercoder Agreement method as described by Campbell et al. [13]. In Fig. 2, an overview of the final categorization is visible.

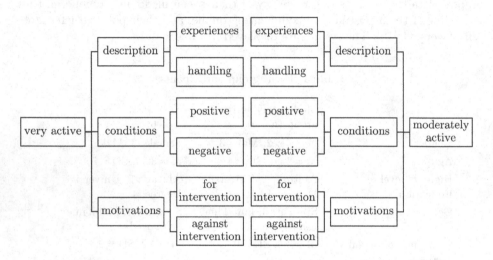

Fig. 2. Overview of the final categorization

3   Results

As Fig. 2 shows, we contrasted the results of both groups for each category, (*description*, *conditions* and *motivations*). As our research question focusses on predictors, only a quick overview will be given for the category *description*.

For the sake of brevity, in the following sections these terms will be used: *Hater:* The perpetrator of the hate speech, *victim(s):* the recipient(s) or subject(s) of the hate speech, and *adversary victim(s):* victim(s) or subject(s) of hate speech that represent a group the participant politically or personally opposes.

3.1   Description: Experiences with Hate Speech and Handling Hate Speech

When describing their experiences with hate speech, both groups mention similar attributes of hate speech (e.g., the online *spaces* where they have most often observed it). However, while four of the six very active participants report to have themselves been victims of hate speech, only one moderately active participant does so as well. There are also notable differences in the way participants of both groups handle hate speech: While participants in the moderately active group tend to look at hateful comments only for entertainment value or avoid looking at comments at all, many participants in the very active group actively seek out hate speech comments in order to fight it.

3.2   Conditions: When to Engage in Counter Speech

For a given situation, participants describe both conditions that make it more likely that they engage in counter speech (*positive conditions*) as well as conditions that make it less likely (*negative conditions*). As mentioned above, the participants in the moderately active group reported to only seldom engage in counter speech at all, much less counter speech favoring *adversary victims*, i.e., politically opposed users that are targetted by hate speech. Therefore, most of the conditions listed are to be understood as conditions for counter speech in general. The only exception is the subcategory *positive conditions* for the very active group where a differentiation between counter speech in general and counter speech favoring *adversary victims* was possible.

Positive Conditions for Counter Speech Favoring Adversaries. When it comes defending people who they are politically opposed to, the following conditions emerged in the very active group: **1) Offenses against a "culture of discussion"**, i.e., the participant feels that the hater breaks the rules for a respectful debate, **2) offenses against the human dignity**, i.e., the participant feels that the hater debases the victim's human dignity, **3) properties of the victim**, e.g., the participants feels sympathy for the victim, and **4) a personal connection to the topic discussed.**

Positive Conditions for Counter Speech in General.

Properties of the Hate Speech. Concerning the properties of the hate speech or the situation where the hate speech occurs, participants of both groups mention they are more likely to step in when they feel that their **1) counter speech is likely to have an impact**, e.g., there are not that many comments overall. Additionally, participants of the very active group name the space as an important factor. They are more likely to step in when there is hate speech **2) outside of hater-dominated spaces**, e.g., not in a dedicated facebook group, or **3) in a more private space**, e.g., in a personal chat group.

On the other side, participants of the moderately active group mention **4) calls to violence and threats** as well as **5) doxxing**, i.e., finding and disseminating the victim's personal information, as factors making counter speech more likely for them.

Properties of the Victim. Relating to the properties of the victim, both groups mention that they would be more likely to intervene if **1) the victim is a private citizen** or if **2) they know the victim personally**, although that is more important in the moderately active group. Additionally, participants of the very active group would be more likely to engage in counter speech if **3) the victim is an activist**.

Personal Attributes. Participants of both group state that they are more likely to step in if they are **1) well informed about the topic of discussion**. Members of the very active group also name **2) free time and mental energy** as a condition. Some members of the moderately active group, on the other hand, describe **3) feeling frustrated and angry** or **4) having a personal connection** to the topic of discussion as a conductor for counter~speech.

Negative Conditions for Counter Speech in General. Many of the *negative conditions* mentioned in the group are merely negations of the *positive conditions* already listed and will therefore not be reported again.

Properties of the Hate Speech. Members of both group state that they are less likely to engage in counter speech, when **1) both sides of the discussion engage in hate speech** or when **2) the hate speech is entertaining to them**.

Additionally, participants of the very active group are less willing to intervene when they fear **3) personal risk to themselves**.

Properties of the Victim. Apart from the negatives to the *positive conditions* already mentioned, one member of the very active group reports that they would be less likely to intervene if they suspect **the victim is eager to be seen as a victim by the public**.

3.3 Motivations: Why to Engage in Counter Speech

Just as with the conditions, the *motivations* of the participants could also be categorized into *motivations for intervention* and *motivations against intervention*. In this context, *motivations* relate to the participants' attitudes towards counter speech in general. By contrast, the *conditions* listed above relate to specific situations.

Motivations for Intervention. The *motivations for intervention* can be further categorized into *goals and values* and *personal attributes and experiences*.

Goals and Values. Participants of both groups concede that while they might not be able to dissuade the hater from their destructive behavior, they still **1) hope to positively influence the audience**. Members of the very active group are additionally motivated by the desire to **2) fight disinformation, 3)** motivate critical thinking in other users, 4) create a better culture of discussion in online spaces and 5) engage politically. Some of the very active participants describe viewing their counter speech activity as a form of activism.

Moderately active participants, on the other hand, worry that *online hate might spark offline violence*.

Personal Attributes and Experiences. When it comes to their personal attributes and experiences that motivate them to engage in counter speech, participants of both groups mention 1) a strong sense of justice and 2) a sense of responsibility.

In addition, very active participants name 1) enjoying debating, 2) their own experiences with bullying and discrimination, 3) enjoying self-promotion, as well as 4) being thanked and admired by others, e.g., by site administrators, as motivators.

Motivations Against Intervention. Members of both groups name one main motivation not to engage in counter speech: They think it is 1) not worth the effort. On top of that, members of the very active group mainly mention 2) fatigue with fighting hate speech in general as something that demotivates them from engaging in counter speech.

Among the moderately active participants, a considerable number more motivations are named: 1) A general unwillingness to participate in online communication, 2) a preference for alternative approaches to hate speech, e.g. blocking the perpetrator or even reporting them to the police, 3) their perception of the chance to be successful as too small and 4) their own tendency to avoid reading comments at all.

4   Discussion and Conclusion

Notably, a vast difference in engagement levels between the participants was found. While some would not engage in online discourse at all and consequently would not engage in counter speech either, others were hyperactive on social media, placing a lot of value on political discourse in online spaces. Participants in the latter group reported a much higher likelihood to engage in counter speech, be it on behalf of opponents or in general.

Overall, the relationship between the counter speaker and the victim which we focussed on in our research question (*In social media discussions, what motivates users to engage in counter speech in support of political adversaries?*) seems to be less important than the willingness to engage in counter speech in general. While we collected and categorized the predictors for counter speech reported by our participants in *conditions*, i.e., situational predictors, and *motivations*, i.e., general predictors, there is only a small number of predictors from the subset *conditions* strictly in answer to our research question:

Three basic motivations for users to engage in counter speech in support of political adversaries can be differentiated: Firstly, the hater violates norms or values that are more important to the counter speaker than political affiliation. Values named here were a "culture of discussion", i.e., an implicit set of rules for a respectful debate, and "human dignity". These conditions tie somewhat into other findings about counter speakers placing high importance on morality [30, 46]. Interestingly, they also mirror the vision of the internet as a place for public deliberation [14]. Productive debates can only happen if all participants follow the rules, no matter which side they are on. Secondly, counter speech is more likely if the participants feels sympathetic towards the victim. This is similar to results from cyber-bullying research [30]. Thirdly, participants are more likely to intervene when they feel a personal connection to the topic of discussion. Both the second and the third motivation are limited in their generalizability. Sympathies are likely to wane the larger the distance on the political spectrum gets. And in many occurrences of hate speech, there will be no connection to a tangible discussion topic.

The other predictors we found refer to counter speech in general and therefore do not strictly answer the research question. However, as posited above, we did not observe the expected divide between people engaging in counter speech only for friends or members of their in-group and people engaging in counter speech for everyone—including adversaries. Rather, the divide was between people engaging in counter speech for everyone, regardless of political or group affiliation, and people not generally engaging in counter speech. As such, we feel that the *motivations* of the very active group questioned also partly answer the question of what motivates counter speakers.

The most important *motivations* we found were deep-seated moral convictions and a feeling of responsibility to uphold those convictions. This does not only match the findings by on the importance of morality by Wilhelm and Joeckel [46] and Lambe et al. [30]. The acceptance of responsibility also matches the bystander model of intervention often used to describe bystander behavior in cyber-bullying incidents (e.g., [37]). Moreover, the participants felt that online discourse is an important part of political participation [14]. Many of the active counter speakers we talked to saw their actions as a form of activism. One of their major goals was not to change the behavior of the people engaging in hate speech, but to positively influence the broader audience. This matches what Buerger and Wright [11] call the contagion effect.

In conclusion, when looking at what motivates a person to regularly engage in counter speech, their relationship to the victim appears to be secondary. Of greater importance seems to be what part morality plays in that person's self-image and how willing they are to accept and defend online spaces as a place for public deliberation.

Finally, some limitations have to be noted: Firstly, although we tried to emphasize the relationship aspect (i.e., counter speech *in favor of adversaries*) in our research design, stressing this emphasis during the focus groups proved challenging. Rather, participants tended to talk about their experiences with counter speech *in general*. This holds especially true for the participants of the moderately active group, many of whom never had engaged in counter speech at all. Therefore, our results are not suitable to evaluate whether there are differences between predictors for counter speech *in favor of adversaries* and counter speech *in general*. Secondly, our sample was comparatively young, highly educated and politically left-aligned. It is entirely possible that other predictors not mentioned here are important with counter speakers who are, e.g., more politically right-leaning. In any case, the predictors identified in this study should be further tested in a quantitative study. Thirdly, the predictors identified in this study as well as most other studies listed in Sect. 1.3 are self-reported. Conducting an experiment could shed light on whether or not these translate to actual defending behavior.

Acknowledgements. We would like to thank Maximilian Geulen and Merten Wothge for their help in developing the research design as well as collecting the data. This research was supported by the Digital Society research program funded by the Ministry of Culture and Science of the German State of North Rhine-Westphalia. We would further like to thank the authors of the packages we have used. We used the following packages to create this document: `knitr` [49], `tidyverse` [45], `rmdformats` [4], `kableExtra` [50], `rmdtemplates` [12], `citr` [2].

References

1. Álvarez-Benjumea, A., Winter, F.: Normative change and culture of hate: an experiment in online environments. Eur. Sociol. Rev. **34**(3), 223–237 (2018). https://doi.org/10.1093/esr/jcy005. ISSN: 0266–7215, 1468–2672
2. Aust, F.: citr: RStudio add-in to insert markdown citations. R package version 0.3.2. (2019). https://CRAN.R-project.org/package=citr
3. Awan, I.: Islamophobia on social media: a qualitative analysis of the Facebook'S walls of hate (2016). https://doi.org/10.5281/ZENODO.58517
4. Barnier, J.: rmdformats: HTML output formats and templates for 'rmarkdown' documents. R package version 0.3.6. (2019). https://CRAN.R-project.org/package=rmdformats
5. Benesch, S., et al.: Dangerous speech: a practical guide (2020). https://dangerousspeech.org/guide/
6. Bennett, W.L., Livingston, S.: The disinformation order: disruptive communication and the decline of democratic institutions. Eur. J. Commun. **33**(2), 122–139 (2018). https://doi.org/10.1177/0267323118760317. ISSN: 0267-3231, 1460-3705
7. Borah, P.: Does it matter where you read the news story? interaction of incivility and news frames in the political blogosphere. Commun. Res. **41**(6), 809–827 (2014). https://doi.org/10.1177/0093650212449353. ISSN: 0093–6502, 1552–3810
8. Boulianne, S.: Twenty years of digital media effects on civic and political participation. Commun. Res. (2018). ISSN: 0093–6502, 1552–3810. https://doi.org/10.1177/0093650218808186
9. Brennan, R.L., Prediger, D.J.: Coefficient kappa: some uses, misuses, and alternatives. Educ. Psychol. Meas. **41**(3), 687–699 (1981)
10. Breyer, B.: Left-right self-placement (allbus) (2015)
11. Buerger, C., Wright, L.: Counterspeech: a literature review (2019)

12. Valdez, A.C.: rmdtemplates: rmdtemplates – an opinionated collection of rmark-down templates. R package version 0.3.3.0001 (2019). https://github.com/statisticsforsocialscience/rmd_templates

13. Campbell, J.L., et al.: Coding in-depth semistructured interviews: problems of unitization and intercoder reliability and agreement. Sociol. Methods Res. **42**(3), 294–320 (2013). https://doi.org/10.1177/0049124113500475. ISSN: 0049-1241, 1552-8294

14. Chen, G.M.: Online Incivility and Public Debate. Springer, Cham (2017). https://doi.org/10.1007/978-3-319-56273-5

15. Coe, K., Kenski, K., Rains, S.A.: Online and uncivil? patterns and determinants of incivility in newspaper website comments. J. Commun. **64**(4), 658–679 (2014). https://doi.org/10.1111/jcom.12104. ISSN: 00219916

16. Colleoni, E., Rozza, A., Arvidsson, A.: Echo chamber or public sphere? predicting political orientation and measuring political homophily in twitter using big data: political homophily on twitter. J. Commun. **64**(2), 317–332 (2014). https://doi.org/10.1111/jcom.12084. ISSN: 00219916

17. Dickter, C.L.: Confronting hate: heterosexuals' responses to anti-gay comments. J. Homosex. **59**(8), 1113–1130 (2012). https://doi.org/10.1080/00918369.2012.712817. ISSN: 0091-8369, 1540-3602

18. Dickter, C.L., Newton, V.A.: To confront or not to confront: non-targets' evaluations of and responses to racist comments: responses to racist comments. J. Appl. Soc. Psychol. **43**, E262–E275 (2013). https://doi.org/10.1111/jasp.12022. ISSN: 00219029

19. Erjavec, K.: Readers of online news comments: why do they read hate speech comments? Ann. Series historia et sociologia **24**(3), 451–462 (2014)

20. Erjavec, K., Kovačič, M.P.: You don't understand, this is a new war!' analysis of hate speech in news web sites' comments. Mass Commun. Soc. **15**(6), 899–920 (2012). https://doi.org/10.1080/15205436.2011.619679. ISSN: 1520-5436, 1532-7825

21. Feezell, J.T.: Predicting online political participation: the importance of selection bias and selective exposure in the online setting. Polit. Res. Q. **69**(3), 495–509 (2016). https://doi.org/10.1177/1065912916652503. ISSN: 1065-9129, 1938-274X

22. Gagliardone, I., et al.: Countering online hate speech. Technical report, UNESCO (2015)

23. Gensing, P.: Grünen-Politikerin Roth: Im Visier des Hasses. de (2018). http://www.tagesschau.dehttp://faktenfinder.tagesschau.de/inland/kampagnen-roth-101.html

24. Hambauer, V., Mays, A.: Wer wählt die AfD? – Ein Vergleich der Sozialstruktur, politischen Einstellungen und Einstellungen zu Flüchtlingen zwischen AfD-WählerInnen und der WählerInnen der anderen Parteien de. Z. Vgl. Polit. Wiss **12**(1), 133–154 (2018). https://doi.org/10.1007/s12286-017-0369-2. ISSN: 1865-2646, 1865-2654

25. Hwang, H., Kim, Y., Huh, C.U.: Seeing is believing: effects of uncivil online debate on political polarization and expectations of deliberation. J. Broadcast. Electron. Media **58**(4), 621–633 (2014). https://doi.org/10.1080/08838151.2014.966365. ISSN: 0883-8151, 1550-6878

26. Hwang, H., et al.: Does civility matter in the Blogo– sphere? examining the interaction effects of incivility and disagreement on citizen attitudes. In: Annual Convention of the International Communication Association Montreal, Canada (2008)

27. Jubany, O.: Backgrounds, experiences and responses to online hate speech: an ethnographic multi-sited analysis. In: 2nd Annual International Conference on Social Science and Contemporary Humanity Development (SSCHD 2016). Atlantis Press(2016). ISBN: 978-94-6252-227-5. https://doi.org/10.2991/sschd-16.2016.143

28. Kazerooni, F., et al.: Cyberbullying bystander intervention: the number of offenders and retweeting predict likelihood of helping a cyberbullying victim. J. Comput. Mediated Commun. **23**(3), 146–162 (2018). https://doi.org/10.1093/jcmc/zmy005. ISSN: 1083-6101

29. Kim, Y., Kim, Y.: Incivility on facebook and political polarization: the mediating role of seeking further comments and negative emotion. Comput. Hum. Behav. **99**, 219–227 (2019). https://doi.org/10.1016/j.chb.2019.05.022. ISSN: 07475632

30. Lambe, L.J., et al.: Standing up to bullying: a social ecological review of peer defending in offline and online contexts. Aggression Violent Behav. **45**, 51–74 (2019)

31. Lees, C.: The 'alternative for Germany': the rise of right-wing populism at the heart of Europe. Politics **38**(3), 295–310 (2010). https://doi.org/10.1177/0263395718777718. ISSN: 0263-3957, 1467-9256

32. MacPhail, C., et al.: Process guidelines for establishing intercoder reliability in qualitative studies. Qual. Res. **16**(2), 198–212 (2016). https://doi.org/10.1177/1468794115577012. ISSN: 1468-7941, 1741-3109

33. Mader, M., Schoen, H.: The European refugee crisis, party competition, and voters' responses in Germany. West Eur. Polit. **42**(1), 67–90 (2019). https://doi.org/10.1080/01402382.2018.1490484. ISSN: 0140-2382, 1743-9655

34. Mayring, P.: Qualitative content analysis: theoretical foundation, basic procedures and software solution. Klagenfurt (2014)

35. Molina, R.G., Jennings, F.J.: The role of civility and metacommunication in facebook discussions. Commun. Stud. **69**(1), 42–66 (2018). https://doi.org/10.1080/10510974.2017.1397038. ISSN: 1051-0974, 1745-1035

36. Munger, K.: Tweetment effects on the tweeted: experimentally reducing racist harassment. Polit. Behav. **39**(3), 629–649 (2017). https://doi.org/10.1007/s11109-016-9373-5. ISSN 0190-9320, 1573-6687

37. Naab, T.K., Kalch, A., Meitz, T.G.K.: Flagging uncivil user comments: effects of intervention information, type of victim, and response comments on bystander behavior. New Media Soc. **20**(2), 777–795 (2018). https://doi.org/10.1177/1461444816670923. ISSN: 1461-4448, 1461-7315

38. Papacharissi, Z.: Democracy online: civility, politeness, and the democratic potential of online political discussion groups. New Media Soc. **6**(2), 259–283 (2004). https://doi.org/10.1177/1461444804041444. ISSN: 1461-4448, 1461-7315

39. Papacharissi, Z.: The virtual sphere: the internet as a public sphere. New Media Soc. **4**(1), 9–27 (2002). https://doi.org/10.1177/14614440222226244. ISSN: 1461-4448, 1461-7315

40. Rains, S.A., et al.: Incivility and political identity on the internet: intergroup factors as predictors of incivility in discussions of news online: incivility and political identity online. J. Comput. Mediated Commun. **22**(4), 163–178 (2017). https://doi.org/10.1111/jcc4.12191. ISSN: 10836101

41. Schulz, M., Mack, B., Renn, O. (eds.): Fokusgruppen in Der Empirischen Sozialwissenschaft: Von Der Konzeption Bis Zur Auswertung. Springer VS, Wiesbaden (2012). https://doi.org/10.1007/978-3-531-19397-7. ISBN: 978-3-531-19396-0

42. Selting, M., et al.: A system for transcribing talk-in-interaction: GAT 2 translated and adapted for english by elizabeth couper-kuhlen and dagmar barth-weingarten. Gesprächsforschung - Online-Zeitschriftzur verbalen Interaktion **12**, 1–51 (2011). ISSN: 1617-1837
43. Volksverhetzung: Hunderte Anzeigen Gegen AfD-Fraktionsvize von Storch — ZEIT ONLINE (2018). https://www.zeit.de/politik/2018-01/volksverhetzungbeatrix-von-storch-strafanzeigen-silvester
44. Waldron, J.: The Harm in Hate Speech. Harvard University Press, USA (2012). ISBN: 978-0-674-06589-5
45. Wickham, H.: tidyverse: easily install and load the 'tidyvers'. R package version 1.3.0. (2019) . https://CRAN.R-project.org/package=tidyverse
46. Wilhelm, C., Joeckel, S.: Gendered morality and backlash effects in online discussions: an experimental study on how users respond to hate speech comments against women and sexual minorities. Sex Roles **80**(7), 381–392 (2018). https://doi.org/10.1007/s11199-018-0941-5. ISSN: 0360-0025, 1573-2762
47. Wong, R.Y.M., Cheung, C.M.K., Xiao, B.: Combating online abuse: what drives people to use online reporting functions on social networking sites. In: 2016 49th Hawaii International Conference on System Sciences (HICSS), pp. 415–424. IEEE (2016). ISBN: 978-0-7695-5670-3. https://doi.org/10.1109/HICSS.2016.58
48. Wright, L., et al.: Vectors for counterspeech on twitter. In: Association for Computational Linguistics, pp. 57–62 (2017). https://doi.org/10.18653/v1/W17-3009
49. Xie, Y.: knitr: a general-purpose package for dynamic report generation in R. R package version 1.26 (2019). https://CRAN.Rproject.org/package=knitr
50. Zhu, H.: kableExtra: Construct Complex Table with 'kable' and Pipe Syntax. R package version 1.1.0 (2019). https://CRAN.R-project.org/package=kableExtra

Automatically Identifying Political Ads on Facebook: Towards Understanding of Manipulation via User Targeting

Or Levi[1]([✉]), Sardar Hamidian[2], and Pedram Hosseini[2]

[1] AdVerif.ai, Amsterdam, Netherlands
or@adverifai.com
[2] The George Washington University, Washington, USA
{sardar,phosseini}@gwu.edu

Abstract. The reports of Russian interference in the 2016 United States elections brought into the center of public attention concerns related to the ability of foreign actors to increase social discord and take advantage of personal user data for political purposes. It has raised questions regarding the ways and the extent to which data can be used to create psychographical profiles to determine what kind of advertisement would be most effective to persuade a particular person in a particular location for some political event; Questions which have not been explored yet due to the lack of publicly available data. In this work, we study the political ads dataset collected by ProPublica, an American nonprofit newsroom, using a network of volunteers in the period before the 2018 US midterm elections. With the help of the volunteers, it has been made possible to collect not only the content of the ads but also the attributes that were used by advertisers to target the users. We first describe the main characteristics of the data and explore the user attributes including age, region, activity, and more, with a series of interactive illustrations. Furthermore, an important first step towards understating of political manipulation via user targeting is to identify politically related ads, yet manually checking ads is not feasible due to the scale of social media advertising. Consequently, we address the challenge of automatically classifying between political and non-political ads, demonstrating a significant improvement compared to the current text-based classifier used by ProPublica, and study whether the user targeting attributes are beneficial for this task. Our evaluation sheds light on questions, such as how user attributes are being used for political ads targeting and which users are more prone to be targeted with political ads. Overall, our contribution of data exploration, political ad classification and initial analysis of the targeting attributes, is designed to support future work with the ProPublica dataset, and specifically with regard to the understanding of political manipulation via user targeting.

Keywords: Political advertising · User targeting · Social media

M. van Duijn et al. (Eds.): MISDOOM 2020, LNCS 12259, pp. 95–106, 2020.
https://doi.org/10.1007/978-3-030-61841-4_7

1   Introduction

Social media platforms are collecting a great amount of personal user data. While the data can be used to improve the effectiveness of ad recommendation, as demonstrated by previous works [5–7], it also raises concerns related to user privacy, especially when it comes to political ads; Concerns, which have been amplified by the reports of Russian interference in the 2016 United States elections, when fake accounts linked to a Russian troll farm bought advertisements targeting millions of Facebook users prior to the election. These concerns were further amplified by the Facebook-Cambridge Analytica data scandal, when it was revealed that Cambridge Analytica harvested the personal data of millions of people's Facebook profiles without their consent and used it for political purposes.

Despite the growing public interest, the effect of political ad targeting on social media has not been explored yet due to the lack of publicly available data. Facebook has made available[1] an archive of ads related to politics but that has included only the content of the ads. In an effort to promote ad transparency and hold advertisers including political groups accountable, ProPublica, an American nonprofit newsroom, has collected a dataset of political ads in the period before the 2018 US midterm elections. Readers were asked to install a browser extension that automatically collected advertisements shown to them on Facebook without collecting personal information. With the help of the volunteers it has been made possible to collect not only the content of the political ads but also the attributes that were used by advertisers to target the users.

This work is the first to study the ProPublica political ads data and the use of targeting attributes, such as age, region, activity, and interests, for political advertising on social media. First, we describe the main properties of the dataset and provide a series of interactive illustrations by leveraging the targeting attributes, in addition to election information collected from online resources.

Second, in order to study the potential to manipulate users for political purposes via the targeting attributes, it is important to initially identify which ads, and advertisers, are politically oriented. We are motivated by the increasing efforts of both social media platforms, and investigative journalism organizations, to improve the transparency and scrutiny around political advertising and study their effect on the spread of misinformation and social discord. However, given the large scale of social media advertising, manually checking ads is impractical.

Consequently, we address the challenge of automatically classifying between political and non-political ads. While the data released by ProPublica contains only ads that were identified as political by an existing classifier, we notice there is still a great amount of disagreement compared to the judgments by the volunteers, and aim to improve the text classification.

In addition to identifying language differences, we also consider the following research question: can the targeting attributes be used for identification of political ads? In other words, are there differences in the patterns of user targeting

---

[1] https://www.facebook.com/ads/archive/.

between political and non-political ads? The evaluation of our method sheds light on how user attributes are being used for political ads targeting and what kind of user profiles are more likely to be targeted. For instance, we find that political advertisers are more likely to use location targeting, and that users in battleground states are more likely to be targeted with political ads.

2   Related Work

Previous works have demonstrated the effectiveness of targeting attributes for ad recommendation, based on user behavior [6,7], user demographics [8] or a combination of the two. For instance, Bagherjeiran et al. [5] proposed to build a generic user profile with demographic and behavioral information about the user, and learned a mapping from non-textural user features to the textual space of ads that helped to improve the click rate on ads.

Another related line of work is the classification of political orientation from text on social media. [3,4,9]. Pennacchiotti et al. [10] proposed to automatically construct user profiles, to identify the political affiliation of users, based on features related to profile information, messaging behavior, linguistic content and social connections. Similarly, Boutet et al. [11] used the number of Twitter messages referring to a particular political party to identify the political leaning of users. In this work we focus on a different task. Rather than identifying a political orientation, we aim to distinguish between political and non-political ads. For this task, we use the novel targeting attributes, that were used by advertisers to target users and have been made available only recently, with the release of the ProPublica dataset.

3   The ProPublica Dataset

The ProPublica political ads dataset[2] includes information regarding the content of the ads, such as title, message and images; the number of users who voted it as political or not political; and the targeting attributes, as described in Fig. 1. Overall, the data includes more than 68,000 ads from 5,700 different advertisers collected in the period between August 2017 and October 2018.

To manifest a better insight into the properties of the data, we provide a series of interactive illustrations[3] by leveraging the targeting attributes, in addition to election information collected from online resources. Figure 2 is one of the graphs from this dashboard illustrating the distribution of political ads on Facebook based on geographical information collected from the targeting attributes. According to the map, users in highly populated states (Darker green relative to high regional population) like California, New York, Texas, and Washington are more prone to be targeted by political ads.

---

[2] https://propublica.org/datastore/dataset/political-advertisements-from-facebook.
[3] https://tabsoft.co/2RErMBD.

Attribute	Count	Unique	Examples
Age	61,463	266	"18 and older", "30 and older"
MinAge	59,196	49	"18", "30"
Region	52,323	77	"California", "Texas"
Retargeting	15,184	3	"similar to their customers", "recently near their business"
Interest	13,684	1135	"Democratic Party", "Bernie Sanders"
City	9,029	723	"Washington", "New York"
State	9,029	68	"California", "New York"
Like	5,371	2	Boolean
Segment	3,876	77	"US politics (very liberal)", "a family-based household"
Gender	3,095	3	"women", "men"
MaxAge	2,966	43	"54", "64"
Agency	432	6	"Experian", "Epsilon"
Language	244	5	"English (US)", "Spanish"

Fig. 1. The Targeting Attributes. For each attribute we present the number of occurrences in the data, the number of unique values and a couple of examples.

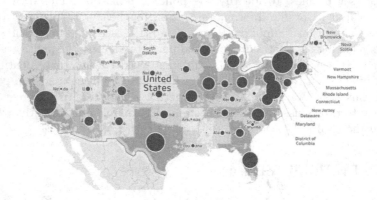

Fig. 2. The distribution of political ads on Facebook in different states based on population. Circle size is the percentage calculated by number of ads in the state divided by total number of ads in the US.

Figure 3 shows the number of political ads for each of the targeting attributes. According to this chart, the top two targeting attributes used in political ads are the age and the region of the Facebook users. More than 70% of the time Facebook users are targeted by political ads is because they meet a certain age and location criteria, as opposed to language, agency, and gender with only 2%.

Region is the second most important attribute used in political ads. As shown in Fig. 4, Facebook users in California, Texas, Florida and New York are almost 10 times more likely to be targeted with political ads than states like Indiana, Montana or even Virginia.

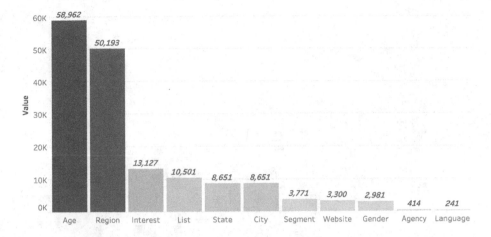

Fig. 3. Number of political ads for each of the targeting attributes.

After age and region, interest is the third most important attribute for political ad targeting. Figure 5 shows the top 10 interest topics used by advertisers. According to the chart, Facebook users with interest in the "Democratic Party", "Bernie Sanders" and "Barack Obama" are more prone to be targeted by political ads than the other interest topics.

Figure 6 shows the number of political ads for each of the battleground states, in addition to the election outcome on the map. There appears to be no significant correlation between the election outcome and the number of ads in battleground states.

4   Method

To study the effects of political manipulation via user targeting, we first address the challenge of automatically classifying between political and non-political ads. The classification labels are based on the 'political' and 'not political' fields in the data, which reflect the number of volunteers who have voted an ad as political or not political. Ads with more 'political' votes are classified as political and vice versa. We disregard ads with equal amounts of 'political' and 'not political' votes.

To classify political ads, ProPublica have been using a text classifier, such that the dataset contains only ads that were identified as political with a probability greater than 70% (see 'political probability' field). However, a quick examination of the probabilities assigned by the classifier compared to the judgments by the volunteers shows still a great amount of disagreement. For instance, there are examples where the classifier picks up on a keyword like 'vote' but it is used in a non-political context. We hypothesize that using bigrams together with a tree-based classifier could help with these false positives and improve the performance of the classifier. A key consideration is also to provide a simple method that will be computationally inexpensive.

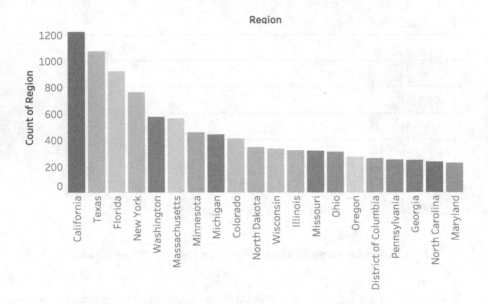

Fig. 4. The distribution of political ads in different states.

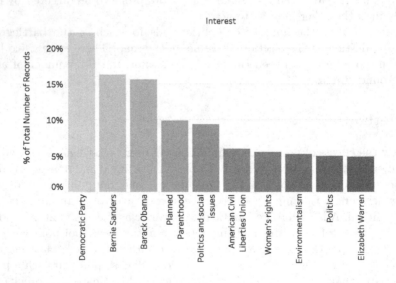

Fig. 5. Top 10 Interest topics used for targeting the political ads.

Given that the data made available by ProPublica contains only ads that were already identified by the current classifier, political ads, as judged by the volunteers, outnumber non-political ads with a 9:1 ratio. To address this challenge we use an imbalance correction method, giving a penalty to the over-represented

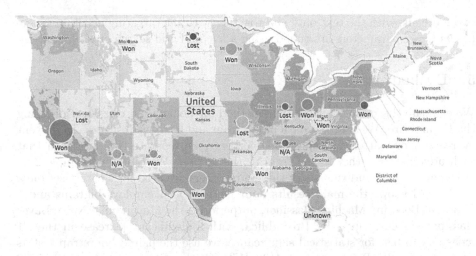

Fig. 6. Incumbent status for battleground states vs. the volume of political advertising, represented by the circle size.

class, with a weight that is inversely proportional to the class frequencies in the input data:

$$Weight(y) = \frac{n\_samples}{n\_samples(y)} \tag{1}$$

where $n\_samples$ and $n\_samples(y)$ is the number of samples in general, and from class y, respectively.

We next turn to study our research question with regard to the potential of the targeting attributes to help with identifying political ads. The 'targets' field holds the targeting attributes of each ad. As part of the data pre-processing, we transform this field into separate columns, each representing one of the targeting attributes. Since the 'Region' and 'State' attributes are mostly overlapping, we drop the 'State' and use the 'Region', which occurs in more entries. We drop the sparse attributes 'Engaged with Content', with only 9 entries, and 'Language', with only 4 Non-English entries. Instead of the 'Age' attribute, which represents the targeted age range, we use the 'MinAge' and 'MaxAge' attributes, which represent the range limits. All the attributes are treated as categorical variables and transformed using one-hot encoding, except for the numerical attributes 'MinAge' and 'MaxAge'. Note that this still supports cases of users with multiple values for the same attribute, e.g. multiple interests, given that each interest is represented by a separate binary feature.

The ad text is obtained by concatenating the 'title' and 'message' fields of the ad. We use a TF-IDF vector representation as implemented by the sci-kit learn toolkit with Snowball stemming and stop words removed.

The baseline method by ProPublica uses a Multinomial Naive Bayes classifier. For the tree-based classification model, we use the Gradient Boosting Decision Tree (GBDT) as implemented by the LightGBM toolkit [12]. We test two methods, with the text only and together with the targeting attributes. The model hyper-parameters are tuned using a five-fold grid search cross validation.

5   Evaluation

We evaluate the performance of our method for political ad classification using the F1 measure. We split the data into a train and held-out test sets. To prevent over-fitting on patterns of specific advertisers, we separate the data such that each advertiser is either in the train or the test set. We randomly sample 20% of the advertisers and the ads of these advertisers are used for the test set only.

Table 1 shows the main results. Our method, that employs bigrams and a Gradient Boosting Machine classifier, outperforms the Multinomial Naive Bayes classifier currently used by ProPublica, with a significant increase in the F1 measure. To test for statistical significance, we use the paired bootstrap test as recommended by Reichart et al. [13]. With the bootstrap test, we draw 1000 different samples. The size of each sample is the same as the full data, and the train and test sets are obtained using the above-mentioned split by advertisers. For each sample we evaluate the F1 score of the baseline and our method. The scores are then used to check the statistical significance via the bootstrap test implemented by Dror et al.[4] with a 0.05 significance level.

Further to our research question, the evaluation also shows that using the targeting attributes for classification of political ads can further improve the performance, compared the text-only methods. Even though the improvement is not large, it gives motivation to further investigate differences in the patterns of targeting users between political and non-political ads.

Table 1. Main Results. Our method, with the Gradient Boosting Machine classifier, achieves significant improvement on the F1 measure compared to the existing ProPublica classifier. Also, using the targeting attributes outperforms the text only based methods. Bold: best result among methods. Statistically significant differences with the ProPublica baseline and the GBM text only classifier are marked with '*' and '**', respectively.

Method	Precision	Recall	F1
MultinomialNB: Text Only (ProPublica)	88.75	96.65	92.53
GBM: Text Only	90.33	99.25	94.58*
GBM: Text + Targeting attributes	**90.83**	**99.68**	**95.05****

---

[4] https://github.com/rtmdrr/.

To study the feature importance to our LightGBM model, we use Tree SHAP [1], a fast algorithm to compute SHAP values [2] for trees, as implemented by Lundberg et al.[5]. Figure 7 shows the most important keywords, sorted by the sum of SHAP value magnitudes over all training samples. The list includes terms that can be expected to be associated with political ads, such as "trump", "senate", "congress" and more.

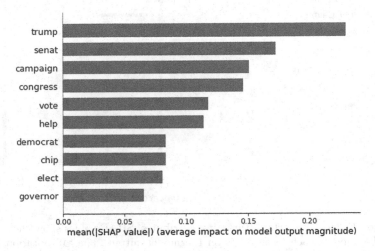

Fig. 7. Top 10 Most Important Keywords. The list contains terms that can be expected to be associated with political ads.

Figure 8 shows the most important targeting attributes. It uses SHAP values to show the distribution of the impacts each feature has on the model output. The color represents the feature value: high (red) or low (blue), which is simply 1 or 0 for the binary attributes.

The most important attribute is the 'MinAge'. We can see that above a certain threshold, higher age values increase the chance of seeing a political ad. Further examination (not presented herein) reveals that this threshold corresponds to '18', which is also the legal voting age in the US. We can also see that users with interest related to 'Barack Obama', 'Bernie Sanders' or the 'Democratic Party' are more likely to see political ads. Lastly, this analysis reveals that non-political advertisers are less likely to use the 'Region' attribute for targeting. This could be expected since politicians are more likely to target the state that elects them. On the other hand, users located in 'Texas', 'California', 'Minnesota', 'Florida' and 'New York' are more likely to be targeted with political ads. A comparison with the list provided by Ballotpedia.org[6] reveals that all the states except 'New York' are considered as battleground states.

---

[5] https://github.com/slundberg/shap.
[6] https://ballotpedia.org.

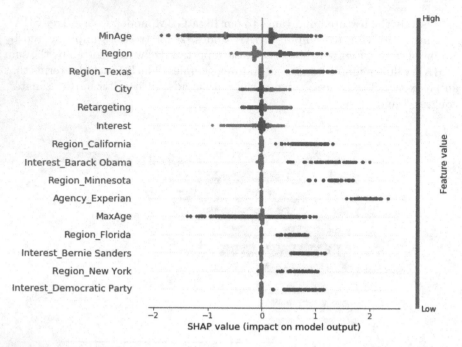

Fig. 8. Top 15 Most Important Targeting Attributes. SHAP values show the distribution of the impacts each feature has on the model output. The '_0' notation is used for features representing an attribute with a missing value. We observe that certain Regions and Interests are more likely to be targeted with political ads. (Color figure online)

6   Conclusion and Future Work

This work is the first to study the ProPublica political ads dataset. The uniqueness of the data lies in the targeting attributes that were used by advertisers to target users on social media. We first described the main characteristics of the data and explored the targeting attributes with a series of interactive illustrations. Then, as a first step towards understating of political manipulation via user targeting, we addressed the challenge of automatically identifying political ads. Our method outperformed the current text-based classifier used by ProPublica with a significant improvement in the F1 measure. We also demonstrated the potential for further improvement in identifying political ads by using the targeting attributes. Lastly, we studied the feature importance of our method and pointed out interesting insights with regard to language differences between political and non-political ads, and the use of targeting attributes in political advertising, such as that users in battleground states are more likely to be targeted.

We consider several avenues for future work. First, the dataset contains additional information that has not been utilized in this work. For example, the ad images could potentially be helpful for the classification of political ads. A key consideration for us has been to provide a simple and scalable solution. This leaves room for future work to experiment with more sophisticated methods, such as learning user-based embeddings based on the targeting attributes to potentially show even greater improvement in performance compared to the text-only methods. Moreover, the identification of political ads allows for future work to explore the rich data provided by the targeting attributes in more detail. For example, to investigate which political ads were associated with which users and which targeting attributes, and specifically with regard to regional targeting which we found to be important. Overall, we hope these preliminary results will help to spark future work on understanding of political manipulation via user targeting and ways of addressing it.

References

1. Lee, S.-I., Lundberg, S.M., Erion, G.G.: Consistent individualized feature attribution for tree ensembles. ArXiv e-prints (2018)
2. Lee, S.-I., Lundberg, S.M.: A unified approach to interpreting model predictions. In: Advances in Neural Information Processing Systems (2017)
3. Van Durme, B., Volkova, S., Copper-smith, G.: Inferring user political preferences from streaming communications. In: Proceedings of the 52nd Annual Meeting of the Association for Computational Linguistics (2014)
4. Lim, E.-P., Hoang, T.-A., Cohen, W.W.: Politics, sharing and emotion in microblogs. In: Proceedings of the 2013 IEEE/ACM International Conference on Advances in Social Networks Analysis and Mining (2013)
5. Bagherjeiran, A., Joshi, A.: User demographic and behavioral targeting for content match advertising. In: 5th International Workshop on Data Mining and Audience Intelligence for Advertising (ADKDD 2011) (2011)
6. Bagherjeiran, A.: Learning to target: what works for behavioral targeting. In: CIKM 2011 Proceedings of the 20th ACM International Conference on Information and Knowledge Management (2011)
7. Vucetic, S., Grbovic, M.: Generating ad targeting rules using sparse principal component analysis with constraints. In: Proceedings of the Companion Publication of the 23rd International Conference on World Wide Web Companion (2014)
8. Solomon, L., Jansen, B.J.: Gender demographic targeting in sponsored search. In: Proceedings of the 28th International Conference on Human Factors in Computing Systems (2010)
9. Funk, A., Maynard, D.: Automatic detection of political opinions in tweets. In: The Semantic Web: ESWC 2011 Workshops (2011)
10. Popescu, M.P.: Democrats, republicans and star bucks afficionados: user classification in twitter. In: Proceedings of the 17th ACM SIGKDD International Conference on Knowledge Discovery and Data Mining (2011)
11. Kim, H., Boutet, A., Yoneki, E.: What's in your tweets? i know who you sup-ported in the UK 2010 General Election. In: Proceedings of the Sixth International AAAI Conference on Weblogs and Social Media (2012)

12. Finley, T., et al.: LightGBM: a highly efficient gradient boosting decision tree. In: Advances in Neural Information Processing Systems (2017)
13. Reichart, R., Dror, R.: Recommended statistical significance tests for NLP tasks. In: Proceedings of the 56th Annual Meeting of the Association for Computational Linguistics (2018)

Identifying Political Sentiments on YouTube: A Systematic Comparison Regarding the Accuracy of Recurrent Neural Network and Machine Learning Models

Daniel Röchert[(✉)], German Neubaum, and Stefan Stieglitz

University of Duisburg-Essen, 47057 Duisburg, Germany
daniel.roechert@uni-due.de

Abstract. Since social media have increasingly become forums to exchange personal opinions, more and more approaches have been suggested to analyze those sentiments automatically. Neural networks and traditional machine learning methods allow individual adaption by training the data, tailoring the algorithm to the particular topic that is discussed. Still, a great number of methodological combinations involving algorithms (e.g., recurrent neural networks (RNN)), techniques (e.g., word2vec), and methods (e.g., Skip-Gram) are possible. This work offers a systematic comparison of sentiment analytical approaches using different word embeddings with RNN architectures and traditional machine learning techniques. Using German comments of controversial political discussions on YouTube, this study uses metrics such as F1-score, precision and recall to compare the quality of performance of different approaches. First results show that deep neural networks outperform multiclass prediction with small datasets in contrast to traditional machine learning models with word embeddings.

Keywords: Deep learning · Machine learning · Text classification · Word embeddings · Computational science

1 Introduction

On social media platforms such as YouTube, Facebook, or Twitter, a mass of people interact with each other on a daily basis, commenting on media content such as videos and exchanging their viewpoints on different issues. Since politically and civically relevant communication is becoming more and more prevalent on social media, identifying opinion climates and optimizing approaches remains as an important task for research. To identify the most appropriate method that detects sentiments in political discussions is of pivotal relevance when it comes to grasp dysfunctional communication processes online. For instance, knowing how different opinions are related to each other contributes to assess to what

© The Author(s) 2020
M. van Duijn et al. (Eds.): MISDOOM 2020, LNCS 12259, pp. 107–121, 2020.
https://doi.org/10.1007/978-3-030-61841-4_8

extent politically homogeneous/heterogeneous cocoons exist. Besides this, identifying sentiments among social media users could also help to asses the opinion climate toward misinformation and to examine that dynamics such misinformation can induce in certain networks. Cross-user generated content such as comments, likes, dislikes or related videos are exchanges of information on a specific topic, also in multi-language context and contain many additional metadata that can be used to analyze user behavior and their current sentiment of a specific topic. Sentiment analysis (SA) also known as opinion mining as a particular form of natural language processing (NLP) is a common tool to grasp communication patterns on social media and is becoming progressively relevant in the research area of social media analytics [34]. Challenges in the area of NLP refer to understanding and processing human communication by machines, not by fixed rules or dictionaries, but rather by training them to learn these complex natural languages. The utilization of SA has become an important method in various domains: product reviews, movie reviews, election campaigns, stock market prediction and social media behavior analysis. The usage of SAs in social media might be used for the decision-making process of companies in order to trace more accurate product strategies based on the customers' current opinions. The more precise the outcome of the SA with regard to product or service reviews, the more effectively strategies can be deployed to prevent crises or to adapt customer requirements. Employing a machine learning approach, a recent study estimated that approx. 60–80% of YouTube comments contain opinions [31]. This makes it highly attractive to identify opinion climates with SA techniques investigating not only public opinion on political issues but also brands and products. Given these numbers, the present study relies on user comments gathered on the platform YouTube. We chose YouTube as a communication platform for our study due to the given prevalence of opinion expressions and its worldwide popularity. The present work applied a comparison of deep learning (subset of machine learning) and traditional machine learning techniques for the categorical classification task to predict the user sentiment score in political YouTube comments and their replies with own input weights of pre-trained word embeddings. Artificial neural models have successfully established themselves in other text classification tasks and achieved good results [26]. However, studies systematically comparing different sentiment analytical combinations are still scarce, especially on the social media platform YouTube with German YouTube comments. With this work, we aim to fill this gap and offer one of the first analyses of German comments on YouTube by using different machine learning techniques. Moreover, this study examines which of those techniques provides better results by combining them with recurrent neural networks and machine learning models. To formalize the overall goals of this paper, the following questions are guiding this research:

RQ1. What is the difference in performance of sentiment classification between recurrent neural networks and traditional machine learning methods?

RQ2. Which of the generated word embedding techniques yields the most accurate results for classification and are any differences detectable among these techniques?

First we crawled YouTube data through the YouTube API, pre-processed the comments and replies by removing inconsistent data and transform them into sentences. Afterwards we transformed all of these sentences into one high dimensional vector also called word embedding which amplifies a dense distributed representation for each word in a high dimension space with the frameworks word2vec and fastText by applying two different techniques such as Skip-Gram and Continuous Bag of Words (CBOW). These word embeddings learned the semantic of their surrounding words and will help to train the deep neural network model as well as the machine learning models.

2   Theoretical Background

2.1   Related Work

Social media have become important communication channels for public interactions in today's digital society. Especially, the investigation of political communication on social platforms, which are examined by means of user-generated comments, plays an increasingly important role in different research areas such as hate speech, misinformation, or political homogenization and polarization. These areas are particularly concerned with the dark side of social media and the ever-growing threat to democracy in society [35]. In particular, the topic of hate speech in social media has generated a lot of attention worldwide in the last few years and is still a current problem for service providers. A study analyzed user comments on the refugee crisis in Germany in 2015/2016 on various news portals [15]. In the study, a binary classifier has been trained using logistic regression, which has achieved a F1-score of 0.67. Further, the researchers have been able to show that many hate words refer to political topics. In addition to the mono-linguistic identification of hate speech, there have been attempts to identify hate speech in different languages using deep-learning techniques and compare them to traditional machine-learning methods [23]. Another aspect that relates to the political context of social media is that these platforms are more often portrayed as a threat to democracy, as they allow interactions between like-minded people. A recent study has examined the YouTube discussion network of comments using opinion-based homogeneity to identify the climate of opinion [29]. The results of the study show that YouTube users reply less on political comments that reflects their own position than on comments that reflect a different opinion. A further problem with social media is that it allows any person to spread claims without any fact-checking. Previous research has shown that the use of social media can increase the impact of fake news and that the main purpose of social media is to influence public opinion as well as political events [18]. In order to prevent this spread of misinformation, several studies focus on the dissemination and detection of misinformation. A recent study has investigated the identification of fake news from text and images on Twitter using convolutional neural networks and recurrent neural networks [1]. The recurrent neural network has achieved the best performance, thereby making it possible to identify relevant features that are classified as fake news. These "hot topics" in computational research indicate that there is a need to identify those analytical approaches that yield the best classification of sentiments within the large amount of communication data in social media.

2.2 Recurrent Neural Network

Recurrent Neural Networks (RNN) [30] are used for processing sequential information such as language modeling, machine translation, time series prediction or image captioning. The general idea of RNNs is to create a kind of "memory" by performing the same operations on every input values in a feedback connection. This process allows to remember the network from previous processed information by sharing the same weights (parameter sharing) across several time steps in the hidden state and perform the output which depends on the passed information to next network [7]. Especially in NLP, this feature is quite helpful to process sequence of sentences because they mainly follow the same rules across the sequence. Parameter sharing makes it possible to perform the same task at each time-step with different input sequences of variable length and makes it therefore more powerful and dynamic compared to normal feed forward neural networks. It reduces the total number of parameters, which means the RNN does not have to learn the same rules of sequences again and already knows their weights. The formula for processing of sequences of a vector x at every time step looks as follow:

$$h_t = fW(h_{t-1}, x_t) \tag{1}$$

where the activation function f will depend on weights W, which accepts the previous hidden state h_{t-1} as well as the input at the current state x_t. This output will the updated hidden state called h_t.

2.3 Word Embeddings

In 1954, Zellig Harris established the hypothesis that the difference in meaning correlates with the difference in distribution, also known as the distributional hypothesis [10]. This hypothesis is grounded by distributional semantics, which is an active area of research in natural language processing to develop new techniques to capture various semantic phenomena, by computing semantic similarities between words based on their distributional properties in the corpus. One of these techniques is called word embedding and describes the mapping process of words from a vocabulary into a high dimensional vector spaces by keeping semantically related words close together. It uses an embedding matrix $E \in \mathbb{R}^{|V| \times d_w}$ where d_w is the dimensionality of the embedding space and $|V|$ is the size of the vocabulary. In previous research, this technique is an efficient way to improve and simplify many NLP applications such as machine translation [20,39], spelling correction [13] or SA [4,17]. In the context of a SA with classification problem, word embeddings are mainly used to include the semantic connections of words in the analysis to develop better and more accurate predictions. A widely used unsupervised word embedding algorithm is called word2vec[1], which has been developed by Mikolov et al. from Google and contains a two-layer neural network, which uses text data as input and transforms the output as a set of high dimensional vectors [19]. Another unsupervised distribution semantic model is called fastText[2] which has been developed by Facebook and is essentially an extension of word2vec model. The main difference of both methods is that the fastText algorithm supports the use of n-grams, which improve the syntatics tasks by taking morphological information into account [3]. Both models have implemented the CBOW and the Skip-Gram methods for computing vector representations of words and are based on hierarchical softmax and negative sampling. The Skip-Gram method has been introduced by Mikolov et al. and predicts potential neighboring words based on a target word [19]. Whereas the CBOW technique uses the context of the neighboring words and predicts the target word. Negative sampling is a modification of an approach called Noise Contrastive Estimation (NCE) [8]. The main idea of the sampling-based approach is to reduce the performance of computational by noise contrastive estimation with several negative examples. An experiment has shown that the negative sampling method is the most efficient algorithm independent from the language used [22]. The present work is intended to compare different combinations of techniques (word2vec and fastText) and methods (Skip-Gram and CBOW), generating unique word vectors that represent the projection of YouTube comments in a continuous vector space.

3 Research Method

This section deals with the sentiment analysis by using deep leaning methods such as RNN to analyze two controversial topics in Germany that were discussed on the social media platform YouTube. The following Fig. 1 demonstrates the process structure of the approach. First, we crawled YouTube data through the YouTube API, preprocessed the comments and replies by removing inconsistent data and transform them into sentences. Afterwards, we transformed all of these sentences into one high dimensional vector also called word embedding which amplifies a dense distributed representation for each word in a high dimension space with the frameworks word2vec and fastText by applying two different techniques such as Skip-Gram and CBOW. These word embeddings learned the semantic of their surrounding words and will help to train the model. The recurrent neural network has been used to initialize these embedding weights to train the network and to create a classifier for further predictions.

---

[1] https://code.google.com/archive/p/word2vec/.
[2] https://fasttext.cc.

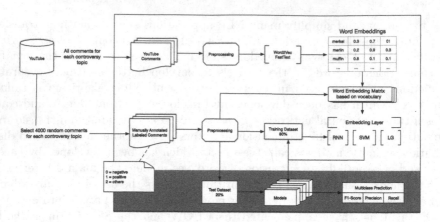

Fig. 1. Process of training and evaluation.

3.1 Data Acquisition

The data of this study were gathered on YouTube crawled by the YouTube API and conducted on May 15th 2018. The data comprised comments and replies of two controversial topics in Germany. The first crawl started with the search criterion: "Kopftuchverbot in Deutschland - Headscarf ban in Germany", for this search we collected 320 unique videos with a maximum number of 48,354 comments and replies. The debate "Wearing religious headscarves" is met with supporters who claim that to fulfil freedom of religion it needs to be allowed while opponents state that headscarves are a symbol for female oppression. For the second query, we used the search terms: "Adoptionsrecht für homosexuelle Paare - Adoption rights for homosexual couples" and contains 15,889 comments and replies with 266 unique videos. In Germany, the debate "Adoption rights for homosexual couples" continues to cause debate. Advocates argue that there is no reason to not allow joint adoption for homosexual partners, whereas opponents argue that every child needs a mother and a father, reflecting their normative ideas of family life. Both topics were selected because they highlight current and controversial issues in society and thus have a lot of potential for discussion in social media. We assume that both controversial topics exhibit a sentiment diversity (i.e. a similar distribution of pros and cons). YouTube labels each video with their own categoryID[3], in this case we use categoryID of 25, which stands for "Politics and News" in the YouTube API. After filtering the comments and replies for both search criterion's, we had a data pool of 14,277 comments and replies for the first dataset "Headscarves" and 8,443 comments and replies for the second dataset "Adoption rights".

---

[3] https://developers.google.com/youtube/v3/docs/videoCategories.

3.2 Annotator Agreement

We selected two well trained independent annotators who received the same dataset with 4,000 randomly selected comments and replies for each topic. The term "well trained" refers to annotators who have received personal instruction on the topics presented. Furthermore, the explanation of the coding scheme included example sentences and their coding was outlined and clarified. Through the personal instruction, questions and problems could be clarified to eliminate inconsistencies. The data were labelled with one of three classes which were mutually exclusive: *negative*, *positive* and *others* based on an existing coding scheme [29]. While there was 86.6% percent agreement for the topic of headscarf ban, 82.5% of percent agreement was reached for the topic of adoption right for homosexual couples. In order to ensure better results for all machine learning models, we have decided to use only those records that have an equal match between both annotators for later analysis.

3.3 Data Preparation

Besides the labeling process, another complex task is the cleaning of unstructured data. In terms of data preparation, cleaning unstructured data guarantees that algorithms can classify better and compute more accurate results with the pre-prepared data [34]. Therefore, the main workflow of cleaning the text by regular expression includes: removing hyperlinks and usernames; removing special symbols and numerical values; converting words into lowercase and assigning smilies into three different word categories such as "emotionhappy", "emotionsad", "emotionlaugh."

After cleaning the text, it is necessary to split it into sentences or paragraphs, which is required for the word embedding models word2vec and fastText in Python. For the supervised learning problem, it is required to separate the entire dataset into the training and test datasets. Each dataset is split into training set (80%) and test set (20%). This separation has to be randomized to guarantee that there is no noise in the dataset. We used 5-fold cross-validation on the training dataset to evaluate the performance of all models with a fixed combination of manual-based hyperparameters.

3.4 Unsupervised Learning

In our approach, we used a Python implementation of the word2vec and fastText from Gensim, which is used for NLP task like topic modeling, document indexing and similarity retrieval [27]. We decided to generate our own word embeddings because recent studies have shown that the creation of domain-specific word embeddings such as (crisis, patent) in particular can enhance the performance of the classification, compared to the pre-trained embeddings of Wikipedia or Google News, which are more suitable for more general classification tasks [16, 28]. We created for each method 300 high dimensional word embeddings on basis of the comments and replies of the whole corpus where the words represent as unigrams. As mentioned earlier, both models word2vec and fastText apply Skip-Gram and CBOW techniques and use the same parameter settings to make them comparable afterwards in the evaluation of the sentiment model. The applied parameters with a brief description of their functionalities are presented in the following:

1. *size: represents the dimension of the feature vectors.*
2. *min_count: represents the minimum frequency per token to filter rare words.*
3. *alpha: represents the learning rate of the network.*
4. *iter: represents the epoch over the corpus to update the weights.*
5. *sample: represents the threshold for configuring which higher-frequency words are randomly downsampled.*
6. *negative: represents the amount of how many "noise words" should be included during training.*

The final parameters that have been used for all word embeddings are *size* with a value of 300, *min_count* with a value of 5, *alpha* with a value of 0.01, *iter* with a value of 15, *sample* with a value of 0.05, and *negative* with a value of 15. Since our vocabulary has a size of 11,435 and the dataset contains 126,362 clean sentences with 1,939,663 tokens, we have deliberately opted for a larger dimension (300). For the further process, we chose negative sampling as baseline in this work, which can improve the computation of word embeddings for frequent words and also decrease the performance of training speed of the neural network [21]. Table 1 demonstrates the representation of the embedding matrix to find the top four most similar entities for the word "kopftuch" (headscarf) and "homosexuell" (homosexual). Looking at the results of the two methods, it is noticeable that the most similar words of word2vec are rather different, but nevertheless relevant to the context. On the other hand, the entities of fastText consist of many variations that are very close to the actual word. It is therefore relevant to examine to what extent which of the two methods delivers the better results in the prediction.

3.5   Supervised Learning

For the supervised learning task, we implemented our model based on Keras with a TensorFlow backend [5]. Keras is a Python library for developing deep neural networks. The baseline models have been implemented as well in Python, but with the sci-kit library for machine learning in Python [24]. The implementation and configuration of all recurrent neural networks share all the same parameters to make them comparable with the different combination of word embeddings. We used a many-to-one model for our architecture, where the input of the network is characterized by sentences with variably sized and multiple words. The first layer of our sequential model is the embedding layer initialized by a dimension 300 and an input length of 100. After this layer, we set a recurrent layer with 64 hidden units, an internal dropout rate of 0.1 and a recurrent dropout of 0.1. The main reason for the regularization of a neural network is the increase

Table 1. Word similarities of the words "kopftuch" and "homosexuell".

	word2vec	
	CBOW	**SkipGram**
	hijab (0.68)	tragen (0.66)
	koptuch (0.66)	hijab (0.60)
	kopftücher (0.60)	koptuch (0.59)
Target word: kopftuch	tuch (0.57)	minirock (0.59)
	FastText	
	kopftuchs (0.97)	kopftuchzwang (0.82)
	kopftuchgebot (0.97)	kopftuchfrau (0.82)
	kopftuchzwang (0.96)	kopftuchs (0.81)
	Koftuch (0.94)	kopftuchgebot (0.8)
	word2vec	
	schwul (0.80)	schwul (0.62)
	heterosexuell (0.79)	lesbisch (0.60)
	bisexuell (0.73)	heterosexuell (0.60)
Target word: homosexuell	lesbisch (0.72)	bisexuell (0.59)
	FastText	
	homosexuel (0.97)	homosexuel (0.93)
	homosexuele (0.97)	homosexuele (0.93)
	homosexuelle (0.95)	homosexuellen (0.82)
	homosexuelles (0.95)	homosexuelle (0.82)

in performance and its applicability to unseen data beyond the training data and to avoid overfitting. Especially for small datasets, neural networks are more inclined to overfit than on large datasets because they are used to learn from large data. For regularization of our network, we decided to employ to usual methods: applying dropout to the networks [11], using L_2 weight regularization as well as class weights. The general idea of dropout is to avoid co-adaptations by applying random dropout units during the training of the neural network [33]. Using dropout can greatly reduce overfitting in RNNs [37]. Besides the dropout regularization, we used L_2 weight decay to reduce the complexity of the softmax function. Readjustment of the class weights have been applied to re-balance the classes and make them more reasonable and equally considered during the training. Classes that appear in the dataset often achieve low weights, whereas infrequent classes receive higher weights to re-balance the training. As an optimization function to train our network, we choose the extension to stochastic gradient descent called Adam [14] with the categorical cross entropy loss function, suited to multi-class classification problems. The output layer are characterized by three neurons with a softmax activation function for predicting the probability distribution for each class. Further, we trained the model with a mini-batch size of 10 and set the number of epochs of 100. Because our dataset is small for training and testing we chose a small training batch size, as well as small hidden units of the neural networks to increase the accuracy of the prediction.

3.6 Baseline Models

We have also implemented traditional machine learning models, so that we can identify how neural networks perform in comparison to methods which can perhaps better handle smaller datasets. In a study where Chinese short texts with public financial documents were classified, it was shown that the support vector machines as well as logistic regressions achieved the best results of the performance of the prediction [36]. More precisely, by comparing machine learning models, it was shown that logistic regression in the area of product reviews [25] or BBC news [32] achieved better results than other classical machine learning models such as k-nearest-neighbors or random forest. Apart from logistic regression, there exist also several studies showing that the Support Vector machine was successfully applied for text classification and reached the best performance in multi-class prediction [16,38]. Based on the positive results of the previously stated studies, we have decided to use SVM and logistics regression as baseline machine learning techniques. In general, machine learning models such as support vector machines or logistic regression cannot directly handle word embeddings, which are represented in a high-dimensional space, therefore we have to prepare our 300 dimensional word embeddings into one dimensional by using the average value of each word vectors. This allows us to represent each word by an average value and have been successfully implemented on other studies [2]. The following machine learning techniques have been performed:

- Support Vector Machines (SVM): are based on the margin maximization principle and used for non-linear and linear regression and classification tasks. The SVM uses a penalty parameter C of the value of 100, which is characterized as the error term, the smaller the value, the stronger is the regulation of the model. As well, we applied a *linear* kernel and balanced class weights to the model.
- Logistic Regression (LG): as well as SVM, logistic regression is a supervised learning algorithm to estimates the probability of a categorical dependent variables by computing the sigmoid function. Like for the recurrent neural networks, we avoided overfitting by applying L_2 weights regularization with the *saga* solver. Also we used balanced class weights to adjust the imbalanced distribution of classes.

4 Results

Since the models have been trained successfully, the information of the models can be extracted and used for analysis. The results for the prediction on the test datasets are shown in Table 2. We used precision, recall and F1-score to measure the performance of three different classes. For multi-class tasks which are imbalanced, it is recommended to apply weighted F1-score, which computes the average for each class. The results for the performance F1-score reveal two main features. First, the results show that in general all recurrent neural networks outperform the machine learning models. The best performance was achieved with RNNs obtained by combining word2vec with CBOW for both datasets. Second, focusing on the different word embedding methods like Skip-Gram and CBOW, the results indicate that CBOW performs better than Skip-Gram, especially for RNNs, but this does not apply to the remaining results. Looking at the results for the individual word embeddings techniques "word2vec" and "fastText", no particular difference is noticeable because the F1-values are generally very similar to each other.

Table 2. Evaluation result of deep learning and traditional machine learning methods on test dataset.

Models	Technique	Method	Adoption rights			Headscarves		
			F1-score	Precision	Recall	F1-score	Precision	Recall
RNN	word2vec	Skip-Gram	0.715	0.726	0.706	0.789	0.794	0.784
		CBOW	**0.746**	**0.748**	**0.744**	**0.823**	**0.815**	**0.835**
	fastText	Skip-Gram	0.724	0.739	0.738	0.754	0.806	0.724
		CBOW	0.741	0.731	0.760	0.755	0.793	0.731
SVM	word2vec	Skip-Gram	0.565	0.717	0.509	0.543	0.798	0.470
		CBOW	0.568	0.721	0.512	0.543	0.798	0.470
	fastText	Skip-Gram	0.567	0.719	0.512	0.544	0.801	0.471
		CBOW	0.560	0.723	0.503	0.552	0.798	0.480
LG	word2vec	Skip-Gram	0.597	0.704	0.550	0.647	0.783	0.585
		CBOW	0.592	0.703	0.544	0.642	0.783	0.577
	fastText	Skip-Gram	0.600	0.710	0.553	0.649	0.783	0.587
		CBOW	0.581	0.699	0.532	0.629	0.773	0.562

5   Discussion

This study offered a systematic comparison of combinations consisting of different sentiment analytical approaches such as deep neural networks and machine learning models. With regard to RQ1, we can conclude that our approach has demonstrated that the artificial neural network models outperform usual machine learning models by embedding high dimensional vectors. In order to have a fair comparison, hyperparameters were kept constant in this study. The fact that deep neural networks generally reach higher F1-scores may be explained by different factors: First, the weaker results of machine learning methods can be explained by the fact that they cannot capture the high-dimensional word vectors during training, but only receive averaged word vectors for all words in the corpus. As a result, important information is no longer provided during the computation and performance deteriorates. Second, deep neural networks might reach a higher level of accuracy when hyperparameters are determined by grid search or random search in accordance with the dataset at hand. Third, it must be noted that the dataset is imbalanced, methods to weight the classes are beneficial, but more effective would be actual datasets with equally distributed classes. Given that the category with the most comments was the *others* class, all methods might benefit more from a dataset that has a larger portion of positive versus negative comments whose context are easier to identify (than from *others* comments). When considering the normalized confusion matrix, the class most frequently predicted in neural networks is "others", which therefore has a positive effect on the F1-score, since this class is most frequently represented in the dataset. Regarding RQ2, it can be concluded that word embeddings have significantly improved the performance of RNN compared to the traditional ML models. Due to the different models, however, it is not possible to determine exactly which method and technique is the best because the different combinations of word embeddings have computed relatively similar outcomes.

6   Further Research

To conclude, the present study revealed that with small datasets of user comments on YouTube, deep neural networks outperform machine learning models. For future work, it would be interesting to improve some features to achieve more precise results in the prediction. The first improvement in analysis might consist of applying advanced models and techniques to compute even more accurate predictions. Simple RNNs are often used for processing long-term sequences like documents, however studies have shown that RNNs are mainly suitable for short term dependencies because of the vanishing gradient or exploding gradient problem [12], which makes them inaccurate for tasks that require long-term sequences. This problem appears when training deep neural networks to learn dependencies by backpropagation through time over long time steps, which can reach extremely high or exponentially small values of gradients. To avoid this kind of problem, it is commendable to apply other recurrent neural network architectures such as long-short term memory. For further research, it would be advisable to implement and compare the improved RNNs like long-short term memory networks as well. Furthermore, it would be a reasonable idea to utilize further machine learning algorithms such as naive bayes or random forest, which are not based on word embeddings but on term frequency times inverse document frequency vectors to extend the systematic comparison and test which combined approaches offer more accurate results. It does not require word embedding but is also used for SA [6,9]. While word embedding links the semantics of sentences, term frequency times inverse document frequency computes the importance of a term inside a comment by their frequency of the entire dataset. In addition, a further aspect that should be considered when using word embeddings in future research is the comparison with already existing pre-trained models such as Wikipedia or Google News to be able to make semantic comparisons between these and own domain-specific models and to take into account which models are better suited for classification. Another necessary step is to perform SA with other languages in order to achieve greater diversity and compare them against each other. In addition to political and controversial topics, it would also be appropriate to collect data from product reviews or unboxing videos and evaluate the comments with the aid of SA to gain experience in this field as well.

Acknowledgments. This research was supported by the Digital Society research program funded by the Ministry of Culture and Science of the German State of North Rhine-Westphalia (Grant Number: 005-1709-0004), Junior Research Group "Digital Citizenship in Network Technologies" (Project Number: 1706dgn009).

References

1. Ajao, O., Bhowmik, D., Zargari, S.: Fake news identification on twitter with hybrid CNN and RNN models. In: Proceedings of the 9th International Conference on Social Media and Society, pp. 226–230 (2018). https://doi.org/10.1145/3217804. 3217917
2. Bayot, R.K., Gonçalves, T.: Author profiling using SVMS and word embedding averages. In: CLEF (Working Notes), pp. 815–823 (2016)
3. Bojanowski, P., Grave, E., Joulin, A., Mikolov, T.: Enriching word vectors with subword information. Trans. Assoc. Comput. Linguist. **5**, 135–146 (2017)
4. Bowman, S.R., Angeli, G., Potts, C., Manning, C.D.: A large annotated corpus for learning natural language inference. arXiv preprint arXiv:1508.05326 (2015)
5. Chollet, F., et al.: Keras (2015). https://keras.io
6. Ghag, K., Shah, K.: SENTITFIDF - sentiment classification using relative term frequency inverse document frequency. Int. J. Adv. Comput. Sci. Appl. **5**(2) (2014). https://doi.org/10.14569/IJACSA.2014.050206
7. Goodfellow, I., Bengio, Y., Courville, A., Bengio, Y.: Deep Learning, vol. 1. MIT Press, Cambridge (2016)
8. Gutmann, M., Hyvärinen, A.: Noise-contrastive estimation: a new estimation principle for unnormalized statistical models. In: Proceedings of the Thirteenth International Conference on Artificial Intelligence and Statistics. Proceedings of Machine Learning Research, vol. 9, pp. 297–304. PMLR (2010). http://proceedings.mlr. press/v9/gutmann10a.html
9. Haddi, E., Liu, X., Shi, Y.: The role of text pre-processing in sentiment analysis. Procedia Comput. Sci. **17**, 26–32 (2013). https://doi.org/10.1016/j.procs.2013.05. 005
10. Harris, Z.S.: Distributional structure. Word **10**(2–3), 146–162 (1954). https://doi. org/10.1080/00437956.1954.11659520
11. Hinton, G.E., Srivastava, N., Krizhevsky, A., Sutskever, I., Salakhutdinov, R.R.: Improving neural networks by preventing co-adaptation of feature detectors. arXiv preprint arXiv:1207.0580 (2012)
12. Hochreiter, S.: The vanishing gradient problem during learning recurrent neural nets and problem solutions. Int. J. Uncertainty, Fuzz. Knowl.-Based Syst. **6**(02), 107–116 (1998). https://doi.org/10.1142/S0218488598000094

13. Kilicoglu, H., Fiszman, M., Roberts, K., Demner-Fushman, D.: An ensemble method for spelling correction in consumer health questions. In: AMIA Annual Symposium Proceedings. vol. 2015, p. 727. American Medical Informatics Association (2015)
14. Kingma, D.P., Ba, J.: Adam: A method for stochastic optimization. CoRR abs/1412.6980 (2015)
15. Köffer, S., et al.: Discussing the value of automatic hate speech detection in online debates. Multikonferenz Wirtschaftsinformatik (MKWI 2018): Data Driven X-Turning Data in Value, Leuphana, Germany (2018)
16. Li, H., Caragea, D., Li, X., Caragea, C.: Comparison of word embeddings and sentence encodings as generalized representations for crisis tweet classification tasks. en. In: New Zealand p. 13 (2018)
17. Li, Q., Shah, S., Liu, X., Nourbakhsh, A., Fang, R.: Tweetsift: tweet topic classification based on entity knowledge base and topic enhanced word embedding. In: Proceedings of the 25th ACM International on Conference on Information and Knowledge Management, pp. 2429–2432. ACM (2016). https://doi.org/10.1145/2983323.2983325
18. Marwick, A., Lewis, R.: Media Manipulation and Disinformation Online. Data & Society Research Institute, New York (2017)
19. Mikolov, T., Chen, K., Corrado, G., Dean, J.: Efficient estimation of word representations in vector space. arXiv preprint arXiv:1301.3781 (2013)
20. Mikolov, T., Le, Q.V., Sutskever, I.: Exploiting similarities among languages for machine translation. arXiv preprint arXiv:1309.4168 (2013)
21. Mikolov, T., Sutskever, I., Chen, K., Corrado, G.S., Dean, J.: Distributed representations of words and phrases and their compositionality. In: Proceedings of the 26th International Conference on Neural Information Processing Systems. NIPS 2013, vol. 2. pp. 3111–3119 (2013)
22. Naili, M., Chaibi, A.H., Ghezala, H.H.B.: Comparative study of word embedding methods in topic segmentation. Procedia Comput. Sci. **112**, 340–349 (2017). https://doi.org/10.1016/j.procs.2017.08.009
23. Ousidhoum, N., Lin, Z., Zhang, H., Song, Y., Yeung, D.Y.: Multilingual and multi-aspect hate speech analysis. In: Proceedings of the 2019 Conference on Empirical Methods in Natural Language Processing and the 9th International Joint Conference on Natural Language Processing (EMNLP-IJCNLP), pp. 4675–4684. Association for Computational Linguistics (2019). https://doi.org/10.18653/v1/D19-1474
24. Pedregosa, F., et al.: Scikit-learn: machine learning in Python. J. Mach. Learn. Res. **12**, 2825–2830 (2011)
25. Pranckevicius, T., Marcinkevicius, V.: Comparison of Naive Bayes, random forest, decision tree, support vector machines, and logistic regression classifiers for text reviews classification. Balt. J. Mod. Comput. **5** (2017). https://doi.org/10.22364/bjmc.2017.5.2.05
26. Rao, A., Spasojevic, N.: Actionable and political text classification using word embeddings and LSTM. CoRR abs/1607.02501 (2016)
27. Řehůřek, R., Sojka, P.: Software framework for topic modelling with large corpora. In: Proceedings of the LREC 2010 Workshop on New Challenges for NLP Frameworks, pp. 45–50. ELRA, May 2010. https://doi.org/10.13140/2.1.2393.1847
28. Risch, J., Krestel, R.: Domain-specific word embeddings for patent classification. Data Technol. Appl. (2019). https://doi.org/10.1108/DTA-01-2019-0002

29. Röchert, D., Neubaum, G., Ross, B., Brachten, F., Stieglitz, S.: Opinion-based homogeneity on YouTube. Comput. Commun. Res. **2**(1), 81–108 (2020). https://doi.org/10.5117/CCR2020.1.004.ROCH
30. Rumelhart, D.E., Hinton, G.E., Williams, R.J.: Learning representations by back-propagating errors. Nature **323**(6088), 533 (1986). https://doi.org/10.1038/323533a0
31. Severyn, A., Moschitti, A., Uryupina, O., Plank, B., Filippova, K.: Multi-lingual opinion mining on YouTube. Inf. Process. Manage. **52**(1), 46–60 (2016). https://doi.org/10.1016/j.ipm.2015.03.002
32. Shah, K., Patel, H., Sanghvi, D., Shah, M.: A comparative analysis of logistic regression, random forest and KNN models for the text classification. Augmented Hum. Res. **5**(1), 1–16 (2020). https://doi.org/10.1007/s41133-020-00032-0
33. Srivastava, N., Hinton, G., Krizhevsky, A., Sutskever, I., Salakhutdinov, R.: Dropout: a simple way to prevent neural networks from overfitting. J. Mach. Learn. Res. **15**, 1929–1958 (2014)
34. Stieglitz, S., Mirbabaie, M., Ross, B., Neuberger, C.: Social media analytics-challenges in topic discovery, data collection, and data preparation. Int. J. Inf. Manage. **39**, 156–168 (2018). https://doi.org/10.1016/j.ijinfomgt.2017.12.002
35. Sunstein, C.R.: # Republic: Divided Democracy in the Age of Social Media. Princeton University Press, Princeton (2018)
36. Wang, Y., Zhou, Z., Jin, S., Liu, D., Lu, M.: Comparisons and selections of features and classifiers for short text classification. IOP Conf. Ser. Mat. Sci. Eng. **261**, 012018 (2017). https://doi.org/10.1088/1757-899x/261/1/012018
37. Zaremba, W., Sutskever, I., Vinyals, O.: Recurrent neural network regularization. arXiv preprint arXiv:1409.2329 (2014)
38. Zhang, M., Ai, X., Hu, Y.: Chinese text classification system on regulatory information based on SVM. IOP Conf. Ser. Earth Environ. Sci. **252**, 022133 (2019). https://doi.org/10.1088/1755-1315/252/2/022133
39. Zou, W.Y., Socher, R., Cer, D., Manning, C.D.: Bilingual word embeddings for phrase-based machine translation. In: Proceedings of the 2013 Conference on Empirical Methods in Natural Language Processing, pp. 1393–1398 (2013)

Abusive Comments in Online Media and How to Fight Them
State of the Domain and a Call to Action

Marco Niemann[(✉)], Jens Welsing, Dennis M. Riehle, Jens Brunk, Dennis Assenmacher, and Jörg Becker

University of Münster – ERCIS, Leonardo-Campus 3, 48149 Münster, Germany
marco.niemann@ercis.uni-muenster.de

Abstract. While abusive language in online contexts is a long-known problem, algorithmic detection and moderation support are only recently experiencing rising interest. This survey provides a structured overview of the latest academic publications in the domain. Assessed concepts include the used datasets, their language, annotation origins and quality, as well as applied machine learning approaches. It is rounded off by an assessment of meta aspects such as author collaborations and networks as well as extant funding opportunities. Despite all progress, the domain still has the potential to improve on many aspects: (international) collaboration, diversifying and increasing available datasets, careful annotations, and transparency. Furthermore, abusive language detection is a topic of high societal relevance and requires increased funding from public authorities.

Keywords: Abusive language · Comment moderation · Machine learning · Review

1 Introduction

Abusive language[1] (and especially hate speech as one of its most extreme manifestations) in online communities is becoming more and more prevalent. What has been a fringe phenomenon in the early days of the web, is now affecting the lives of millions of individuals [17,20,24]. These phenomena, which are often discussed under trivializing names such as "(hate) speech" and "(abusive) language", are not only mere inconveniences but issues that have been proven to be detrimental to the mental health of individuals and even societies at large scale [4,23]. Consequentially, these forms of inadequate communication are typically subject to legal regulations prohibiting their utterance as well as the display in

---

[1] We are aware that there are multiple terms and concepts, such as "abusive language", "hate speech", "offensive language", and many more. For this publication, we will use the term "abusive language", as it receives increasing acceptance in the domain (cf., the "Workshop on Abusive Language Online" conducted annually) and is sufficiently generic to account for a multitude of equally problematic types of language.

© Springer Nature Switzerland AG 2020
M. van Duijn et al. (Eds.): MISDOOM 2020, LNCS 12259, pp. 122–137, 2020.
https://doi.org/10.1007/978-3-030-61841-4_9

public (e.g., in Germany it is illegal to post any form of hate speech as well as to tolerate such comments on your platform once you are made aware of their existence [13]). Hence, platform operators have multiple incentives to keep their discussion spaces clean, as they otherwise risk getting sued and/or lose visitors and as a consequence traffic as well. The initial response of many outlets has been to close down their discussion spaces (in Germany up to 50% of the newspapers took this step [30]), as manual moderation results in considerable personnel cost that is not linked to any direct income [18]. Aside from the apparent issues for open societies and democracies, which arise from silencing people, journalists and media companies struggle with these radical decisions, as they limit user engagement [8] and therefore have the same detrimental potential as the abusive comments they try to avoid [18].

To address this issue, people from different computer science domains such as machine learning (ML) and natural language processing (NLP) have started working on (semi-)automated solutions. They are supposed to reduce the workload of journalists and community managers through both automated pre-filtering as well as moderation support (e.g., highlighting problematic parts of comments). Work is done by academics as well as practitioners, and over the last decade, a lively stream of research developed around the topic of abusive language detection. With the constant growth of the domain, it gets increasingly difficult for the individual researcher to keep track of the progress. Hence, as with any other rapidly growing domain, review papers are getting more and more important to streamline ongoing research. Prior survey and review papers typically addressed issues such as used definitions of abusive language, applied ML algorithms, conducted preprocessing, and sources for datasets [14,29]. While we will follow up on most of these aspects, we introduce several additional meta aspects such as extant author networks, funding parties, and annotator qualifications.

The remainder of this work is structured as follows: In Sect. 2, we outline our survey approach, including search and analysis strategies. The subsequent Sect. 3 is used to analyze the identified literature for aspects such as Author Analysis, Datasets and ML Approaches. As a wrap-up of this publication, we summarize our findings in Sect. 4 with a call for future action.

2   Research Approach

To understand the current state of research on computer-assisted detection of abusive speech online, it is mandatory to review the recent developments in that area carefully. The method of choice is a structured literature review according to the principles of Webster and Watson [33] and vom Brocke et al. [7]. According to the taxonomy of Cooper [10] (see Fig. 1), we focus on the synthesis and integration of central findings and problems of the abusive language detection domain. Given the conference format, our coverage is representative in nature and mainly addresses the scholars active in the domain.

To conduct the search, we composed the search string depicted below. It combines the central concept of our survey ("abusive language") with the often

Characteristic	Categories			
Focus	research outcome	research method	theories	applications
Goal	integration	criticism	central problems	
Organization	historical	conceptual	methodological	
Perspective	neutral representation		espousal of position	
Audience	specialized scholars	general scholars	practitioners/politicians	general public
Coverage	exhaustive	exhaustive and selective	representative	central/pivotal

Fig. 1. Categorization of our research in the taxonomy of [10]

synonymously used concept of "hate speech". As we want to focus on works that propose novel approaches to tackle the problem of abusive language online, we add the keywords "detection" and "classification" to limit results to papers working on (semi-)automated solutions. To avoid duplicating work already conducted by, e.g., Fortuna et al. [15], we restrict the search to the years 2018 and 2019 by using the following search criterion:

("abusive language" OR "hate speech") AND ("detection" OR "classification") AND PUBYEAR $\in \{2018, 2019\}$

As search engines, we considered *Scopus*, *Microsoft Academic*, and the *Web of Science*, which have been found to excel through broad coverage in general and for the topic at hand. *Google Scholar* was excluded as despite its massive portfolio it still lacks a lot of search and filter functionality plus its Google heritage subjects it to the Google algorithm which performs context-specific optimizations and hence does not allow reproducibility [5]. Beyond this initial search, we additionally conducted a forward- and backward-search on works standing out through their constant appearance in the papers we found using a structured search.

3   State of the Domain

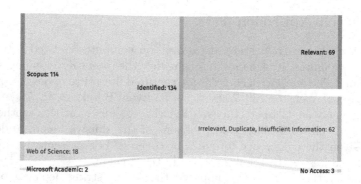

Fig. 2. Literature search results breakdown

As depicted in Fig. 2, our structured literature search returned 134 results, of which 69 were identified as relevant for our research. 62 publications were excluded as they are either duplicates or without an individual approach to automated abusive language detection (i.e., other literature reviews, ...).

The traditional approach of Webster and Watson [33] and vom Brocke et al. [7] suggests the use of concept matrices to assess the identified material. Figure 3 presents the concepts evaluated within this chapter and the reasoning for their selection. Based on the chosen concepts, we decided against using traditional table-based concept matrices and will instead make use of more visual means as, e.g., networks are hard to depict in text-based formats.

Concept	Reasoning
Authors	To assess the level of collaborative work on the domain and to identify potentially leading researchers a network analysis of the paper authors is included.
Funding	Identifying leading public and/or private sponsors of research.
Languages	Outlining the state of research for different languages and identifying extant gaps (or potentially difficult to assess languages).
Datasets	Used datasets, data sources, and the usage patterns (reuse vs. one-off creation of novel sets) impact not only the comparability of research but also the coverage of analyzable material.
Annotation	To assess the impact of different annotation strategies on the annotation quality as a major determinant of ML model quality.
ML Approaches	Identifying popular and successful ML methods.

Fig. 3. Selected concepts for analysis

3.1 Author Analysis

To conduct the analysis, we used the VOSviewer [12], which is one of the standard tools for the creation and visualization of bibliographic networks. At first, we created a map for the overall authorscape of the identified publications, which is depicted in Fig. 4.

Looking at Fig. 4, the most striking feature is the abundance of mostly disconnected author groups. The only larger cluster can be found at the center of the figure and revolves around the four Italian authors Tommaso Caselli, Nicole Novielli, Viviana Patti, and Paolo Rosso. Taking a closer look at the cluster (see Fig. 5) and the associated publications, the underlying bond can be identified as the "Evalita 2018 Hate Speech Detection Task" (EVALITA). Most of the collaborating authors are—as to be expected—of Italian origin, respectively, working for Italian research institutions [6]. Nevertheless, the proceedings also contain several international authors from countries with similar languages [14], respectively, several who contributed through mixed tasks (detection of English and Italian) [16]. Since the only two remaining larger clusters only contain Italian[2] respectively Indonesian authors, this is indeed the only identified occasion of large-scale international collaboration and knowledge exchange.

---

[2] The authors are interestingly not linked to the other Italian author cluster, indicating a somewhat lacking national collaboration.

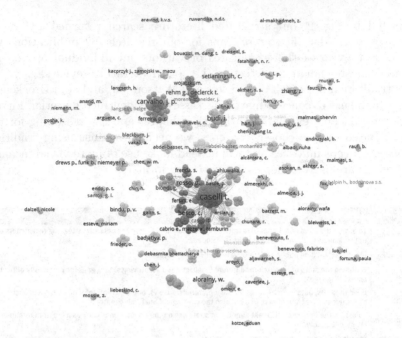

Fig. 4. VOSviewer distance-based label view of the co-author relationships. Node size depends on the number of co-authors. Distance (and edges) between nodes indicate the strength of co-author relationships; colors the automatically identified clusters [12]. (Color figure online)

Given the prevalence of the issue of abusive language and the maturing stage of the domain, it is surprising to observe this level of disconnection. Even though partially separated by language, the structural approaches and issues in the domain are typically shared and should consequently provide ample opportunity for collaboration.

3.2 Funding

Given the massive social, legal, and economic impacts of abusive language, it is receiving attention from both public bodies as well as private institutions. Hence, it is interesting to see whether this interest mirrors into corresponding funding programs and whether certain institutions are taking significant influence on the research carried out.

Out of the assessed 69 publications, 38 (approx. 55%) state that they received some form of funding/financial support. Despite the unambiguous relevance for media companies, only one of these 38 publications officially received support from a private entity: Fortuna et al. [14] have been supported by Google's DNI grant. The remaining 37 funded publications received public money from various ministries or societies. Amongst these, no dominant organization could be

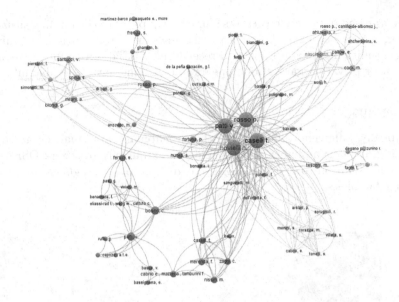

Fig. 5. Literature search results breakdown

identified as only a few sponsors are linked to more than one publication. Interestingly the "Directorate Research and Community Services of the Universitas Indonesia", a Spanish, and a Portuguese ministry, are amongst the most stated sponsors (cf., Fig. 6). This is interesting, since Indonesian, Spanish, Portuguese have not been among the most assessed languages in the domain so far. The EU—while heavily investing in AI and related technology—is only supporting three publications through Horizon 2020 grants.

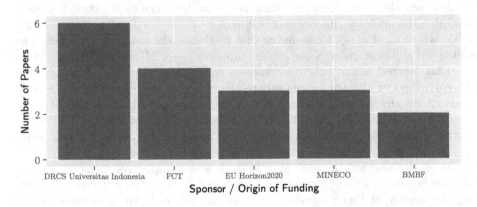

Fig. 6. Most influential sponsors of abusive language detection research

The assessed data only represents a limited snapshot of the funding situation; however, it can be acknowledged that the issue of abusive language online is having a sufficient societal impact to receive substantial public funding. So far, no public or private organization appears to be taking any noticeable influence.

3.3 Languages

Undoubtedly, languages differ a lot in their vocabulary, grammar, usage, and at times even in their alphabet. Consequently, it is unlikely to see an OSFA (one size fits all) solution to abusive language detection for all languages or even for language families.

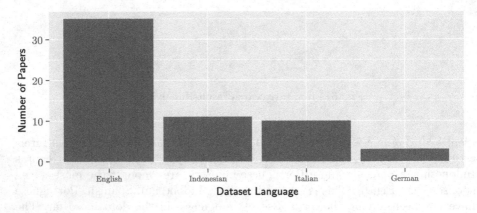

Fig. 7. Distribution of publications among most common languages

Amongst the 69 assessed publications—as in the majority of extant papers— English is the predominant working language solutions are developed for (50.72% = 35 papers; cf., Fig. 7). Considering that English is the most common language online [31] and that many of the leading universities for ML and NLP (e.g., Stanford) are located in the US, this comes as no surprise. However, differing from the early days of abusive language detection research, approx. 50% of the publications are already working on different languages—which again indicates the globality of the problem as well as the increasing promise of ML and NLP given their spread to less common and often more complex languages (e.g., German; cf. [25]).

As all the assessed research aims at finding automated solutions to uncover abusive language, we are furthermore interested in potential differences regarding the quality of those solutions. Conducting an in-depth assessment of the approaches and the underlying linguistic structure of the languages would be beyond the scope of this review. Instead, we focus on the achieved $F1$-score.

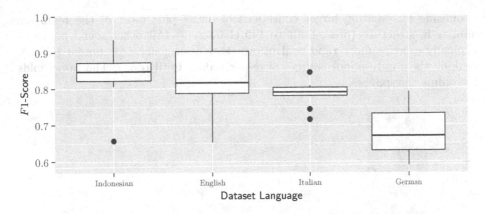

Fig. 8. F1-scores achieved for different languages

As a proxy, it captures both the derived automated solution's quality and the "simplicity" of the underlying language. In Fig. 8, we plotted the F1-scores of the most commonly assessed languages—and surprisingly, the so far rather under-researched, Indonesian turns out to perform best. English as the most popular language has a slightly worse median performance; however, the variance is higher with individual publications reaching F1-scores of up to 0.9 [27,35]. The performance of abusive language detection for German is substantially worse, with a median of only 0.675 and a maximum of under 0.8. This is in line with the observations of individual authors, who observed that German tends to be comparatively complex to analyze and work with [25]. A final interesting observation can be made considering the performance of Italian: The majority of the publications there worked on the ELVITA dataset and stand out through their low variance. This is an indication that not only the language itself makes a difference but also the dataset and the type of language used.

3.4 Datasets

The traditional approach towards the detection of abusive language through ML is based on the sub-class of supervised machine-learning. Training and performance of this class of algorithms substantially depend on the kind and quality of the employed training data [2]. Hence, we take a look at both data sources as well as datasets[3] used in recent publications.

The first observation that can be made is that the majority of the datasets used are still curated based on Twitter data (see Fig. 9; in our sample in 40 papers out of 69 use datasets made up of Tweets), as already observed by prior reviews [15]. Even though most data in the web is more or less freely accessible, Twitter offers a comparatively easy to use and unrestricted API making it rather

---

[3] Each recombined dataset (combined of $n \geq 2$ already existent ones) is considered a novel dataset of its own right.

promising for creating larger collections of data—plus most of the texts are similar in structure (prev. limit to 140 characters). All other social networks typically exercise more rigid control over their user-generated content (UGC), making them only minor sources of research data until today. The same holds for online newspapers.

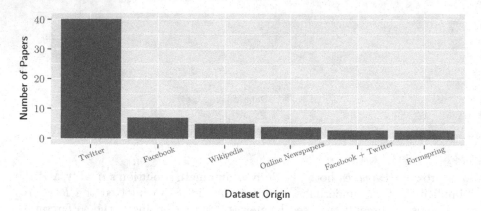

Fig. 9. Most common dataset origins (occurrences >1)

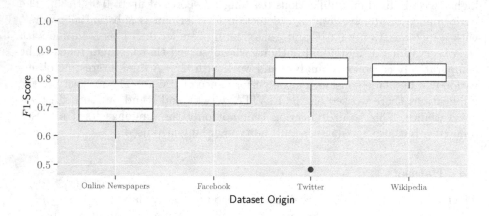

Fig. 10. $F1$-scores for common dataset origins

Assessing the data origins further and comparing the classification results which are achieved based on them, especially Twitter but also Wikipedia stand out (see Fig. 10): In both cases, the best performing half of the publications performs better than at least 75% of the publications using sources such as Facebook or online newspapers. Overall, it appears to be most complicated to correctly classify comments from online newspapers, which is the only source with a median $F1$-score being lower than 0.8 (with $F1 = 0.69$). However, given the smaller sample ($n = 4$), these results are to be treated with caution.

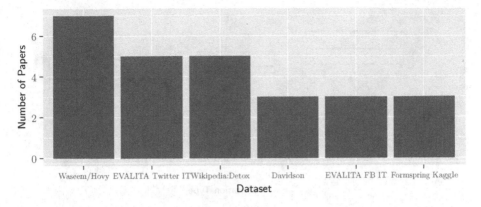

Fig. 11. Distribution of datasets across publications (occurrences >1)

Differing from prior reviews such as the one by Fortuna and Nunes [15] (one reused dataset in 17 assessed publications; 6%), the share of research reusing published datasets has been rising to ~56% (39 out of 69) so that only 28 publications use a novel, self-created dataset. Three of the largest datasets (the ones by [32,34], and [11]; cf. Fig.11) are already 2–3 years old, which corresponds to classical academic publishing cycles and might explain their slow uptake. While this development is good for comparability between different publications, a certain amount of scrutiny should be kept. Considering that, e.g., Twitter data is not representative for UGC on the web, an excess reliance on these kinds of datasets might turn out to be problematic—especially considering that other data sources appear harder to work with (cf. above and Fig. 10).

3.5 Annotation

Another side-effect that comes with the use of supervised machine-learning is the necessity to use so-called labeled or annotated ground-truth data: To train suitable classifiers, it is insufficient to use raw comments. Instead, for each comment, an annotation indicating its type (e.g., abusive vs. clean) is needed. However, comments are not labeled by their original creators; hence, this task is typically done by a third party—often crowd workers, researchers, or student assistants. As such, annotations are subjective and laden with emotions [21], obtaining an agreed-upon annotation is complex with potential repercussions to the final classification [26].

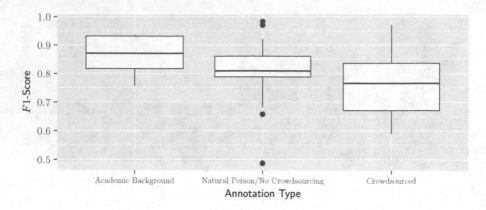

Fig. 12. $F1$-scores for different annotation types

Given the high investments (of time or money) in annotated datasets, it is vital to understand which investment delivers the best value. In Fig. 12 we depict the $F1$-scores reached with datasets annotated by a) people with a stated academic background, b) crowd workers, and c) natural persons without further specification of their educational background. The primary finding from this assessment is that a controlled group of annotators with a scientific background delivers more usable annotations than crowd workers from diverse backgrounds[4]. However, the larger variance on the crowdsourced datasets indicates that they hold potential: For example, Albadi et al. [1] used upfront quizzes and continuous control questions to ensure that each partaking crowd worker had a correct understanding of the concepts in question.

Another metric that is usually put under scrutiny is the agreement between annotators or inter-rater agreement[5], which is an indication of annotation reliability given coders' shared understanding of the labels [3]. For the assessed 69 papers, we found varying agreement scores, which, however, did not show any substantial correlation with the final $F1$-scores ($\rho = 0.2088$). This is in line with observations made by Koltsova [21]. Consequently, alternative approaches to label data (e.g., using multiple labels per comment) (cf. [25]) might help to overcome the inherent subjectivity of traditional approaches while improving classification quality.

3.6   ML Approaches

One of the most diverse areas is the selection of classification algorithms. As many of the extant approaches such as recurrent neural networks (RNNs) or decision trees (DTs) exist in various flavors and configurations, we decided to

---

[4] Datasets with all annotation strategies would have to be subjected to a testbed of multiple classifiers to ensure the improved performance is due to the chosen strategy.
[5] For commonly used measures such as Krippendorff's alpha, this should be around 0.8 or higher [22]. However, other measures can have different scales.

group algorithmically similar approaches ending up with six larger groups: SVM, Ensembles of Classifiers, RNNs (incl. LSTMs, GRUs, ...), DTs (incl. random forests), Logistic Regression (LR), and vanilla Neural Networks (NNs).

Despite their extensive coverage in public media [28], NNs are not the most common approach to classify comments in our selection (cf., Fig. 13). Instead, SVMs are still taking the first place as the most used algorithmic approach, closely followed by the classifier ensembles. Only in places 3 and 6, we can find RNNs and NNs, split by DTs and LR-based solutions.

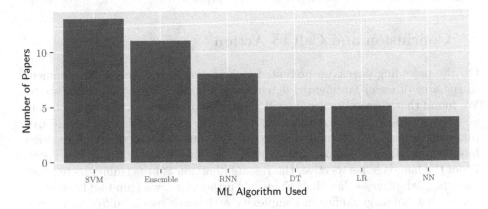

Fig. 13. Distribution of ML approaches

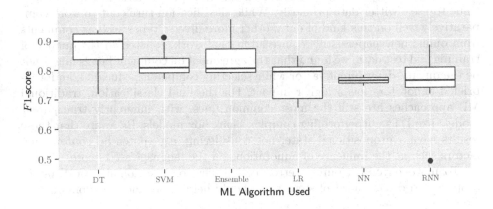

Fig. 14. F1-scores for different ML approaches

Based on the performance assessment plotted in Fig. 14, there are two algorithmic winners: The first is the DTs with a median F1-score of approx. 0.9 (with the limitation of being computed based on only four publications). This is somewhat surprising, as DTs can be considered as a promising approach to classification, as they avoid the often introduced algorithmic black-box. The second winning group is the classifier ensembles, which have a slightly reduced median performance, but the best overall performance. From a theoretical perspective, this should not be surprising since ensemble classifiers have the benefit of combining multiple algorithms simultaneously, giving them the ability to smoothen potential weaknesses of individual algorithms [2,19].

So far, there appears to be no set of dominating algorithmic approaches. The vivid, ongoing experimentation, however, indicates that classic ML algorithms and ensembles are especially promising. Impact factors such as used features or dataset sizes were not considered for this analysis.

4   Conclusion and Call to Action

On the preceding pages, we presented a short overview of recent developments in the area of (semi-)automated detection of abusive language in online spaces. We found that currently, there is still very collaborative work: There are heterogeneous micro-clusters of authors who, however, rarely work with people from different clusters, which limits knowledge exchange. One of the few exceptions has been an Italian competition bringing together a larger group of experts. From the language perspective, the research horizon is broadening, increasingly including languages other than English. Furthermore, we found additional evidence that languages differ in complexity and hence require different levels of investigation. Public funding is only applied (or at least acknowledged) sparsely, also from administrations claiming to work heavily on AI-supported systems (e.g., Germany and the EU). Regarding the data perspective, researchers continue to use Twitter data primarily. While classification turns out to work comparatively well on this kind of data, other more diverse types such as comments from online newspapers still require additional work. Related to the quality of training and test data, we found that the agreement on comment labels might not be the quality-determining factor while selecting competent, educated, and well-briefed annotators has a higher impact. For the final classification, traditional ML approaches are still the most common ones, with inherently transparent models like DTs outperforming complex black box models. Be aware that these results have a propositional state, not considering, e.g., potential confounding factors such as the influence of annotations on the language's $F1$-score.

To move beyond a purely retrospective view on the domain, we want to propose and discuss a set of steps that should help to advance the domain:

- Inclusion of competitions (like the ELVITA one) or paper-a-thons on domain conferences to further (international) collaboration and exchange. This would help to transfer extant knowledge to junior researchers as well as those working on so far under-researched languages.
- Additional focus on complex languages (such as German).
- Publish more datasets from diverse sources (other than Twitter). This goes beyond the data-related aspects such as collection, storage, curation, and release, but has a legal (adjust copyrights to enable releases for research)

and social (create awareness researchers are not stealing property but reusing published items to reduce abusive content) component. As a starting point, all publicly funded research that generates new datasets should be obliged to release the data.

- Ensure careful annotation. This ranges from the provision of proper labels to the thorough annotation through professional annotators. Furthermore, the awareness for accurate annotation should be risen, as they are the baseline for "algorithmic moderators" (to avoid issues such as censorship claims).
- Incentivize further research on models that trade-off between predictive quality (already comparatively high) and transparency. Academic outlets should also start assessing algorithmic transparency as one criterion of eligibility for publishing to avoid a shift towards highly optimized black box models.
- Increase the amount of public funding for abusive language research. SME media companies otherwise lack the resources to gain access to competitive ML-assisted moderating solutions (cf. [9]). Beyond that, many of the above-stated goals also require a substantial financial commitment that is otherwise hardly bearable for public research institutions.

Acknowledgments. The research leading to these results received funding from the federal state of North Rhine-Westphalia and the European Regional Development Fund (EFRE.NRW 2014–2020), Project: **MODERAT!** (No. CM-2-2-036a).

References

1. Albadi, N., Kurdi, M., Mishra, S.: Investigating the effect of combining GRU neural networks with handcrafted features for religious hatred detection on Arabic Twitter space. Soc. Netw. Anal. Min. **9**(1), 1–19 (2019). https://doi.org/10.1007/s13278-019-0587-5
2. Alpaydin, E.: Introduction to Machine Learning, 3rd edn. The MIT Press, Cambridge (2014)
3. Artstein, R., Poesio, M.: Inter-coder agreement for computational linguistics. Comput. Linguist. **34**(4), 555–596 (2008)
4. Benesch, S.: Countering dangerous speech to prevent mass violence during Kenya's 2013 elections. Tech. rep., Dangerous Speech Project (2013)
5. Boeker, M., Vach, W., Motschall, E.: Google scholar as replacement for systematic literature searches: good relative recall and precision are not enough. BMC Med. Res. Methodol. **13**(1), 131 (2013)
6. Bosco, C., Sanguinetti, M., Dell'Orletta, F., Poletto, F., Tesconi, M.: Overview of the EVALITA 2018 hate speech detection task. In: Sixth Evaluation Campaign of Natural Language Processing and Speech Tools for Italian, EVALITA 2018, Turin, Italy, pp. 1–8 (2018)
7. vom Brocke, J., Simons, A., Niehaves, B., Riemer, K., Plattfaut, R., Cleven, A.: Reconstructing the giant: on the importance of rigour in documenting the literature search process. In: Proceedings of 17th European Conference on Information Systems, ECIS 2009, Verona, Italy, pp. 2206–2217 (2009)
8. Brunk, J., Mattern, J., Riehle, D.M.: Effect of Transparency and Trust on Acceptance of Automatic Online Comment Moderation Systems. In: Proceedings of 21st IEEE Conference on Business Informatics, Moscow, Russia, pp. 429–435 (2019)

9. Brunk, J., Niemann, M., Riehle, D.M.: Can analytics as a service save the online discussion culture? - The case of comment moderation in the media industry. In: Proceedings of 21st IEEE Conference on Business Informatics, CBI 2019, Moscow, Russia, pp. 472–481 (2019)
10. Cooper, H.M.: Organizing knowledge syntheses: a taxonomy of literature reviews. Knowl. Soc. **1**(1), 104–126 (1988)
11. Davidson, T., Warmsley, D., Macy, M., Weber, I.: Automated hate speech detection and the problem of offensive language. In: Proceedings of Eleventh International Conference on Web and Social Media, ICWSM-2017, Montreal, Canada, pp. 512–515 (2017)
12. van Eck, N.J., Waltman, L.: Software survey: VOSviewer, a computer program for bibliometric mapping. Scientometrics **84**(2), 523–538 (2010)
13. Ellis, J.: What happened after 7 news sites got rid of reader comments (2015). https://www.niemanlab.org/2015/09/what-happened-after-7-news-sites-got-rid-of-reader-comments/
14. Fortuna, P., Bonavita, I., Nunes, S.: Merging datasets for hate speech classification in Italian. In: Proceedings of the Sixth Evaluation Campaign of Natural Language Processing and Speech Tools for Italian, EVALITA 2018, Turin, Italy, pp. 1–6 (2018)
15. Fortuna, P., Nunes, S.: A survey on automatic detection of hate speech in text. ACM Comput. Surv. **51**(4), 1–30 (2018)
16. Frenda, S., Ghanem, B., Guzmán-Falcón, E., Montes-y Gómez, M., Villaseñor-Pineda, L.: Automatic expansion of lexicons for multilingual misogyny detection. In: Proceedings of Sixth Evaluation Campaign of Natural Language Processing and Speech Tools for Italian, EVALITA 2018, Turin, Italy, pp. 1–6 (2018)
17. Gardiner, B., Mansfield, M., Anderson, I., Holder, J., Louter, D., Ulmanu, M.: The dark side of guardian comments (2016). https://www.theguardian.com/technology/2016/apr/12/the-dark-side-of-guardian-comments
18. Green, M.: No comment! why more news sites are dumping their comment sections (2018). https://www.kqed.org/lowdown/29720/no-comment-why-a-growing-number-of-news-sites-are-dumping-their-comment-sections
19. Hastie, T., Tibshirani, R., Friedman, J.: Additive models, trees, and related methods. The Elements of Statistical Learning. SSS, pp. 295–336. Springer, New York (2009). https://doi.org/10.1007/978-0-387-84858-7_9
20. Hine, G.E., et al.: Kek, cucks, and god emperor trump: a measurement study of 4chan's politically incorrect forum and its effects on the web. In: Proceedings of 11th International Conference on Web and Social Media, ICWSM-2017, Montral, Canada, pp. 92–101 (2017)
21. Koltsova, O.: Methodological challenges for detecting interethnic hostility on social media. In: Bodrunova, S.S., et al. (eds.) INSCI 2018. LNCS, vol. 11551, pp. 7–18. Springer, Cham (2019). https://doi.org/10.1007/978-3-030-17705-8_1
22. Krippendorff, K.: Content Analysis: An Introduction to its Methodology, 2nd edn. SAGE Publications Inc., Thousand Oaks (2004)
23. Langham, J., Gosha, K.: The classification of aggressive dialogue in social media platforms. In: Proceedings of 2018 ACM SIGMIS Conference on Computers and People Research, SIGMIS-CPR 2018, Buffalo-Niagara Falls, NY, USA, pp. 60–63 (2018)
24. Mansfield, M.: How we analysed 70m comments on the guardian website (2016). https://www.theguardian.com/technology/2016/apr/12/how-we-analysed-70m-comments-guardian-website

25. Niemann, M.: Abusiveness is non-binary: five shades of gray in German online news-comments. In: Proceedings of 21st IEEE Conference on Business Informatics, CBI 2019, Moscow, Russia, pp. 11–20 (2019)
26. Niemann, M., Riehle, D.M., Brunk, J., Becker, J.: What is abusive language? In: Grimme, C., Preuss, M., Takes, F.W., Waldherr, A. (eds.) MISDOOM 2019. LNCS, vol. 12021, pp. 59–73. Springer, Cham (2020). https://doi.org/10.1007/978-3-030-39627-5_6
27. Pitsilis, G.K., Ramampiaro, H., Langseth, H.: Effective hate-speech detection in Twitter data using recurrent neural networks. Appl. Intell. **48**(12), 4730–4742 (2018). https://doi.org/10.1007/s10489-018-1242-y
28. Sample, I.: 'It's able to create knowledge itself': Google unveils AI that learns on its own (2017). https://www.theguardian.com/science/2017/oct/18/its-able-to-create-knowledge-itself-google-unveils-ai-learns-all-on-its-own
29. Schmidt, A., Wiegand, M.: A survey on hate speech detection using natural language processing. In: Proceedings of the Fifth International Workshop on Natural Language Processing for Social Media, SocialNLP 2017, Valencia, Spain, pp. 1–10 (2017)
30. Siegert, S.: Nahezu jede zweite Zeitungsredaktion schränkt Online-Kommentare ein (2016). http://www.journalist.de/aktuelles/meldungen/journalist-umfrage-nahezu-jede-2-zeitungsredaktion-schraenkt-onlinekommentare-ein.html
31. W3Techs: Historical trends in the usage statistics of content languages for websites, February 2020. https://w3techs.com/technologies/history_overview/content_language
32. Waseem, Z., Hovy, D.: Hateful symbols or hateful people? Predictive features for hate speech detection on Twitter. In: Proceedings of NAACL Student Research Workshop, Stroudsburg, PA, USA, pp. 88–93 (2016)
33. Webster, J., Watson, R.T.: Analyzing the past to prepare for the future: writing a literature review. MIS Q. **26**(2), xiii–xxiii (2002)
34. Wulczyn, E., Thain, N., Dixon, L.: Ex machina. In: Proceedings of 26th International Conference on World Wide Web, WWW 2017, Perth, Australia, pp. 1391–1399 (2017)
35. Zhang, Z., Luo, L.: Hate speech detection: a solved problem? The challenging case of long tail on Twitter. Semant. Web **10**(5), 925–945 (2019)

Fake News Detection on Twitter Using Propagation Structures

Marion Meyers$^{(\boxtimes)}$, Gerhard Weiss, and Gerasimos Spanakis

Department of Data Science and Knowledge Engineering, Maastricht University,
Maastricht, The Netherlands
marion.meyers@hotmail.com,
{gerhard.weiss,jerry.spanakis}@maastrichtuniversity.nl

Abstract. The growth of social media has revolutionized the way people access information. Although platforms like Facebook and Twitter allow for a quicker, wider and less restricted access to information, they also consist of a breeding ground for the dissemination of fake news. Most of the existing literature on fake news detection on social media proposes user-based or content-based approaches. However, recent research revealed that real and fake news also propagate significantly differently on Twitter. Nonetheless, only a few articles so far have explored the use of propagation features in their detection. Additionally, most of them have based their analysis on a narrow tweet retrieval methodology that only considers tweets to be propagating a news piece if they explicitly contain an URL link to an online news article. By basing our analysis on a broader tweet retrieval methodology that also allows tweets without an URL link to be considered as propagating a news piece, we contribute to fill this research gap and further confirm the potential of using propagation features to detect fake news on Twitter. We firstly show that real news are significantly bigger in size, are spread by users with more followers and less followings, and are actively spread on Twitter for a longer period of time than fake news. Secondly, we achieve an 87% accuracy using a Random Forest Classifier solely trained on propagation features. Lastly, we design a Geometric Deep Learning approach to the problem by building a graph neural network that directly learns on the propagation graphs and achieve an accuracy of 73.3%.

Keywords: Fake news · Twitter · Propagation

1 Introduction

The way people access information and news has radically shifted since the rise of social networks. From being platforms centered around creating and maintaining better social connections, applications such as Facebook and Twitter have become news providers for many of their users [3]. Twitter, with its 326 million monthly active users, has become more than just a social platform but has re-invented how citizens interact with each other and access information about the

© Springer Nature Switzerland AG 2020
M. van Duijn et al. (Eds.): MISDOOM 2020, LNCS 12259, pp. 138–158, 2020.
https://doi.org/10.1007/978-3-030-61841-4_10

world [11,19]. As those platforms constitute a place where any opinion can be expressed and shared, they are also highly exposed to the dissemination of fake information. While traditional media sources such as newspapers and the television have a one-to-many structure, information on social media is shared on a many-to-many fashion hence making the monitoring of the information being diffused a much more complicated task.

The term *fake news* has been the subject of much controversy in the past years. Many definitions exist but none is universally accepted. It often encompasses notions such as manipulation, disinformation (information purposefully misleading), misinformation (information that is verifiably fake) and rumors [14]. In order to remain consistent throughout this article, the terms *fake news*, *fake information* and *fake fact* will be used interchangeably and their definitions will be restricted to claims that are verifiably false. Similarly, *real news*, *real information* and *real fact* will refer to claims that are verifiably true.

Fake news are referred to by many institutions and governments as one of the most dangerous threats to our current society [12], for example because of their influence on elections' results [6,9,10,15,16,23]. As the power and dangers of fake news are increasingly acknowledged, many groups are taking actions against their diffusion, but a systematic way to detect them on social media is still lacking. Most approaches to fake news detection make use of user and content-based features. However, a recent study showed that fake and real news have significantly different propagation patterns [28]. This suggests that propagation features could be successfully used as a basis for classification. Additionally, compared to content-based features, propagation characteristics present the key advantage of being language independent. However, only a few studies so far have leveraged these features for the fake news detection task. Additionally, they have only done so on URL-restricted data sets, defined throughout this research as data sets created by a tweet retrieval methodology where a tweet is only considered to be propagating a news piece if it explicitly contains an URL link to an online news article. In contrast, we define a non-URL-restricted data set as one created by a tweet retrieval methodology that also allows tweets without an URL link to be considered as propagating a news piece.

Building on the apparent potential of propagation features to detect fake news on Twitter, and considering the narrow definition of news used in most of the research so far, this paper contributes to filling this research gap by answering the following research question: given a news graph G, defined here as a set of tweets and retweets that have been associated to a specific news item using a non URL-restricted retrieval methodology, how significant are propagation features at classifying G as a real or a fake piece of information?

This paper answers this question in 2 ways. On one hand, it does so by further investigating the significant differences in the propagation of real and fake information on a non URL-restricted Twitter data set. On the other, it evaluates the performance of 2 different types of classifiers that solely leverage propagation information: a Random Forest Classifier trained on manually extracted features from the propagation graphs, and a Geometric Deep Learning approach directly applied on the full graphs representation. Our code is available via GitHub[1]

2   Related Work

Approaches to fake news detection typically make use of 3 types of information: user-based, news-based and propagation-based [26].

First, user-based approaches have shown promising classification results. Indeed, features extracted from user profiles such as their amount of followers and followings, their time since creation as well as their activity rate have shown to differ between real and fake information [2,22]. Additionally, user-based approaches to fake news detection have been further supported by the evidence that fake accounts play a great role in the dissemination of fake information on social media [6,20,23,24]. Hence, detecting fake accounts on social media is a valuable proxy for attempting to detect fake news [4].

Second, some approaches discriminate real and fake information on social media based on the content of the message being spread. This entails the topic being discussed in the post but also the type of words used, the sentiment portrayed and the 'non-linguistic' information such as the number of question marks or exclamation points employed. [2] for example showed that tweets displaying a stronger sentiment, containing many question marks or smiling emoticons were more likely to be related to non-credible news.

Third, propagation-based approaches classify real and fake information based on their respective diffusion patterns on social media. They are built on a theoretical framework of news diffusion on social media to which a considerable amount of research has been dedicated [21,27,30,31]. Propagation models generally represent tweets (or users) as nodes of a graph and social connections (follower, following) or influence paths (retweet, mention, comments, etc.) as edges. Throughout this article, those graphs will interchangeably be referred to as propagation graphs, propagation models, propagation structures or propagation networks. While user-based and content-based approaches have been the main focus in the existing literature, considerably less research has been dedicated to applying propagation features to the fake news detection task. However, some articles have successfully proved that fake and real news present significantly different propagation patterns on Twitter. [28] discovered that real news take about 6 times as long as fake news to reach 1500 users, consistently reach less users in total and were less retweeted. Additionally, [13] proved that fake news have a more fluctuated temporal diffusion. Then, a few attempts to make use of propagation features to detect fake news on Twitter have been developed. [2] combined different types of features (message-based, user-based, topic-based and propagation-based) and demonstrated that network features such as the number of tweets in the graph and the average node degree played a key role in their classifier's performance. Furthermore, [13] showed that the temporal features extracted from the propagation graphs allowed their classifier to achieve

---

[1] https://github.com/MarionMeyers/fake_news_detection_propagation.

better results than the baseline performance. Together, those articles suggest that propagation structures seem like promising features for classifying real and fake information on Twitter.

However, a more novel approach to graph classification that aims to optimize the use of propagation features has recently been applied to the problem. [5] makes use of the recent advances in Geometric Deep Learning to classify news directly on their Twitter propagation graphs and achieves state-of-the-art classification results (92.7% AUC_ROC). The field of 'Geometric Deep Learning' refers to methods that adapt deep learning approaches to higher dimensional data such as graphs and manifolds. Indeed, most machine learning approaches only work on Euclidian data, ie. 2-dimensional lists of features. When applied on graphs, this means reducing and discarding parts of the information through the manual choice of the 2D features to extract. Geometric Deep Learning approaches counter this limitation by designing neural networks able to learn directly from the 3D representation of the input: Graph Neural Networks. This entails the creation of layers able to cope with a varying input size since the training graphs have a different number of nodes and edges: Graph Convolutional Layers [29]. The success of this approach once again supports the relevance of using propagation features to classify real and fake news [17].

Lastly, both [28] and [5] gather news on Twitter by collecting URL links relating to a news article from fact-checking websites such as Snopes.com or Politifact.com[2,3]. Those websites collect news and score them on a veracity scale based on extensive investigation by independent journalists. Next, they either gather all tweets containing these URL links together with their corresponding retweets [5], or gather all reply tweets containing those URL links together with the original tweet and its associated retweets [28]. Both approaches lead to the creation of a data set where each array of tweets relating to a certain news item is labelled real or fake depending on the veracity of the article they are sharing. As previously defined, their approaches both present a URL-restricted tweet retrieval methodology.

3 Dataset

3.1 Dataset Collection

In our research we make use of the FakeNewsNet data set created in response to a clear lack of existing fake news data sets [25]. Their approach to data collection is to gather news articles from fact-checking organizations (Politifact and Gossipcop) together with their truth label assigned by independent journalists. From those labelled news articles, the headline is extracted and separated into a set of keywords. Then, those keywords are concatenated into a query for the Twitter API. For each news article, labelled real or fake, different kinds of information are then accessed:

---

[2] www.politifact.com.
[3] www.snopes.com.

- news content: the body of the article, images, publish date
- tweets: the list of tweets containing the article headline keywords
- retweets: the list of retweets of all tweets previously retrieved
- user information: the profile information (user id, creation date, 200 most recent published tweets, list of followers and friends) of all users that have posted a tweet or retweet related to the news article.

Not only does this data set provide us with the necessary information to create the propagation graphs detailed in the following section, but it also uses a non URL-restricted tweet retrieval methodology. Indeed, instead of collecting tweets that explicitly contain the URL link to the news piece, it gathers all tweets that contain the keywords associated with the article's headline.

The data set downloaded contains 347 fake news graphs and 310 real ones for a total of 518,684 tweets and 686,245 retweets.

Due to retrieval rate limitations imposed by Twitter, some parts of the data set require a very long time to be collected and were hence not included in this research. This includes both followers and followings information. Additionally, this limitation also led us to restrict the data set only to the Politifact website.

3.2 Propagation Graphs Creation

The propagation graphs, derived from the set of tweets and retweets corresponding to a labelled piece of information, are defined as follows:

- Let V be the set of nodes of the graph. A node can be of two types:
  1. A tweet node: the node stores the tweet and its associated user. A tweet belongs to a news graph if it contains the keywords extracted from the headline of the news article.
  2. A retweet node: the node stores the retweet and its associated user. All retweets of a tweet node are present in the graph.
- Let E be the set of edges of the graph. Edges are drawn between a tweet and its retweets. Edges contain a time weight that corresponds to the time difference between the tweet and retweet publish times.

Then $G = (V,E)$ is the news graph. G is then a composition of non-connected sub-graphs where each sub-graph comprises a tweet and its associated retweets. It is important to note that Twitter is designed in such a way that a retweet of a retweet will point back to the original tweet. Hence, the depth of the graph is never more than 1.

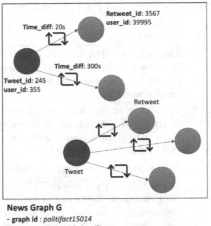

News Graph G
- **graph id** : *politifact15014*
- **corresponding article headline**:
BREAKING: First NFL Team Declares Bankruptcy Over Kneeling Thugs
- **label**: *False*

Fig. 1. Example of a propagation graph

4   Our Approach

Our research consists of two main steps:

1. Manually extract features from the propagation graphs in order to further
   investigate the possible significant differences between how real and fake information propagate on Twitter.
2. Build 2 classifiers trained on the propagation graphs (1) a classifier trained
   on the manually extracted features (2) a Geometric Deep Learning approach
   trained on the propagation graphs themselves.

4.1   Manual Extraction of Propagation Features

Table 1 presents all features extracted from the propagation graphs. Once
extracted from all graphs, we perform a t-test statistical analysis on the means
of the features in the real news and fake news graphs with a 0.05 significant
level. Additionally, we perform an outlier analysis for several features in order
to gain a better understanding of our data. Lastly, we look more in depth at
the propagation of the tweets and retweets over time and analyze the temporal
characteristics of their spread.

Table 1. Features Extracted From Each News Graph.

Scope	Feature	Description
User/Social Context Features	Avg number of followers	For each user that has either posted a tweet or a retweet in the graph, his amount of followers is retrieved. Those counts are then averaged over all users involved in the news graph
	Avg number of following	For each user that has either posted a tweet or a retweet in the graph, his amount of following (friends) is retrieved. Those counts are then averaged over all users involved in the news graph
Network Features	Retweet Percentage	This is measured through the following equation: $$\frac{number\ of\ retweets}{number\ of\ tweets + number\ of\ retweets}$$
	Average Time Diff	This measures the average time between a tweet and a corresponding retweet. Since each edge of the graph has a time weight on it, it is computed by making the average of all the edge weights of the graph
	Number of tweets	
	Number of retweets	
	Time_first_last or News lifetime	This measure is obtained by computing the time difference between the first and last recorded publish dates of tweets (or retweets) in the graph
	Average favorite count	For each node, its number of favourites is retrieved. Those counts are then averaged over all nodes in the graph
	AvgRetCount	For each tweet, its number of retweets is retrieved. Those counts are then averaged over all tweets in the graph
	UsersTouched 10 h	Starting from the first post recorded in the graph, all posts that happened in the first 10 h of the diffusion are retrieved. From those posts, the amount of unique users involved in the spread is then calculated
	PercPosts1hour	This feature is calculated by the following equation: $$\frac{number\ of\ tweets\ and\ retweets\ in\ the\ first\ hour}{total\ number\ of\ tweets\ and\ retweets\ in\ the\ graph}$$

4.2 Classification Approaches

Approach to the Classification on Manually Extracted Features. Our approach to the creation and the analysis of a classifier trained on manually extracted features from the graphs can be separated into 2 steps (1) Compare and select the best type of classifier for the problem (2) Analyze the importance of the different features in the classification.

Compare and Select the Best Type of Classifier

Different classifiers were trained using a 10-fold cross validation method. Namely, the algorithms tried are: Random Forest, Decision Tree, Linear Discriminant Analysis, Bayes Neural Network, Logistic Regression, K-Nearest Neighbors, Quadratic Discriminant Analysis and Support Vector Machine. As the data set is slightly unbalanced, it is important to evaluate if this significantly impacts the classification performance. Hence, the performance of all classifiers is not only recorded on the full data set but also on 5 different under-sampled balanced versions of the data set. Their results are then compared and the algorithm yielding the highest accuracy will be chosen for further analysis.

Analyze the Importance of Different Features

To evaluate the importance given to each feature by the classifier, we record its performance over all possible subsets of features. Given that there are 11 features in total, the power set hence contains 2048 unique subsets (including the empty set). For each set size, we then record which feature (or combination of features) lead to the highest performance score. We do this for the best accuracy, best f1 score and best AUC_ROC. This approach not only allows us to understand what set size typically reaches the highest performance, but also which features play key roles in the classification.

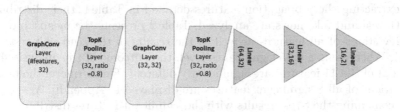

Fig. 2. GDL network architecture.

Geometric Deep Learning Approach. While most existing graph neural networks have been developed for the node classification task, the problem tackled here is that of graph classification. However, [1] and [8] have adapted current successes from the node to the graph classification task. They make use of the graph convolutional layer described in [18] as this layer was shown to be applicable to social networks and molecule graphs classification. In out research, this layer is combined with a specific pooling layer developed in [8], the topk pooling layer, that reduces the size of the graph at each iteration by choosing the top k best nodes and dropping the remaining ones. The choice of nodes to drop or keep is based on their inner features.

The neural network architecture used in this research is described more in details in Fig. 2.

The data fed into the network has to be specifically structured for the task. Indeed, not only are the graph connections themselves used for learning, but relevant features can also be encoded in both the nodes and the edges. Hence, nodes will be characterized by the following information:

- Number of followers of the user
- Number of friends (following) of the user
- Number of favorites of the tweet/retweet

- Number of retweets of the tweet (0 if the node is a retweet)
- Node type (either a tweet or a retweet)

Edges are characterized by the time difference between the tweet and its associated retweet. It is to be noted that all features inserted in the nodes are features that are also available to the classifier trained on manually extracted features in order for the future performance comparison to be applicable. In order to build our architecture, we have been using the recently released Pytorch Geometric library that had already implemented the different layers we are utilizing [7]. The network is using a 10-fold cross validation method on a balanced version of the data set (using under-sampling).

5   Experimental Results

5.1   Manually Extracted Propagation Features Analysis

After extracting the propagation features detailed in Table 1, their distribution for both real and fake news are analyzed. Table 2 presents the means and standard deviations of all features as well as the results of the student t-tests performed. When using a 0.05 significance level, the outcome of the analysis shows that 8 out of the 11 features are significantly different. Furthermore, the boxplot distributions of all 8 significant features are displayed in Appendix A.

By combining the t-test results with the significant features distribution presented in Appendix A, different conclusions can be drawn on the data set and the differences in propagation between real and fake information on Twitter.

Real News Are 'bigger' Than Fake News. Real news have an average of 1212 tweets and 1796 retweets while fake news have on average 411 tweets and 372 retweets. From the statistical analysis displayed in Table 2, it is observed that the means of both features are significantly different. By further analyzing

Table 2. Features Summary.

	mean real	mean fake	std real	std fake	t	pValue	signif
followerAvg	34607.0280	8835.2657	73084.3660	14107.1257	6.1079	0.0000	Y
followingAvg	3386.4674	4535.2654	3998.6284	3201.5401	−4.0336	0.0001	Y
retweetPerc	0.4132	0.3730	0.2262	0.2214	2.2969	0.0219	Y
avgTimeDiff (in seconds)	372966.1338	320420.5629	1956157.2011	1451788.9476	0.3872	0.6988	N
numTweets	1212.3710	411.6686	2824.1935	1600.1888	4.4005	0.0000	Y
numRetweets	1796.6161	372.6052	4927.2753	1969.8602	4.7600	0.0000	Y
avgFav	.1861	1.3384	5.9917	4.5917	2.0175	0.0441	Y
avgRetCount	3.1288	3.1925	8.6245	15.7255	−0.0653	0.9480	N
news lifetime (in seconds)	115662880.1871	27737159.8963	97964001.7070	45342932.5034	14.4778	0.0000	Y
usersTouched10hours	71.6710	57.7666	192.7123	150.3321	1.0225	0.3070	N
percPosts1hour	0.1528	0.0720	0.2521	0.1269	5.0940	0.0000	Y

the 4 highest outliers in the number of tweets (2 real and 2 fake), a limitation to the data collection protocol used in this research was discovered. Indeed, they all have an extremely large number of tweets because the list of keywords used to extract the relevant twitter information is very broad and leads to the retrieval of many posts that do not correspond to the original news. For example, a query that lead to the retrieval of 24,338 tweets is 'One in Four – Congressman Joe Pitts'. Initially referring to an article written by the Congressman Joe Pitts on addiction rate in Pennsylvia, the broad query led to the retrieval of many unrelated tweets such as "In Chinese universities, students sleep four to a dorm room. I would not have survived it. One was difficult enough...".

Real News Stay Longer 'in the Loop'. The news lifetime was shown to be significantly different for real and fake graphs (see Table 2). Real news stay on average 4.16 times longer on Twitter than fake ones (1338 vs 321 days). By looking at the boxplots in Appendix A, it is interesting to note that while the lifetime of fake news presents a certain amount of outliers, the real news lifetime is more spread but doesn't show any outlier. A deeper look at the fake news outliers proves once again that very broad queries lead to the retrieval of many more tweets than intended. For example, the query 'Sid Miller', initially referring to a fake image of the politician spread on Twitter in 2016, encompassed a tweet dating from 2011 that used the same keywords, thereby yielding an abnormally large lifetime for the fake news. We also note the possibility of recurrent fake news that lead to an abnormally long lifetime. This is the case for a fake news that emerged both in 2012 and 2017 involving Barack Obama's face being printed on one-dollar bills.

Two hypothesis can then be formulated to try to explain why real news show a longer lifetime on Twitter. First, real news could present queries that are more likely to be used at different points in time hence augmenting their probability of showing a larger news lifetime average. In comparison, fake news would show a more novel and rare set of keywords that are less likely to be re-used in other news items. Second, the lifetime of fake news could be shorter due to the fact that once they are proven to be misleading, their spread is more likely to be halted.

Users Spreading Real News Tend to Have More Followers but to Follow Less Accounts. On average, users involved in the propagation of real information have 34,607 followers while fake news propagators only have 4,535. The statistical results in Table 2 confirm that those means are significantly different. A quick look at the real news outliers in follower counts shows that they seem to be shared by trustworthy accounts such as the NY Times (43,254,008 followers) or the Huffington Post (11,477,200 followers). On the contrary, real news propagators follow on average less accounts than fake news propagators do. While accounts linked to spreading real news follow on average 3386.47 other accounts, fake news propagators follow on average 4535.27 accounts. Once again, this difference has been statistically proven to be significant.

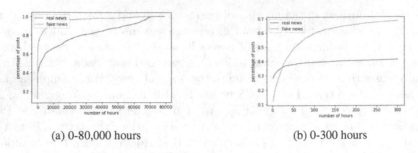

(a) 0-80,000 hours   (b) 0-300 hours

Fig. 3. Average Percentage of Posts over Time

Temporal Spread Analysis. Figure 3 presents an average of the percentage of tweets and retweets posted over time for fake and real news. Firstly, we see on the first graph of Fig. 3 that fake news reach 100% of their posts earlier than real news (30,000 vs 70,000 h). This corresponds to our previous finding that the lifetime of real news is bigger than that of fake news.

Secondly, the shapes of the two curves are very different. The fake news curve shows a strong increase in the its beginning before increasing in a more moderate manner and remaining relatively stable from about 15,000 h on. The real news curve also shows an steep increase at the beginning but quickly evolves into a more moderate increase over time, to only reach its 100% at about 70,000 h. In order to better visualize and compare the early increases of the two curves, the second graph of Fig. 3 presents the same curves on a shorter amount of time. We observe that although real news already reach 30% of their posts in the first hour of spread, fake news quickly overtake and reach 70% of their posts after 300 h. By then, the real news have only reached 40% of their posts.

This analysis allows us to visually represent our previous finding that fake news have a shorter lifetime than real news. Indeed, we see that while real news have a slower increase over time and thereby a larger lifetime, fake news reach the end of their spread faster, hence have a shorter lifetime. It is also important to note that our previous finding about the news size are likely to have impacted the results of this temporal analysis. Indeed, as real news are significantly bigger in size, they are more likely to take a longer time to be spread.

5.2   Classification Results

Classifier on Manually Extracted Features
Compare And Select The Best Type Of Classifier Appendix B presents the scores of all classifiers attempted. Firstly, we only observe a small difference in the accuracy of the classifiers when applied on the full data sets or on the balanced versions. Looking at the Random Forest Classifier, its accuracy on the balanced data sets oscillates between 83.5% and 86.5%, and obtains an accuracy of 85% on the full data set. We then conclude that the slightly unbalanced characteristic of the data set does not have a concrete influence on the classification performance.

The Random Forest Classifier ranked the highest in all scores and was hence selected as classification algorithm for the rest of the analysis.

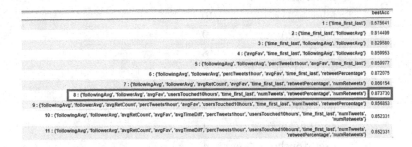

	bestAcc
1 : ('time_first_last')	0.675641
2 : ('time_first_last', 'followerAvg')	0.814499
3 : ('time_first_last', 'followingAvg', 'followerAvg')	0.829580
4 : ('avgFav', 'time_first_last', 'followingAvg', 'followerAvg')	0.859953
5 : ('followingAvg', 'followerAvg', 'percTweets1hour', 'avgFav', 'time_first_last')	0.859977
6 : ('followingAvg', 'followerAvg', 'percTweets1hour', 'avgFav', 'time_first_last', 'retweetPercentage')	0.872075
7 : ('followingAvg', 'followerAvg', 'avgRetCount', 'avgFav', 'time_first_last', 'retweetPercentage', 'numRetweets')	0.866154
8 : ('followingAvg', 'followerAvg', 'avgFav', 'usersTouched10hours', 'time_first_last', 'numTweets', 'retweetPercentage', 'numRetweets')	0.873730
9 : ('followingAvg', 'followerAvg', 'avgRetCount', 'percTweets1hour', 'avgFav', 'usersTouched10hours', 'time_first_last', 'numTweets', 'retweetPercentage')	0.856853
10 : ('followingAvg', 'followerAvg', 'avgRetCount', 'avgFav', 'avgTimeDiff', 'percTweets1hour', 'usersTouched10hours', 'time_first_last', 'numTweets', 'numRetweets')	0.852331
11 : ('followingAvg', 'followerAvg', 'avgRetCount', 'avgFav', 'avgTimeDiff', 'percTweets1hour', 'usersTouched10hours', 'time_first_last', 'numTweets', 'retweetPercentage', 'numRetweets')	0.852331

Fig. 4. Set of features reaching the highest accuracy per subset size

Analyze The Importance Of Different Features Firstly, we observe in Fig. 4 that the random forest classifier reaches its highest accuracy on the full data set when using a set of 8 features. While it reaches 85% accuracy using the 11 features, the performance goes up to 87% when using the following set of features: *followingAvg, followerAvg, avgFav, usersTouched10hours, news lifetime, numTweets, retweetPercentage, numRetweets*.

Secondly, Table 3 presents a summary of the number of occurrences of each feature in all the best subsets presented in Fig. 4. We observe that the news lifetime is present in all of them, followed by the average number of followers present in 10 out of 11 subsets. We also see in Fig. 4 that these two features combined already accurately classify 81.44% of all graphs. This leads us to conclude that they are both of major importance in the classification. Additionally, both the following average and the average number of favourites seem to be important as they are present in respectively 8 and 9 of all best subsets.

Thirdly, we note without surprise that the 3 features that were proven to be non-significant (*avgTimeDiff, usersTouched10hours* and *avgRetCount*) don't contribute much to the classification performance.

Lastly, we observe that the number of tweets and retweets are only present in 4 of the best subsets. Although the features were both shown to be significant, the median of both features were very similar between the real and fake sets of graphs, which might explain why the random forest classifier did not give them a strong importance.

5.3   Geometric Deep Learning

Before training the algorithm, the pre-processing step of normalizing the features is performed. Then, the neural network is trained using a 10-fold cross validation method. A mini-batch size of 1 and a learning rate of 0.001 were found to be yielding the best results. When trained for 400 epochs, the neural network

Table 3. Number of occurrences of each feature in all best subsets

	Number of Occurrences
newsLifetime	11
followerAvg	10
followingAvg	9
avgFav	8
retweetPerc	5
numTweets	4
numRetweets	4
avgRetCount	4
usersTouched10hours	4
percPosts1hour	3
avgTimeDiff	1

achieved the results displayed in Fig. 5. On average over the 10 folds, the accuracy recorded on the last epoch is 73.29%, with a standard deviation of 0.0746 which proves the robustness of the model.

Our Geometric Deep Learning approach has only been tried on one neural network architecture, which leads us to conclude that a gdl-based detection of fake news seems like a promising approach given the satisfactory results presented above. However, a systematic comparison of gdl models is needed in order optimize the model for this specific task instead of utilizing a model proven to be successful in other classification tasks.

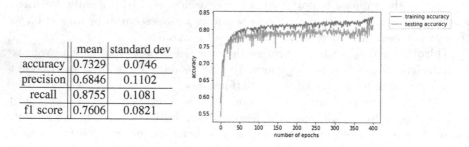

	mean	standard dev
accuracy	0.7329	0.0746
precision	0.6846	0.1102
recall	0.8755	0.1081
f1 score	0.7606	0.0821

Fig. 5. Geometric Deep Learning approach scores over 400 epochs

6   Discussion

The experiments performed in this paper led us to gain insights on how fake and real news propagate on Twitter. It is then interesting to compare our findings with those achieved by previous research. Firstly, [28] has found that fake news propagate wider, faster and deeper than real news. More specifically, they discovered that real news take about 6 times as long as fake news to reach 1500 users, consistently reach less users in total and were less retweeted. However, our conclusions somehow contradict their findings since we have observed that real news present more tweets and retweets. However, both the average retweet count and the users touched in the first 10 h feature are not significant in our results hence preventing us from fully arguing against their finding. It is however important to note that while our results have been discovered on an entire news graphs composed of non-connected sub-graphs, their conclusions are drawn from individual retweet cascades. This methodological contrast might contribute to the evident disaccord between our results. Secondly, both [2] and [28] support our finding that real news are spread by users with more followers than those spreading fake information. However, our results about the number of followings is opposite to theirs. While both their analysis show that real news propagators follow more people, our research shows that fake news propagators actually have more followings. Lastly, to the best of our knowledge, no previous work seems to make use of 'lifetime' as classification feature thereby preventing us from making any comparison.

The last section of the experiments entailed the application and evaluation of a Geometric Deep Learning approach to the problem, which achieved an accuracy of 73.3%. The only other application of Geometric Deep Learning to fake news detection had achieved an AUC_ROC of 92.7% on their URL-wise classification but their network had the advantage of containing social connections and influence paths [5].

Before summarizing the final conclusions of our research paper, it is necessary to underline its major limitations. First of all, although using a non URL-restricted news definition distinguishes our research from most of the existing literature on fake news classification, it brings up the issue of using a definition that is very broad. As explained in Sect. 5, using the keywords from the articles headlines leads in some cases to the retrieval of many tweets that are unrelated to the original news piece. This also causes some graphs to cover periods of time that seem unrealistic. This limitation is hard to circumvent when dealing with fake news detection research. One the one hand, our choice of data is restricted by the very limited availability of Twitter labelled news data sets. On the other hand, none of these data sets agree on a precise methodology to retrieve tweets that correspond to a news piece. Although the majority has been following the URL-restricted approach defined earlier, this methodology also has major limitations. Second of all, all news analysed come from a single source of information, Politifact, that mainly includes American political news. This hence prevents us from generalizing our findings to other news topics.

7 Conclusion

This paper demonstrated the potential of using propagation features to discriminate real from fake news on Twitter by analyzing a non URL-restricted data set. More specifically, it firstly discovers the following significant differences in the propagation of the real and fake news: real news graphs are bigger in size, are spread by users with more followers and less followings, and stay longer on Twitter than fake news. Secondly, it achieves a 87% detection accuracy using a Random Forest Classifier solely trained on propagation features, hence further confirming the latter assumption. Lastly, by developing a graph neural network trained directly on the 3D representation of the propagation graphs, it achieves an accuracy of 73.3%. Overall, the significant differences discovered as well as the good performances achieved by the 2 algorithms trained on propagation information lead us to conclude that propagation features are a relevant and important asset to the fake news detection task on Twitter.

Further research should firstly be dedicated to the evaluation of our classification approaches on the early detection of fake news instead of at the end of their diffusion. Secondly, further efforts should go into refining our data set in order to counter the negative impact of our broad definition of news on the reliability of our results. In order to do that, a time limit on the retrieval of the tweets could be set, or the analysis could be performed on the tweet cascades (the set of one tweet and its corresponding retweets) instead of on the entire news graph. Thirdly, it would be interesting to apply our approach to other news topics than political news in order to evaluate if the same conclusions on the propagation patterns can be drawn. Lastly, the GDL experiments were only performed on one type of convolutional and pooling layers, while many more have been shown to be successful in various applications. Further research should hence be dedicated to trying different versions of this neural network and hopefully improve the classification performance by finding the optimal combination of convolutional and pooling layers.

Appendix

Appendix A: Significant Features Distribution

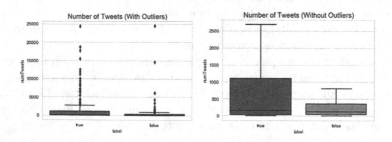

Fig. 6. Number of Tweets Distribution.

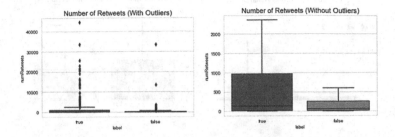

Fig. 7. Number of Retweets Distribution.

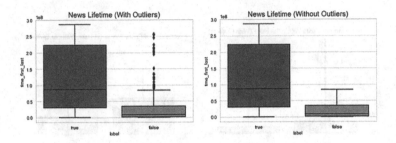

Fig. 8. News Lifetime (time_first_last) Distribution.

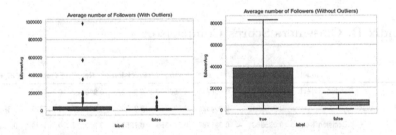

Fig. 9. Average Number of Followers Distribution.

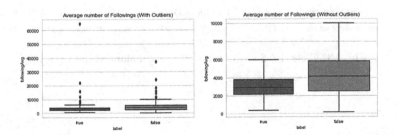

Fig. 10. Average Number of Followings Distribution.

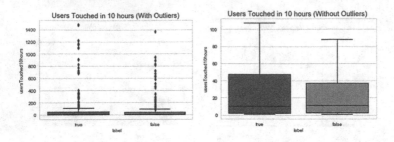

Fig. 11. Number of Users Touched Within the First 10 h Distribution.

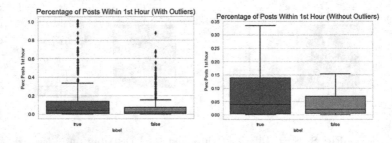

Fig. 12. Percentage of Posts In The First Hour Distribution.

Appendix B: Classifiers Scores Comparison

	Model	Fitting time	Scoring time	Accuracy	Precision	Recall	F1_score	AUC_ROC
5	Random Forest	0.019847	0.009275	0.850000	0.855226	0.850000	0.849355	0.917950
3	Linear Discriminant Analysis	0.002991	0.004322	0.799767	0.813922	0.799767	0.797219	0.891538
1	Decision Tree	0.005983	0.005187	0.782258	0.785503	0.782258	0.781449	0.782258
4	Quadratic Discriminant Analysis	0.001796	0.004787	0.762903	0.786729	0.762903	0.757126	0.852549
7	Bayes	0.001394	0.004387	0.751613	0.791883	0.751613	0.741174	0.856400
6	K-Nearest Neighbors	0.001183	0.014667	0.738710	0.742815	0.738710	0.737370	0.788450
0	Logistic Regression	0.004387	0.004888	0.635484	0.733380	0.635484	0.574515	0.866389
2	Support Vector Machine	0.177230	0.022935	0.503226	0.350820	0.503226	0.340308	0.509677

Fig. 13. Classifier Scores: under-sampled balanced data set 1

	Model	Fitting time	Scoring time	Accuracy	Precision	Recall	F1_score	AUC_ROC
5	Random Forest	0.018745	0.008777	0.864516	0.870510	0.864516	0.863998	0.909209
3	Linear Discriminant Analysis	0.002882	0.003988	0.808077	0.823229	0.808077	0.805685	0.887988
1	Decision Tree	0.005080	0.003392	0.790323	0.795953	0.790323	0.789402	0.790323
4	Quadratic Discriminant Analysis	0.001297	0.003989	0.764516	0.783938	0.764516	0.759388	0.853174
7	Bayes	0.001295	0.003889	0.754839	0.793074	0.754839	0.745782	0.853486
6	K-Nearest Neighbors	0.001292	0.015763	0.750000	0.751943	0.750000	0.749607	0.798075
0	Logistic Regression	0.004004	0.003981	0.685484	0.751533	0.685484	0.651006	0.862019
2	Support Vector Machine	0.150106	0.018250	0.506452	0.451639	0.506452	0.347283	0.512903

Fig. 14. Classifier Scores: under-sampled balanced data set 2

	Model	Fitting time	Scoring time	Accuracy	Precision	Recall	F1_score	AUC_ROC
5	Random Forest	0.018440	0.008182	0.851613	0.854290	0.851613	0.851336	0.909105
3	Linear Discriminant Analysis	0.002771	0.004321	0.806489	0.820166	0.806489	0.804613	0.890859
1	Decision Tree	0.005983	0.003491	0.775806	0.777676	0.775806	0.775449	0.775806
4	Quadratic Discriminant Analysis	0.001396	0.004987	0.762903	0.779588	0.762903	0.759104	0.845578
7	Bayes	0.001306	0.004177	0.751613	0.787460	0.751613	0.743435	0.847242
6	K-Nearest Neighbors	0.001200	0.016457	0.730645	0.732476	0.730645	0.730079	0.783351
0	Logistic Regression	0.003804	0.003679	0.722581	0.785927	0.722581	0.700066	0.869823
2	Support Vector Machine	0.184508	0.020855	0.508065	0.402091	0.508065	0.350243	0.509677

Fig. 15. Classifier Scores: under-sampled balanced data set 3

	Model	Fitting time	Scoring time	Accuracy	Precision	Recall	F1_score	AUC_ROC
5	Random Forest	0.019647	0.009072	0.835484	0.842741	0.835484	0.834513	0.904214
3	Linear Discriminant Analysis	0.002881	0.004211	0.800233	0.813652	0.800233	0.797959	0.886793
1	Decision Tree	0.004981	0.003592	0.793548	0.797135	0.793548	0.792968	0.793548
4	Quadratic Discriminant Analysis	0.001696	0.003989	0.774194	0.792638	0.774194	0.770666	0.845369
7	Bayes	0.001495	0.005094	0.758065	0.793220	0.758065	0.750942	0.853382
6	K-Nearest Neighbors	0.001379	0.016767	0.741935	0.744589	0.741935	0.740953	0.787929
0	Logistic Regression	0.003390	0.003092	0.674194	0.747914	0.674194	0.636437	0.856712
2	Support Vector Machine	0.157588	0.017446	0.506452	0.451639	0.506452	0.347283	0.512903

Fig. 16. Classifier Scores: under-sampled balanced data set 4

	Model	Fitting time	Scoring time	Accuracy	Precision	Recall	F1_score	AUC_ROC
5	Random Forest	0.016362	0.008080	0.854839	0.860123	0.854839	0.854257	0.917430
3	Linear Discriminant Analysis	0.002658	0.003324	0.805182	0.822330	0.805182	0.802539	0.890440
1	Decision Tree	0.005385	0.004289	0.796774	0.800022	0.796774	0.796213	0.796774
4	Quadratic Discriminant Analysis	0.001799	0.005084	0.761290	0.777300	0.761290	0.757422	0.857232
7	Bayes	0.001595	0.003989	0.756452	0.790125	0.756452	0.748277	0.853278
6	K-Nearest Neighbors	0.001502	0.015652	0.720968	0.724078	0.720968	0.719957	0.784183
0	Logistic Regression	0.003094	0.003595	0.645161	0.711975	0.645161	0.602609	0.859001
2	Support Vector Machine	0.157389	0.018448	0.503226	0.350820	0.503226	0.340308	0.509677

Fig. 17. Classifier Scores: under-sampled balanced data set 5

	Model	Fitting time	Scoring time	Accuracy	Precision	Recall	F1_score	AUC_ROC
5	Random Forest	0.021441	0.009176	0.850793	0.854662	0.852197	0.850523	0.921442
3	Linear Discriminant Analysis	0.002992	0.003657	0.809689	0.826785	0.803407	0.806346	0.884708
1	Decision Tree	0.006286	0.003791	0.785408	0.789165	0.786788	0.784979	0.786788
4	Quadratic Discriminant Analysis	0.001795	0.005387	0.777669	0.793786	0.771159	0.772636	0.851762
7	Bayes	0.001610	0.004280	0.765571	0.802432	0.755701	0.755153	0.851277
6	K-Nearest Neighbors	0.001399	0.020044	0.736503	0.739172	0.734965	0.735711	0.792261
0	Logistic Regression	0.003697	0.004182	0.730326	0.778263	0.737258	0.712641	0.867978
2	Support Vector Machine	0.197067	0.026137	0.534219	0.465700	0.506452	0.378318	0.512903

Fig. 18. Classifier Scores: full data set

Appendix C: Feature Importance Analysis

bestAcc

1 : {'time_first_last'} 0.675641
2 : {'time_first_last', 'followerAvg'} 0.814409
3 : {'time_first_last', 'followingAvg', 'followerAvg'} 0.829580
4 : {'avgFav', 'time_first_last', 'followingAvg', 'followerAvg'} 0.859953
5 : {'followingAvg', 'followerAvg', 'percTweets1hour', 'avgFav', 'time_first_last'} 0.859977
6 : {'followingAvg', 'followerAvg', 'percTweets1hour', 'avgFav', 'time_first_last', 'retweetPercentage'} 0.872075
7 : {'followingAvg', 'followerAvg', 'avgRetCount', 'avgFav', 'time_first_last', 'retweetPercentage', 'numRetweets'} 0.860154
8 : {'followingAvg', 'followerAvg', 'avgFav', 'usersTouched10hours', 'time_first_last', 'numTweets', 'retweetPercentage', 'numRetweets'} 0.873730
9 : {'followingAvg', 'followerAvg', 'avgRetCount', 'percTweets1hour', 'avgFav', 'usersTouched10hours', 'time_first_last', 'numTweets', 'retweetPercentage'} 0.856653
10 : {'followingAvg', 'followerAvg', 'avgRetCount', 'avgFav', 'avgTimeDiff', 'percTweets1hour', 'usersTouched10hours', 'time_first_last', 'numTweets', 'numRetweets'} 0.852331
11 : {'followingAvg', 'followerAvg', 'avgRetCount', 'avgFav', 'avgTimeDiff', 'percTweets1hour', 'usersTouched10hours', 'time_first_last', 'numTweets', 'retweetPercentage', 'numRetweets'} 0.852331

bestF1

1 : {'time_first_last'} 0.674648
2 : {'time_first_last', 'followerAvg'} 0.814333
3 : {'time_first_last', 'followingAvg', 'followerAvg'} 0.820350
4 : {'avgFav', 'time_first_last', 'followingAvg', 'followerAvg'} 0.859503
5 : {'followingAvg', 'followerAvg', 'percTweets1hour', 'avgFav', 'time_first_last'} 0.859818
6 : {'followingAvg', 'followerAvg', 'percTweets1hour', 'avgFav', 'time_first_last', 'retweetPercentage'} 0.871508
7 : {'followingAvg', 'followerAvg', 'avgRetCount', 'percTweets1hour', 'avgFav', 'usersTouched10hours', 'time_first_last'} 0.865884
8 : {'followingAvg', 'followerAvg', 'avgFav', 'usersTouched10hours', 'time_first_last', 'numTweets', 'retweetPercentage', 'numRetweets'} 0.873385
9 : {'followingAvg', 'followerAvg', 'avgRetCount', 'percTweets1hour', 'avgFav', 'usersTouched10hours', 'time_first_last', 'retweetPercentage', 'numRetweets'} 0.856470
10 : {'followingAvg', 'followerAvg', 'avgRetCount', 'avgFav', 'avgTimeDiff', 'percTweets1hour', 'usersTouched10hours', 'time_first_last', 'numTweets', 'numRetweets'} 0.851886
11 : {'followingAvg', 'followerAvg', 'avgRetCount', 'avgFav', 'avgTimeDiff', 'percTweets1hour', 'usersTouched10hours', 'time_first_last', 'numTweets', 'retweetPercentage', 'numRetweets'} 0.851748

bestROC

1 : {'time_first_last'} 0.749588
2 : {'time_first_last', 'followerAvg'} 0.856440
3 : {'time_first_last', 'followingAvg', 'followerAvg'} 0.891854
4 : {'avgFav', 'time_first_last', 'followingAvg', 'followerAvg'} 0.912940
5 : {'followingAvg', 'followerAvg', 'avgFav', 'usersTouched10hours', 'time_first_last'} 0.914363
6 : {'followingAvg', 'followerAvg', 'percTweets1hour', 'avgFav', 'time_first_last', 'retweetPercentage'} 0.928215
7 : {'followingAvg', 'followerAvg', 'percTweets1hour', 'avgFav', 'time_first_last', 'retweetPercentage', 'numRetweets'} 0.924078
8 : {'followingAvg', 'followerAvg', 'avgFav', 'usersTouched10hours', 'time_first_last', 'numTweets', 'retweetPercentage', 'numRetweets'} 0.927014
9 : {'followingAvg', 'followerAvg', 'avgRetCount', 'percTweets1hour', 'avgFav', 'usersTouched10hours', 'time_first_last', 'numTweets', 'numRetweets'} 0.922370
10 : {'followingAvg', 'followerAvg', 'avgRetCount', 'avgFav', 'avgTimeDiff', 'percTweets1hour', 'usersTouched10hours', 'time_first_last', 'retweetPercentage', 'numRetweets'} 0.923094
11 : {'followingAvg', 'followerAvg', 'avgRetCount', 'avgFav', 'avgTimeDiff', 'percTweets1hour', 'usersTouched10hours', 'time_first_last', 'numTweets', 'retweetPercentage', 'numRetweets'} 0.909439

Fig. 19. Best Subsets Analysis Full Data Set

References

1. Cangea, C., Veličković, P., Jovanović, N., Kipf, T., Liò, P.: Towards sparse hierarchical graph classifiers. arXiv preprint arXiv:1811.01287 (2018)
2. Castillo, C., Mendoza, M., Poblete, B.: Information credibility on twitter. In: Proceedings of the 20th International Conference on World Wide Web, pp. 675–684. ACM (2011)
3. Center, P.R.: News use across social media platforms 2018 (2018). https://www.journalism.org/2018/09/10/news-use-across-social-media-platforms-2018/. Accessed 03 June 2019
4. Davis, C.A., Varol, O., Ferrara, E., Flammini, A., Menczer, F.: Botornot: a system to evaluate social bots. In: Proceedings of the 25th International Conference Companion on World Wide Web, pp. 273–274. International World Wide Web Conferences Steering Committee (2016)
5. Federico, M., Fabrizio, F., Davide, E., Damon, M.: Fake news detection on social media using geometric deep learning. arXiv preprint arXiv:1902.06673 (2019)
6. Ferrara, E.: Disinformation and social bot operations in the run up to the 2017 french presidential election (2017)
7. Fey, M., Lenssen, J.E.: Fast graph representation learning with PyTorch Geometric. In: ICLR Workshop on Representation Learning on Graphs and Manifolds (2019)
8. Gao, H., Ji, S.: Graph u-net (2019). https://openreview.net/forum?id=HJePRoAct7
9. Gorodnichenko, Y., Pham, T., Talavera, O.: Social media, sentiment and public opinions: Evidence from# brexit and# uselection. Technical report, National Bureau of Economic Research (2018)
10. Guardian, T.: Bolsonaro business backers accused of illegal whatsapp fake news campaign (2018). https://www.theguardian.com/world/2018/oct/18/brazil-jair-bolsonaro-whatsapp-fake-news-campaign. Accessed 03 Aug 2019
11. Iqbal, M.: Twitter revenue and usage statistics (2018). http://www.businessofapps.com/data/twitter-statistics/. Accessed 03 June 2019
12. Kalsnes, B.: Fake news, May 2019. https://oxfordre.com/communication/view/10.1093/acrefore/9780190228613.001.0001/acrefore-9780190228613-e-809
13. Kwon, S., Cha, M., Jung, K., Chen, W., Wang, Y.: Prominent features of rumor propagation in online social media. In: 2013 IEEE 13th International Conference on Data Mining, pp. 1103–1108. IEEE (2013)
14. Lazer, D.M., et al.: The science of fake news. Science **359**(6380), 1094–1096 (2018)
15. Leonhardt, D., Thompson, S.A.: Trump's lies (2017). https://www.nytimes.com/interactive/2017/06/23/opinion/trumps-lies.html, archived from the original on 23 June 2017
16. Marwick, A., Lewis, R.: Media Manipulation and Disinformation Online. Data & Society Research Institute, New York (2017)
17. Monti, F., Boscaini, D., Masci, J., Rodola, E., Svoboda, J., Bronstein, M.M.: Geometric deep learning on graphs and manifolds using mixture model CNNS. In: Proceedings of the IEEE Conference on Computer Vision and Pattern Recognition, pp. 5115–5124 (2017)
18. Morris, C., et al.: Weisfeiler and leman go neural: Higher-order graph neural networks. arXiv preprint arXiv:1810.02244 (2018)
19. Nielsen, R.K.: News media, search engines and social networking sites as varieties of online gatekeepers. In: Rethinking Journalism Again, pp. 93–108. Routledge (2016)

20. Review, M.T.: First evidence that social bots play a major role in spreading fake news (2017). https://www.technologyreview.com/s/608561/first-evidence-that-social-bots-play-a-major-role-in-spreading-fake-news/. Accessed 03 June 2019
21. Sadikov, E., Martinez, M.M.M.: Information propagation on twitter. CS322 project report (2009)
22. Shao, C., Ciampaglia, G.L., Flammini, A., Menczer, F.: Hoaxy: a platform for tracking online misinformation. In: Proceedings of the 25th International Conference Companion on World Wide Web, pp. 745–750. International World Wide Web Conferences Steering Committee (2016)
23. Shao, C., Ciampaglia, G.L., Varol, O., Flammini, A., Menczer, F.: The spread of fake news by social bots. arXiv preprint arXiv:1707.07592 pp. 96–104 (2017)
24. Shao, C., Ciampaglia, G.L., Varol, O., Yang, K.C., Flammini, A., Menczer, F.: The spread of low-credibility content by social bots. Nat. Commun. 9(1), 4787 (2018)
25. Shu, K., Mahudeswaran, D., Wang, S., Lee, D., Liu, H.: Fakenewsnet: A data repository with news content, social context and dynamic information for studying fake news on social media. arXiv preprint arXiv:1809.01286 (2018)
26. Shu, K., Sliva, A., Wang, S., Tang, J., Liu, H.: Fake news detection on social media: a data mining perspective. ACM SIGKDD Explorations Newsletter 19(1), 22–36 (2017)
27. Tambuscio, M., Ruffo, G., Flammini, A., Menczer, F.: Fact-checking effect on viral hoaxes: a model of misinformation spread in social networks. In: Proceedings of the 24th International Conference on World Wide Web, pp. 977–982. ACM (2015)
28. Vosoughi, S., Roy, D., Aral, S.: The spread of true and false news online. Science 359(6380), 1146–1151 (2018)
29. Wu, Z., Pan, S., Chen, F., Long, G., Zhang, C., Yu, P.S.: A comprehensive survey on graph neural networks. arXiv preprint arXiv:1901.00596 (2019)
30. Xiong, F., Liu, Y.: Opinion formation on social media: an empirical approach. Chaos: An Interdisciplinary J. Nonlinear Sci. 24(1), 013130 (2014)
31. Xiong, F., Liu, Y., Zhang, Z.J., Zhu, J., Zhang, Y.: An information diffusion model based on retweeting mechanism for online social media. Phys. Lett. A 376(30–31), 2103–2108 (2012)

#ArsonEmergency and Australia's "Black Summer": Polarisation and Misinformation on Social Media

Derek Weber[1,2(✉)] , Mehwish Nasim[1,3,5,6] , Lucia Falzon[2,4] ,
and Lewis Mitchell[1,5]

[1] University of Adelaide, Adelaide, South Australia, Australia
{derek.weber,lewis.mitchell}@adelaide.edu.au
[2] Defence Science and Technology Group, Adelaide, Australia
derek.weber@dst.defence.gov.au
[3] Data61, Commonwealth Science and Industry Research Organisation,
Adelaide, Australia
mehwish.nasim@data61.csiro.au
[4] School of Psychological Sciences, University of Melbourne, Melbourne, Australia
lucia.falzon@unimelb.edu.au
[5] ARC Centre of Excellence for Mathematical and Statistical Frontiers,
Adelaide, Australia
[6] Cyber Security Cooperative Research Centre, Adelaide, Australia

Abstract. During the summer of 2019–2020, while Australia suffered unprecedented bushfires across the country, false narratives regarding arson and limited backburning spread quickly on Twitter, particularly using the hashtag *#ArsonEmergency*. Misinformation and bot- and troll-like behaviour were detected and reported by social media researchers and the news soon reached mainstream media. This paper examines the communication and behaviour of two polarised online communities before and after news of the misinformation became public knowledge. Specifically, the *Supporter* community actively engaged with others to spread the hashtag, using a variety of news sources pushing the arson narrative, while the *Opposer* community engaged less, retweeted more, and focused its use of URLs to link to mainstream sources, debunking the narratives and exposing the anomalous behaviour. This influenced the content of the broader discussion. Bot analysis revealed the active accounts were predominantly human, but behavioural and content analysis suggests Supporters engaged in trolling, though both communities used aggressive language.

Keywords: Social media · Information campaigns · Polarisation · Misinformation · Crisis

---

The original version of this chapter was revised: An error in Table 2 was corrected and Section 3.1 and the Conclusion were updated accordingly. The correction to this chapter is available at https://doi.org/10.1007/978-3-030-61841-4_19

© Commonwealth of Australia 2020, corrected publication 2021
M. van Duijn et al. (Eds.): MISDOOM 2020, LNCS 12259, pp. 159–173, 2020.
https://doi.org/10.1007/978-3-030-61841-4_11

1   Introduction

People share an abundance of useful information on social media during a crisis situation [5,6]. This information, if analysed correctly, can rapidly reveal population-level events such as imminent civil unrest, natural disasters, or accidents [26]. Not all content is helpful, however: different entities may try to popularise false narratives using sophisticated social bots and/or humans. The spread of such misinformation not only makes it difficult for analysts to use Twitter data for public benefit [21] but may also encourage large numbers of people to believe false narratives, which may then influence public policy and action, and can be particularly dangerous during crises [18].

This paper presents a case study of the dynamics of misinformation propagation during one such crisis. The 2020 Australian 'Black Summer' bushfires burnt over 16 million hectares, destroyed over 3,500 homes, and caused at least 33 human and a billion animal fatalities[1], and attracted global media attention. We show that:

– Significant Twitter discussion activity accompanied the Australian bushfires, influencing media coverage.
– In the midst of this, narratives of misinformation began to circulate on social media, including that:

• the bushfires were caused by arson;
• preventative backburning efforts were reduced due to green activism;
• Australia commonly experiences such bushfires; and
• climate change is not related to bushfires.

All of these narratives were refuted, e.g., the arson figures being used were incorrect[2], preventative backburning has limited effectiveness[3], the fires are "unprecedented"[4], and climate change is, in fact, increasing the frequency and severity of the fires[5]. The Twitter discussion surrounding the bushfires made use of many hashtags, but according to research by Graham and Keller [13] reported on ZDNet [25], the arson narrative was over-represented on *#ArsonEmergency*, likely created as a counter to the pre-existing *#ClimateEmergency* [2]. Furthermore, their research indicated that *#ArsonEmergency* was being boosted by

---

[1] https://www.abc.net.au/news/2020-02-19/australia-bushfires-how-heat-and-drought-created-a-tinderbox/11976134.

[2] https://www.abc.net.au/radionational/programs/breakfast/victorian-police-reject-claims-bushfires-started-by-arsonists/11857634.

[3] https://www.theguardian.com/australia-news/2020/jan/08/hazard-reduction-is-not-a-panacea-for-bushfire-risk-rfs-boss-says.

[4] The Australian Academy of Science's statement: https://www.science.org.au/news-and-events/news-and-media-releases/statement-regarding-australian-bushfires.

[5] Science Brief, on 14 January 2020, reports on a survey of 57 papers on the matter conducted by researchers from the University of East Anglia, Imperial College, London, Australia's CSIRO, the Univerity of Exeter and the Met Office Hadley Centre, Exeter: https://sciencebrief.org/briefs/wildfires.

bots and trolls. This attracted widespread media attention, with most coverage debunking the arson conspiracy theory. This case thus presents an interesting natural experiment: the nature of the online narrative before the publication of the ZDnet article and then after these conspiracy theories were debunked.

We offer an exploratory mixed-method analysis of the Twitter activity using the term 'ArsonEmergency' around (±7 days) the publication of the ZDNet article, including comparison with another prominent contemporaneous bushfire-related hashtag, #AustraliaFire. A timeline analysis revealed three phases of activity. Social network analysis of retweeting behaviour identifies two polarised groups of Twitter users: those promoting the arson narrative, and those exposing and arguing against it. These polarised groups, along with the unaffiliated accounts, provide a further lens through which to examine the behaviour observed. A content analysis highlights how the different groups used hashtags and other sources to promote their narratives. Finally, a brief analysis of bot-like behaviour then seeks to replicate Graham & Keller's findings [13].

Our contribution is two-fold: 1) we offer an original, focused dataset from Twitter at a critical time period covering two eras in misinformation spread[6]; and 2) insight into the evolution of a misinformation campaign relating to the denial of climate change science and experience in dealing with bushfires.

1.1 Related Work

The study of Twitter during crises is well established [5,6,11], and has provided recommendations to governments and social media platforms alike regarding its exploitation for timely community outreach. The continual presence of trolling and bot behaviour diverts attention and can confuse the public at times of political significance [7,15,21,22] as well as creating online community-based conflict [8,16] and polarisation [12].

Misinformation on social media has also been studied [17]. In particular, the disinformation campaign against the White Helmets rescue group in Syria is useful to consider here [24]. Two clear corresponding clusters of pro- and anti-White Helmet Twitter accounts were identified and used to frame an investigation of how external references to YouTube videos and channels compared with videos embedded in Twitter. They found the anti-White Helmet narrative was consistently sustained through "sincere activists" and concerted efforts from Russian and alternative news sites. These particularly exploited YouTube to spread critical videos, while the pro-White Helmet activity relied on the White Helmets' own online activities and sporadic media attention. This interaction between supporter and detractor groups and the media may offer insight into activity surrounding similar crises.

1.2 Research Questions

Motivated by our observations, we propose the following research questions about Twitter activity during the 2019–20 Australian bushfire period:

---

[6] https://github.com/weberdc/socmed_sna.

RQ1. To what extent can an online misinformation community be discerned?

RQ2. How did the spread of misinformation differ between the identified phases, and did the spread of the hashtag #ArsonEmergency differ from other emergent discussions (e.g., #AustraliaFire)?

RQ3. How does the online behaviour of those who accept climate science differ from those who refute or question it? How was it affected by media coverage exposing how the #ArsonEmergency hashtag was being used?

RQ4. To what degree was the spread of misinformation facilitated or aided by troll and/or automated bot behaviour?

In the remainder of this paper, we describe our mixed-method analysis and the datasets used. A timeline analysis is followed by the polarisation analysis. The revealed polarised communities are compared from behavioural and content perspectives, as well as through bot analysis. Answers to the research questions are summarised and we conclude with observations and proposals for further study of polarised communities.

2   Dataset and Timeline

The primary dataset, 'ArsonEmergency', consists of 27,456 tweets containing this term posted by 12,872 unique accounts from 31 December 2019 to 17 January 2020. The tweets were obtained using Twitter's Standard search Application Programming Interface (API)[7] by combining the results of searches conducted with Twarc[8] on 8, 12, and 17 January. As a contrast, the 'AusFire' dataset comprises tweets containing the term 'AustraliaFire' over the same period, made from the results of Twarc searches on 8 and 17 January. 'AusFire' contains 111,966 tweets by 96,502 accounts. Broader searches using multiple related terms were not conducted due to time constraints and in the interests of comparison with Graham and Keller's findings [13]. Due to the use of Twint[9] in that study, differences in dataset were possible, but expected to be minimal. Differences in datasets collected simultaneously with different tools have been previously noted [27]. Live filtering was also not employed, as the research started after Graham and Keller's findings were reported.

This study focuses on about a week of Twitter activity before and after the publication of the ZDNet article [25]. Prior to its publication, the narratives that arson was the primary cause of the bushfires and that fuel load caused the extremity of the blazes were well known in the conservative media [2]. The ZDnet article was published at 6:03am GMT (5:03pm AEST) on 7 January 2020, and was then reported more widely in the MSM morning news, starting around 13 hours later. We use these temporal markers to define three dataset phases:

– *Phase 1*: Before 6am GMT, 7 January 2020;

---

[7] https://developer.twitter.com/en/docs/tweets/search/api-reference/get-search-tweets.

[8] https://github.com/DocNow/twarc.

[9] https://github.com/twintproject/twint.

– *Phase 2*: From 6am to 7pm GMT, 7 January 2020; and
– *Phase 3*: After 7pm GMT, 7 January 2020.

Figure 1 shows the number of tweets posted each hour in the 'ArsonEmergency' dataset, and highlights the phases and notable events including: the publication of the ZDNet article; when the story hit the MSM; the time at which the Rural Fire Service (RFS) and Victorian Police countered the narratives promoted on the *#ArsonEmergency* hashtag; and the clear subsequent day/night cycle. The RFS and Victorian Police announcements countered the false narratives promoted in political discourse in the days prior.

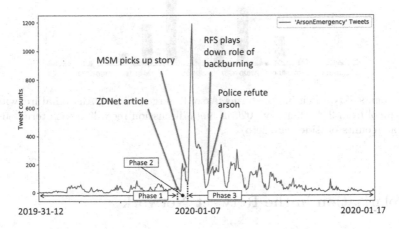

Fig. 1. Tweet activity in the 'ArsonEmergency' dataset, annotated with notable real-world events and the identified phases.

Since late September 2020, Australian and international media had reported on the bushfires around Australia, including stories and photos drawn directly from social media, as those caught in the fires shared their experiences. No one hashtag had emerged to dominate the online conversation and many were in use, including *#AustraliaFires*, *#ClimateEmergency*, *#bushfires*, and *#AustraliaIsBurning*.

The use of *#ArsonEmergency* was limited in Phase 1, with the busiest hour having around 100 tweets, but there was an influx of new accounts in Phase 2. Of all 927 accounts active in Phase 2 (responsible for 1,207 tweets), 824 (88.9%) of them had not posted in Phase 1 (which had 2,061 active accounts). Content analyses revealed 1,014 (84%) of the tweets in Phase 2 were retweets, more than 60% of which were retweets promoting the ZDNet article and the findings it reported. Closer examination of the timeline revealed that the majority of the discussion occurred between 9pm and 2am AEST, possibly inflated by a single tweet referring to the ZDNet article (at 10:19 GMT), which was retweeted 357 times. In Phase 3, more new accounts joined the conversation, but the day/night cycle indicates that the majority of discussion was local to Australia (or at least its major timezones).

The term 'ArsonEmergency' (sans '#') was used for the Twarc searches, rather than '#ArsonEmergency', to capture tweets that did not include the hashtag but were relevant to the discussion. Of the 27,546 tweets in the 'Arson-Emergency' dataset, only 100 did not use it with the '#' symbol, and only 34 of the 111,966 'AustraliaFire' tweets did the same. Figure 2 shows the emergence of the reflexive discussion generated by those conversing about the discussion on *#ArsonEmergency* without promulgating the hashtag itself.

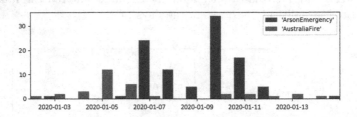

Fig. 2. Counts of tweets using the terms 'ArsonEmergency' and 'AustraliaFire' without a '#' symbol from 2–15 January 2020 in meta-discussion regarding each term's use as a hashtag (counts outside were zero).

3   Polarisation in the Retweet Network

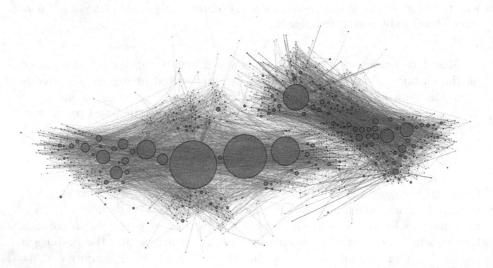

Fig. 3. Polarised retweets graph about the arson theory. Left(blue): *Opposers*, right(red): *Supporters* of the arson narrative. Nodes represent users. An edge between two nodes means one retweeted the tweet of the other. Node size corresponds to degree centrality (Color figure online).

There is no agreement on whether retweets imply endorsement or alignment. Metaxas *et al.* [19] studied retweeting behaviour in detail by conducting user surveys and studying over 100 relevant papers referring to retweets. Their findings conclude that when users retweet, it indicates interest and agreement as well as trust in not only the message content but also in the originator of the tweet. This opinion is not shared by some celebrities and journalists who put a disclaimer on their profile: "retweets ≠ endorsements". Metaxas *et al.* [19] also indicated that inclusion of hashtags strengthens the agreement, especially for political topics. Other motivations, such as the desire to signal to others to form bonds and manage appearances [10], serve to further imply that even if retweets are not endorsements, we can assume they represent agreement or an appeal to likemindedness at the very least.

We conducted an exploratory analysis on the retweets graph shown in Fig. 3. The nodes indicate Twitter accounts. An edge between two accounts shows that one retweeted a tweet of the other. Using conductance cutting [4], we discovered two distinct well-connected communities, with a very low number of edges between the two communities. Next, we selected the top ten accounts from each community based upon the degree centrality (most retweeted), manually checked their profiles, and hand labelled them as *Supporters* and *Opposers* of the arson narrative[10]. The accounts have been coloured accordingly in Fig. 3: red nodes are accounts that promoted the narrative, while blue nodes are accounts that opposed them.

#ArsonEmergency had different connotations for each community. Supporters used the hashtag to reinforce their existing belief about climate change, while Opposers used this hashtag to refute the arson theory. The arson theory was a topic on which people held strong opinions resulting in the formation of the two strongly connected communities. Such polarised communities typically do not admit much information flow between them, hence members of such communities are repeatedly exposed to similar narratives, which further strengthens their existing beliefs. Such closed communities are also known as *echo chambers*, and they limit people's information space. The retweets tend to coalesce within communities, as has been shown for Facebook comments [20].

These two groups, Supporters and Opposers, and those users unaffiliated with either group, are used to frame the remainder of the analysis in this paper.

3.1 Behaviour

User behaviour on Twitter can be examined through the features used to connect with others and through content. Here we consider how active the different groups were across the phases of the collection, and then how that activity manifested itself in the use of mentions, hashtags, URLs, replies, quotes and retweets.

Considering each phase (Table 1) Supporters used *#ArsonEmergency* nearly fifty times more often than Opposers, which accords with Graham & Keller's

---

[10] Labelling was conducted by the first two authors independently and then compared.

Table 1. Activity of the polarised retweeting accounts, by interaction type broken down by phase.

	Group		Tweets	Accounts	Hashtags	Mentions	Quotes	Replies	Retweets	URLs
Phase 1	Supporters	Raw count	1,573	360	2,257	2,621	185	356	938	405
		Per account	4.369	—	1.435	1.666	0.118	0.226	0.596	0.257
	Opposers	Raw count	33	21	100	35	8	2	20	9
		Per account	1.571	—	3.030	1.061	0.242	0.061	0.606	0.273
Phase 2	Supporters	Raw count	121	77	226	159	11	29	74	24
		Per account	1.571	—	1.868	1.314	0.091	0.240	0.612	0.198
	Opposers	Raw count	327	172	266	476	7	14	288	31
		Per account	1.901	—	0.813	1.456	0.021	0.043	0.881	0.095
Phase 3	Supporters	Raw count	5,278	474	7,414	7,407	593	1,159	3,212	936
		Per account	11.135	—	1.405	1.403	0.112	0.220	0.609	0.177
	Opposers	Raw count	3,227	585	3,997	3,617	124	95	2,876	359
		Per account	5.516	—	1.239	1.121	0.038	0.029	0.891	0.111
Overall	Supporters	Raw count	6,972	497	9,897	10,187	789	1,544	4,224	1,365
		Per account	14.028	—	1.420	1.461	0.113	0.221	0.606	0.196
	Opposers	Raw count	3,587	593	4,363	4,128	139	111	3,184	399
		Per account	6.049	—	1.216	1.151	0.039	0.031	0.888	0.111

findings that the false narratives were significantly more prevalent on that hashtag compared with others in use at the time [13, 25]. In Phase 2, during the Australian night, Opposers countered with three times as many tweets as Supporters, including fewer hashtags, more retweets, and half the number of replies, demonstrating different behaviour to Supporters, which actively used the hashtag in conversations. Content analysis confirmed this to be the case. This is evidence that Supporters wanted to promote the hashtag to promote the narrative. Interestingly, Supporters, having been relatively quiet in Phase 2, produced 64% more tweets in Phase 3 than Opposers, using proportionately more of all interactions except retweeting, and many more replies, quotes, and tweets spreading the narrative by using multiple hashtags, URLs and mentions. In short, Opposers tended to rely more on retweets, while Supporters engaged directly and were more active in the longer phases.

The concentration of narrative from certain voices requires attention. To consider this, Table 2 shows the degree to which accounts were retweeted by the different groups by phase and overall. Unaffiliated accounts relied on a smaller pool of accounts to retweet than both Supporters and Opposers in each phase and overall, which is reasonable to expect as the majority of Unaffiliated activity occurred in Phase 3, once the story reached the mainstream news, and therefore had access to tweets about the story from the media and prominent commentators.

Table 2. Retweeting activity in the dataset, by phase and group.

Phase	Supporters			Opposers			Unaffiliated		
	Retweets	Retweeted accounts	Retweets per account	Retweets	Retweeted accounts	Retweets per account	Retweets	Retweeted accounts	Retweets per account
1	938	77	12.182	20	8	2.500	1,659	105	15.800
2	74	21	3.524	288	31	9.290	652	60	10.867
3	3,212	290	11.076	2,876	228	12.614	11,807	532	22.194

Of the top 41 retweeted accounts, which retweeted 100 times or more in the dataset, 17 were Supporters and 20 Opposers. Supporters were retweeted 5,487 times (322.8 retweets per account), while Opposers were retweeted 8,833 times (441.7 times per account). Together, affiliated accounts contributed 93.3% of the top 41's 15,350 retweets, in a dataset with 21,526 retweets overall, and the top 41 accounts were retweeted far more often than most. This pattern was also apparent in the 25 accounts most retweeted by Unaffiliated accounts in Phase 3 (accounts retweeted at least 100 times): 8 were Supporters and 14 were Opposers. Thus Supporters and Opposers made up the majority of the most retweeted accounts, and arguably influenced the discussion more than Unaffiliated accounts.

3.2 Content

When contrasting the content of the two affiliated groups, we considered the hashtags and external URLs used. A hashtag can provide a proxy for a tweet's topic, and an external URL can refer a tweet's reader to further information relevant to the tweet, and therefore tweets that use the same URLs and hashtags can be considered related.

Hashtags. To discover *how* hashtags were used, rather than simply *which* were used, we developed co-mention graphs (Fig. 4). Each node is a hashtag, sized by degree centrality; edges represent an account using both hashtags (not necessarily in the same tweet); the edge weight represents the number of such accounts in the dataset. Nodes are coloured according to cluster detected with the widely used Louvain method [3]. We removed the *#ArsonEmergency* hashtag (as nearly each tweet in the dataset contained it) as well as edges having weight less than 5. Opposers used a smaller set of hashtags, predominantly linking *#AustraliaFires* with *#ClimateEmergency* and a hashtag referring to a well-known publisher. In contrast, Supporters used a variety of hashtags in a variety of combinations, mostly focusing on terms related to 'fire', but only a few with 'arson' or 'hoax', and linking to *#auspol* and *#ClimateEmergency*. Manual review of Supporter tweets included many containing only a string of hashtags, unlike the Opposer tweets. Notably, the *#ClimateChangeHoax* node has a similar degree to the *#ClimateChangeEmergency* node, indicating Supporters' skepticism of the science, but perhaps also attempts by Supporters to join or merge the communities.

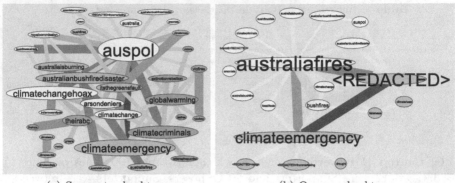

(a) Supporter hashtags.   (b) Opposer hashtags.

Fig. 4. Co-mentioned hashtags of Supporters and Opposers. Hashtag nodes are linked when five or more accounts tweeted both hashtags, and are coloured by cluster. < REDACTED> hashtags include identifying information. Heavy edges (with high weight) are thicker and darker.

Manual inspection of Supporter tweets revealed that replies often consisted solely of "*#ArsonEmergency*" (one Supporter replied to an Opposer 26 times in under 9 mins with a tweet just consisting of the hashtag, although in six of the tweets @mentions of other influential Twitter accounts were also included). This kind of behaviour, in addition to inflammatory language in other Supporter replies, suggests a degree of aggression, though aggressive language was also noted among Opposers. Only 1.7% of Opposer tweets included more than 5 hashtags, while 2.8% of Supporter ones did, compared with 2.1% unaffiliated.

External URLs. URLs in tweets can be categorised as *internal* or *external*. Internal URLs refer to other tweets in retweets or quotes , while external URLs are often included to highlight something about their content, e.g., as a source to support a claim. By analysing the URLs, it is possible to gauge the intent of the tweet's author by considering the reputation of the source or the argument offered.

We categorised[11] the top ten URLs used most by Supporters, Opposers, and the unaffiliated across the three phases, and found a significant difference between the groups. URLs were categorised into four categories:

NARRATIVE. Articles used to emphasise the conspiracy narratives by prominently reporting arson figures and fuel load discussions.

CONSPIRACY. Articles and web sites that take extreme positions on climate change (typically arguing against predominant scientific opinion).

DEBUNKING. News articles providing authoritative information about the bushfires and related misinformation on social media.

OTHER Other web pages.

---

[11] Categorisation was conducted by two authors and confirmed by the others.

URLs posted by Opposers were concentrated in Phase 3 and were all in the DEBUNKING category, with nearly half attributed to Indiana University's Hoaxy service [23], and nearly a quarter referring to the original ZDNet article [25] (Fig. 5a). In contrast, Supporters used many URLs in Phases 1 and 3, focusing mostly on articles emphasising the arson narrative, but with references to a number of climate change denial or right wing blogs and news sites (Fig. 5b).

Figure 5(c) shows that the media coverage changed the content of the unaffiliated discussion, from articles emphasising the arson narratives in Phase 1 to Opposer-aligned articles in Phase 3. Although the activity of Supporters in Phase 3 increased significantly, the unaffiliated members appeared to refer to Opposer-aligned external URLs much more often.

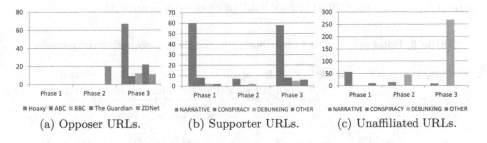

(a) Opposer URLs.   (b) Supporter URLs.   (c) Unaffiliated URLs.

Fig. 5. URLs used by Opposers, Supporters and unaffiliated accounts.

Supporters used many more URLs than Opposers overall (1,365 to 399) and nearly twice as many external URLs (390 to 212). Supporters seemed to use many different URLs in Phase 3 and overall, but focused much more on particular URLs in Phase 1. Of the total number of unique URLs used in Phase 3 and overall, 263 and 390, respectively, only 77 (29.3%) and 132 (33.8%) appeared in the top ten, implying a wide variety of URLs were used. In contrast, in Phase 1, 72 of 117 appeared in the top ten (61.5%), similar to Opposers' 141 of 212 (66.5%), implying a greater focus on specific sources of information. In brief, it appears Opposers overall and Supporters in Phase 1 were focused in their choice of sources, but by Phase 3, Supporters had expanded their range considerably.

4   Botness Analysis

The analysis reported in ZDNet [25] indicated widespread bot-like behaviour by using `tweetbotornot`[12]. Our re-analysis of this finding had two goals: 1) attempt to replicate Graham & Keller's findings in Phase 1 of our dataset; and 2) examine the contribution of bot-like accounts detected in Phase 1 in the other phases. Specifically, we considered the questions:

---

[12] https://github.com/mkearney/tweetbotornot.

– Does another bot detection system find similar levels of bot-like behaviour?
– Does the behaviour of any bots from Phase 1 change in Phases 2 and 3?

We evaluated 2,512 or 19.5% of the accounts in the dataset using Botometer [9], including all Supporter and Opposer accounts, plus all accounts that posted at least three tweets either side of Graham and Keller's analysis reaching the MSM.

Botometer [9] is an ensemble bot classifier for Twitter accounts, relying on over a thousand features drawn from six categories. It includes a "Complete Automation Probability" (CAP), a Bayesian-informed probability that the account in question is "fully automated". This does not accommodate hybrid accounts [14] and only uses English training data [21], leading some researchers to use conservative ranges of CAP scores for high confidence that an account is human (<0.2) or bot (>0.6) [22]. We adopt that categorisation.

Table 3. Botness scores and contribution to the discussion across the phases.

Category	CAP	Total	Active accounts			Tweets contributed		
			Phase 1	Phase 2	Phase 3	Phase 1	Phase 2	Phase 3
Human	0.0–0.2	2,426	898	438	1,931	2,213	674	11,700
Undecided	0.2–0.6	66	20	6	56	28	11	304
Bot	0.6–1.0	20	9	4	11	23	6	84

Table 3 shows that the majority of accounts were human and contributed more than any automated or potentially automated accounts. This contrast with the reported findings [25] may be due to a number of reasons. The CAP score is focused on non-hybrid, English accounts, whereas `tweetbotornot` may provide a more general score, taking into account troll-like behaviour. The content and behaviour analysis discussed above certainly indicates Supporters engaged more with replies and quotes, consistent with other observed trolling behaviour [16] or "sincere activists" [24]. The collection tool used, Twint, may have obtained different tweets to Twarc, as it explicitly avoids Twitter's APIs. It is possible its avoidance of the API reveals more bot-like behaviour. Finally, it is unclear what Graham and Keller's collection strategy was; if it focused on the particular accounts which drew their attention to #ArsonEmergency to begin with, it may not have included the wider range of behaviour evident in our dataset.

5 Discussion

We are now well-placed to address our research questions:

RQ1. *Discerning a misinformation-sharing community.* Analysis revealed two distinct polarised communities. The content posted by the most influential accounts in these communities shows Supporters were responsible for the majority of arson-related content, while Opposers countered the arson narrative.

RQ2. *Differences in the spread of misinformation across phases and other discussions.* Considering URL and hashtag use in Phase 1 and 3, while the number of active Supporters grew from 360 to 474, the number of unique external URLs they used more than doubled, from 117 to 263. This was possibly due to the increased traffic on *#ArsonEmergency*. The number of hashtags increased from 182 hashtags used 2,257 times to 505 hashtags used 7,414 times. This implies Supporters attempted to connect *#ArsonEmergency* with other hashtag-based communities. In contrast, Opposer activity increased from 33 hashtags used 100 times to 182 hashtags used 3,997 times, but Fig. 4b shows Opposers focused the majority of their discussion on a comparatively small number of hashtags.

RQ3. *Behavioural differences over time and the impact of media coverage.* Supporters were more active in Phase 1 and 3 and used more types of interaction than Opposers, especially replies and quotes, implying a significant degree of engagement, whether as trolls or as "sincere activists" [24]. Opposers and Supporters made up the majority of retweeted accounts overall, and made up 22 of the top 25 accounts retweeted by una liated accounts in Phase 3. Supporters' use of interaction types remained steady from Phase 1 to 3. While behaviour remained relatively similar, activity grew for both groups after the story reached the MSM. The vast majority of accounts shared articles debunking the false narratives. The ZDNet article also affected activity, spurring Opposers and others to share the analysis it reported.

RQ4. *Support from bots and trolls.* We found very few bots, but aggressive troll-like behaviour was observed in the Supporter community. Aggressive language was observed in both affiliated groups. Distinguishing deliberate baiting from honest enthusiasm (even with swearing), however, is non-trivial [24].

The *#ArsonEmergency* activity on Twitter in early 2020 provides a unique microcosm to study the growth of a misinformation campaign before and after it was widely known. Our study reveals the following:

- Two clear polarised communities with distinct behaviour patterns and use of content were present.
- Supporters were more active and more engaged. Opposers relied on retweeting more, and focused on a few prominent hashtags, while Supporters used many. This was possibly to widely promote their message, or due to non-Australian contributors being unfamiliar with which hashtags to use for an Australian audience.
- The majority of Phase 1 *#ArsonEmergency* discussion referred to articles relevant to the arson narratives, but after the story reached the MSM, only the Supporter community continued to use such links.
- The majority of unaffiliated accounts shifted focus from CCD narrative-related articles in Phase 1 to debunking sites and articles in Phase 3. It is unclear whether the change in behaviour was driven by accounts changing opinion or the influx of new accounts.
- The *#ArsonEmergency* growth rate followed a pattern similar to another related hashtag that appeared shortly before it (*#AustraliaFire*).

– The influence of bot accounts appears limited when analysed with Botometer [9]. It classified 0.8% (20 of 2,512) of accounts as bots, and 96.6% (2,426 of 2,512) of the remaining accounts confidently as human. Graham and Keller had found an even spread of bot scores, with an average score over 0.5. Only 20% of accounts had a score ≤ 0.2 and 46% ≥ 0.6 [25].

Further research is required to examine social and interaction structures formed by groups involved in spreading misinformation to learn more about how such groups operate and better address the challenge they pose to society. Future work will draw more on social network analysis based on interaction patterns and content [1] as well as developing a richer, more nuanced understanding of the Supporter community itself, including more content and behaviour analysis.

Acknowledgment. The work has been partially supported by the Cyber Security Research Centre Limited whose activities are partially funded by the Australian Government's Cooperative Research Centres Programme.

Ethics. All data was collected, stored and analysed in accordance with Protocols H-2018-045 and #170316 as approved by the University of Adelaide's human research ethics committee.

References

1. Bagrow, J.P., Liu, X., Mitchell, L.: Information flow reveals prediction limits in online social activity. Nat. Hum. Behav. **3**(2), 122–128 (2019)
2. Barry, P.: Broadcast 3rd February 2020: News Corps Fire Fight. Media Watch, Australian Broadcasting Corporation, 2020(1), February 2020
3. Blondel, V.D., Guillaume, J.-L., Lambiotte, R., Lefebvre, E.: Fast unfolding of communities in large networks. J. Stat. Mech. Theory Experiment **2008**(10), P10008 (2008)
4. Brandes, U., Gaertler, M., Wagner, D.: Engineering graph clustering: Models and experimental evaluation. ACM J. Experimental Algorithmics, **12**, 1.1:1–1.1:26 (2007)
5. Bruns, A., Burgess, J.: #qldfloods and @QPSMedia: Crisis communication on Twitter in the 2011 South East Queensland Floods. Research Report 48241, ARC Centre of Excellence for Creative Industries and Innovation, January 2012
6. Bruns, A., Liang, Y.E.: Tools and methods for capturing Twitter data during natural disasters. First Monday **17**(4), (2012)
7. CREST. Russian interference and influence measures following the 2017 UK terrorist attacks. Policy Brief 17–81-2, Centre for Research and Evidence on Security Threats, Cardiff University, December 2017
8. Datta, S., Adar, E.: Extracting inter-community conflicts in Reddit. In: ICWSM, pp. 146–157. AAAI Press (2019)
9. Davis, C.A., Varol, O., Ferrara, E., Flammini, A., Menczer, F.: BotOrNot: A system to evaluate social bots. In: WWW (Companion Volume), pp. 273–274. ACM (2016)
10. Falzon, L., McCurrie, C., Dunn, J.: Representation and analysis of Twitter activity: A dynamic network perspective. In: ASONAM, pp. 1183–1190. ACM (2017)

11. Flew, T., Bruns, A., Burgess, J., Crawford, K., Shaw, F.: Social media and its impact on crisis communication: Case studies of Twitter use in emergency management in Australia and New Zealand. In: 2013 ICA Shanghai Regional Conference: Communication and Social Transformation, November 2014

12. Garimella, V.R.K., Morales, G.D.F., Gionis, A., Mathioudakis, M.: Polarization on social media. In: WWW (Tutorial Volume). ACM (2018)

13. Graham, T., Keller, T.R.: Bushfires, bots and arson claims: Australia flung in the global disinformation spotlight, January 2020. https://theconversation.com/bushfires-bots-and-arson-claims-australia-flung-in-the-global-disinformation-spotlight-129556. (Accessed on 2020-02-07)

14. Grimme, C., Assenmacher, D., Adam, L.: Changing perspectives: Is it sufficient to detect social bots? In: Meiselwitz, G. (ed.) SCSM 2018. LNCS, vol. 10913, pp. 445–461. Springer, Cham (2018). https://doi.org/10.1007/978-3-319-91521-0_32

15. Keller, F.B., Schoch, D., Stier, S., Yang, J.: How to manipulate social media: Analyzing political astroturfing using ground truth data from South Korea. In: ICWSM, pp. 564–567. AAAI Press (2017)

16. Kumar, S., Hamilton, W.L., Leskovec, J., Jurafsky, D.: Community interaction and conflict on the Web. In: WWW, pp. 933–943. ACM (2018)

17. Kumar, S., Shah, N.: False information on web and social media: A survey. CoRR, abs/1804.08559 (2018)

18. Kušen, E., Strembeck, M.: You talkin' to me? Exploring human/bot communication patterns during riot events. Inf. Process. Manage. **57**(1), 102126 (2020)

19. Metaxas, P.T., Mustafaraj, E., Wong, K., Zeng, L., O'Keefe, M., Finn, S.: What do retweets indicate? Results from user survey and meta-review of research. In: ICWSM, pp. 658–661. AAAI Press (2015)

20. Nasim, M., Ilyas, M.U., Rextin, A., Nasim, N.: On commenting behavior of Facebook users. In: HT, pp. 179–183. ACM (2013)

21. Nasim, M., Nguyen, A., Lothian, N., Cope, R., Mitchell, L.: Real-time detection of content polluters in partially observable Twitter networks. In: WWW (Companion Volume), pp. 1331–1339. ACM (2018)

22. Rizoiu, M.-A., Graham, T., Zhang, R., Zhang, Y., Ackland, R., Xie, L.: #DebateNight: The role and influence of socialbots on Twitter during the 1st 2016 U.S. Presidential debate. In: ICWSM, pp. 300–309. AAAI Press (2018)

23. Shao, C., Ciampaglia, G.L., Flammini, A., Menczer, F.: Hoaxy: A platform for tracking online misinformation. In: WWW (Companion Volume), pp. 745–750. ACM (2016)

24. Starbird, K., Wilson, T.: Cross-Platform Disinformation Campaigns: Lessons Learned and Next Steps. Harvard Kennedy School Misinformation Review, January 2020

25. Stilgherrian. Twitter bots and trolls promote conspiracy theories about Australian bushfires — ZDNet, January 2020. https://www.zdnet.com/article/twitter-bots-and-trolls-promote-conspiracy-theories-about-australian-bushfires/. Accessed 28 Jan 2020

26. Tuke, J., et al.: Pachinko Prediction: A Bayesian method for event prediction from social media data. Inf. Process. Manage. **57**(2), 102147 (2020)

27. Weber, D., Nasim, M., Mitchell, L., Falzon, L.: A method to evaluate the reliability of social media data for social network analysis. In: ASONAM, ACM (2020). Accepted

How Identity and Uncertainty Affect
Online Social Influence
An Agent-Based Approach

Christina Mason[✉], Peter van der Putten, and Max van Duijn

Media Technology, Leiden Institute of Advanced Computer Science (LIACS),
University of Leiden, Snellius Building, Room 122, Niels Bohrweg 1, 2333 CA Leiden,
The Netherlands
c.h.mason@umail.leidenuniv.nl

Abstract. Computer simulations have been used to model psychological and sociological phenomena in order to provide insight into how
they affect human behavior and population-wide systems. In this study,
three agent-based simulations (ABSs) were developed to model opinion dynamics in an online social media context. The main focus was
to test the effects of 'social identity' and 'certainty' on social influence. When humans interact, they influence each other's opinions and
behavior. It was hypothesized that the influence of other agents based
on ingroup/outgroup perceptions can lead to extremism and polarization under conditions of uncertainty. The first two simulations isolated
social identity and certainty respectively to see how social influence would
shape the attitude formation of the agents, and the opinion distribution
by extension. Problems with previous models were remedied to some
extent, but not fully resolved. The third combined the two to see if the
limitations of both designs would be ameliorated with added complexity. The combination proved to be moderating, and while stable opinion
clusters form, extremism and polarization do not develop in the system
without added forces.

Keywords: Social influence · Social identity · Certainty · Opinion
dynamics · Online social networks · Facebook · Agent-based models ·
Attitude formation · Abelson diversity problem · Polarization ·
Extremism · Misinformation

1 Introduction

On social media websites like Facebook, information is disseminated differently
from traditional media outlets, as it is negotiated by a network of "friends".
This means that users' personal social networks affect what information they
are exposed to. As a consequence, social influence has become a major factor
in how information is distributed in this context, affecting societal and political
opinions.

© Springer Nature Switzerland AG 2020
M. van Duijn et al. (Eds.): MISDOOM 2020, LNCS 12259, pp. 174–190, 2020.
https://doi.org/10.1007/978-3-030-61841-4_12

Social influence is the process by which people adjust their opinions based on their interactions with other people [1]. This study aims to explore social influence insofar as social identity and uncertainty contribute to it. This is conceptually driven by the idea that attitudes[1] are embedded in a social context, and that people base them around their social ties [2]. Furthermore, their susceptibility to influence is mediated by how certain they feel about their own views, with less certain agents being more vulnerable to changing their opinion [3]. The key aim of this study is to see if these two factors in a social media communication structure will affect the extent to which agents are socially influenced in their attitude formation. Attitude formation is the process by which an individual goes from unstable, ambivalent or ambiguous attitudes about a certain subject to a stable opinion. Once an attitude is formed, it becomes the standard by which an individual uses to evaluate the attitudes of others [4].

Humans form groups based on their social identity. In this study, social identity is operationalized as the set of groups an individual subscribes to, and includes demographic traits like gender, race, and nationality but also cultural traits such as ethnicity, religion, and political affiliation (cf. [5]). It is assumed that group structures affect how information is distributed. Therefore social identity is used as a variable to see what effect it has on system-wide opinion dynamics. Uncertainty refers to the confidence with which an agent holds an opinion, and it is shown to be affected by group membership [2,6]. Group membership is an important concept driving social influence, because people are more likely to be influenced by those who they consider to have the same group membership as themselves, or their ingroup. Conversely, those who identify as a different social category are considered outgroup members and are less influential [7].

While some models have combined uncertainty and social identity [8], the context of their social interactions are dyadic (an interaction between two agents), unlike online social networks. Multiadic communication (one agent communicating to many other agents at once), which is how information is shared on Facebook, has not been extensively studied. While fewer studies have modeled online social networks [9,10], they have not taken into account the specific factors studied here. Furthermore, simulations of extremism and polarization often insert extremist agents into the population, suggesting that extremism does not arise from the same cognitive motivations held by the rest of the population [10,11]. In this study, it is assumed that this is not necessarily the case: it is tested if extremism can arise from these models without inserting a few agents who perpetuate it with unique behaviors.

An important motivation for studying social influence is that it can add to our understanding of the problem of 'fake news' and potentially inform future counter strategies. If agents are vulnerable to social influence, injecting misinformation into a social network can lead to large-scale information disorders, such as the emergence and persistence of polarization and extremism [12,13]. It is estimated that the average American encountered between one and three fake

---

[1] In the literature, 'attitude' and 'opinion' are often used interchangeably.

articles daily in the month before the 2016 presidential election, with the vast majority reported being seen on Facebook [12]. The fact that Russia has used Facebook as a propaganda tool for political influence demonstrates the severity of the problem and the great need for research into helping to understand the dynamics of how information influences peoples' attitudes. Furthermore, Facebook networks, like real-world networks, can be highly segregated [14], contributing to the formation of small groups who communicate among each other with little or no exposure to contrasting opinions (so-called echo chambers), which compound the problem of the spread and circulation of misinformation. The models discussed in this paper are based on the communication structure of such online social media sites. Section 2 will discuss previous agent-based models of opinion dynamics. Subsequently, Sect. 3 will give an overview of the present study while Sects. 4, 5 and 6 will describe the three models developed for this study in detail, with the results of each model following their description. Finally, Sect. 7 provides a discussion of the findings from all three models. It is beyond the scope of this paper to compare the conclusions drawn based on the models with real-world data. However, in the final section various leads for future research along such lines are discussed.

2   Background

2.1   Modelling Opinion Dynamics

The typical way of modelling opinion dynamics in ABMs is using a continuous opinion model, where opinions are represented on a continuous scale (say, between 0 and 1), and the similarity between any two opinions is defined by how close they are on the continuum. This allows for social influence by agent's pulling (or pushing) each others opinions along the spectrum through interaction according to the rules of the model. This continuum represents moderate opinions in the center, and extremist views on either end [15,16]. When combining social influence and opinion dynamics, these models have four potentials for distributing opinions: consensus, polarization, strong diversity or weak diversity. Consensus is agreement on one opinion, and polarization on two opposing opinions. Strong diversity refers to the representation of many opinions along the spectrum, and weak diversity is so-called "opinion clustering", where only several opinions are represented [15].

The fundamental problem with this type of representation is the so-called Abelson's Diversity Puzzle, which says that social influence represented on a spectrum with opinions being pulled towards each other will always lead to consensus unless there are perfectly separate agents who enact zero influence on one another [17,18]. In a highly connected world it is unreasonable to assume that there are entirely isolated groups of individuals who receive no influence from other groups [19], so there must be another explanation for the persistence of a diversity of attitudes in connected networks like Facebook.

2.2 Solutions in Modelling

The most prominent and perhaps successful solution to this problem is the bounded confidence model [20,21]. Bounded confidence models assign 'boundaries' between what agents can be influenced by who and in what direction. Agents have an opinion and a threshold (the 'bound of confidence') on either side of their opinion, where if another agent's opinion is within this threshold, then it can be influenced, if it is outside, it can no longer be influenced. Relative Agreement Models are an augmentation on this, where the amount of agreement between agents will determine the extent of the influence, and agents with lower thresholds (equated with less "uncertainty" surrounding their opinion) will proportionately have more influence in the model [21,22]. This is taken to be a more faithful representation of real influence, because influence is proportional to the certainty of that agent (and not a binary only taking account the distance of opinion), so that confident agents can be more convincing despite how different their opinion is from a less certain agent [22].

There are two major issues with these models. Firstly, if there is even a slight probability that an agent will influence another agent outside of its bound of confidence, the system degrades to consensus (Fig. 1) [23]. Secondly, the clustering of agents are a mathematical necessity determined by their initialized distance from each other and agents only interact on the basis of this distance, which is unrealistically oversimplified even for a reductive model of human behavior.

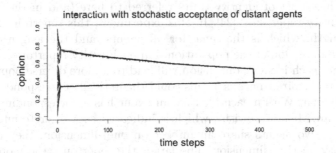

Fig. 1. Probability of acceptance outside of bounds of confidence of .0001 will eventually lead to consensus (from [23]).

3   Present Study

The models described here are also models of social influence, but social influence is mediated by social identity and certainty. Three models were developed for experimentation. In the first model, instead of agents forming groups because of attitude proximity (as with the BC model), they will form groups based on similarity of social identity, following the identity repertoire construct [24]. The second model takes the BC model as is, but uses certainty as a negotiator for group formation as well as stochastic noise, to see if this affects the mathematical rigidity of the original model. Finally, the two models are combined to see if a combination of them creates a more faithful representation of attitude formation, and see what tweaking the parameters of this system results in. If it is possible for stable opinion clustering to form (that is, a heterogeneous distribution) given the Abelson Diversity Problem, can extremism or polarization be modelled by the design of these models given the variables in question?

4   Model 1: Social Identity

This model relies conceptually on the idea of ingroup/outgroup perceptions, where an agent can only be influenced by another agent if they are perceived of as their ingroup. What is being manipulated here is how many identity dimensions agents are comparing themselves on, and how many possible identities exist within these dimensions. The combination of these two factors determines the composition of the population, and therefore how diverse it is. The goal here is to see if there is some combination where ingroup sizes will facilitate clustering, but not into groups of agents who share all traits.

4.1   Design

Each agent has a set of identity traits referred to here (and in the literature) as their 'identity repertoire' [24]. In this experiment, this repertoire is a set of arbitrary length, which is the same for all agents, and the length of the set affects the composition of the population. Larger identity repertoires, and more options within each identity dimension will lead to a more diverse population. If the identity repertoire length is 3, this could theoretically correspond to gender, race, and religion. Within each identity an agent has a corresponding category (e.g.. Christian/Muslim/Jewish), which is indicated as a discrete integer. This means that if two agents share an integer on one dimension, they are of the same category on this dimension. The larger the repertoire, the more possible 'types' and the more possible combinations for an individual agent. For example, consider a population which has an identity repertoire of 2 (they compare themselves on 2 dimensions) and each dimension has 2 categories (0 or 1). This basic combination means that there are 4 possible types: 00, 01, 10, 11. Agents in this construct may share no traits in common (00 and 11), one trait in common (00 and 01), or all traits in common (00 and 00). Whether or not an agent considers another agent their ingroup is defined by how many traits they share in common, which is also a variable named the 'similarity threshold'.

The model is fully connected to the extent that each agent is exposed to the attitude of any other, so that it can be considered an unbiased system. On each time step, a random agent is chosen to 'broadcast' it's opinion, which is then received by all agents in the network. If this agent is in a particular agent's ingroup, it will be influenced by this agent to some degree, k_u, the 'influence factor'. If x is an agents attitude and x' is the influencing agents attitude, the change in the agents attitude, Δx, is calculated as follows:

$$\Delta x = x + k_u |x' - x| \tag{1}$$

Where x moves towards x' by the difference between x and x' times k_u. The influence factor k_u is a modified version of Deffuant et al. [11] which includes the uncertainty of the influencing agent (which will be used in Model 2) and is calculated as follows:

$$k_u(x, x', u, u') = (1 - u')(e^{-(x-x'u)^2}) \tag{2}$$

Where u is the agents uncertainty and u' is the influencing agent's uncertainty. This equation moderates the degree to which an agent will go towards another agent's opinion. If the agent is very certain, k_u will be smaller, and the more quickly the graph of possible influence given the difference between the two attitudes will go to zero. Also, the larger the distance between the two agent's attitudes, the faster the equation goes to 0 generally.

This basic formula will be used throughout the models, however as mentioned this particular model does not take uncertainty into account. For these simulations, both u and u' will be set to .5 for all agents and will not vary as a result of influence. The equation (graphed in Fig. 2) is as follows:

$$k_u(x, x') = .5(e^{-(x-x'.5)^2}) \tag{3}$$

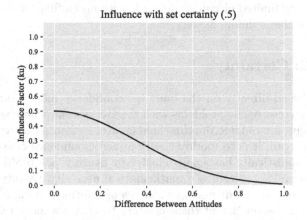

Fig. 2. Influence when certainty is set to .5.

In order to maintain the integrity of the model conceptually (in terms of the Abelson Diversity Puzzle), agents who are under no chance of influence are altered. That is, if an agent does not share enough similarities with any agent to consider them the ingroup (and therefore are immune to social influence), their similarity threshold is lowered until they are ensured to have at least one ingroup member.

4.2 Results

When agents must share all traits in common to be considered an ingroup, stable opinion clusters occur. They are essentially small consensus islands whereby each type of agent is excluded from influence from any agent who does not share all of their traits. However, as with the Abelson Diversity Problem, in populations which are not sufficiently diverse, if agents consider anything less than sharing all traits in common, the population will converge to consensus (Fig. 3). The solution to this, then, is to increase the identity repertoire and the complexity of each dimension, and to find the optimum number of traits by which agents compare each other and see what the resulting opinion clusters are. There are only a few scenarios which create any semblance of a reasonable amount of clustering, or a balance between consensus and complete anomie (Fig. 3). The diversity has to be large enough whereby there are no 'types' for agents to separate into, so that they form groups with others based on overlapping, uncorrelated traits.

The problem with this system is that it is not realistic. Having one similarity threshold for basically the entire population is not how people identify their ingroups, some people are more or less open than others. There are no strict rules as to how people choose to identify with each other, and on what grounds. If the amount of similarities is loosened in either direction, or the threshold is randomized, the result is either anomie if it is too constrained, or consensus if it is too open or random. There are many other factors which could affect how influence works are not taken into account in this model, therefore, it is encouraging that at least under very limited circumstances, identity and affiliation itself can have some effect on stable opinion clusters.

5 Model 2: Certainty

This model is based directly on the bounded confidence model, but this study does not claim to resolve the problems with the BC system, where small random amounts of acceptance outside the threshold creates consensus, as with the Abelson problem. Instead, it is to modify the Bounded Confidence construct, which by design deterministically has agents cluster by nearest 'acceptable' neighbors, creating stable opinion clusters as a mathematical necessity. By introducing certainty, it is hoped that the diversity of sources of information circulating in the system will affect the quality of these clusters to create a more realistic set of opinion dynamics. "More realistic" means specifically:

- A system where the diversity of information being circulated affects the overall certainty of the system, and the length of time for the system to stabilize.
- A system which agents do not cluster according to their "uniform" distribution as with BC models.

The certainties of the agents will be negotiated by the source of the information being broadcast (whether it is from their ingroup or their outgroup), so

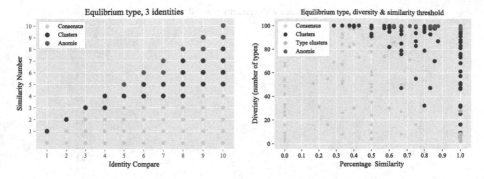

Fig. 3. (Left) Depending on the amount of identities, the similarity number must be a bit higher than 50% to avoid consensus. (Right) Clustering occurs when the diversity is higher, and the requirement for similarities is relatively high. Type clusters occur at strict similarity requirements (100%), with low levels of diversity. Typically, similarity requirements below 50% will lead to consensus, although requirements as high as 75% can lead to consensus in low diversity populations.

that it is the exposure to information which makes an agent more or less certain [25]. The reason this is important in studying social influence in identity is that in moments of uncertainty, people default to the opinions of others [6].[2] This tendency facilitates misinformation, because when an individual defaults without question, their beliefs can be reinforced by others regardless of the validity of that attitude, or the consequences of believing it [1].

5.1   Design

In this model, agents still broadcast their opinion at random, but their opinions can change randomly based on their certainty. Certainty is a number between 0 and 1 which describes how committed the agent is to the opinion it holds. Low certainties allow for a greater likelihood of random opinion change, or noise.

Two principles are borrowed from Grow [8] which are drawn from psychological research and used in their model on certainty and social influence:

1. Certainty is inversely related to the ability to be influenced.
2. Certainty is directly related to the amount of agreement among peers (social cohesion).

Equation 1 ensures that agents who are more certain will be less influenced by agents whose opinion is farther from them on the spectrum, thereby fulfilling principle 1 (Fig. 4).

Principle 2 describes the process of certainty changing as a result of the (non-linear) interactions among agents. Therefore, it was fulfilled using a series

---

[2] Classical studies in psychology have also long confirmed this tendency. See [26] for social norms, [27] for social comparison theory, [28] for conformity, [29] for affiliation and [30] for social categorization theory. For a summary see [6] pg 770.

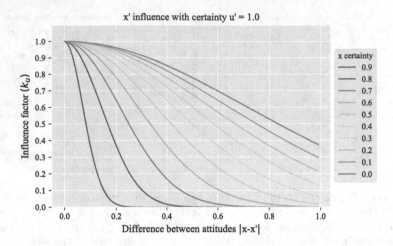

Fig. 4. As the certainty of x increases, the influence factor drops quickly to zero as the difference between their opinions ($|x - x'|$) increases.

of coefficients which change the certainty of the agent depending which agent is broadcasting at a particular time step.

Table 1. Receiving broadcast weights

	Ingroup		Outgroup
Change attitude	(1)$\mu = +1$		(2)$\mu = -.01$
	Agree	Disagree	(5)$\mu = -.01$
	(3)$\mu = +1$	(4)$\mu = -1$	

Values of μ for each possible scenario of receiving information. (1) If an agent changes its mind it can only do so if the broadcast is from the ingroup. (2) (5) A small change happens from not agreeing with your outgroup which makes the system less stable the more opinions are broadcasted. (3), (4) The weight of not changing an attitude is equal but opposite whether you agree or disagree. Groups are punished if they do not agree, so the larger majority is dismantled if there are more opinions within the ingroup (4).

All of these results have a population of 100 agents and are measured first with a uniform starting certainty of .5. The reason for this is twofold: first, if agents all begin with the same certainty the resulting groupings will not be affected by the initial state and second, .5 certainty will ensure the system begins in a state of enough certainty that noise will not take over and equilibrium can be reached. To adjust certainty as described above, agent x with uncertainty u adjusts its certainty at each time step as follows:

$$u_{(t+1)} = u + \varepsilon\mu \tag{4}$$

Table 2. Broadcast weights

Change attitude	$\mu = 1$
Do not change attitude	$\mu = .01$

Broadcasting has a higher weight when the agent changes their mind. Attitudes which are expressed generally get a small change, meaning certainty increases over time.

Where $\varepsilon = .01$, and μ varies depending on the communication (Table 1). ε is a measure of the speed of certainty change, and has been chosen as .01 for practical purposes of simulation duration (ε varies with the number of agents and is calculated by the percent of the population of a single agent, with a population of 100, this is 1% or .01). μ is a weight value that when varied promotes different dynamics in the simulation (Tables 1 and 2).

Finally, agents with low certainty can change their opinion at random with a probability defined by the following equation, which is a function of the agent's uncertainty u:

$$p(u) = (ue^{-(1-u)})^2 \tag{5}$$

5.2   Results

The resulting system is one where the "pressure to conform" is high enough that extremism, and indeed small groups in general, can only persist in situations which have a diverse enough opinion cluster that majority pressures do not overcome small ingroup stability. That is, since large groups of agents are consistently confirming each others opinions, if they are large enough they will destabilize small groupings. The stability of cluster formation, then, is related to the number and population of each opinion group, which is consistent with the literature on social groups and attitude certainty [31].

First, an information space where certainty (on average) is less given the amount of information being circulated is demonstrated in Fig. 5. To start, Fig. 5 (left) shows simply the more clusters the longer the system takes to stabilize, with a Pearson's correlation of .49. Figure 5 (right) shows that average certainty after 100 stable runs is significantly smaller given a larger amount of clusters, which demonstrates that more information in the system leads to less certain agents overall (more clusters = more attitudes). This trend diminishes after longer runs, but this is because for a cluster to be stable, the average certainty is always increasing, if the average certainty were always decreasing, the cluster would be vulnerable to random opinion change and would no longer remain stable. Furthermore, the certainty increasing over time when unchallenged is considered a feature of certainty under normal conditions [31,32].

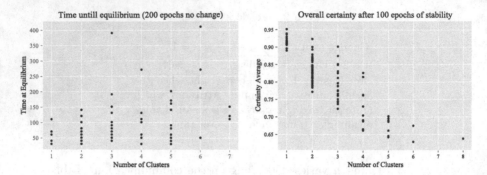

Fig. 5. (Left) Time until equilibrium is reached and number of clusters at equilibrium. Each dot represents one simulation run. (Right) Average certainty of clusters over the course of the simulation. Each dot represents one simulation run.

6   Model 3: Combination

This model is a combination of the two former models. It is hoped that combining both can resolve issues with the previous by virtue of its complexity, and produce a more flexible model by employing both certainty and identity.

6.1   Design

This model uses all of the former methods, running essentially in parallel. Here, however, the similarity threshold was able to be lowered to less than 50% similarities, and the difference tolerance (essentially the 'bound of confidence'), will also be randomized between 0 and 1. This creates a heterogeneous population of more and less 'open' agents who nevertheless operate by the same basic rules as the previous implementations. Heterogeneity is a desirable feature in agent-based models generally in that it is more reflective of human populations [33]. Also, 'relaxing' the strict parameters required in the first models addresses the limitations of those models in hopes that this simulation will produce clustering with less rigid restrictions.

6.2   Results

As was hoped, the relaxation of the parameters from the first two models allows for stable clusters in this iteration. Namely, the amount of similarities required for agents to be considered ingroup members could be lowered to less than half of the repertoire length. Formerly, this would lead to consensus inevitably, however, because of the added difference threshold, this would be resisted. The difference threshold can also be flexible, and is initialized at random between 0 and 1 for each agent, which would have lead to consensus in Model 2. This combination of these two models, then, successfully allows for a relatively more realistic representation of identity and certainty, while still maintaining stable clusters over time. This is significant, because it suggests that adding variables on top of each other can provide solutions to the Abelson Diversity Problem without adding a disintegrating force.

The simulation gives rise to extremism, but by and large only if there are agents which are initialized as extreme. This would imply that a system can become extreme when an extremist is inserted, but does not say anything about the system being able to produce extremism. In order to test this, agents were initialized with attitudes considered moderate (between .2 and .8), and the resulting population of extremists was found once the system arrived at equilibrium (Table 3).

Table 3. 10 run averages for different attitude ranges

Initial attitude range	Initial extremist population	Final extremist population	Difference	Final average extremist certainty	Initial mean/ standard deviation	Final Mean/ standard deviation	Difference
(1) 0–1	38.3	23.8	−14.5	0.80	0.495/0.281	0.510/0.215	+.015/−.066
(2) .2−.8	0.0	2.3	+2.3	0.27	0.493/0.169	0.496/ 0.124	+.003/−.045

(1) With initial extremists and (2) Without initial extremists (extremists as being defined by attitudes < .2 or > .8).

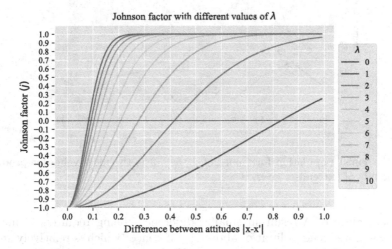

Fig. 6. Johnson factor for different values of λ ($\beta = 1$).

The system in itself, then, does not lead to extremism in any meaningful way due to large pressures towards moderation by the majority of agents. To push the system to its limits and determine if there are conditions whereby polarization or extremism can be produced with an initially moderate population, another parameter was experimented with. Named the Johnson factor, it is based on

186   C. Mason et al.

a theory by Donald Johnson in his 1940 paper *Confidence and the Expression of Opinion* [34], postulating that extreme attitudes tend to become confident because they are able to reject more opinions which are farther away from their own than those who hold more moderate opinions. The Johnson factor moderates the certainty of agents on any broadcast (see (2) (5) Table 1). Instead of the confidence decreasing by $\varepsilon\mu$ (μ is negative here) in the event of an outgroup broadcast, certainty will decrease by the Johnson factor j, which is defined by the following equation:

$$j(x, x') = \beta(2 * e^{-\lambda(x-x')^2} - 1) \qquad (6)$$

Where x is the agent's attitude and x' is the broadcasting agent's attitude, β is a scaling factor determining the magnitude of j and λ is a variable describing at what threshold of attitude difference there will be zero change in certainty (the x-intercept in Fig. 6).

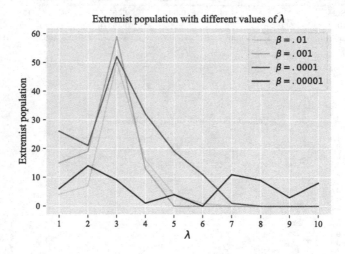

Fig. 7. Extremist population for values of λ. $\lambda = 3$ is the ideal value for producing large amounts of extremists given $\beta > \mu$.

Higher values of λ result in smaller differences being required to increase confidence, and reaches a limit of about .1 difference (which is relatively small), in order for confidence to be increased. Where $\lambda = 0$, μ remains unchanged and the simulation runs as before. Figure 7 shows that the extremist population increases until $\lambda = 3$ for all values of β which were tested. As λ gets larger than 3, the difference required to increase certainty is much smaller, and the certainty of the population rises proportionally despite whether the agent's opinion resides in the extremes. For $\lambda >= 5$, this is about a difference of 1.5, meaning that many agents will have a difference of opinion which is larger than this. In these cases, certainty increases for all agents and there is not enough uncertainty to produce the noise required for agents to become extreme. Interestingly, larger values of λ actually safeguard against extremism. As β goes towards .0001 it is approaching the original μ, which means it has a very small effect and results in small amounts of extremists due to slightly lower uncertainty.

7 Discussion and Conclusion

The main questions of this study were, are the variables of social identity and uncertainty able to affect social influence and result in complex opinion dynamics (including extremism and polarization) as observed in online social networks such as Facebook? Furthermore, given the constraints of the Abelson Diversity Puzzle, do stable opinion clusters form?

Model 1 demonstrated that social identity is able to produce stable opinion clusters as long as the amount of connections is limited and the population is somewhat diverse. Model 2 did successfully allow for certainty to be negotiated by ingroup size, and therefore added a level of complexity to the rigidity of the bounded confidence model. This supports the theory that certainty is a negotiator of group dynamics, as is suggested by the literature, and this basis for a model could be used for further investigation of these concepts (see uncertainty identity theory as described in [35] pages 943–45). Model 3 demonstrated that while clustering occurs, moderating forces are strong, and extremism or polarization do not result from the system alone. One option was experimented with to see if extremism resulted, showing the virtues of the design of Model 3 as a testing ground to isolate variables outside of social influence and certainty. The aim of this research is not to systematically test other theories, but it is hoped that the results of this experiment suggests the potentials of the model design.

Ultimately, given the Abelson Problem, these models demonstrate that opinion distributions other than consensus can exist in systems where everyone is connected. That is, since Facebook is not a network where everyone agrees on one opinion, these models are successful to the extent that they were able to reproduce a myriad of opinions on a macro level, while maintaining influence connections between groups of agents. Because of this, social identity and certainty can be considered possible explanations for the formation of social connections, and for how people are influenced by others.

Therefore, these models can tentatively say that if Facebook facilitated an open broadcast of opinions open to all members of the network, it seems to have a moderating effect overall. Encouraging open information exchange, where people are exposed to many diverse opinions, could help to mitigate information disorders, as has been observed in offline social networks [36]. As the messages in these models are all weighted equally, that is, no message is more persuasive than any other, it is hard to extrapolate these results to include things like propaganda. Considering these factors would be a fruitful starting point in future research and could be possible contributors in polarization and extremism, as well as other information disorders.

There are several reasons why the design and results are not completely descriptive of the effects of social influence on Facebook. For example, Model 1 does not allow for similarities between agents which are flexible and less than half of the identity repertoire. This is due to the constraints of opinion dynamic models with regard to the Abelson Diversity Problem. Nevertheless, the attempts to reconcile this problem were somewhat successful. The fact that Model 3 allowed for the relaxation of both the bound of confidence principle and the similarity threshold is very encouraging, and suggests that the interaction of these factors is a fruitful starting point both with regards to agent-based model design, and a possible factor in swaying opinion dynamics in the real world.

A key future challenge for all three models is comparison with real-world data. Indeed, the veracity of the models themselves cannot be confirmed without this, even though on an abstract level it can be concluded that they succeeded to reproduce macro-level trends of opinion diversity (i.e. avoiding consensus). A thorough collection of relevant data, either from mining the Facebook API (which is limited due to privacy restrictions) or by gathering it via an application, was beyond the scope of this present study. Given these results, though, follow up research focusing on empirical data and using the modeling methods outlined in this paper would be beneficial to further examining the results and moving forward with more complex models. Nevertheless, this process of building systems and combining them appears to be a sufficient method for exploring the effects of the factors described here in isolation, and could be used to test other possible interacting variables in the psychology of attitude formation.

References

1. Moussaïd, M., Kämmer, J.E., Analytis, P.P., Neth, H.: Social influence and the collective dynamics of opinion formation. PLoS ONE **8**(11), e78433(2013)
2. Hogg, M.A., Smith, J.R.: Attitudes in social context: a social identity perspective. Eur. Rev. Soc. Psychol. **18**(1), 89–131 (2007)
3. Tormala, Z.L.: The role of certainty (and uncertainty) in attitudes and persuasion. Curr. Opin. Psychol. **10**, 6–11 (2016)
4. Sherif, M., Cantril, H.: The psychology of 'attitudes': Part I. Psychol. Rev. **52**(6), 295 (1945)
5. Abrams, D., Hogg, M.A.: Social Identifications: A Social Psychology of Intergroup Relations and Group Processes. Routledge, London (2006)
6. Smith, J.R., Hogg, M.A., Martin, R., Terry, D.J.: Uncertainty and the influence of group norms in the attitude-behaviour relationship. Br. J. Soc. Psychol. **46**(4), 769–792 (2007)
7. Abrams, J.R., Barker, V., Giles, H.: An examination of the validity of the subjective vitality questionnaire. J. Multilingual Multicultural Dev. **30**(1), 59–72 (2009)
8. Grow, A., Flache, A.: How attitude certainty tempers the effects of faultlines in demographically diverse teams. Comput. Math. Organ. Theory **17**(2), 196 (2011)

9. Quattrociocchi, W., Caldarelli, G., Scala, A.: Opinion dynamics on interacting networks: media competition and social influence. Sci. Rep. **4**, 4938 (2014)
10. Madsen, J.K., Bailey, R.M., Pilditch, T.D.: Large networks of rational agents form persistent echo chambers. Sci. Rep. **8**(1), 1–8 (2018)
11. Deffuant, G.: Comparing extremism propagation patterns in continuous opinion models. J. Artif. Soc. Soc. Simul. **9**(3) (2006)
12. Lazer, D.: vd. (2018). The science of fake news. Science 359(6380), 1094–1096 (2018)
13. Lewandowsky, S., Ecker, U.K., Seifert, C.M., Schwarz, N., Cook, J.: Misinformation and its correction: continued influence and successful debiasing. Psychol. Sci. Publ. Interest **13**(3), 106–131 (2012)
14. Hofstra, B., Corten, R., Van Tubergen, F., Ellison, N.B.: Sources of segregation in social networks: a novel approach using Facebook. Am. Sociol. Rev. **82**(3), 625–656 (2017)
15. Duggins, P.: A psychologically-motivated model of opinion change with applications to American politics. arXiv preprint arXiv:1406.7770 (2014)
16. Flache, A., et al.: Models of social influence: towards the next frontiers. J. Artif. Soc. Soc. Simul. **20**(4) (2017)
17. Abelson, R.P.: Mathematical models of the distribution of attitudes under controversy. In: Contributions to Mathematical Psychology (1964)
18. DeGroot, M.H.: Reaching a consensus. J. Am. Stat. Assoc. **69**(345), 118–121 (1974)
19. Mäs, M., Flache, A., Helbing, D.: Individualization as driving force of clustering phenomena in humans. PLoS Comput. Biol. **6**(10) (2010)
20. Hegselmann, R., Krause, U., et al.: Opinion dynamics and bounded confidence models, analysis, and simulation. J. Artif. Soc. Soc. Simul. **5**(3), 3–33 (2002)
21. Deffuant, G., Neau, D., Amblard, F., Weisbuch, G.: Mixing beliefs among interacting agents. Adv. Complex Syst. **3**, 87–98 (2000)
22. Meadows, M., Cliff, D.: Reexamining the relative agreement model of opinion dynamics. J. Artif. Soc. Soc. Simul. **15**(4), 4 (2012)
23. Kurahashi-Nakamura, T., Mäs, M., Lorenz, J.: Robust clustering in generalized bounded confidence models. J. Artif. Soc. Soc. Simul. **19**(4), 7 (2016)
24. Lustick, I.S., et al.: Agent-based modelling of collective identity: testing constructivist theory. J. Artif. Soc. Soc. Simul. **3**(1), 1 (2000)
25. Visser, P.S., Mirabile, R.R.: Attitudes in the social context: the impact of social network composition on individual-level attitude strength. J. Pers. Soc. Psychol. **87**(6), 779 (2004)
26. Sherif, M.: The psychology of social norms. Harper (1936)
27. Festinger, L.: A theory of social comparison processes. Hum. Relat. **7**(2), 117–140 (1954)
28. Asch, S.E.: Studies of independence and submission to group pressure: I. A minority of one against a unanimous majority. Psychol. Monogr. **70**(9), 417–427 (1956)
29. Schachter, S.: The Psychology of Affiliation: Experimental Studies of the Sources of Gregariousness. Stanford University Press, Stanford (1959)
30. Turner, J.C., Hogg, M.A., Oakes, P.J., Reicher, S.D., Wetherell, M.S.: Rediscovering the Social Group: A Self-categorization Theory. Basil Blackwell, Oxford (1987)
31. Petrocelli, J.V., Tormala, Z.L., Rucker, D.D.: Unpacking attitude certainty: attitude clarity and attitude correctness. J. Pers. Soc. Psychol. **92**(1), 30 (2007)
32. Tormala, Z.L., DeSensi, V.L., Clarkson, J.J., Rucker, D.D.: Beyond attitude consensus: the social context of persuasion and resistance. J. Exp. Soc. Psychol. **45**(1), 149–154 (2009)

33. Epstein, J.M.: Generative Social Science: Studies in Agent-Based Computational Modeling. Princeton University Press, Princeton (2006)
34. Johnson, D.M.: Confidence and the expression of opinion. J. Soc. Psychol. **12**(1), 213–220 (1940)
35. Levine, J.M., Hogg, M.A.: Encyclopedia of Group Processes and Intergroup Relations, vol. 1. Sage, Los Angeles (2010)
36. Stroud, N.J.: Media use and political predispositions: revisiting the concept of selective exposure. Pol. Behav. **30**(3), 341–366 (2008)

Do Online Trolling Strategies Differ in Political and Interest Forums: Early Results

Henna Paakki[1]([✉]), Antti Salovaara[2], and Heidi Vepsäläinen[3]

[1] Department of Computer Science, Aalto University, Espoo, Finland
henna.paakki@aalto.fi
[2] Department of Design, Aalto University, Espoo, Finland
antti.salovaara@aalto.fi
[3] Department of Computer Science, University of Helsinki, Helsinki, Finland
heidi.vepsalainen@helsinki.fi

Abstract. This study compares the effectiveness of different trolling strategies in two online contexts: politically oriented forums that address issues like global warming, and interest-based forums that deal with people's personal interests. Based on previous research, we consider trolling as context-bound and suggest that relevance theory and common grounding theory can explain why people may attend and react to certain types of troll posts in one forum, but pay scant attention to them in another. We postulate two hypotheses on how successful (i.e., disruptive) trolling varies according to context: that trolls' messaging strategies appear in different frequencies in political and interest forums (H1), and that context-matching strategies also produce longer futile conversations (H2). Using Hardaker's categorization of trolling strategies on a covert–overt continuum, our statistical analysis on a dataset of 49 online conversations verified H1: in political forums covert strategies were more common than overt ones; in interest forums the opposite was the case. Regarding H2 our results were inconclusive. However, the results motivate further research on this phenomenon with larger datasets.

Keywords: Trolling strategies · Political forum · Interest forum · Relevance theory · Common grounding.

1 Introduction

Online discussion platforms, such as online forums and news articles' comment sections, connect millions of people daily. There are platforms and topics for everyone, hosting discussions ranging from seeking advice for personal trouble to heated debates on political matters. Many discussion platforms are vulnerable to malicious and disruptive behavior, which wreaks havoc in conversations and causes emotional distress to the people involved. Although online trolling is a diverse phenomenon, and perceptions towards it vary [9, pp. 65–89], the consensus is that it is ubiquitous and mainly disruptive, particularly because of the

© The Author(s) 2020
M. van Duijn et al. (Eds.): MISDOOM 2020, LNCS 12259, pp. 191–204, 2020.
https://doi.org/10.1007/978-3-030-61841-4_13

recent developments in using trolls to amplify polarization and political agendas, as well as to disrupt unwanted conversations and to spread disinformation [1,5].

Considering the widespread agreement that Internet trolling can cause significant societal harm, it is surprising how little is known about the conversational strategies that trolls use. Evidence suggests, though, that trolling may manifest differently across contexts [9,25]. Therefore, the trolling strategies used commonly in interest-oriented discussion forums may differ from the ones used in political debates. Most effective trolls may even be able to adapt their trolling strategies when they switch from one forum or discussion topic to another. Being aware of such differences in trolling strategies would be important in order to combat the ways by which trolls destroy civic conversations.

This paper's findings come from a research project that has been launched to address the problem of trolling. Under the course of our research, we have made an initial observation that trolls seem to use different trolling strategies in political and interest discussions. Using a small dataset of 68 online discussions around political or societal themes (climate change, Brexit) and interest themes (cats, fitness), all of which included successful (i.e., response-inducing) trolling, we tested two hypotheses: that successful trolling strategies would indeed be applied with different frequencies depending on the topic of discussion (H1), and that the reply chains to trolls would also differ in their length, depending on the strategy used by the troll (H2). For distinguishing different trolling activities, we utilized the already well-established categorization by Hardaker [15] that describes six different trolling strategies along a covert–overt continuum.

The amount of data is so far limited, but our analysis suggest that H1 holds. We found a statistically significant difference between successful trolling strategies in political vs. interest discussions: in political discussions trolls apply covert strategies (i.e., subtle and non-apparent) more often than in interest discussions, where the strategies contrariwise are predominantly overt (i.e., noticeable and direct). On the other hand, we could not confirm H2 about reply chain lengths. The limited amount of data, however, pointed towards the direction predicted by the hypothesis: that covert trolling would lead to longer derailed discussions in political discussions, while overt strategies would do the same for interest discussion. The lack of confirmation to H2 notwithstanding, our findings have both academic and real-life implications, which we will cover in the Discussion.

2   Theory

Our hypotheses did not result from serendipitous discoveries but had a theoretical backing that sensitized us to pay attention to their possible existence.

Trolls take advantage of the ambiguities of computer-mediated communication and the vulnerabilities of internet discussion communities to lure others into fruitless, frustrating or circular discussions and to waste their time [16]. Trolling involves a process of learning the social practices of a community, assimilating to them, and then violating these practices to create disruption [8,25]. Trolling behaviors and perceptions of trolling are context-bound: they differ according to platform and community [9,16,25]. The motivations for trolling are similarly heterogeneous, including both amusement and political influence [3,16]. Therefore, also the most common strategies used to successfully troll other participants on a discussion forum are context-dependent.

Previous studies have illustrated various types of trolling. They have often oriented to analyzing and understanding one type of trolling at a time, such as memorial page trolling [22], signalling of in-group/out-group membership [11], LOL trolling [17], and political trolling [1,9]. In more generalizing depictions, differences between trolling styles have been illustrated e.g. by distinguishing between light or humorous trolling vs. (malevolent) serious trolling or ideological trolling [9,10]. Community norms [19], platform, conversational style, motivations, and enabling factors all have an effect on the differences in trolling behaviors, as well as how they are interpreted by community members [9]. Therefore, considering the context-bound nature of trolling, it makes sense to study how trolling strategies vary according to context, and whether trolls behave differently in light conversations as opposed to more serious political conversations. While many of the above-listed studies have not presented typologies of different trolling strategies or styles, Hardaker's [15] categorization of six comparable categories (Table 1) does that, and places different strategies onto a continuum ranging from covert trolling strategies to more overt ones. In our study, we adopt this categorization to classify our data, and to analyze the differences in trolling styles on political and interest forums.

Table 1. Hardaker's [15] six trolling strategies on a covert-overt continuum

Strategy type	Strategy	Definition
Covert	Digression	Luring others into off-topic discussions by spamming, partaking in cascades or introducing tangential topics (e.g., as in [16]).
	(Hypo)criticism	Excessive criticism of others, e.g. on their punctuation while possibly committing the same errors oneself.
	Antipathy	Creation of a sensitive or antagonistic context through purposeful provocation, in order to manipulate others to produce emotional responses.
	Endangering	Giving out poor advice under an innocent guise, and others are compelled to respond in order to protect others.
	Shocking	Posting about taboos or sensitive subjects, such as religion, death or human rights.
Overt	Aggression	Deliberate and open aggressing of others into retaliating (e.g., by name-calling or foul language).

2.1 Hypothesis 1: The Frequencies of Trolling Strategies Are Different in Political and Interest Forums

The relevance of a comment in an online forum depends on the content that has started the conversation. For example, a discussion in an online newspaper's comment section happens in the context of the related news article. Similarly, in Reddit (a popular online news aggregator and discussion forum) a message is visible in relation to a "subreddit" (a discussion section) and an original post within it. Therefore the boundaries for the discussions that unfold are set to a specific topic that also sets the conversational context [18,20]. This affects the expectations people have about the discussion and its style, and thus they tend to accommodate their posts to this context [29].

Relevance theory [26], which builds on Gricean maxims [12,13], may help to illustrate why some posts on these forums manage to attract people's attention far better than others. A post's relevance is determined by not only its relevance to the assigned topic and the on-going conversation, but also its understandability. Relevance theory states that human cognitive mechanisms have a universal tendency of selecting most potentially relevant stimuli out of a variety, and to maximize the relevance of processed inputs, therein using the available processing resources most efficiently [26, Ch. 3.1–2]. The cognitive principle of relevance deems some messages more appealing or understandable than others, also making them more relevant [26]. We argue that along with contextual norms assigned by the discussion topic, relevance also dictates the conversation's flow – in particular what type of posts (and thus trolling strategies) are deemed more relevant, and which posts incite more subthreads.

Compared to other less serious arenas, political forums discussing larger societal issues orientate more strongly toward more serious deliberative discourse or debate, and exhibit higher levels of interactivity and topical coherence [28] . They are to some extent similar to content-based and knowledge-based discussions on social media [18], and show less off-topic posts, as users' contributions to the discussions are more likely to address previous posts in a manner befitting a real debate [28, pp. 15–17]. News discussion is largely opinion-based, and so participants also expect to be communicating with people coming from varying or opposing viewpoints [18,27]. Thus, the general style of political forum discussion is different compared to interest topics. *Consequently, we believe that political forum discussions are more vulnerable to covert trolling attempts by being more neutral, information-centered and less personal.*

Contrarily to political arenas, interest forums serve as spaces for bonding with people with similar interests, beliefs or hobbies [4,21]. Central motivations for joining these communities include information exchange, social support, and most of all friendship [24]. Essential for many such groups is creating an environment of camaraderie and supportive solidarity to enhance fun and a sense of belonging, which is why insults are taboo and confrontation minimized [4]. In general, interest forums invite contemplation on personal experiences, friendly exchange of feelings and anecdotes, and supportive information-sharing about the hobby or interest with other enthusiasts [4,14,20,24]. We argue that due to the high relevancy of posts containing friendly support or personal experiences in this context, posts violating its taboos (e.g., insulting others) are also more cognitively relevant. This is because resolving and condemning such posts contributes to maintaining the key elements of the forum, such as a safe and friendly environment. Of course, conversations on online newspapers' comment sections under interest-related articles do not necessarily form even a loose community. However, we consider it likely that these conversational arenas maintain some similar functional features as more close-knit communities like r/cats on Reddit. This is why *we maintain that interest forums match with overt strategies*, i.e. they are more vulnerable to more personal and visible overt trolling attempts like direct insults. Therefore, in summary, we hypothesize that:

H1: The frequencies of covert and overt trolling strategies are different in political and interest forums.

In particular, we hypothesize that covert trolling is common in political discussion while overt trolling is common in interest forums.

2.2   Hypothesis 2: Trolls Can Derail Others into Longer Futile Discussions by Choosing Trolling Strategies According to the Type of the Forum

Our second hypothesis is derived from the first one. If trolls match their trolling strategy to the type of the online forum, this may be because they know (consciously or sub-consciously) it will be more effective. One method for measuring the effectiveness of trolling is to measure the amount of engagement that a message manages to garner from others in the discussion.

Along with relevance theory, the *theory of common grounding* [6,7] provides a theoretical justification for why trolls succeed in capturing other people into long unfruitful discussions. In well-intended communication, conversational parties engage in common grounding – a 'collective process by which the participants try to reach a mutual belief that they have understood what each other meant' [6, p. 223]. Following the premises of this psycholinguistics-derived theory, all contributions to a conversation need to be grounded, i.e. turned into mutual knowledge, by providing evidence that the message has been understood [6,7]. All participants in the conversation are also expected to engage in resolving breakdowns in the case of possible misunderstandings. An unintelligible action thus calls for an explanation from its performer. This requirement for providing an explanation, in turn, is highly amenable for exploitation if one wishes to act as a troll. By resisting the norms of common grounding and accountability, a troll can prolong the time their posts attract attention.

As mentioned, contextual differences require learning the conversational conventions of a given online forum in order to gain access to the type of interaction others on the forum usually deem relevant [8,9,26]. Similarly, we state that relevant posts are seen as worth the collaborative efforts of grounding in case of breakdowns; in an asynchronous discussion space with a multitude of overlapping posts only discussion-relevant breakdowns are attended to. Consequently, we argue that participants on political forums are more prone to engaging in long grounding efforts when the conversation breaks down due to issues matching with the functions of the discussion space: misunderstandings or view point differences in informational content or correctness. On the other hand, we claim that people on interest forums are more inclined to engage in long conversations on personal experiences and issues related to the individual participant, which is why more collaborative effort will be expended on resolving the matching overt trolling attempts like unintelligible actions or attacks against a participant's person. Therefore, our hypothesis H2 is, as already stated in the section's title:

H2: The quantity of replies to trolls will vary in different types of forums depending on the employed trolling strategy.

In particular, covert strategies would incite longer conversations on political forums, whereas overt strategies would have the same effect on interest forums.

3   Data

Through selective sampling of online forums, we have manually acquired a corpus of conversations containing trolling. Keeping in mind our two hypotheses, we have selected several differing platforms to increase the heterogeneity of conversational and trolling styles. The corpus covers several discussion areas on *Reddit* and comment sections on English language online newspapers, including *the Telegraph*, *the Guardian* and *the Washington Post*. Having a large readership, these are influential media platforms that are likely to be targeted by trolls.

Considering our interest in both political and interest online discussions (see Sect. 2), our corpus includes two kinds of conversation topics: one around political issues (*climate change* and *Brexit*) and the other around interest discussions (*cats* and *fitness*). Important political topics, especially climate issues and Brexit , are likely to attract serious or ideological trolls wishing to disrupt or polarize the dialogue (e.g., [2,3,23]) Interest topics, in turn, such as apolitical and more everyday hobby-related discussions, may be vulnerable to "light" trolls if the topic is dear to the community (e.g., horses [14] or soap operas [4]).

In this data collection process, we have continued browsing the above-listed forums and their topic-specific discussion spaces until we have identified 2–5 conversation threads for each topic on each platform. We have particularly looked for activity-rich discussions in order to find successful trolling that has managed to elicit a lot of responses. Here successful trolling has referred to managing to formulate posts and/or responses to others' posts that provoke others into responding directly or indirectly. Comments like 'Don't answer him, he's a troll.' and troll-triggered off-topic arguments among other participants have also qualified as responses. For the online newspaper comment sections, successful trolling has typically meant 8–15 response posts in a thread triggered by the troll, while on Reddit the range has been 15–20 replies. The differing numbers are due to the average number of replies having been smaller in newspaper comment sections as compared to Reddit, and the need for context-sensitivity as some topics inspired more replies in general than others, even within the same platform.

Finally, we have tagged all the trolling content in this dataset following Hardaker's [15] six-category typology (see Table 1) where the trolling strategies can be located on an covert–overt continuum. We have used both conversationalist and researcher intuition to recognize what would have qualified as trolling in Hardaker's study, labeling instances of trolling according to her categorization to gain a comprehensive dataset [14,15].

4   Results

Most trolling styles in Hardaker [15] could be found in each of the selected topics, with Brexit and climate change on the political axis, and fitness and cats on the interest axis. Table 2 presents examples.

Table 2. Examples of trolling using different strategies.

Strategy	Example start of discussion
Digression	*Political (climate change):* Makes me wonder what flat earthers think since the flat earth is surrounded by ice walls. – *AccelHunter, Reddit, April 2019*
Hypocriticism	*Political (Brexit):* @Peter Wayde Peter, if you can't even punctuate a sentence "why should we take notice you?" (heavy sarcasm) PS, "the causes will be the causes" is terrible syntax. – *Charles Hinton, the Telegraph, 16 May 2019*
Antipathy	*Political (climate change):* It's comments like this that make me realize how ignorant the Western left really is To you, the two sides are "the side I agree with personally" and "the side that is inherently wrong and evil". There's no middle ground. Everything is black and white and that's that. – *Dreamcast3, Reddit, May 2019*
Endangering	*Interest (fitness):* Im forced to take steroids to keep lifting Nothing will help my knees pain, been living with this life breaking pain for 10+ years, if i want to keep doing what i love, i have to take steroids. – *postashio, Reddit, June 2017*
Shocking	*Interest (cats):* Let people have cats but just remove the cats claws and teeth. – *Viking76, the Telegraph, 12 June 2019*
Aggression	*Interest (cats):* Why are cat owners less happy, you ask? Many cat owners are angry, man-hating, feminist spinsters - who cannot be happy. – *Yankees_Fan, the Washington Post, 5 April 2019*

4.1   Are the Frequencies of Covert and Overt Trolling Strategies Different in Political and Interest Forums (H1)?

Our first hypothesis (H1), more specifically, was that trolls would be more likely to use covert trolling strategies (digression, (hypo)criticism or antipathy) in political discussions and overt strategies (endangering, shocking or aggression) in interest forums. To evaluate this hypothesis, we counted the frequency of each trolling strategy used in each discussion in our sample. We created two larger groups of trolling (covert and overt) by pooling together the frequencies of the three first and the three last strategies. This resulted in a 2×2 frequency matrix whose values are presented in the sub-totals in Table 3.

In the preparation of this table, we removed the following cases that would have confounded our analysis. First, 13 discussions could be classified both as covert and overt trolling. After their removal, each discussion represented exclusively either covert or overt trolling. Second, there were 4 trolls (identified by their nickname) that appeared several times in our data (in 9 discussions altogether). To remove the possibility that their behaviors would be over-represented and would thus skew our data, we used a random number generator to sample only one discussion from each troll in our analysis. In one case, both confoundments were present within the same discussion. As a result, altogether we removed 19 discussions from the analysis. Table 3's content is what remained after these preparations.

Table 3. Examples of trolling using different strategies.

Trolling strategy		Political discussions		Interest discussions	
		Brexit	Climate change	Cats	Fitness
Covert	Digression	3	4	0	1
	Hypocriticism	2	0	0	2
	Antipathy	3	8	1	2
	Total (covert)		19^a		5
Overt	Endangering	0	1	2	1
	Shocking	0	0	1	0
	Aggression	3	1	12	5
	Total (overt)		5		20^b
Total					49

^{a} The count sums to 19 instead of 20 because one discussion exhibited both hypocriticism and antipathy which was counted as one discussion only in the total.
^{b} The count sums to 20 instead of 21 because one discussion exhibited both endangering and aggression which was counted as one discussion only in the total.

Already with a plain visual inspection of the frequencies, our hypothesis seemed to be true: there were more discussions in the political-covert quadrant than in the political-overt quadrant (19 vs. 5), and the inverse held in the interest-covert and interest-overt (5 vs. 20) quadrants. We confirmed the hypothesis by comparing frequencies between categories using a Chi-square contingency table analysis: in political discussions, covert trolling was more frequent while the opposite was true for interest discussions ($p < .0001$). Thus *H1 was confirmed*: trolls appear to use more covert trolling styles to (successfully) disrupt political conversations, whereas for invading interest conversations they use more overt styles.

We also studied how the removal of the fore-mentioned 13 discussions (where trolls had applied both overt and covert trolling strategies) had possibly skewed our findings. We included the removed discussions in our analysis by assigning them either to an overt or covert category. We implemented the assignment so that the frequencies between the categories would come as close to each other as possible, thus making it maximally difficult to find differences in a statistical test. Out of the 13 discussions 8 were political, 1 of which included a troll who had also appeared in another discussion in our data. We assigned the resulting 7 discussions to the overt trolling category, resulting in a 19 vs. 12 comparison between covert and overt strategies in political discussions (instead of 19 vs. 5; see Table 3). The remaining 5 discussions that had been removed were interest-based discussions, where covert strategies had been rare. We assigned all the 5 discussions to the covert group, thus yielding a 10 vs. 20 comparison (instead of the earlier 5 vs. 20). We finally repeated our test for frequency differences, and again found a statistically significant difference ($p < .05$), thus further confirming H1.

A closer look at Table 3 suggests that covert digression and antipathy strategies were particularly common in politically oriented discussions. Aggress trolling was also found in some cases (see Table 3), but the proportional amount of aggress trolling behavior was smaller than in interest conversations. In interest topics, in turn, successful trolls seemed to commonly exploit overt aggress and endanger strategies, attacking others directly or feigning concern about endangering issues like steroid use. It must be noted that in fitness discussions the difference between covert and overt strategies was very small, arguably because trolling instances were harder to find. With a larger dataset the above-stated possibilities may be studied further.

4.2   Can Trolls Derail Others into Longer Futile Discussions Choosing Trolling Strategies According to the Type of the Forum (H2)?

As a follow-up for hypothesis H1, we specifically predicted in hypothesis H2 that the matching pairs of trolling strategy and discussion type (i.e., covert–political, overt–interest) would not only be more frequent but also, from the troll's point of view, more "successful" in luring others into longer arguments. The success could be measured by the number of replies that others would post to the troll's messages. Long chains of replies would best serve the trolls' interest of creating havoc and destroying civic discussion in online spaces. The length of individual posts was not considered due to the fact that it may vary in online discussions for several reasons which cannot be controlled here.

To evaluate hypothesis H2, we counted the number of replies that others had posted to the discussion thread after the trolls' original message. If the trolls themselves engaged in these subsequent discussions, we excluded their messages from these counts. We then compared the lengths of the reply chains in the 2×2 quadrants consisting of covert vs. over trolling and political vs. interest discussions. For this comparison, we used ANOVA, which is a method suited for analyzing differences between scalar values between categories.

Table 4 presents the data used in the analysis. Similarly with H1, also here a visual inspection suggests that the hypothesis could indeed hold: the covert-political and overt-interest matches have longer reply chains than the other pairs. However, this time we could not confirm this impression statistically: in a one-way ANOVA on political discussions, covert trolling did not lead to longer chains than overt trolling ($p = .279$). In the same analysis on interest discussions, overt trolling did not lead to longer chains than covert trolling ($p = .284$). We also carried out a two-way ANOVA with the strategy type (covert/overt) and the theme (political/interest) as factors, with an interest in the test's interaction term that could test if the length variable's relationship is inverted when analyzing the two different discussion topics. The interaction term was closer to a statistical significance, but not sufficient for any conclusions ($p = .129$). Correcting the length variable distributions' skewness by square root transformation, or using non-parametric U tests did not yield significant results either. Thus, *H2 was not confirmed*.

Table 4. Lengths and standard deviations of the reply chains to troll's posts.

General trolling strategy	Average reply chain length	
	Political discussions	Interest discussions
Covert	15.6 ($sd = 11.5$)	10.8 ($sd = 5.2$)
Overt	9.8 ($sd = 2.0$)	18.4 ($sd = 15.1$)[a]

[a] One discussion was excluded due to an excessive number of replies (590).

The reason for this failure becomes apparent when one inspects the numbers of cases in each quadrant. The earlier-presented Table 3 shows that the data contained only 5 cases of mismatching strategy–discussion pairs (i.e., political–overt and interest–covert). Statistically significant findings were not attainable with such a small dataset size.

5   Discussion

To recap, our first hypothesis was that commonly used successful trolling strategies differ according to the conversational context of the forum: political–covert or interest–overt. It was validated by a *Chi*-square analysis, which encourages further studies on the phenomenon with larger datasets. The second hypothesis was that covert strategies produce longer futile conversations in political arenas, whereas overt strategies drag on longer arguments in interest conversations. This claim was not supported by our statistical analyses at this point, but the data suggest it plausible for larger datasets to yield better results.

A better dataset would include a larger number or conversations, ranging through a greater variety of topics on the political and interest axes, including also unsuccessful troll posts. It would also allow for a more specific analysis of different trolling strategies, like the ones that Hardaker [15] identified. Our data is, of course, insufficient at the moment due to its size and the limitations of sampling trolling based on conversation-inherent dynamics. For the moment, classification into a category of trolling strategies per Hardaker [15, p. 68] requires several posts from the troll to determine whether the poster could be trolling others. This requirement means that our analysis addresses only successful trolling attempts where even the smallest attempt has led to a desired effect (from the troll's point of view). Sampling and analyzing also unsuccessful trolling is a problem to be resolved in future research, and will allow more conclusive findings.

We also have other considerations that future research needs to address. First, how exactly the nature of the conversational space and its norms (as theorized by Kirman et al. [19]) affects communicational breakdowns. Now, the results of this study already implicate that transgression of contextual norms involves using a matching trolling strategy: trolls create posts that have high cognitive relevance in the discussion space. They also show that trolling style is not bound to individual and unique situations only; there are more general patterns in trolling that transcend forum and topic boundaries (e.g. Brexit), and certain types of forums can be expected to be vulnerable to matching trolling strategies. In political discussions, this means assimilating to the fact-based style, seeming (superficially) well-informed and topically coherent, citing (pseudo-)scientific sources and referring to field specific terminology, while baiting others for instance with antagonistic interpretations of related information, epistemological controversy or incoherence. In contrast, the interest context seems to give focus to trolling that attacks the friendly and supportive discussion's main functions: here successful trolls do not require fact-based or topic-related expertise, high topical coherence or objectivity, but can instead overtly violate contextual boundaries by striking an emotional chord within the community. Thus, in the constant and multi-sided flow of posts with different and possibly overlapping agendas, the cognitive principle of relevance seems to dictate that posts matching with the functions of the discussion space gain most attention and manage to launch further discussions. The relatedness of more general contextual features and (successful) trolling strategies needs to be addressed more carefully in further research.

This also gives rise to further considerations beyond those that we put forward in our hypotheses. In particular, we find it worthwhile to consider relevance theory more broadly in the context of analyzing trolling. A relevance theoretical approach helps to further explicate the relationship between trolling and expectations of context-specific posts. Firstly, why some troll posts are noticed in the discussion while others receive very little attention, and secondly, why people engage in selected communicational breakdowns, despite their redundancy, provocativeness and frustrating effects. In interest discussions, for instance, participants seem to pay attention to overt troll posts because they seek to resolve norm-violations in order to reach common grounding and to maintain the friendly atmosphere. Arguably, participants on political forums put emphasis on factual correctness and enjoy sharing knowledge, which is why they are more inclined to be baited by epistemic incoherence or challenges against information they have provided. Thus, another possible course for future studies could involve deepening our understanding on how exactly discussion spaces give higher cognitive relevance to certain trolling strategies than others, e.g. why exactly certain posts are relevant to the people partaking in given discussions.

An issue to be aware of is that the results of the research presented in this paper, and in more extensive studies in the future, might be used for malicious purposes by aspiring trolls and bodies who are interested in large-scale misinformation campaigns. However, we believe that the results we presented here are mostly known to trolls already, whereas other discussants on online forums are probably less informed about trolling strategies. This makes them more vulnerable, which is why the results should yield positive results in raising awareness.

Assuming that the finding from H1 survives the test with a larger dataset, and H2 can eventually be proved, the implications are that we can expect certain types of online forums to be vulnerable to specific types of trolling strategies. The findings of this study already take us a step closer to identifying a given forum's weak spots that enable trolling behaviors, thus helping in predicting and detecting trolling attempts. Developing awareness of the type of lures trolls use to attack different conversational groups would arguably also improve conversants' resistance to trolls' harassment. Future studies with larger sets of data will likely enhance the opportunities for identifying trolling patterns out of larger collections of online conversations, and therefore take us closer to more accurate automatizations of trolling detection and prevention, and moderation practices. Considering the recent developments in organized trolling of political discussions, detecting trolling patterns in these arenas on a larger scale would help in battling trolling used in information operations and to ensure democratic public spaces for online civic discussion. On the other hand, this would also help in ensuring that minority groups, for instance, will have safe spaces for meeting others with similar experiences, not having to be terrorized by trolls who seek only to amuse themselves or to oppress others.

Acknowledgments. This work has been supported by Academy of Finland (grant nr. 320694).

References

1. Akhtar, S., Morrison, C.M.: The prevalence and impact of online trolling of UK members of parliament. Comput. Hum. Behav. **99**, 322–327 (2019). https://doi.org/10.1016/j.chb.2019.05.015
2. Antonio, R.J., Brulle, R.J.: The unbearable lightness of politics: climate change denial and political polarization. The Sociol. Q. **52**(2), 195–202 (2011). https://doi.org/10.1111/j.1533-8525.2011.01199.x
3. Badawy, A., Ferrara, E., Lerman, K.: Analyzing the digital traces of political manipulation: the 2016 Russian interference Twitter campaign. In: 2018 IEEE/ACM International Conference on Advances in Social Networks Analysis and Mining (ASONAM), pp. 258–265. IEEE, Barcelona (2018). https://doi.org/10.1109/ASONAM.2018.8508646
4. Baym, N.K.: Tune in, Log on: Soaps, Fandom, and Online Community. SAGE Publications, Thousand Oaks (2000). https://doi.org/10.4135/9781452204710
5. Bennett, W.L., Livingston, S.: The disinformation order: disruptive communication and the decline of democratic institutions. Eur. J. Commun. **33**(2), 122–139 (2018). https://doi.org/10.1177/0267323118760317
6. Clark, H.H., Brennan, S.E.: Grounding in communication. In: Resnick, L.B., Levine, J.M., Teasley, S.D. (eds.) Perspectives on Socially Shared Cognition, pp. 127–149. American Psychological Association, Washington (1991). https://doi.org/10.1037/10096-006
7. Clark, H.H., Schaefer, E.F.: Contributing to discourse. Cogn. Sci. **13**(2), 259–294 (1989). https://doi.org/10.1016/0364-0213(89)90008-6
8. Cruz, A.G.B., Seo, Y., Rex, M.: Trolling in online communities: a practice-based theoretical perspective. Inf. Soc. **34**(1), 15–26 (2018). https://doi.org/10.1080/01972243.2017.1391909
9. Fichman, P., Sanfilippo, M.R.: Online Trolling and its Perpetrators: Under the Cyberbridge. Rowman and Littlefield, Lanham (2016)
10. Fuller, G., Wilson, J., McCrea, C.: Troll theory? Fibreculture J. **22**, 1–15 (2013)
11. Graham, E.: Boundary maintenance and the origins of trolling. New Media Soc. **21**(9), 2029–2047 (2019). https://doi.org/10.1177/1461444819837561
12. Grice, H.P.: The causal theory of perception. In: Dancy, J. (ed.) Aristotelian Society Supplementary Volume, vol. 35, pp. 121–168. Oxford University Press (1988)
13. Grice, H.P.: Studies in the Way of Words. Harvard University Press, Cambridge (1989)
14. Hardaker, C.: Trolling in asynchronous computer-mediated communication: From user discussions to academic definitions. J. Politeness Res. Lang. Behav. Cult. **6**(2), 215–242 (2010). https://doi.org/10.1515/jplr.2010.011
15. Hardaker, C.: Uh.... not to be nitpicky, but...the past tense of drag is dragged, not drug.: an overview of trolling strategies. J. Lang. Aggress. Confl. **1**(1), 58–86 (2013)
16. Herring, S., Job-Sluder, K., Scheckler, R., Barab, S.: Searching for safety online: Managing "trolling" in a feminist forum. Inf. Soc. **18**(5), 371–384 (2002). https://doi.org/10.1080/01972240290108186
17. Hopkinson, C.: Trolling in online discussions: from provocation to community-building. Brno Stud. Engl. **39**(1), 5–25 (2013). https://doi.org/10.5817/BSE2013-1-1
18. Johansson, M.: Everyday opinions in news discussion forums: public vernacular discourse. Discourse, Context & Media **19**, 5–12 (2017). https://doi.org/10.1016/j.dcm.2017.03.001

19. Kirman, B., Lineham, C., Lawson, S.: Exploring mischief and mayhem in social computing or: how we learned to stop worrying and love the trolls. In: Proceedings of the 2012 ACM Annual Conference Extended Abstracts on Human Factors in Computing Systems, pp. 121–130. ACM Press, Austin (2012). https://doi.org/10.1145/2212776.2212790

20. Kollock, P., Smith, M.: Managing the virtual commons: cooperation and conflict in computer communities. In: Herring, S.C. (ed.) Pragmatics & Beyond New Series, vol. 39, p. 109. John Benjamins Publishing Company, Amsterdam (1996). https://doi.org/10.1075/pbns.39.10kol

21. Pew Research Center: Pew Internet and American Life Project (2001). https://www.pewinternet.org

22. Phillips, W.: LOLing at tragedy: Facebook trolls, memorial pages and resistance to grief online. First Monday 16(12) (2011). https://doi.org/10.5210/fm.v16i12.3168

23. Phillips, W.: This Is Why We Can't Have Nice Things: Mapping the Relationship Between Online Trolling and Mainstream Culture. The MIT Press, Cambridge (2015)

24. Ridings, C.M., Gefen, D.: Virtual community attraction: why people hang out online. J. Comput. Mediat. Commun. 10(1) (2006). https://doi.org/10.1111/j.1083-6101.2004.tb00229.x

25. Sanfilippo, M., Yang, S., Fichman, P.: Trolling here, there, and everywhere: perceptions of trolling behaviors in context. J. Assoc. Inf. Sci. Technol. 68(10), 2313–2327 (2017). https://doi.org/10.1002/asi.23902

26. Sperber, D., Wilson, D.: Relevance: Communication and Cognition, 2nd edn. Blackwell Publishers, Cambridge (1986)

27. Stromer-Galley, J.: Diversity of political conversation on the internet: users' perspectives. J. Comput. Mediat. Commun. 8(3) (2006). https://doi.org/10.1111/j.1083-6101.2003.tb00215.x

28. Stromer Galley, J., Martinson, A.M.: Coherence or fragmentation?: comparing serious and social chat online. In: Proceedings of the Association for Internet Researchers Annual Conference, Sussex (2004)

29. Welbers, K., de Nooy, W.: Stylistic accommodation on an Internet forum as bonding: do posters adapt to the style of their peers? Am. Behav. Sci. 58(10), 1361–1375 (2014). https://doi.org/10.1177/0002764214527086

On the Robustness of Rating Aggregators Against Injection Attacks

Angelo Spognardi[1] and Marinella Petrocchi[2,3(✉)]

[1] Department of Computer Science, Università di Roma La Sapienza, Rome, Italy
spognardi@di.uniroma1.it
[2] Institute of Informatics and Telematics (IIT-CNR), Pisa, Italy
marinella.petrocchi@iit.cnr.it
[3] IMT School for Advanced Studies, Lucca, Italy

Abstract. For a decade now, Academia has been researching refined techniques to detect fake reviews. In this article, rather than proposing a new detection methodology, we propose to contain the consequences of an attack launched by a fake reviewer who attaches arbitrary scores to the review target. We demonstrate that, by simply changing the score aggregator, the review site can withstands smart and targeted attacks, even carried out for an extended period of time. While experimentation is carried on on real data from a popular e-advice website, our approach is general enough to be applied in any other information service where voting and ratings need to be aggregated.

Keywords: Reviews analysis · Fake reviews · Outlier confinement · Slotted aggregators

1 Introduction

User opinions about past transactions are an important information to help a customer and a vendor to evaluate pros and cons of the buying/selling when they interact. Given the importance of opinions, a deplorable practice is to write unfair opinions, to promote own products or to disparage products of competitors. This is not only morally regrettable, but also punishable by law, see, e.g., [20], the first Italian judgment that convicts both financially and criminally a natural person for selling fake review packages. Nevertheless, the plague of fake reviews is far from being eradicated. In September 2019, Tripadvisor published the first Review Transparency Report: the platform declared that, although many junk judgments have been blocked in 2018, the battle still goes on [21].

The important challenge of detecting unfair opinions has attracted and attracts the scientific community. The majority of studies deals with the detection of suspicious reviews through a supervised classification approach, where

Partially supported by MIUR (Italian Ministry of Education, University, and Research) under grant "Dipartimenti di eccellenza 2018–2022" of the Department of Computer Science of Sapienza University, by the European Union's Horizon 2020 project n.830892 SPARTA and by IMT Scuola Alti Studi Lucca: Integrated Activity Project TOFFEe 'TOols for Fighting FakEs'.

© Springer Nature Switzerland AG 2020
M. van Duijn et al. (Eds.): MISDOOM 2020, LNCS 12259, pp. 205–217, 2020.
https://doi.org/10.1007/978-3-030-61841-4_14

a ground truth of a priori known genuine and fake reviews is needed. Then, features about the labeled reviews, the reviewers and the reviewed products are engineered.

There is however a less traveled way in the literature, which aims to contain outliers rather than unveil fake reviews. In many e-reviews sites, in fact, products and services are presented to the user in order of score. Fake reviewers who aim to knock down an opponent's product, or to promote a service that they support, can act in groups, inserting bursts of reviews with very high scores (to promote) or very low scores (to discredit). Considering scores' aggregators, the mean is adopted by the most popular websites for e-advice. The median has been proposed in the literature as a metric less susceptible than the mean to outliers and bias, see, e.g., [6,7,9]. Defining, and playing with, other aggregators, work in [5] showed so-called *slotted aggregators*, considering scores as divided into temporal slots of equal length, are more robust to certain types of attacks. This work contributes with a wider analysis of robustness: We show that not only slotted aggregators are able to contain an attacker who inserts outlier scores in the most recent slot, i.e., working in real time and for once on the review, but also the 'patient' attacker, who possibly understands the strategy on which the slotted aggregators are based to contain the false votes, waits diligently and introduces outliers in multiple slots.

In this work, the use of alternatives to rating aggregators is experimented within a popular hotel review platform, where users give their rating to hotels. It is worth noticing, however, that the use of the proposed aggregators can be also easily be generalized to any information service that relies on voting and rating, including posts and news (i.e., Reddit, Disqus, and alike).

Upon introducing useful notions, we will show experiments and results in Sect. 3). We then conclude with related work and final remarks.

2 Background

This section introduces useful notions, as the definition of the rating aggregators, the dataset under investigation, and the kind of attacks we consider in the rest of the paper. Without loss of generality, we introduce the main terminology within the context of an e-advice platform rating hotels. However, we stress the fact that all the concepts are general enough to be easily adapted to other contexts.

2.1 Aggregator Essentials

Given a hotel h_j, the set of ratings X_j received by h_j (with $|X_j| = n_j$), we denote μ_j as the mean of such ratings, and M_j as their median. The mean μ_j is the average of the ratings in X_j, namely $\mu_j = \frac{1}{n_j} \sum_{r \in X_j} r$. The *median* M_j is obtained ordering the ratings $r \in X_j$, from the lowest to the highest, in a sequence $x_1, \ldots, x_{n_j}$ and picking

$$M_j = \begin{cases} x_{[\frac{n_j}{2}]} & \text{if } n_j \text{ is odd} \\ \frac{1}{2}\left(x_{[\frac{n_j}{2}]} + x_{[\frac{n_j}{2}]+1}\right) & \text{if } n_j \text{ is even} \end{cases} \tag{1}$$

where $[\frac{n_j}{2}]$ is the greatest integer less than or equal to $\frac{n_j}{2}$. In practice, if the sample size is an odd number, the median is defined to be the middle value of the ordered samples; if the sample size is even, the median is the average of the two middle values [18].

2.2 Slotted Aggregators

A usually public metadata associated to an online rating is the date of the review, namely, when the rating has been cast by the reviewer. This provides another way to sort the ratings and enables the definition of another type of aggregators, which consider all the ratings divided into temporal *slots* of equal length. Here, we remind the notion of *slotted mean* $S\mu_s$, introduced in [5], as the mean of the means of the ratings over a set S of slots s of a same amount of time. As in Fig. 1, if we denote with a_i the mean of the ratings received by the hotel h_j during slot i, we define $S\mu_s = \frac{1}{|S|}\sum_{i \in S} a_i$, omitting the slots with no ratings. For example, to evaluate the *weekly* slotted mean $S\mu_w$, we consider all the means of the ratings received during all the weeks and we average those means. Similarly, we can consider the *monthly* slotted mean $S\mu_m$, or any other period of time. The slotted mean shows many similarities with the "moving average", typical of time series analysis [23]: both the metrics consider the time when the measurements are collected and the average of such measurements. However, the moving average captures the trend of a phenomenon, reducing the effects of fluctuations, whereas the slotted mean gives a representative, but static, value of the phenomenon.

Work in [5] also considers the *slotted median SM*, i.e., the mean of the medians of the ratings over temporal slots of the same amount of time [5]. In the following, we will consider both the *weekly slotted median* SM_w and the *monthly slotted median* SM_m. Figure 1 depicts the relation between the ratings, the slots and the considered slotted aggregators. The weekly slotted mean considers the average of the simple means a_i of each slots, while the weekly slotted median considers the average of the medians M_i of each slot. When the slots are months, the single slots are bigger, since clearly they consider more ratings (for example $r_1, r_2, \ldots, r_9$, instead of r_1, r_2 for the first slot).

For a more rigorous definition of the robustness of an aggregator, we refer the interested reader to the concept of *breakdown point*, defined in robust statistics [1].

2.3 Dataset

The analyses presented in this work are launched over a dataset consisting of 447,659 reviews about hotels in Paris, gathered from Booking.com. The reference period for data gathering is September 23, 2011–11 July, 2013. Table 1 summarizes the amount of collected data. At time of data collection, reviewers could post numerical sub-scores regarding six hotels parameters (cleanness, comfort, services, staff, value for money, and location). The average of the six sub-scores

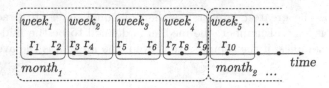

$$S\mu_w = \frac{1}{n} \sum_{i=1}^{n} a_i, \text{ where } a_1 = \frac{r_1+r_2}{2}, a_2 = \frac{r_3+r_4}{2} \ldots$$
$$SM_w = \frac{1}{n} \sum_{i=1}^{n} M_i, \text{ where } M_1 = med(r_1, r_2), M_2 = med(r_3, r_4) \ldots$$
$$S\mu_m = \frac{1}{n} \sum_{i=1}^{n} a_i, \text{ where } a_1 = \frac{r_1+r_2+\ldots+r_9}{9}, a_2 = \frac{r_{10}+\ldots}{\ldots} \ldots$$
$$SM_m = \frac{1}{n} \sum_{i=1}^{n} M_i, \text{ where } M_1 = med(r_1, r_2, \ldots, r_9), M_2 = med(r_{10}, \ldots) \ldots$$

Fig. 1. Slotted aggregators equations: week-slot and month-slot

Table 1. Dataset for hotels in Paris from *Booking.com*, updated at July 2013

City	Hotels	Reviews	Number of ratings			
			Avg	Stddev	Min	Max
Paris	1915	447659	278	281	3	2750

represented the reviewer score. The totality of reviewer scores for one hotel is then averaged to obtain the *global score* for that hotel: all the collected scores are in the range $[2.5, 10]$. Hotels are ranked by Booking.com according to global scores, from the hotel with the highest score, to the one with the lowest one. Hereafter, we may refer to global scores as simply *scores* or *ratings*.

2.4 Attacks and Analyses

We consider an attacker that injects scores at the extremes of the value scale, as in [7]: for the sake of readability we say that, by injecting the highest value (10), we perform a *push* attack and, by injecting the lowest value (2.5), a *nuke* attack [11]. We consider two types of analysis of the robustness of the aggregators: 1) one that considers how many outliers are needed to affect the rank of a hotel and 2) one that considers the effects of bursts of injections. For each hotel in the dataset, we compare its ranking against a static ranked list of the remaining hotels. In particular, the first experiment (*Altering the ranking*) is similar to the one in [7]: for each hotel, we count the number of outliers required to alter the ranking of the hotel, gaining or losing at least one position. In the second experiment (*Burst of injections*), for each hotel with at least 4 ratings, we inject 5%, 10%, and 20% of outer scores (with respect to the number of actual ratings) and count the number of lost/acquired positions. For example, for a hotel with 30 scores, we inject 1, 3, and 6 outer scores, respectively. We exclude those hotels having less than 4 ratings, since even 1 outlier would exceed the 20% of the actual ratings.

In this section, we consider the attacker to inject ALL the ratings in one single slot, namely the one with the most recent (w.r.t. the date) genuine ratings. In

Table 2. Average rank alteration made with burst of injections

Attack type	Injection rate	μ	M	$S\mu_w$	SM_w	$S\mu_m$	SM_m
Push	5%	61.88	50.81	24.98	15.77	43.54	34.01
	10%	121.18	107.67	30.38	19.53	65.81	41.42
	20%	226.18	203.50	39.48	27.30	91.00	49.37
Nuke	5%	139.01	32.05	51.40	13.91	91.89	24.07
	10%	266.25	62.54	62.69	18.81	140.37	29.42
	20%	456.81	123.74	80.66	27.25	192.80	44.13

the next section, we will take into account the more general case of an attacker spreading the injections within multiple slots.

The slotted versions of the mean and median have been already proved, under certain circumstances, more robust against bursts of outliers injections. Indeed, as long as the outliers fall within a single slot, the impacts of the attack are effectively mitigated, and the two aggregators can also ultimately avoid the modification of the ranking. In other words, it can happen that, regardless the number of outliers we try to inject, it is impossible to alter the ranking of an hotel. We say this condition a *no-win* situation, that recalls the concept of *breakdown point*, common in robust statistics: This has been proved in [5] and it also happens for some of our experiments considering in the next section.

Table 2 reports the average alteration in the global ranking, experienced by the hotels of Paris when we inject a number of outliers, which depends on the whole set of ratings for each hotel. As the injection rate increases, the pace at which the average rank alteration increases varies considerably for the different aggregators.

Considering the upper part of the table, the simple mean μ and the median M have the largest rank alterations, since the effect of the outliers keeps increasing as the injection rate grows. For the slotted aggregators, instead, the effects are clearly mitigated: since the injections are only confined in a single slot (simulating a massive burst of injections), the rank alteration is lower. The aggregator that better resists against massive injections is the slotted weekly median SM_w.

The lower part of Table 2, instead, considers injection of 2.5 (*nuke* attack). The alterations experienced by the simple mean are severely higher, even for the slotted mean aggregators $S\mu_w$ and $S\mu_m$. The median M, instead, appreciably reduces the average alterations (with respect to the *push* attack).

All in all, the slotted aggregators based on the median exhibit the best resilience against both *push* and *nuke* attacks.

To conclude this analysis, we report in Table 3 the ratio of hotels that do not change their position in the global ranking, after the burst of injections. The rankings based on the mean-based aggregators nearly always experience a position alteration. On the contrary, the rankings that rely on the median are more stable and exhibit significant alterations only with large bursts of injections (*i.e.*, 10% and 20%). Overall, the most stable ranking is obtained using slotted weekly median SM_w.

Table 3. Ratio of hotels whose rank does not change after attacks made with burst of injections.

Attack type	Injection rate	μ	M	$S\mu_w$	SM_w	$S\mu_m$	SM_m
Push	5%	0	0.75	0.05	0.55	0.01	0.34
	10%	0	0.53	0.05	0.55	0.01	0.32
	20%	0	0.20	0.05	0.54	0.01	0.32
Nuke	5%	0	0.74	0	0.62	0	0.56
	10%	0	0.54	0	0.61	0	0.54
	20%	0	0.20	0	0.61	0	0.53

3   Injection Attacks in an Extended Period of Time

To extend the evaluation of the robustness of the various aggregators, we consider a more general type of attack that injects the outliers in a longer period, namely in more than one slot. As previously observed, the time-based nature of the slotted aggregators has the beneficial effect to slow down the impact of the attacks, when compared to the simple mean. In this work, we consider a 'patient' attacker, operating on more than one time slot. As an additional conservative assumption, in all the experiments we do not take into account the –likely– event of legitimate users adding their scores to the hotels, interfering with the attacker.

Altering the Ranking. In this experiment, we keep injecting the outliers scores in a given number of slots, namely the most recent n slots, while holding the rank of all the other hotels fixed, until the target hotel changes its rank. Figures 2 and 3 show the results for the *altering the rank* experiment considering the slotted aggregators and multiple slot injection (from 2 to 12). We injected the outliers in a round robin fashion, distributing them from the newest (the most recent) slot to the oldest one: for example, if we had to inject 14 outliers in 6 slots, we placed three outliers in the two most recent slots and two in the remaining ones (i.e., 3, 3, 2, 2, 2, 2).

We can observe that the average number of outlier injections needed to change the rank noticeably varies w.r.t. the slotted mean and the slotted median. In Fig. 2, the number of outliers required is very low for the weekly slotted mean $S\mu_w$ and it is almost constant (slightly above 1), independently from the number of slots used for the injection. The weekly slotted median SM_w, instead, has a more variable trend, since the scores required to alter the rank severely change as the number of slots increases. However, the plot has to be evaluated also looking at the related *no-win ratio*, introduced in Sect. 2.4. The no-win ratio is defined as the ratio of hotels for which the alteration is not possible, because of a *no-win* situation: namely, independently from the number of outliers one can inject, the limited number of slots for injection eventually makes the alteration impossible. Consequently, a higher no-win ratio means a higher resistance against the attack.

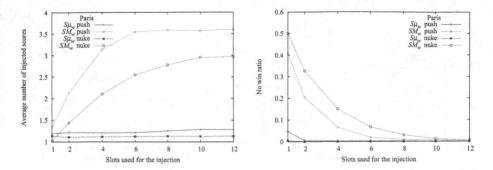

Fig. 2. Week-slot aggregators: altering the ranking with injections in multiple slots

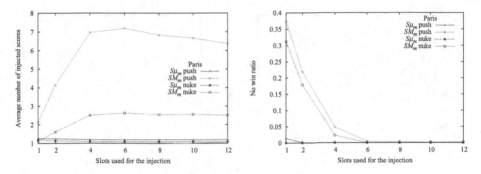

Fig. 3. Month-slot aggregators: altering the ranking with injections in multiple slots

In the right plot of Fig. 2, we can observe that, for the weekly slotted median SM_w, the no-win ratio decreases as the number of slots increases, together with the number of required injections. It is interesting to observe that while the *push* attacks are less effective than the *nuke* attacks for the weekly slotted median SM_w, they are essentially equal for the weekly slotted mean $S\mu_w$. This is even more evident for the monthly slotted aggregators, as shown in Fig. 3. Observing the plots, we can again notice that the number of injections required when considering multiple slots does not change for the monthly slotted mean $S\mu_m$, with the same trend of the single slot attack, while it significantly varies for the median counterpart SM_m.

From the above results, it is evident as the slotted aggregators relying on the median are considerably more robust when compared to those based on the mean. Moreover, as suggested by the no-win ratio plots, we also observe, as expected, that the multislot attacks are more effective than the single slot injections. However, we recall that this type of attack would require a considerable longer period to be realized.

Burst of Injections. We repeat the *burst of injections* experiment, considering an attacker that introduces outliers in several slots, varying the number of slots

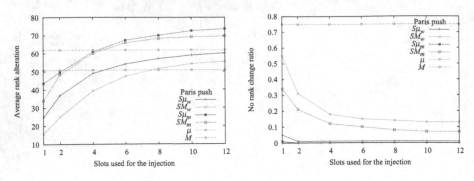

(a) Average rank alterations and no rank change ratio, 5% injection rate

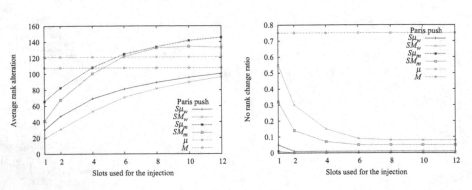

(b) Average rank alterations and no rank change ratio, 10% injection rate

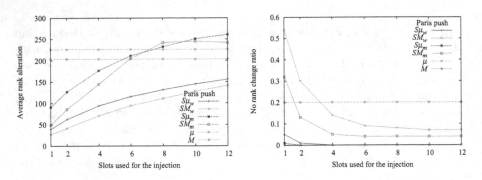

(c) Average rank alterations and no rank change ratio, 20% injection rate

Fig. 4. Rank alteration for a multislot *push* attack with bursts of injections.

from 1 to 12. Again, we fix the original rank of all the other hotels, while performing the injections. The outliers are injected in a round robin fashion, from the newest (the most recent) slot to the oldest one. For each setting (5%, 10% and 20% of injected outliers), we report in Fig. 4 and in Fig. 5 the average num-

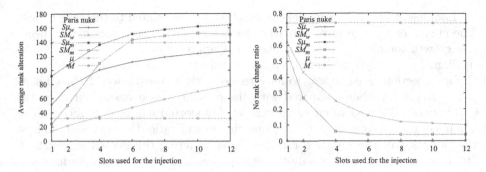

(a) Average rank alterations and no rank change ratio, 5% injection rate

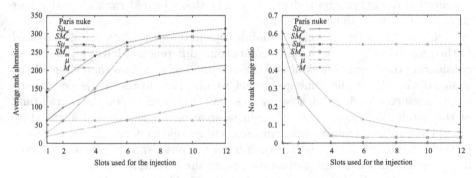

(b) Average rank alterations and no rank change ratio, 10% injection rate

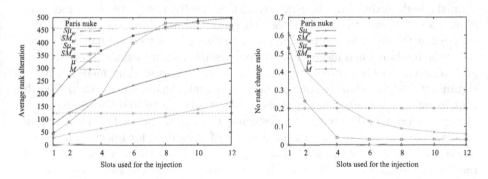

(c) Average rank alterations and no rank change ratio, 20% injection rate

Fig. 5. Rank alteration for a multislot *nuke* attack with bursts of injections.

ber of rank alterations and the no-win ratio for the *push* and the *nuke* attack, respectively. For the sake of comparison, we also plotted the results of the simple mean and the median in the single slot experiment, as reported in Table 2.

Looking at Fig. 4, we can make some observations related to the *push* attack. The curves of average rank alteration for the slotted aggregators have a peculiar growth for all the injection rates, that approaches the ones of mean and median, for weekly-based ones, and overhauls them, for monthly-based ones. Higher injection rates appear to have reduced effects on the weekly-based slotted aggregators, when compared with the monthly-based ones. Moreover, the gap between the median curve and the weekly slotted aggregators increases as the injection rate increases. Concerning the no-win ratio, the curves are almost the same for all the injection rates, when considering the slotted aggregators. However, it is evident that only the aggregators based on the median have significant no rank change ratios, that never reach 0, even when the number of injection slots is the highest. It is also evident that the median is almost always dominating the other aggregators, since it is able to avoid rank alterations for several hotels in all the experiments.

The above observations can be mainly repeated for the plots in Fig. 5, related to the *nuke* attack, but we can also remark some differences. Firstly, all the curves considering the average rank alterations assume higher values than those of the *push* attack. This is the same event that we observed in the single slot experiment, when considering that lower scores have higher effects on the overall rank of the hotels. We argue that the main motivation for the slotted aggregators being more robust against push, but more vulnerable to nuke attacks, is related to the distribution of ratings that each hotel receives. Namely, the large majority of the hotels has a high variability among the reviewers scores, but –almost always– the average of the scores is higher than 7. This means that each injected low outlier (for the *nuke* attack) is able to influence the aggregated value more than the high outlier (for the *push* attack). Secondly, the curve of the median is almost always lower than that of the other aggregators, with relevant differences only when the injection rate is 20% and the weekly slotted median SM_w overtakes the median when more than 10 slots are used for injections. Moreover, the gap between weekly slotted mean $S\mu_w$ and the corresponding median SM_w is significantly higher than the one of the *push* attack. Again, when considering the no-win ratio, the slotted aggregators based on the mean and the simple mean always undergo rank alterations, resulting to curves constantly with 0 value. Similarly to the *push* attack, as the number of slots used for injection increases, the ratio decreases for the slotted aggregators based on the median. The simple median, instead, always shows a solid resistance against the rank modification, for any injection rate.

In conclusion, we can summarize some considerations. Firstly, injections in multiple slots clearly reduce the effectiveness of the slotted aggregators to resist against bursts of injections. This leads to say that the resilience of the proposed aggregators is spent to make the attacks spanning in longer periods: the hotels that undergo the attacks change their rank, but only after weeks or months of injections. Secondly, the slotted aggregators based on week-slots appear to be more resistant than the monthly based, but those based on median also exhibit a significant no change ratio: the weekly slotted median SM_w can be considered the most robust slotted aggregator, since it performs better than all the others. When compared with the median, it is clearly less robust, but it has the ability to slow down the effectiveness of the injection attacks.

4   Related Work

This work examines the robustness of different types of aggregators, i.e., metrics whose value determines the formation of the ranking of products and services, based on the reputation that users declare on them by means of online reviews. The robustness is tested by introducing anomalous values, at the extremes of the reference range, to establish how many 'outliers' are needed to subvert the original ranking. In this respect, the work falls under the umbrella of so called outlier analysis.

'Outliers' - or anomalies - are instances that do not conform to the norm of a dataset'[1]. The analysis of outliers implies several goals, first of all their detection, and the definition of outliers depends strongly on the considered scenario. For example, the literature has dealt and currently deals with contexts such as intrusion and fraud detection, or disease condition detection, just to cite a few. In this regard, we recall the contributions in [15,17], which provide, respectively, 1) access to a large collection of outlier detection datasets with ground truth, ranged over security attacks, anomalies, and event detection; and 2) a methodology based on Sequential Ensemble Learning for outlier detection.

The existence of spam reviews has been known since the early 2000 s, when e-commerce and e-advice sites began to be popular. In the literature, the issue has been mostly addressed through the automatic classification of reviews, based on a series of features of the reviews and of the reviewer who writes them. In his seminal work [10], Liu lists three approaches to automatically identify opinion spam: the supervised, unsupervised, and group approaches. Standard supervised approaches have been proved to achieve good results with common algorithms such as Naive Bayes and Support Vector Machines [13]. Unfortunately, a ground truth of *a priori* known genuine and fake reviews is needed. This leads to two main drawbacks: the need to have annotated datasets and the possibility that a model trained on a dataset is not valid for others (i.e., for datasets of different domains).

Machine learning algorithms usually take as input a set of features of the data to be examined. Regarding reviews, the most common features come from characteristics of the reviewer and the review itself [8]. Features that have been proven to be valid for opinion spam detection are, e.g., the linguistic ones [4]. Also, an analysis of anomalous practices with respect to the average behavior of a genuine reviewer led to good results. Anomalous behavior of the reviewer may be related to general and early rating deviation [10] or temporal dynamics [24].

In recent years, a behavioral analysis of the target under investigation has been proven to be useful not only to discover individual fake users, but also

---

[1] http://odds.cs.stonybrook.edu/about-odds/ Accessed April 30, 2020.

to detect the coordinated and synchronized behavior that characterizes groups o malicious users. In the field of electronic word of mouth, researchers have highlighted how it is possible to find reviewers, in this case real humans, paid to review the same product with predefined schemes and timing [3]. Fake reviewers' coordination can emerge by mining frequent behavioral patterns and ranking the most suspicious ones, as done in [12,22].

Depending on the particular context, some of the above mentioned approaches can be preferred with respect to other ones. We emphasize that, whatever the approach used for fake reviews detection, this involves a phase of data pre-processing, to calculate features that commonly concern reviews, reviewers and reviewed products. As an example, in [16], Rayana et al. offer a holistic approach, called SPEAGLE, that utilizes features from the review meta-data (text, timestamp, rating) as well as relational data (the reviewers' network). A massive feature engineering process is also considered by very recent work, like that proposed by Barbado et al. in [2], which deals with the reviewers' activity and their social relationships, or that by Noekhah et al. [14], which enriches an already abundant features' set with novel ones such as the 'Review Group agreement', the 'Sentiment-Rate difference', and the 'Similar rating reviews'.

Although the article contribution does not have the ability to spot fake reviews, we remark the advantage to work at the score level only, as other authors have done before with other types of aggregators, see, e.g., [9]. Here, we prove that the adoption of slotted aggregators significantly contains those attacks manipulating the score of the review. It is known that the average user stops at the first results of an online search [19]. In the common case where products are shown to the user by rating, changing the aggregator with those suggested in this work confines the attacker's abilities and minimizes the satisfaction of the attack target.

5   Conclusions

In this study, we performed some experiments to evaluate the robustness and demonstrate the usefulness of adopting slotted aggregators for e-commerce and e-advice platforms. We showed that not only such aggregators are able to contain massive injection attacks, but also to slow down a very motivated and 'patient' attacker, that spans the attack over a long period. The proposed aggregators are effective and efficient alternatives to the standard mean, then, they can be applied to any information service that relies on voting and rating. As a future direction, we argue that slotted aggregators should be compared with other, more complex, aggregators, like the weighted mean and clustering algorithms.

References

1. Analytical Methods Committee, et al.: Robust statistics-how not to reject outliers. part 1. basic concepts. Analyst **114**(12) (1989)

2. Barbado, R., Araque, O., Iglesias, C.A.: A framework for fake review detection in online consumer electronics retailers. Inf. Process. Manag. **56**(4), 1234–1244 (2019). https://doi.org/10.1016/j.ipm.2019.03.002
3. Why I write fake online reviews (2019). https://www.bbc.com/news/uk-47952165
4. Crawford, M., Khoshgoftaar, T.M., Prusa, J.D., Richter, A.N., Al Najada, H.: Survey of review spam detection using machine learning techniques. J. Big Data **2**(1), 1–24 (2015). https://doi.org/10.1186/s40537-015-0029-9
5. Di Pietro, R., Petrocchi, M., Spognardi, A.: A lot of slots - outliers confinement in review-based systems. In: Web Information Systems Engineering, pp. 15–30 (2014)
6. Garcin, F., Faltings, B., Jurca, R., Joswig, N.: Rating aggregation in collaborative filtering systems. In: Recommender Systems, RecSys 2009, pp. 349–352. ACM (2009)
7. Garcin, F., et al.: Aggregating reputation feedback. In: ICORE (2009)
8. Jindal, N., Liu, B.: Analyzing and detecting review spam. In: Seventh IEEE International Conference on Data Mining (ICDM 2007), pp. 547–552 (October 2007). https://doi.org/10.1109/ICDM.2007.68
9. Jurca, R., Garcin, F., Talwar, A., Faltings, B.: Reporting incentives and biases in online review forums. TWeb **4**(2), 5:1–5:27 (2010)
10. Liu, B.: Sentiment Analysis and Opinion Mining. Morgan and Claypool, San Rafael (2012)
11. Mobasher, B., Burke, R., Bhaumik, R., Williams, C.: Toward trustworthy recommender systems: an analysis of attack models and algorithm robustness. ACM Trans. Internet Technol. **7**(4), 23-es (2007)
12. Mukherjee, A., et al.: Spotting fake reviewer groups in consumer reviews. In: 21st World Wide Web Conference, pp. 191–200 (2012)
13. Mukherjee, A., et al.: Spotting opinion spammers using behavioral footprints. In: 19th Knowledge Discovery and Data Mining, pp. 632–640. ACM (2013)
14. Noekhah, S., binti Salim, N., Zakaria, N.H.: Opinion spam detection: using multi-iterative graph-based model. Inf. Process. Manag. **57**(1), 102140 (2020)
15. Rayana, S.: ODDS library (2016). http://odds.cs.stonybrook.edu
16. Rayana, S., Akoglu, L.: Collective opinion spam detection: bridging review networks and metadata. In: Proceeding of the 21st ACM SIGKDD International Conference on Knowledge Discovery and Data Mining, KDD 2015 (2015)
17. Rayana, S., Zhong, W., Akoglu, L.: Sequential ensemble learning for outlier detection: a bias-variance perspective. In: Proceeding of IEEE International Conference on Data Mining, ICDM 2016 (2016)
18. Rice, J.: Mathematical Statistics And Data Analysis, vol. Duxbury Advanced, p. 3. Cole CENGAGE Learning, Brooks (2007)
19. How far down the search engine results page will most people go? (2017). https://www.theleverageway.com/blog/how-far-down-the-search-engine-results-page-will-most-people-go/
20. Investigations Spotlight: Jail Time for Review Fraud (2019). https://www.tripadvisor.com/TripAdvisorInsights/w4237
21. TripAdvisor Review Transparency Report (2019). https://www.tripadvisor.com/TripAdvisorInsights/w5144
22. Viswanath, B., et al.: Strength in numbers: robust tamper detection in crowd computations. In: Online Social Networks, pp. 113–124. ACM (2015)
23. Wei, W.W.S.: Time Series Analysis, 2nd edn. PEARSON Addison-Wesley, Boston (2006)
24. Xie, S., et al.: Review spam detection via temporal pattern discovery. In: 18th Knowledge Discovery and Data Mining, pp. 823–831. ACM (2012)

FakeYou! - A Gamified Approach for Building and Evaluating Resilience Against Fake News

Lena Clever[1]([⊠])[iD], Dennis Assenmacher[1][iD], Kilian Müller[1][iD],
Moritz Vinzent Seiler[1][iD], Dennis M. Riehle[1][iD], Mike Preuss[2][iD],
and Christian Grimme[1][iD]

[1] Department of Information Systems, University of Münster, Leonardo-Campus 3,
48149 Münster, Germany
lena.clever@wi.uni-muenster.de
[2] University of Leiden, Niels Bohrweg 1, 2333 CA Leiden, The Netherlands

Abstract. Nowadays fake news are heavily discussed in public and political debates. Even though the phenomenon of intended false information is rather old, misinformation reaches a new level with the rise of the internet and participatory platforms. Due to Facebook and Co., purposeful false information - often called fake news - can be easily spread by everyone. Because of high data volatility and variety in content types (text, images,...) debunking of fake news is a complex challenge. This is especially true for automated approaches, which are prone to fail validating the veracity of the information. This Work focuses on a gamified approach to strengthen the resilience of consumers towards fake news. The game FakeYou motivates its players to critically analyze headlines regarding their trustworthiness. Further, the game follows a "learning by doing strategy": by generating own fake headlines, users should experience the concepts of convincing fake headline formulations. We introduce the game itself, as well as the underlying technical infrastructure. A first evaluation study shows, that users tend to use specific stylistic devices to generate fake news. Further, the results indicate, that creating good fakes and identifying correct headlines are challenging and hard to learn.

Keywords: Fake news · News · Game · Mobile game · Misinformation

1 Introduction and Motivation

Besides text, images are a traditional and mighty vehicle to transport (wrong) information into peoples minds [2] making them most attractive for the purpose of intended misinformation - also called *fake news*. While some researchers report on images being of significant importance for reaching a wider audience [9], others show that information transported through (fabricated) images can change or even manipulate memories of viewers [15,22]. This is supported by

M. van Duijn et al. (Eds.): MISDOOM 2020, LNCS 12259, pp. 218–232, 2020.
https://doi.org/10.1007/978-3-030-61841-4_15

some cognitive factors which render mentally digested misinformation resistant to correction [13, 20]. Very recent evidence confirms that multimodal disinformation, i.e., disinformation comprising text- and image-based information is more credible than just textual information [11].

Fig. 1. Fake image, that claims the corona virus breakout of 2019 in China could be cured by consuming cocaine. The image was debunked by the Mimikama project, https://www.mimikama.at/allgemein/cocaine-kills-corona-virus/.

Image fabrication has for long been a skill only feasible for experts but modern computers or simple-to-use online services enable virtually everybody to make up fake images. An example for the simplicity of image-based fake news generation is shown in Fig. 1. Using the online service *BreakYourOwnNews*[1], a breaking news fake was produced that transported this misleading message.

With the rise of fake news [5], projects like *Mimikama*[2] started to search for false messages in order to expose and debunk them. Much of their work focuses on images [10]. Already before, research on *Facebook* [8] showed that especially image-based fakes cascade more deeply into social networks than correcting content. And of course, manual correction and research on each and every image is very time consuming making debunking permanently lagging behind. Also automation approaches for detecting fake news are not sufficient to solve the problem, as they are usually unable to validate textual as well as image-based content. Thus, current automation mainly addresses originality issues of images by trying to find whether an image was tempered or fabricated [7, 16].

In this work, we focus on consumer resilience as another important building block of fighting fake news in practice. Instead of relying on external services like debunking and automated detection of manipulated images, we aim for a gamified approach

---

[1] https://breakyourownnews.com/.
[2] https://www.mimikama.at.

1. to sensitize social media consumers for the issue of multimodal (image- and text-based) fake news in general,
2. to demonstrate the individual challenges in evaluating presented information pieces in a restricted environment (like social media or news aggregator apps), and
3. to enable consumers to experience and possibly develop techniques of generation for misleading information.

All aspects are integrated into a single mobile application, in which users annotate original press photographs and images extracted from real news articles with fake text headlines. At the same time, users have to find the true headline in a multiple choice competition among fakes produced by other users. Both, successfully deceiving others and finding out the truth are rewarded.

As an intended side effect, this app is able to store any produced content and interaction data of users for further evaluation. As such, we provide this app as an education and evaluation platform for fostering and investigating resilience against fake news. The present work introduces the architecture and concept of this application and demonstrates a perspective for future research within a small case study with $N = 53$ participants.

The work is structured as follows: Sect. 2 gives a short overview on some current perspectives on fake news, the reception of misinformation and current research in the context of this work. Thereafter, Sect. 3 provides a glimpse into the game rules and concept, before Sect. 4 introduces the aspects of the software's architecture and components. Section 5 presents a case study on how user interaction and user generated content can be evaluated to learn about challenges in fake news detection and generation. The paper is concluded in Sect. 6.

2   Related Work

The distribution and deceiving use of wrong or fabricated information is a rather old phenomenon [2]. Historians in the pre-printing era used them as vehicles to influence the view of generations on a leader or emperors deeds [6] and information twisting certainly increased with the invention of printing techniques and the rise of mass media [17]. However, during the last decade and specifically with the emergence of the internet and social media, the term *fake news* appeared in the public sphere.

In principle, the term still relates to false or fabricated information (misinformation) used for a specific, often disinformation-related, purpose. However, it is important to note that the understanding and usage of the term fake news have started to bifurcate. As Quandt et al. state, the term is now also used as "a derogatory term denouncing media and journalism" [18].

Apart from the increasingly blurry use of the term, three important factors changed compared to the pre-internet eras: (1) the fabrication of misinformation has become very simple due to computer and software technology advancements, (2) the global spreading of (mis)information is accessible to virtually everybody, and (3) information has become a commodity in modern life [2]. This paves the ground for a massive increase of false information spread in social media, which is observable over the last years [2].

With the increasing relevance of intended misinformation, research focuses on different aspects of fake news definitions [21] and cognitive effects but recently also on means for suppression and debunking. Due to the existence of misinformation long before the term fake news was coined, research is far more advanced in the investigation of cognitive effects of false information to the human memory and capabilities to process corrections. Consequently, cognitive sciences are quite sure that misinformation transported by images is capable of changing memories of viewers [15, 22]. At the same time, cognitive processes seem to fill gaps in consumer memories with fake information and support conclusion models that are rather immune against correction efforts [13, 20]. Additionally, there is some evidence that repeated exposure to rumors and misinformation strengthen the belief in them [1, 4]. Consequently, action as well as research on countering the effect of fake news addresses the exposure of consumers. While some favor fact checking [10] and information correction [13] as reaction to fake news, Barrera et al. [3] find that fact checking alone is not sufficient to change peoples mind. A more technical approach is followed by those who try to use machine learning and image forensics techniques in order to detect fabricated images by learning manipulation patterns [7, 16].

Both streams (understanding of fake effects and mechanisms as well as technological support) are also addressed in gamified research projects that integrate consumers of information. Rozenbeek et al. [19] design a browser-based serious game[3] that demonstrates users how polarisation, emotions, conspiracy theory, trolling, and impersonation are used for fake news production and spread. They use the gaming data of about 15,000 participants to demonstrate that the game helps in increasing resilience of participants against fake news. However, the gameplay is rather sophisticated and based on a time consuming click-through simulated game flow, as well as on mostly text messages. With the intention of studying the influence of guidance in gameplay, Lutzke et al. [14] exposed participants – one group with guidelines on how to deal with information, a control group without guidelines – in an online experiment to fake news. The authors find, that guided participants had a reduced likelihood to share or like fake messages afterwards. Katsaounidou et al. [12] provide the MAthE fake news game, a serious game that addresses verification and correction techniques/services. Therefore, the game provides a simulated search engine, reverse image search, an image verification assistant, and a debunking site. The authors find preliminary indications for raised awareness regarding authentication and verification tools.

However, each fake news game has a rather sophisticated gameplay and usually a strong educational focus on fake news production techniques or verification to direct player attention as well as learning processes. In this work, we try to combine both fake news production and evaluation in a very simple rule set

---

[3] https://getbadnews.com/.

222 L. Clever et al.

and highly competitive gameplay to increase player dedication. Players are not guided through an educational program but should get aware of the simplicity of faking and the complexity of evaluating multimodal information in a restricted (app) environment indirectly by playing.

3 Game Rule Set

In the following, we will briefly introduce the game FakeYou. The two main goals of a player in the game FakeYou are:

1. Create a convincing fake headline for a given newspaper article image.
2. Figure out the correct headline of this image, by choosing one of 3 candidates, where one headline is the original headline of the newspaper article, and the others are given by two opponents.

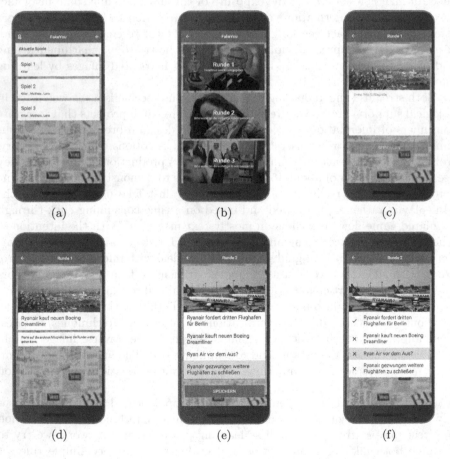

Fig. 2. The steps from (a) to (f) schematically describe the flow of the game and the ruleset of FakeYou.

After registration with an unique user name, the user accesses the game lobby (Fig. 2a). The game lobby consists of a list of started and finished games, as well as a button (+) in the right upper corner to start a new game. When a new game is started, the player has to wait until two other players opt to start a new game. As soon as three players are available, they are assigned to a new game and forwarded to the game page. Each game consits of three rounds. They are presented to user in an overview page, see Fig. 2b. After selecting a round, the player can insert a suitable fake headline for the given image (Fig. 2c). The goal is to create a fake headline, which is believed true by other players. When all three players inserted their headline, the round is forwarded to the evaluation step (Fig. 2d and e).

Here, the correct headline has to be chosen out of three possible options (the two inserted headlines of the opponents and the original headline scarped with the picture). Picking the correct headline is scored by 2 points and fooling a player with a fake headline is scored by 3 points. After each player picked a headline, results are presented to the players (Fig. 2f).

In the following section, a brief overview over the technical implementation and components of FakeYou is given.

4   Architecture

The general architecture of the game consists of a front end and a back end, as depicted in Fig. 3, where the back end is divided into different services.

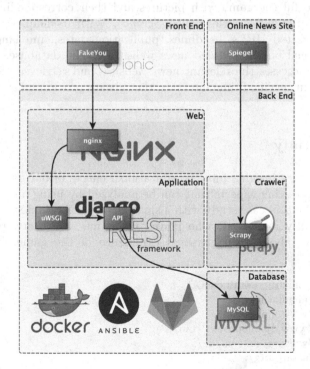

Fig. 3. Architecture of front and back end

FakeYou is designed as a mobile app allowing it to be played online on both personal computers as well as smartphones and tablets. Moreover, we implemented the game as a hybrid app in order to make it possible to play it with different operating systems such as *Android* or *iOS*, thus reaching a wider audience.

As depicted on the left upper corner of Fig. 3, the front end is developed with the help of the *ionic* framework[4]. *Ionic* is an open source framework for the development of hybrid apps, which is built on Angular. *Angular 2*[5] is a *TypeScript*-based, open source web application platform especially developed for front ends. Thus, it structures and connects the different views of the front end as well as offering multiple libraries for encryption and other features.

Apart from the front end and the third party information available on the internet, all information is stored within the back end as shown in the lower part of Fig. 3. Information is accessed, encrypted, and transmitted via a *nginx*[6] web server and a *django*[7] REST framework. While *nginx* acts as a proxy which facilitates the communication between the app and the back end, the django framework handles data access and the database via an API. As database we use *MySQL*[8]. The pictures required for FakeYou are stored on the hard disk, only storing the paths leading to the pictures in *MySQL*. Apart from the pictures, all further important information required for FakeYou e.g.. the user identification, scores, authentication tokens, and statistics are stored in *MySQL*. Neither the app itself nor the web server has direct access to the database. Consequently, the database always delivers a complete and correct picture of all relevant data.

In order to fill the game with pictures and their corresponding headlines, we make use of a web crawler called *Scrapy*[9]. With its help, we are able to store the connected URLs, headlines, publication dates, and languages from articles published on the crawled news websites in the database. The crawler automatically accesses the relevant news websites and retrieves and stores the headline links in specified time intervals, thus always providing new headlines as well as pictures.

5   Case Study

To get preliminary insights into the educational effects of our game and exemplary show interesting aspects that can be analyzed by using our tool, we conducted an evaluation case study with a small number of volunteers (mostly students and faculty members), who played the game and afterwards answered a questionnaire about their personal experience of the game. It should be

---

[4] See: https://ionicframework.com/.
[5] See: https://angular.io/.
[6] See: https://www.nginx.com/.
[7] See: https://www.djangoproject.com/.
[8] See: https://www.mysql.com/de/.
[9] See: https://scrapy.org/.

emphasized that this rather small study with its exploratory analysis is only intended as a showcase, or proof of concept, to motivate the diverse applications of our tool.

5.1   Study Setup and Data

In total, 53 persons participated in the game (75% male, 25% female). The gaming time varied between 30 min up to two hours. However, the number of games the players had played in these specified time intervals varied considerably from player to player. The amount of rounds played by every user during the case study is depicted in Fig. 4 and varied between 1 and 75. Fifty percent of the participants played 12 to 24 rounds which equals 4 to 8 games. There are only a few *super users* who played fake you up to 75 rounds (25 games).

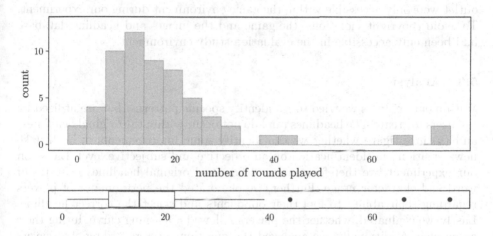

Fig. 4. Deviation of number of rounds played during the evaluation study.

In total, 311 headlines, crawled from a German newspaper website, were used during the evaluation study. The players created 1,080 fake headlines within the study time span of 7 hours. The data collection consisted of two parts. First, we invited the participants to play the game as often as they wanted within a time interval of seven hours. By this, we were able to collect data including the participants fake headlines, their opponents, the correct headlines they were able to detect, the headlines where they were fooled by other users, as well as whom and how often they were able to fool. Additionally, we gathered some metadata such as the number of games played by each user, the scores for every round and some further information like cancelled games.

After playing the game, we asked the participants to complete a questionnaire, which we conducted for two reasons: first, it was our intention to learn more about the players' gaming experience and the handling of the game. Besides, we asked them to provide us with suggestions regarding how we could further improve the app. Secondly, we collected additional relevant data for our analyses such as demographic data of the players (gender and age), their playing times, and how difficult it was for them to come up with fake news and to distinguish fake from real news. Of particular interest for our analyses were the answers concerning whether they were subjectively able to improve in playing the game over time.

5.2   Ethics and Legal Aspects

During the experiment no personal data has been collected or stored. Participants were introduced to choose an artificial user nickname/alias to play the game. We explicitly asked the users to select a name, which has no connection to their real name. Further, it should be emphasized that the game was evaluated within an experimental setting. Images and crawled headlines from the news outlet were only accessible within the game environment during our experiment. To avoid copyright violations, the game and the image- and headline-database had been only accessible in the evaluation study environment.

5.3   Analysis

Within our analyses we tried to (a) identify specific patterns that are utilized by the users to create fake headlines (and do not occur within the original headlines) and (b) investigate whether we can identify some improvements in both, fake news creation and identification on an objective and subjective level. Based on our experiment, we therefore analyzed fake and original headlines in terms of word and character usage. Further, we elaborated the performance of players regarding their ability to fool their opponents and select the correct headline. Lastly, we evaluated, whether the players followed a learning curve during their game play. Additionally, we analyzed the questionnaires regarding the players perceived game experiences.

Figure 5 depicts the amount of words used in both the fake (orange) and the correct (blue) headlines. The amount of words used within a headline is stated on the x-axis, while the y-axis displays the density of both types of headlines. Both distributions are normalized due to the unequal number of fake and original headlines. The two distributions are significantly different according to a conducted Wilcoxon Rank-Sum Test ($p \leq 0.001$). It is noticeable, that although the peaks of both densities are close together, the fake headlines tend to be comprised out of more words than the correct ones (which is also reflected by different means: 6.33 vs 5.21). Furthermore, the correct headlines exhibit a lower variance in the number of words.

In Fig. 6 the usage of punctuation marks and special characters (x-axis) in correct headlines and fake headlines is depicted. The relative number[10] of headlines containing the character or punctuation is displayed on the y-axis.

---

[10] For normalization the number of fake/correct headlines containing the character or punctuation is divided by the total number of fake/correct headlines.

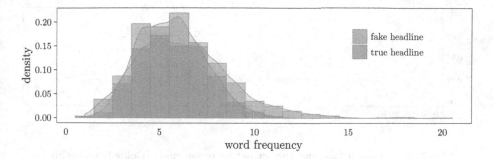

Fig. 5. Word frequency density in fake and correct headlines. (Color figure online)

The relative number of correct headlines is represented in blue, and fake headlines in red. The most prominent finding yielded by this Figure is that colons were a striking stylistic device in fake headlines but never occurred in correct ones.

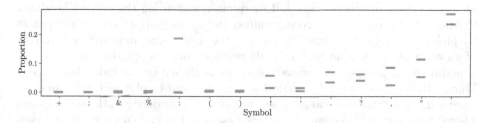

Fig. 6. Usage of punctuation marks and special characters in fake (red) and correct (blue) headlines. (Color figure online)

Even though the differences are much smaller, exclamation marks, question marks, full stops, and hyphens are more frequent in the fake than in the correct headlines. On the other hand, the opposite applies to quotation marks, commas, and apostrophes, which occur more often in the correct headlines. In Fig. 7 the relative score for fooling and correct bets per player are depicted. For normalization purposes, the total number of points achieved by fooling other players is divided by the number of games times the maximum score[11], which can be achieved in one game by fooling other players. The same is done for the total number of points achieved by betting the correct headline. In this case the number of games is multiplied by the maximum score[12], which can be achieved by betting three times the right headline.

---

[11] Fooling two opponents in each of the three rounds sums up in a maximum fake score of 18 (= (3 + 3) * 3).

[12] Betting the correct headline three times in a game leads to a maximum correct bet score of 6 (= 2 * 3).

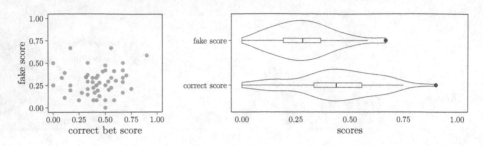

Fig. 7. Deviation of fake and correct bet score per user. (Color figure online)

The left subplot in Fig. 7 consists of a user scatter plot (fake creation vs. true headline identification). The distributions of the data points, indicate that players differ strongly in their skills. There is no strong correlation between the ability to create good fake headlines and identifying a true headline. While most players are located in the middle area of the scales - meaning, that they received a moderate amount of score points by fooling and correct bets - only a few outliers exist. Outliers at the left upper corner represent players, which are good at fooling their opponents, but fail more often in finding the correct headline. Outliers at the right upper corner gained the major part of their score points by picking the right headline. The color of the data points indicates the number of games a player completed. The scale reaches from orange (one game) to blue (maximum 25) games. The number of games is chosen by the individual player. During the evaluation study, participants are allowed to play as much games as they want in a total time range of seven hours. The majority of the participants played between 1 and 6 games. The *super users* of the evaluation study (marked in light blue) are located in the center of the plot, indicating that the relation of their fake score and correct bet score is balanced.

On the right hand side of the Figure, violin plots for the fake and correct bet scores on basis of the individual players are given. Again, score points are normalized by the number of games and the maximum score, which can be achieved. Most of the players chose the right headline in 33 to 56% (median = 44%) of the rounds. In contrast to the achieved fake scores, the distribution of points achieved by betting the correct headline is widely dispersed. The values reach from 0 to 0.9, where the latter represents a player who nearly always chose the correct headline. The distribution of the fake scores is more compressed. The majority of players reach relative scores between 19 and 36% (median = 28%) of the maximum achievable scores for fooling their opponents. The best fake headline creator achieved a relative score of 67%.

Within Fig. 8 the temporal development of the players performance in creating convincing fake headlines and betting the correct headline is depicted. To visualize the players learning rate, we first filtered for users, who played at least 16 rounds (which resembles the mean of the sample). The filtering results in 19 participants. For each of these participants we fitted a linear model, mapping the number of achieved fake and correct bet score points and played rounds.

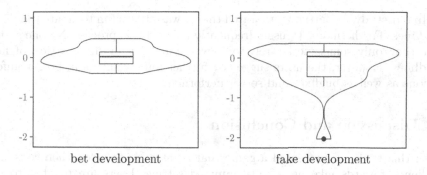

bet development   fake development

Fig. 8. Word frequency density in fake and correct headlines.

In a next step, we extracted the slope out of each linear model and compared the values. The comparison of the fake and correct bet developments are visualized within the two boxplots of Fig. 8. Negative values indicate a negative trend over time, whereas positive values indicate an improvement of the player.

For the bet development, neither a downgrade of scores nor a remarkable improvement can be observed. Interestingly the variance within the fake development is higher. Players tend to get worse in fooling their opponents. Admittedly, the information value of this visualization must be seen critically, as the number of observations is quite small. Further, additional side effects can not be excluded. The game always consists of the two goals "fool opponents" and "bet the correct headline". We do not know, if the ability to chose the right headline might decrease by the fact, that people "learn" to fake, which blurs the results of the performance development.

5.4   Evaluation of the Gameplay

As the evaluation study served as a first test for the FakeYou Game application, we asked participants to fill out an online questionnaire to evaluate the game from a user's perspective. Next to age and gender, participants were asked to state how much they liked the game in terms of design and usability. Further, the participants are obliged to report how they perceived their performance and fun level in betting and the creation of fake headlines. Additionally, we asked whether the participant thinks that he/she became better in figuring out the correct headline. Two participants thought they got better with every round they played. In the eyes of 15 users new rounds frequently improved their ability to find the correct headline. 18 participants stated that new rounds sometimes raised their awareness towards the wrong headlines. A rare improvement was observed by eight users and only two felt no advancement in their capabilities to identify the fake headlines. Interestingly, the majority of the participants perceived at least a small improvement on their ability to figure out the correct headline. Although this perception is only slightly underpinned by the results reported in Fig. 8.

230 L. Clever et al.

In our study, 31 participants stated that it was always fun to create their own headlines. Furthermore, 14 users frequently enjoyed this process. No one stated that they only sometimes, rarely, or never found joy in the creation of fake headlines. However, the users suggested further improvements in both comfort options as well as bugfixes and server performance.

6 Discussion and Conclusion

With this work, we presented a game that is intended to strengthen consumer resilience towards fake news in a gamified setting. Users are pointed to the challenges in detecting fake news and are motivated to think about ways to fake others. The educational effect of both ingredients has to be evaluated further in future work. In order to support further evaluation, the game is designed to collect all game and behavioral data of players.

The case study presented in this paper showcased how the game can be applied to get deeper insights into player behavior. Exemplarily, we found for the special case of the German newspaper headlines and image material that players used different stylistic means for creating headlines.

Regarding player performance, the comparison of fake and correct bet scores of the players indicated large diversity in game play. The majority of players showed a balanced distribution of fake and correct bet scores. Only a few participants gained their major score points by fooling their opponents with convincing fake headlines. Whereas in sum, the results prefigure that betting the correct headline was easier than fooling other players.

As a typical showcase, our study comes with a few limitations. First of all, only one German newspaper website was crawled. Certainly, writing styles of headlines differ between newspapers, which might lead to different results in the analysis, but also in the game play itself. However, adjusting the crawler to other websites is straightforward. the crawler can easily be adjusted in order to gather pictures and headlines from other websites. Furthermore, the case study was conducted with only about 50 participants, which were mainly recruited at university. Certainly, a larger and more representative panel of player need to be evaluated in future work. Additionally, the case study design could be altered in a way, which would allow to relate participants game results with their respective answers to the questionnaire. This would offer further insights, by comparing their perceived improvements with their true performance.

Acknowlegments. The research leading to these results received funding by the Federal Ministry of Education and Research, Germany (Project: PropStop, FKZ 16KIS0495K), the federal state of North Rhine-Westphalia and the European Regional Development Fund (EFRE.NRW 2014–2020, Project: MODERAT!, No. CM-2-2-036a), and the Ministry of Culture and Science of the federal state of North Rhine-Westphalia (Project: DemoResil, FKZ 005-1709-0001, EFRE-0801431). All authors appreciate the support of the European Research Center for Information Systems (ERCIS).

References

1. Balmas, M.: When fake news becomes real: combined exposure to multiple news sources and political attitudes of inefficacy, alienation, and cynicism. Commun. Res. **41**(3), 430–454 (2014). https://doi.org/10.1177/0093650212453600
2. Bannatyne, M., Piekarzewska, A., Koch, C.: If you could believe your eyes: images and fake news, pp. 128–133 (2019). https://doi.org/10.1109/IV-2.2019.00034
3. Barrera, O., Guriev, S., Henry, E., Zhuravskaya, E.: Facts, alternative facts, and fact checking in times of post-truth politics. J. Public Econ. **182**, 104123 (2020). https://doi.org/10.1016/j.jpubeco.2019.104123
4. Berinsky, A.J.: Rumors and health care reform: experiments in political misinformation. Br. J. Polit. Sci. **47**(2), 241–262 (2017). https://doi.org/10.1017/S0007123415000186
5. Bovet, A., Makse, H.A.: Influence of fake news in Twitter during the 2016 US presidential election. Nature Commun. **10**(1), 1–14 (2019). https://doi.org/10.1038/s41467-018-07761-2
6. Burkhardt, J.M.: History of fake news. Libr. Technol. Rep. **53**(8), 5–9 (2017)
7. Dang, L., Hassan, S., Im, S., Moon, H.: Face image manipulation detection based on a convolutional neural network. Expert. Syst. Appl. **129**, 156–168 (2019). https://doi.org/10.1016/j.eswa.2019.04.005
8. Friggeri, A., Adamic, L.A., Eckles, D., Cheng, J.: Rumor cascades. In: Adar, E., Resnick, P., Choudhury, M.D., Hogan, B., Oh, A.H. (eds.) Proceedings of the Eighth International Conference on Weblogs and Social Media, ICWSM 2014, Ann Arbor, Michigan, USA, June 1–4, 2014. The AAAI Press (2014), http://www.aaai.org/ocs/index.php/ICWSM/ICWSM14/paper/view/8122
9. Gunawan, F., Suwandi, V.: Identifying the most influencing characteristics of fake news. ICIC Express Lett. Part B: Appl. **11**(1), 93–101 (2020). https://doi.org/10.24507/icicelb.11.01.93
10. Haigh, M., Haigh, T., Kozak, N.: Stopping fake news: the work practices of peer-to-peer counter propaganda. Journalism Stud. **19**(14), 2062–2087 (2018). https://doi.org/10.1080/1461670X.2017.1316681
11. Hameleers, M., Powell, T.E., Meer, T.G.V.D., Bos, L.: A picture paints a thousand lies? the effects and mechanisms of multimodal disinformation and rebuttals disseminated via social media. Polit. Commun. 1–21 (2020). https://doi.org/10.1080/10584609.2019.1674979
12. Katsaounidou, A., Vrysis, L., Kotsakis, R., Dimoulas, C., Veglis, A.: MathE the game: a serious game for education and training in news verification. Education Sciences **9**(2), 155 (2019). https://doi.org/10.3390/educsci9020155
13. Lewandowsky, S., Ecker, U.K.H., Seifert, C.M., Schwarz, N., Cook, J.: Misinformation and its correction: continued influence and successful debiasing. Psychol. Sci. Public Interest **13**(3), 106–131 (2012). https://doi.org/10.1177/1529100612451018. PMID: 26173286
14. Lutzke, L., Drummond, C., Slovic, P., Árvai, J.: Priming critical thinking: simple interventions limit the influence of fake news about climate change on Facebook. Global Environ. Change **58**, 101964 (2019). https://doi.org/10.1016/j.gloenvcha.2019.101964
15. Nash, R.A., Wade, K.A., Brewer, R.J.: Why do doctored images distort memory? Conscious. Cogn. **18**(3), 773–780 (2009)
16. Parikh, S., Khedia, S., Atrey, P.: A framework to detect fake tweet images on social media, pp. 104–110 (2019). https://doi.org/10.1109/BigMM.2019.00-37

17. Posetti, J., Matthews, A.: A short guide to the history of 'Fake News' and disinformation: a new ICFJ learning module (2018). https://www.icfj.org/news/short-guide-history-fake-news-and-disinformation-new-icfj-learning-module

18. Quandt, T., Frischlich, L., Boberg, S., Schatto-Eckrodt, T.: Fake news, pp. 1–6. American Cancer Society (2019). https://doi.org/10.1002/9781118841570.iejs0128, https://onlinelibrary.wiley.com/doi/abs/10.1002/9781118841570.iejs0128

19. Roozenbeek, J., van der Linden, S.: Fake news game confers psychological resistance against online misinformation. Palgrave Commun. **5**(1), 1–10 (2019). https://doi.org/10.1057/s41599-019-0279-9

20. Sacchi, D.L., Agnoli, F., Loftus, E.F.: Changing history: doctored photographs affect memory for past public events. Appl. Cogn. Psychol. Official J. Soc. Appl. Res. Mem. Cogn. **21**(8), 1005–1022 (2007)

21. Tandoc Jr., E.C., Lim, Z.W., Ling, R.: Defining "Fake News": a typology of scholarly definitions. Digital Journalism **6**(2), 137–153 (2018). https://doi.org/10.1080/21670811.2017.1360143

22. Wade, K.A., Garry, M., Read, J.D., Lindsay, D.S.: A picture is worth a thousand lies: using false photographs to create false childhood memories. Psychon. Bull. Rev. **9**(3), 597–603 (2002)

Combating Disinformation: Effects of Timing and Correction Format on Factual Knowledge and Personal Beliefs

Leonie Schaewitz[1] and Nicole C. Krämer[2]([⊠])

[1] Ruhr-Universität Bochum, 44801 Bochum, Germany
leonie.schaewitz@rub.de
[2] Universität Duisburg-Essen, 47057 Duisburg, Germany
nicole.kraemer@uni-due.de

Abstract. Although the need to understand the mechanisms of disinformation correction has been recognized, research on the effects of different forms of correcting messages is still scarce. Based on assumptions of the continued influence effect, we tested in a 2 (detailed versus simple correction) × 2 (immediate versus belated correction) between-subjects experimental study ($N = 221$) whether more detailed corrections are more effective in reducing misperceptions than simple corrections and whether they are particularly influential when presented belatedly. Results demonstrate that detailed corrections indeed lead to higher recall of correct facts but do not reduce concerns regarding the topic of the disinformation. When more detailed corrections are presented immediately together with the disinformation, they even seem to be counterproductive as they foster personal beliefs that are related to the disinformation. Regarding factual knowledge, the effect is reversed: When presented immediately with the disinformation, detailed corrections lead to a higher recall of correct facts than simple corrections. This suggests that we need to combat the influence of disinformation on factual knowledge and on personal beliefs in different ways.

Keywords: Disinformation · Misinformation · Corrections · Continued influence effect · Fake news

1 Introduction

Combating disinformation on the Internet is important because many individuals nowadays consume (political) news online and use the information found online to build their opinions. Hence, it seems relevant to ensure that citizens are exposed to accurate information and not to *disinformation*, commonly known as *fake news* and defined as fabricated news content that is deliberatively spread to disguise or manipulate (e.g., [1, 8]).

Since it is hardly possible, neither legally nor technically, to completely stop the dissemination of false information on the Internet, one particular strategy to combat the influence of disinformation is fact-checking and providing online users with corrections. With false information spreading broader and faster than true news via social media [19],

© Springer Nature Switzerland AG 2020
M. van Duijn et al. (Eds.): MISDOOM 2020, LNCS 12259, pp. 233–245, 2020.
https://doi.org/10.1007/978-3-030-61841-4_16

there is an increasing research interest in how individuals receive, process, and react to such corrections of false information. More particularly, there is a need to investigate how corrections should be designed and provided to readers in order to effectively reduce the influence of disinformation.

Based on misinformation research and findings on the continued influence effect or misinformation effect (for reviews see [9, 10]), there is ample evidence that it is hard to reduce and potentially impossible to eliminate the influence of false information, as individuals keep on relying on the information even when it has been corrected. Although researchers have, for example, revealed that corrections that provide an alternative cause to an event [7, 12] are more effective in correcting misperceptions than simply stating that a false statement is not true, there are still many open questions left, as for example, how to effectively reduce the belief in completely fabricated events or misleading statements that do not include a cause-effect relationship.

One suggestion is to provide more detailed explanations on why information was false [17]. For example, providing more details or background information and adducing plausible counter-arguments on why something cannot be true could be effective strategies to reduce false beliefs.

In addition, it seems relevant to investigate how important it is that online users receive an immediate update of false information compared to a belated correction. It is possible that corrections are more efficient when they are processed at the same time as false information, because then false information might not make its way into memory in the first place – in the sense that it is not integrated in existing memory structures and the relevant "situation model" [18]. When users, however, receive the corrections at a later time it is necessary to remind them of the false information first in order to correct it. In this case, individuals process the false information twice; hence, the form of the correction (e.g., whether it explains in a plausible and attractive way why information was false) might be more important to reduce the influence of false information.

This paper therefore aims to investigate how different levels of detail in corrective messages as well as the moment at which it is processed influence the belief in false information. By means of an experiment with a 2 × 2 between-subjects design, we specifically examine the effect of simple versus more detailed corrections (type of correction), the effect of corrections presented directly together with false information or belated (time of correction), and the interaction effect of the type and time of the correction.

2 Theoretical Background

The continued influence or misinformation effect [7, 9, 11] describes the phenomenon that individuals keep on relying on false information even when they know that it is wrong. The typical research paradigm for studies on the continued influence effect includes that participants read a scenario about an event (e.g., a fire outbreak) and some receive a correction of a piece of false information that was presented in the course of the story. Although participants acknowledge the presence of a corrective message and even state to believe it, the research shows that they use the false information when they are asked to make inferences about the cause of the event.

2.1 Level of Detail of Correction

A large number of studies on this phenomenon show that there is substantial evidence that a basic retraction of information by simply declaring it as false is not an effective strategy to contain the influence of misinformation (see [9] for an overview). In fact, research has shown that individuals keep on relying on false information after it has been corrected. However, scholars revealed several criteria that can influence this effect: One key condition to reduce the reliance on false information is the provision of an alternative explanation for the cause of an event instead of simply stating that a formally named cause was false [4, 7]. This is also supported by the findings of a recent meta-analysis on the effects of misinformation corrections, which suggests that corrective messages are more effective when they appeal to coherence in terms of plausible alternative causes to misleading information, compared to, for example, simple fact-checking [20]. In addition, a more detailed debunking, such as a correction that provides information on why the original information was false in the first place, was shown to be more effective – especially with regard to remembering facts correctly after a longer time [17].

Other research, however, indicates that more detailed debunking of false information can also be disadvantageous, as it might increase the persistence of misleading information after it has been corrected [2]. In this regard, a popular assumption is that more detailed corrections would necessarily need to include the false information itself and might thereby strengthen its influence. Against the background of the literature on familiarity effects, this argument seems plausible because repetition of information – even when it is repeated to correct it – increases familiarity with the information (see e.g., [15] for more information) and familiar information is more believable [13, 16]. However, recent research on misinformation corrections has shown that corrections, which explicitly repeated the myth, were more effective than corrections without a reminder [3]. In this research, the authors provided an alternative explanation within the correction, which might be a guard against potential negative effects of repetitions. Likewise, Swire et al. [17] found that corrections that repeated a myth were more effective when they provided a more detailed refutation than when they simply negated it.

Hence, there seems to be scientific consensus that corrections of false information should include more than a simple negation; however, it is less clear how detailed a correction should be and what kind of details it should hold in order to reduce the belief in false information and not to enhance its persistence – especially when a statement is completely fabricated and does not include a cause-effect relationship that can be countered with an alternative explanation.

In this regard, it seems likely that the influence of a corrective message does not depend on how long it is per se, but rather on whether the arguments or narratives presented are plausible and attractive to the readers. Against this background, we assume that corrective messages that include reasoned counter-narratives are more effective in generating correct beliefs and less personal concerns regarding the topic of the disinformation than simple retractions without these kinds of counter-arguments. Moreover, we examine the role of perceived credibility of the correction in this relationship.

H1: More detailed corrections are more effective in reducing misperceptions than simple retractions.

H1a: More detailed corrections lead to lower beliefs in disinformation.
H1b. More detailed corrections lead to a higher recollection of facts.

H2: More detailed corrections lead to lower concerns regarding the topic addressed in the disinformation than simple retractions.
RQ1: Does the perceived credibility of the correction mediate the influence of correction type on remembered facts and concerns reading the disinformation topic?

2.2 Timing of the Correction

In addition, it seems relevant to investigate how different correction formats perform in reducing misbeliefs when presented together with the false statement or belated. This would, for example, be relevant for scholars working on automated systems for detecting disinformation, as these might be able to tag and correct disinformation directly in a user's browser application. Moreover, insights on the effects of immediate vs. belated processing of corrections could be used to derive practical implications for the dissemination and display of corrective messages on social media platforms, such as Facebook and Twitter.

Except for the initial work by Johnson and Seifert [7], which found no differences in participants' inferences based on misinformation for when they read the correction directly following misinformation or belated in a story, there is very little research on the effect of the time the correction is processed related to the processing of the false information. One exception is the work by Garrett and Weeks [5] on the effects of real-time corrections. In their experiment, they found that a correction in real-time was modestly more effective than a delayed correction – although the effect was only found for individuals whose prior attitude rejected the false claim.

One assumption, however, for why corrections that are presented separately after false information has already been processed fail to dissolve the influence of false information might be that it is hard for readers to connect the separate pieces of information and to actually override previously read false information. In this regard, research has argued that explicit reminders that highlight the discrepancy between false and corrected information can reduce the continued influence effect [3]. On the other hand, repetitions of the exposure to false information within the correction might increase familiarity with the information that is actually false and thereby increase its believability [13]. In these situations, more detailed corrections that focus on plausible counter-narratives that demonstrate why the information cannot be true might be necessary, while a simple correction might be sufficient to preserve readers from false beliefs when they receive false news and corrections at the same time. When individuals encode the false information and the correction without a time delay, people might be better prepared to discern the correct information and integrate it into memory.

H3: More detailed corrections are particularly more effective in reducing misperceptions when false information is corrected at a later time than when false information and corrections are processed at the same time.

H3a: More detailed corrections lead to lower beliefs in disinformation, especially when it is presented belated.
H3b. More detailed corrections lead to a higher recollection of facts, especially when it is presented belated.

H4: More detailed corrections are particularly more effective in reducing concerns regarding the topic when false information is corrected at a later time than when false information and corrections are processed at the same time.

3 Method

We conducted an online experiment with a 2 (type of correction) × 2 (time of correction) between-subjects design to investigate the hypotheses and research questions. Participants were exposed to mockups of two news posts, the first included false information and the second provided a correction. According to the experimental design, the correction was either simple or detailed and either presented together with the disinformation (directly underneath the disinformation post as a further article) or belated (at a later point in the questionnaire as a separate mockup article). In addition, we varied the news topic to broaden the generalizability of the findings: Participants were either exposed to disinformation and corrections about the prevalence of burglaries or about the prevalence of counterfeit money. The data was collapsed over the two topics (after testing that participants' evaluation of the disinformation articles as well as the corrections did not differ significantly with regard to perceived credibility, plausibility, and attractiveness). The data are available at https://osf.io/nzvc2/.

3.1 Sample

Participants were mainly recruited via online forums, Facebook groups, and the platform surveycircle.com, a platform for scientific studies. As incentive, they were offered the opportunity to take part in a raffle for gift cards of an online store (2 × 100 €, 4 × 50 €). Two hundred and thirty-three participants filled out the questions in the online survey. Of these, one minor person (age < 18) and eleven persons who did not answer the memory task (i.e., "Please provide a short summary of the news information you just read") were excluded. Hence, the final sample includes $N = 221$ participants ($n = 145$ female, $n = 74$ male), who were aged between 18 and 66 ($M = 28.9$, $SD = 9.10$). Most of them were students ($n = 122$) or employees ($n = 68$), and overall the sample was highly educated (most participants indicated to have a high school diploma or university degree). The mean political orientation of the sample (measured on an 11-point scale from $1 = left$, $6 = center$, $11 = right$) is slightly left of the center ($M = 5.11$, $SD = 1.95$) and participants' concerns regarding the issue of crime (measured on a 7-point

238 L. Schaewitz and N. C. Krämer

scale from 1 = *none at all* to 7 = *a great many*) were on a medium level ($M = 4.18$, $SD = 1.65$).

Moreover, with regard to their online news use participants indicated to frequently read news articles online ($M = 4.97$, $SD = 1.69$) and sometimes on social networking sites ($M = 3.62$, $SD = 2.04$). However, they less frequently share news articles on social media (publicly: $M = 1.89$, $SD = 1.36$; privately: $M = 2.58$, $SD = 1.68$), rate or recommend them ($M = 2.67$, $SD = 1.78$), or comment on them ($M = 1.77$, $SD = 1.36$). These items were assessed on a 7-point scale (1 = *never* to 7 = *very often*).

3.2 Stimulus Material

We created two disinformation posts, which provided a wrong statement about a crime statistic (either about the number of domestic burglaries or the prevalence of counterfeit money in circulation). The fictitious posts included a headline, and a short text body (about 50 words) and a symbolic picture. The fake headlines stated: "More and more domestic burglaries in Germany" and "More and more counterfeit money in circulation". The articles (falsely!) claimed that more and more citizens suffer from long-lasting budget cuts in safety issues and that this becomes apparent by the increase in burglaries in German residential districts [by the increasing spread of counterfeit money in Germany and the likelihood of coming in contact with it]. In addition, the text included an appeal to the politics to invest more in safety to impede this increase. Source information was blacked out to not influence participants' credibility assessment of the post. In addition, corresponding correction posts were created in two different versions: The simple corrections basically provided a negation of the prior disinformation in the headlines: "Less and less domestic burglaries in Germany [counterfeit money in circulation]". In the text body the corrections read as follows: "There is currently a false message circulating that the number of domestic burglaries [counterfeit banknotes] in Germany has increased. This message is false. In fact, numbers from the crime statistics show that the number of domestic burglaries in Germany has been falling since 2016 and has fallen by 23% from 2016 to 2017. For 2018, a further decline is prognosticated. [In fact, numbers of the German Central Bank show that the number of counterfeit Euro banknotes is declining and has fallen by 20% from 2017 to 2018]".

The detailed corrections included the text of the simple correction and an additional paragraph providing a reasoned counter-narrative. For the article on burglaries it was, for example, stated that the decline in the number of burglaries can be partly explained by improvements in police work, such as more intensive crime scene work and enhanced evidence collection, as well as by the improved equipment of households with security technology, which was made possible for many citizens through subsidies. For the article on counterfeit money similar rationales were provided. The headlines of the detailed corrections stated: "Security measures show results: Less and less domestic burglaries in Germany [New security arrangements show results: Less and less counterfeit money in circulation]". The correction messages were created based on real news and statistical facts.

3.3 Measures

Credibility and Evaluation of Disinformation and Correction. Participants   rated the disinformation post as well as the correction on seven adjectives (7-point scale from 1 = *does not apply at all*, 7 = *completely applies*). The adjectives "understandable", "comprehensible", and "plausible" were combined to the factor message plausibility (disinformation: Cronbach's α = .80; correction: α = .84); the adjectives "interesting", "informative", and "appealing" were combined to the factor message attractiveness (disinformation: Cronbach's α = .79; correction: α = .82); and the adjective "credible" serves as an indicator for perceived message credibility.

Belief in Disinformation. Participants were asked to indicate whether they believed that the number of domestic burglaries [counterfeit banknotes] in Germany has *decreased* (-1), *stayed the same* (0) or has *increased* (1) in the last year.

Recollection of Facts. For each crime issue [burglaries/counterfeit money], three statements were created: two correct ones based on the information from the correction and one false statement based on the disinformation text. Participants were informed that the statements refer to the information they had read before and asked to indicate for each whether it is correct or incorrect. For each correct statement it was coded with 1 when participants remembered it as correct (otherwise: 0), for the false statement it was coded with 1 when participants remembered it as false (otherwise: 0). Scores for the three questions were summarized, hence, a higher score indicates a better recollection of facts and a lower degree of misperception.

Concerns Regarding Crime and Safety. Eight items were created to measure participants' general concerns regarding the issue of crime in Germany. Each statement was rated on a 7-point scale from 1 = *do not agree at all* to 7 = *completely agree*. Example statements include "I believe that the crime rate in Germany will be higher in five years than it is today." or "The security measures in Germany and the efforts of the policy to provide security are inadequate." The internal consistency of the items is high (α = .93.)

3.4 Procedure

At the beginning of the survey, participants were informed that they will read some news articles, complete some tasks, and fill out some questionnaires. First, we asked for some demographical information (gender, age, education, job, political orientation) as well as their general concerns regarding different areas (e.g., economy, crime, and environment). Then, participants were randomly assigned to one of the experimental conditions. In the condition with a belated correction, the next page presented the disinformation post und asked participants to rate it on the adjectives mentioned above. Afterwards, they answered questions on their news use habits and social media use and filled out questionnaires on the personality traits need for cognition and faith in intuition. These served as filler questions. Then, they were exposed to the correction post and asked to provide an evaluation of it as well. In the condition with an immediate correction, participants first filled out the questionnaires on personality traits and were then exposed to the disinformation and the correction post, presented directly one underneath the other, and asked to evaluate both. After participants (in both conditions) had seen the correction, they attended two distraction tasks (completing numerical series and a word search task), which each was set to three minutes. Then, they answered the questions measuring their concerns regarding crime and safety, their belief in disinformation, for which they were able to provide an explanation for their assessment in an open text box, and answered the factual statements. At the end, they had the opportunity to take part in a raffle for gift cards and were debriefed. The procedure of the study was approved by the local ethical review board (ethics committee of the division of Computer Science and Applied Cognitive Sciences at the Faculty of Engineering, University of Duisburg-Essen).

4 Results

4.1 Effects on Misperceptions

H1 states that more detailed corrections lead to lower misperceptions than simple retractions and H3 proposes that more detailed corrections are particularly more effective in reducing misperceptions when false information is corrected belated.

To test whether participants' belief in disinformation (H1a) differed between the simple vs. detailed correction condition, we conducted a chi-square test. The results show that there was no significant association between the type of correction and whether participants' rather believed in the false information, the correction, or neither of both, $\chi^2(2) = 2.40$, $p = .302$. Overall, $n = 134$ persons (simple: $n = 62$, detailed: $n = 72$) believed the correction, $n = 25$ (simple: $n = 12$, detailed: $n = 13$) believed the disinformation, and $n = 62$ persons (simple: $n = 36$, detailed: $n = 26$) showed neither a belief in the false information nor in the correction (i.e. they indicated to believe that the number of domestic burglaries /counterfeit banknotes stayed the same). Hence, H1a has to be rejected.

In addition, we run loglinear analysis to test whether there is a significant relationship between the three variables type of correction, belief in disinformation, and time of correction (H3a). We found no significant two-way or three-way interactions; hence, H3a is not supported either.

With regard to the recollection of facts (H1b and H3b), an analysis of variance (ANOVA) revealed a significant effect of the type of correction, $F (1, 217) = 5.28$, $p = .023$, $\eta^2 p = .02$. In line with H1b, participants exposed to a more detailed correction evaluated more statements correctly $(M = 2.36, SD = 0.94)$ than participants exposed to a simple correction $(M = 2.05, SD = 1.14)$.

Moreover, the analysis revealed a significant interaction between type and time of correction, $F (1, 217) = 10.61$, $p = .001$, $\eta^2 p = .05$, which shows that more detailed corrections led to a better recollection of facts than simple corrections, especially when corrections are presented on the same page with the false information (see Fig. 1). It has to be noted that the Levine's test revealed unequal homogeneity of variance in the variable recollection of facts; hence, results should be interpreted with caution. Since the interaction of correction type and time shows a pattern other than expected, H3b is not supported by the data. Instead of showing that detailed corrections are especially influential when presented belatedly, they seem to be particularly more effective when presented together with the false information.

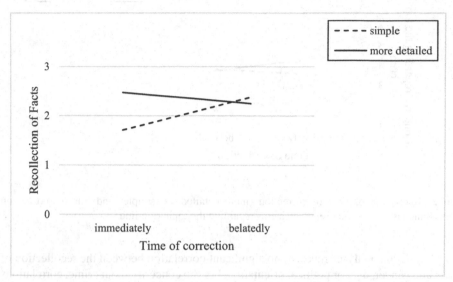

Fig. 1. Interaction of type of correction (more detailed vs. simple) and time of correction (simultaneously vs. belatedly) on the recollection of facts.

4.2 Effects on Concerns Regarding the Topic of Crime

H2 stated that more detailed corrections lead to lower concerns regarding the topic and H4 proposed more detailed corrections are particularly more effective in reducing concerns regarding the topic when false information is corrected at a later time than when false information and corrections are processed at the same time. To test these hypotheses, a two-way ANOVA was conducted, which revealed a marginally significant effect of the type of correction (on the 10% level of significance), $F(1, 217) = 3.88, p = .050$, $\eta^2 p = .02$, and a significant interaction effect of type and time of correction, $F(1, 217) = 6.78, p = .010, \eta^2 p = .03$. The main effect of correction time was not significant. Other than expected, participants exposed to a detailed correction had higher concerns regarding the topic of crime ($M = 4.05, SD = 1.42$) than participants exposed to simple corrections ($M = 3.68, SD = 1.44$). Hence, H2 has to be rejected by this finding. Partly in line with H4, the interaction shows that participants exposed to detailed corrections had lower concerns when the correction was read at a later time; however, the level of detail in the correction seems to make a significant difference only when the correction is presented directly with the disinformation (see Fig. 2).

To explore potential influences of demographical variables and political orientation on the findings, we conducted additional analyses: First, we tested for significant correlations between the recollection of facts as well as the concerns about the topic of crime and the variables age, gender, and political orientation.

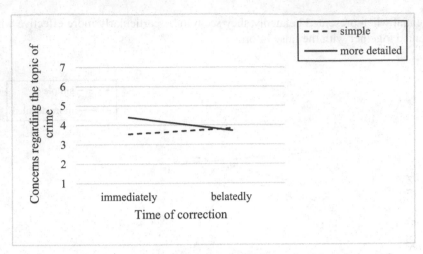

Fig. 2. Interaction of type of correction (more detailed vs. simple) and time of correction (simultaneously vs. belatedly) on concerns regarding the topic of crime.

Correlation analyses revealed no significant correlation between the recollection of facts and gender, age, or political orientation. For the concerns about crime, correlations with gender and age were not significant, but we found a significant positive correlation between concerns and political orientation (Person's $r = .528$, $p < .001$): People with higher concerns had a more right-wing political orientation.

Since this correlation was highly significant, we calculated an additional analysis of covariance (ANCOVA) to investigate the effects of the type and time of the correction on the concerns about the topic of crime, whilst controlling for political orientation, which was included as a covariate. The analysis revealed that the effect of the type of correction on concerns about the topic of crime, $F(1, 216) = 2.63$, $p = .106$, $\eta^2 p = .01$, and the interaction effect of correction type and time, $F(1, 216) = 3.90$, $p = .050$, $\eta^2 p = .02$, were slightly reduced.

To investigate Research Question 1, we conducted two mediation analyses to explore whether the perceived credibility of the correction mediates the effect of correction type on (1) participants' recollection of facts as well as on (2) their concerns regarding the topic of crime. The PROCESS macro for SPSS developed by Hayes [6] was used to conduct the analyses. We used 5000 bootstraps and a 95% level of confidence for all confidence intervals (CI). The results of the analysis for the recollection of facts revealed a significant effect of type of correction on the mediator, $b = .54$, $SE_b = .20$, $t = 2.65$, $p = .009$, and a significant effect of the mediator on the recollection of facts, $b = .15$, $SE_b = .05$, $t = 3.30$, $p = .001$. Moreover, a significant indirect effect of correction type, $b = .08$, $SE_b = .05$, CI [.0111, .1903], on the recollection of facts through perceived credibility of the correction was found. This indicates that more detailed arguments are only recalled when they are credible.

For the outcome variable concerns regarding the topic of crime, the mediation analysis revealed a non-significant effect of the mediator on concerns regarding the topic of crime, $b = -.11$, $SE_b = .06$, $t = -1.69$, $p = .092$. Moreover, we found no significant indirect effect of correction type, $b = -.06$, $SE_b = .04$, CI $[-.1628, .0160]$, on concerns regarding the topic through perceived credibility of the correction.

5 Discussion

The study is situated in the current debate of best solutions to debunk disinformation and aimed to specifically test the effect of level of detail when using corrective messages. Particularly, we address the conditions under which detailed corrective messages are especially influential. Based on previous work on misinformation corrections (e.g., [3]), we derived the assumption that detailed information is especially helpful when it is presented belated, while when presented in parallel with the disinformation it might be sufficient if it is short. As we were especially interested in the interaction effect, we employed a 2 × 2 between subjects experimental setting, in which we varied both, level of detail of the correction as well as timing in the sense of whether the correction was presented immediately or belated.

Results concerning the main effect of detailedness show that its impact is mixed. On the one hand, as expected and as derived from Swire et al. [17], participants remember more facts correctly when the correction is more detailed. However, there was no effect on belief in misinformation and no effect on attitudes (in the sense of concerns about the broader topic of the misleading information). On the contrary, if at all, we found a tendency that more detailed corrections lead to greater concerns. Especially the difference between facts remembered and concerns is interesting. Additional calculations show that the two variables are not correlated ($r = -.075$) – implying that the knowledge of correct facts is not necessarily related to personal beliefs. The finding that more detailed corrections lead to knowing more correct facts but not to less concerns might be interpreted as an effect that although detailed counter information is remembered on a conscious cognitive level, this form of detailedness does not help to counter the building of attitudes that are in line with the misinformation. With other words: the more detailed the information is, the better it reaches people on a cognitive, fact-based level, but that this does not mean that it actually influences their attitudes. Even though people might *know* better, the concern prevails that the misinformation (in this case about rising criminality) is true. This interpretation gains additional plausibility as the mediation analyses show that perceived credibility mediates the influence of the detailedness of the message on recollection of facts but not on concerns – suggesting that information is only remembered when it is assumed to be true, while the credibility is not as important with regard to the building of attitudes. Alternatively, the finding might be explained by reactance. A more detailed correction might be perceived as a stronger persuasion attempt as the simple correction. While it is not threatening one´s freedom when facts are remembered, it is threatening when one´s attitude is about to get changed – when perceived to be forced by longer, more detailed corrections.

With regard to the assumed interaction effects, results are even contrary to what we expected. Here, instead of finding that detailed corrections have a particular impact on the correct remembering of facts when presented belatedly, they seem to be particularly effective when presented together with the false information. Especially when simple corrections are presented directly underneath the disinformation, this leads to a high error rate regarding factual knowledge. Further research will need to investigate whether this is based on heuristic processing. For example, the simple correction might – in the sense of a peripheral cue [14] – be perceived as less convincing compared to a more detailed correction which signals competency. This interpretation is supported by the fact that the perceived credibility of the more detailed correction ($M = 5.13$, $SD = 1.45$) is rated higher than the perceived credibility of the simple correction ($M = 4.59$, $SD = 1.55$). Alternatively, the simple correction potentially draws less attention in comparison to the more detailed one when it is visible directly underneath the original (disinformation) post.

In line with the result that concerns and remembrance of facts show different effects, the interaction effect for concerns shows the reverse pattern compared to the interaction effect for recall of facts. Partly supporting our hypothesis, the interaction shows that participants exposed to more detailed corrections had lower concerns regarding the topic of crime when the correction was read at a later point of time. Regarding the concerns, it was obviously helpful to read the longer – more credible – correction at a later point in time and not in direct proximity to the disinformation.

This study is certainly not without limitations. First of all, the sample consists of comparatively young and highly educated participants, which limits generalizability. Also, although we employed two different versions of stimuli, the chosen topics bear some similarity in the sense that both refer to increased criminal rates. Therefore, results might only be valid for these kinds of contexts. Regarding the results, there is also need for caution: We acknowledged that the Levine's test revealed unequal homogeneity of variance specifically regarding the variable recollection of facts. Moreover, the effects regarding the variable concerns about the topic of the disinformation were slightly reduced when we controlled for the covariate political orientation.

6   Conclusion

In conclusion, this paper shows a surprising difference regarding the effects of disinformation correction on facts and on attitudes. While more detailed corrections (especially when presented directly together with the disinformation) lead to better remembering of facts than simple corrections, they do not help to decrease concerns. More specifically, the influence of detailed corrections on personal beliefs regarding the topic of the disinformation is counterproductive as more details in the correction seem to raise readers' concerns when corrections are presented together with the disinformation.

The results suggest that we have to combat the influence of disinformation on factual knowledge and on personal beliefs in different ways.

Acknowledgements. This research was funded by the German Federal Ministry of Education and Research in the program IT Security ("autonomous and safe in the digitized world", grant number 16KIS0773).

References

1. Allcott, H., Gentzkow, M.: Social media and fake news in the 2016 election. J. Econ. Perspect. **31**(2), 211–236 (2017)

2. Chan, M.S., Jones, C.R., Jamieson, K.H., Albarracín, D.: Debunking: a meta-analysis of the psychological efficacy of messages countering misinformation. Psychol. Sci. 28(11), 1531–1546 (2017)
3. Ecker, U.K., Hogan, J.L., Lewandowsky, S.: Reminders and repetition of misinformation. Helping or hindering its retraction? J. Appl. Res. Mem. Cogn. 6(2), 185–192 (2017)
4. Ecker, U.K.H., Lewandowsky, S., Tang, D.T.W.: Explicit warnings reduce but do not eliminate the continued influence of misinformation. Mem. Cogn. 38(8), 1087–1100 (2010). https://doi.org/10.3758/MC.38.8.1087
5. Garrett, R.K., Weeks, B.E.: The promise and peril of real-time corrections to political mis-perceptions. In: Proceedings of the 2013 Conference on Computer Supported Cooperative Work, pp. 1047–1058 (2013)
6. Hayes, A.F.: Introduction to Mediation, Moderation, and Conditional Process Analysis: A Regression-Based Approach. Guilford Press, New York (2013)
7. Johnson, H.M., Seifert, C.M.: Sources of the continued influence effect. When misinformation in memory affects later inferences. J. Exp. Psychol. Learn. Mem. Cogn. 20(6), 1420–1436 (1994)
8. Lazer, D.M., et al.: The science of fake news. Science 359(6380), 1094–1096 (2018)
9. Lewandowsky, S., Ecker, U.K., Seifert, C.M., Schwarz, N., Cook, J.: Misinformation and its correction. Continued influence and successful debiasing. Psychol. Sci. Public Interest 13(3), 106–131 (2012)
10. Loftus, E.F.: Planting misinformation in the human mind. A 30-year investigation of the malleability of memory. Learn. Mem. 12(4), 361–366 (2005)
11. Loftus, E.F.: Shifting human color memory. Mem. Cogn. 5(6), 696–699 (1977). https://doi.org/10.3758/BF03197418
12. Nyhan, B., Reifler, J.: Displacing misinformation about events. An experimental test of causal corrections. J. Exp. Polit. Sci. 2(1), 81–93 (2015)
13. Pennycook, G., Cannon, T.D., Rand, D.G.: Prior exposure increases perceived accuracy of fake news. J. Exp. Psychol. Gen. 147(12), 1865–1880 (2018)
14. Petty, R.E., Cacioppo, J.T.: The elaboration likelihood model of persuasion. In: Communication and Persuasion. SSSOC, pp. 1–24. Springer, New York (1986). https://doi.org/10.1007/978-1-4612-4964-1_1
15. Schwartz, N., Sanna, L.J., Skurnik, I., Yoon, C.: Metacognitive experiences and the intricacies of setting people straight: implications for debiasing and public information campaigns. Adv. Exp. Soc. Psychol. 39, 127–161 (2007)
16. Skurnik, I., Yoon, C., Park, D.C., Schwarz, N.: How warnings about false claims become recommendations. J. Consum. Res. 31(4), 713–724 (2005)
17. Swire, B., Ecker, U.K., Lewandowsky, S.: The role of familiarity in correcting inaccurate information. J. Exp. Psychol. Learn. Mem. Cogn. 43(12), 1948–1961 (2017)
18. Van Dijk, T.A., Kintsch, W.: Strategies of Discourse Comprehension. Academic Press, New York (1983)
19. Vosoughi, S., Roi, D., Aral, S.: The spread of true and false news online. Science 359(6380), 1146–1151 (2018)
20. Walter, N., Murphy, S.T.: How to unring the bell. A meta-analytic approach to correction of misinformation. Commun. Monogr. 85(3), 423–441 (2018)

Near Real-Time Detection of Misinformation on Online Social Networks

Lennart van de Guchte[1,2]([✉]) [iD], Stephan Raaijmakers[2] [iD], Erik Meeuwissen[2], and Jennifer Spenader[1] [iD]

[1] University of Groningen, 9747 AG Groningen, The Netherlands
lennartvandeguchte@gmail.com
[2] TNO, 2595 DA The Hague, The Netherlands

Abstract. In this paper, we focus on the automatic detection of misinformation articles on online social networks. We study micro-blog posts that propagate news articles and classify these articles as misinformation or trusted information. We do this by extracting a comprehensive set of network and linguistic features and propose a deep learning model that combines both feature types. Experiments on real data demonstrate that our proposed method detects misinformation with an accuracy of 93% in near-real time. Moreover, we compare network and linguistic features with respect to the earliness of detection and combine these features with temporal information about diffusion patterns. We find that combining both feature types is optimal for the detection of misinformation articles in near-real time.

Keywords: Misinformation · Early detection · Online social network · Deep learning

1 Introduction

The massive usage of online social networks has amplified the negative effects that misinformation has on society. To counter misinformation fact-checkers, such as politifact.com or snopes.com, verify news stories and correct inaccurate or false information. However, manual fact-checking cannot keep up with the quantity or speed at which deceptive information is currently propagated. Further, researchers have concluded that correcting misinformation after dissemination is too late to be fully effective e.g. [18], due in part to the "continued-influence effect" [19]: damage caused by exposure to misinformation is hard to undo.

This is why detecting and verifying misinformation in real-time, as it begins to spread, is crucial. In this work, we focus on micro-blog posts that broadcast hyperlinks to news articles, either misinformation or not. We ignore the actual context of these hyperlinks but focus on linguistic and network properties of these

© Springer Nature Switzerland AG 2020
M. van Duijn et al. (Eds.): MISDOOM 2020, LNCS 12259, pp. 246–260, 2020.
https://doi.org/10.1007/978-3-030-61841-4_17

posts. This approach is motivated by the fact that it appears to be difficult and non-trivial to use only the text of an article for detection [27].

Previous efforts to automate misinformation detection have also utilized social context information, such as micro-blog posts, diffusion behaviour and user characteristics, in combination with machine learning methods [27]. Although various studies proved that these features are effective in detecting misinformation after dissemination, only a few studies applied these features to early detection [25]. In this paper, we focus on the effectiveness of network and linguistic features for near real-time detection of misinformation.

Network features are extracted from the information diffusion networks that we deduced from social interactions and include diffusion patterns, user characteristics and social bot indicators, while linguistic features are extracted from micro-blog posts. We study the performance of network and linguistic features when combined with temporal information and propose a deep learning model that combines both feature groups.

The main contribution of this paper consists of tweet volume-independent detection of misinformation in near real-time. Specifically:

- We propose a new method for detecting misinformation articles in near real-time with high accuracy, by combining linguistic and network features that are extracted from an online social network.
- We show the relative strength of network and linguistic features for discriminating misinformation from trusted articles for various detection deadlines, i.e. time after a hyperlink to a news article is broadcast.
- We contribute a novel Twitter dataset that includes tweets related to misinformation and trusted political news articles. The dataset consists of 1300 political related articles and can be used to reconstruct the dissemination of news articles on Twitter.[1]

The rest of this paper is organized as follows. Section 2 presents the relationship to existing work. In Sect. 3 we formulate the problem in detail and Sect. 4 explains our approach. Section 5 describes the experiments we conducted and discusses the results. Finally, in Sect. 6 we draw conclusions and present ideas for future work.

2   Related Work

Online social networks have been investigated extensively for linguistic and network features. Linguistic features are usually extracted from micro-blog posts that propagate misinformation. In [2] a comprehensive set of sentiment words, hashtags, emoticons, orthography and topic related features was successfully used to detect tweets that contain misinformation. In [32], word embeddings techniques were utilized to create linguistic features and combined this with deep learning methods for classification.

---

[1] The dataset is available at https://github.com/lennartvandeguchte/Near-real-time-misinformation-detection.

Previous research has found that misinformation spreads significantly farther, faster, deeper, and more broadly within networks than truthful information [31], in part because of active propagation by social bots [7]. This information is utilized to model the temporal characteristics of news diffusion using propagation paths or diffusion networks. In [16], structural and temporal features were extracted from diffusion networks to successfully detect misinformation on Twitter. It was found that adding linguistic features improved performances.

In [29], linguistic models were studied to classify suspicious tweets and combined this with network features. Linguistic features consisted of syntax, semantic cues, and document embeddings while the network features represented some simple user interactions. It was found that adding network features outperformed all linguistic models and, besides, utilizing a recurrent or convolutional neural network as classifier was better compared to logistic regression. However, these features were extracted after misinformation was already propagated through the network.

Few studies investigated the effectiveness of linguistic and network features over different time windows. In [15], a comprehensive set of linguistic, network, user, and temporal features was evaluated for time windows from 3 till 56 days. They showed that the effectiveness of temporal and network features increases over time while that of linguistic features stayed the same. However, linguistic features outperformed all other feature groups for the smallest time window (3 days). Another interesting finding is that a combination of all features was optimal for the largest time window while for the smallest time window this model was outperformed by a combination of user and linguistic features. The results are evidence that optimal feature selection may depend on the targeted detection time.

Recently, some studies focused on the early detection of misinformation [9]. In [3], linguistic features from a sequence of micro-blog posts are combined with a recurrent neural network that integrates a soft attention mechanism and successfully detects misinformation in an earlier stage. Other research also utilize recurrent neural networks to capture temporal information from propagation paths and combine this with other features such as user characteristics [20] or linguistic content [21]. These deep learning models have shown to outperform competitive methods and detect misinformation in an earlier stage. A limitation of these models is that the earliness of detection depends on the length of the propagation path (e.g. number of retweets). This means that only with abundant data at an early stage of dissemination these models are suitable for early detection. For example, in [20] it has been shown that the proposed model can detect misinformation after 5 min with 92% accuracy, however, to do this they need 40 tweets. Since propagation paths vary in size this approach does not always detect misinformation in 5 min.

A study similar to our current approach where near real-time detection is being investigated along with the relative contribution of different feature sets was carried out in [30]. In this study the detection accuracy was measured as a function of latency for temporal and non-temporal models when using linguistic, user or propagation features. The results showed that when time passed the temporal model and propagation features became stronger while for real-time detection non-temporal and linguistic features slightly outperformed the others, though not very accurate.

3 Problem Statement

We investigate in this paper if near real-time detection is possible by analyzing the linguistic, network and temporal properties of micro-blog posts. To study this we formulate the detection of misinformation as a supervised binary classification problem in which misinformation and trusted articles are being discriminated. An article (A) is represented by the stream of messages (m_t) that post or share this article over time (t): $A(t) = \{m_0, m_1, ..., m_t\}$. For the early classification of an article only a subset of the messages (A_s) is available which depends on the detection deadline (T). A later detection deadline might improve the results since there is more data available but affects the earliness of detection. To find out if there is an optimal moment in time to balance the trade-off between earliness and effectiveness we vary with T.

In contrast with [30], we use different data, features, and classification models and present actual instead of relative detection times. In general, it is difficult to compare different detection approaches because shared datasets are lacking. To overcome this problem, we constructed an up-to-date dataset and make it available to the research community.[2]

4 Approach

4.1 Construction of a Novel Dataset

In line with the majority of research on early misinformation detection we use Twitter data to evaluate our algorithm. The Twitter policy only allows to publish tweet IDs and to reconstruct a data set Twitter's API should be used. However, since Twitter has started to actively remove suspicious accounts and tweets in 2018[3] it has become impossible to fully reconstruct these data sets. Moreover, because the production and dissemination of misinformation is constantly changing detection algorithms should be evaluated using up-to-date data. Therefore we constructed a novel Twitter data set by making use of two publicly available tools:

- Hoaxy [26], for determining whether news content consists of misinformation.
- NewsAnalyzer [1], for scraping trusted news sources.

---

[2] The dataset is available at https://github.com/lennartvandeguchte/Near-real-time-misinformation-detection.

[3] https://www.nytimes.com/2018/07/11/technology/twitter-fake-followers.html.

Since misinformation detection is topic-dependent and over-represented in political news [31] we decided to validate our research by only collecting political-related misinformation articles.

Hoaxy combines web scraping, web syndication and Twitter APIs to collect and analyse misinformation articles. To do this it makes use of a comprehensive list of 120 low-credibility sources in the U.S which is compiled and published by reputable news and fact-checking organizations. These sources are known for frequently publishing hoaxes, rumors, false news, and conspiracy theories, but may also publish accurate rapports.[4] By utilizing the articles URLs Hoaxy collects all tweets that include these URLs. NewsAnalyzer is used to collect trusted information and works similarly as Hoaxy but is able to use a provided list of news sources. To collect trusted articles we rely on previous work that investigated the trustworthiness of various news sources from a republican, democratic and fact-checker perspective [24]. A combined score from all perspectives was given to generate a list of most trusted news sources in the U.S. from which we used 9 as input for NewsAnalyzer: *CBS News, CNN, USA Today, ABC News, The Washington Post, The New York Times, Fox News, NBC News*, and *Huffington Post*. After extracting the data NewsAnalyzer categorized the articles as politics or not-politics if this topic was mentioned in the URL, this was the case for 8 out of 9 news sources. For the last source and for all misinformation articles we build a topic classifier to categorize an article as politics or not-politics.

As classifier we used a multilayer perceptron (MLP) and as input features we created document embeddings by using the Doc2Vec algorithm [17]. We used the implementation of Doc2Vec from Python's Gensim library[5] and trained the algorithm with its default hyper-parameters, except for the number of epochs (100), window size (10), negative size (5), and sampling threshold (1e−5). This resulted in 300-dimensional vectors to represent the articles. To train the Doc2vec and MLP we used 2335 politics and 2469 not-politics articles we collected using NewsAnalyzer that were already categorized as such according to its original news source. This data was divided into a validation set (20%), for hyper-parameter optimization, and a train/test set (80%) to evaluate our model. Performing a 10-fold cross validation resulted in a average accuracy of 94%. After this we trained the model one more time on all available data and used this to classify the misinformation articles, and the trusted articles which were not yet categorized.

Finally, all articles with less than 20 tweets were thrown away to ensure that all articles in the data set have been exposed to a broad audience. This resulted in a data set of 1300 political related articles equally balanced between misinformation and trusted information. The articles are published in 2019 in the period between January 1 and August 1. Each article consists of multiple related tweets from which the amount can vary between 20 and 5000. Since we did not manually check the quality of the data this data set can be considered as silver standard. As a contribution to the research community we made the data set

---

[4] We did not verify to what extend these sources publish misinformation and therefore rely entirely on Hoaxy for our misinformation label.

[5] https://radimrehurek.com/gensim/models/doc2vec.html.

available in the form of a data challenge for the International Conference on Military Information and Communication Systems (ICMCIS) 2020[6] and published it on Github.[7]

4.2 Information Diffusion Network

In order to capture temporal information from the dissemination of news articles we deduced information diffusion graphs from the Twitter data. In these networks the nodes represent tweets and the edges show the relationship between an original tweet and a share (retweet, quoted tweet or reply tweet). Each node has a timestamp that corresponds to the time that has passed since the first tweet in the network was posted. By iterating over different timestamps we can now observe how the network evolves over time. Note that these networks consist solely of multiple star networks with a maximum cascade length of 1, as depicted in Fig. 1. In reality, users could retweet other retweets and therefore create longer cascades. The reason for this is that Twitter's API only provides limited data that points all retweets to the original tweet. Though, approaches have been proposed in which cascades are approximated based on tweet timestamps and friend-follower relationships it appears that this process is time-intensive [30] and therefore not suitable for real-time detection.

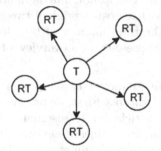

Fig. 1. Example of a star network.

Since the amount of tweets per article can vary a lot (between 20 and 5000 in our data) we transform these variable-length time series into fixed-length time series. This is done by dividing the diffusion network into *snapshots*. Snapshots represent the state of the network at a particular point in time. For example, if the number of snapshots is four ($N_s = 4$) and the detection deadline is four hours ($T = 4$) than a snapshot represents the diffusion network after every hour.

---

[6] https://www.kaggle.com/c/icmcis2020.
[7] https://github.com/lennartvandeguchte/Near-real-time-misinformation-detection.

4.3   Feature Extraction

Utilizing the previous described diffusion networks and tweets we extract two groups of features: network and linguistic features. Network features have been extracted per snapshot while linguistic features were extracted per tweet. The linguistic feature representation per snapshot is computed by averaging over all tweets that are included in the snapshot.

Network Features. The network features can be categorized into the following three categories: *diffusion patterns, followers* and *bots. Diffusion patterns* include the number of nodes (all tweets), original tweets, shares, likes, and cascades over time. To adjust these features to the varying network sizes per article we also computed their relative values by dividing them with the network size of the correlating snapshot. The *Followers* features consist of the number of followers, 'well known users' (>10,000 followers), 'superspreaders' (>100,000 followers), and their relative values. Finally, we used Botometer [5], a state-of-the-art bot detection algorithm for Twitter, to compute bot scores of all users in the network. Botometer uses more than 1,200 features which they categorized as network, content, temporal, user, sentiment, and friend features. For each of these categories, and for all features together, a bot score that indicates the likelihood of an account being a bot is computed. Per bot score we computed the average score for all users in a snapshot. Furthermore we computed two average bot scores for the users that posted original tweets/retweet and used a bot threshold of 0.5 to count the total number of bots for accounts that exceeded this threshold. In Table 1 we presented an overview of all network features.

Linguistic Features. We extracted two types of linguistic features: *tweet embeddings* and *handcrafted features*. First, we preprocessed the tweets by removing the URL (link to the article) and @username to prevent the algorithm from becoming biased. The *tweet embeddings* were then computed using the pre-trained word embeddings from Godin et al. [8]. These embeddings were created by training the Word2Vec [22] algorithm on a Twitter corpus of 400 million tweets. For each tweet, we computed a tweet embedding by averaging the word embeddings for each word in the tweet. If a word did not occur in the pre-trained vocabulary we skipped it.

For the handcrafted features we used a variety of feature shown previously to be effective for misinformation detection (see Table 1 for an overview). We used the sentiment classifier TextBlob[8] to compute polarity and subjectivity scores for every tweet [14]. Furthermore, a group of features regarding the orthography of a tweet was extracted. These features include exclamation marks, capital letters, hashtags, mentions, tweet length and emojis. For the emojis we also used a sentiment map that provide a sentiment score for 751 most used emojis on Twitter [23]. The rest of the features were extracted by utilizing several lexicons. Since these lexicons were developed for formal English words, and tweets

---

[8] https://textblob.readthedocs.io/en/dev/index.html.

Table 1. Overview of all network and handcrafted linguistic features.

Feature	Amount	Representation
Network features		
Number of nodes	1	int
Increase in number of nodes	2	int
Number of original tweets	1	int
Number of shares	1	int
Number of likes	2	int
Number of cascades	2	int
Average like per cascade	2	float
Number of followers	2	int
Number of well known users	2	int
Number of superspreaders	2	int
Average botscores	7	float
Average botscore original tweets	1	float
Average botscore shares	1	float
Percentage of bots	1	float
Handcrafted linguistic features		
Polarity score (TextBlob)	1	float
Subjectivity score (TextBlob)	1	float
Number of exclamation marks	1	int
Percentage exclamation marks	1	float
Number of capital letters	1	int
Number of continuous capital letters	1	int
Hashtags	2	int, binary
Mentions	2	int, binary
Tweet length	1	int
Emojis	1	binary
Emojis sentiment score	1	float
Positive words	2	int, binary
Negative words	2	int, binary
Valence, arousal, dominance	3	float
Weak subjective words	2	int, binary
Strong subjective words	2	int, binary
Hedges	2	int, binary
Assertive verbs	2	int, binary
Factive verbs	2	int, binary
Implicative verbs	2	int, binary
Report verbs	2	int, binary
Verbs of attribution	2	int, binary
Discourse connectives	2	int, binary

contain a lot of informal language, we performed some extra preprocessing. In [6] they studied a variety of preprocessing methods especially used for tweets from which we applied the following in chronological order: replaced slang with formal English, removed integers, punctuation, hashtags and emoticons, replaced contractions by its complete form, and corrected spelling errors/typos by using Norvig's spelling corrector.[9]

To extract features regarding biased and subjective language we use six lexicons that were found to be successful in discriminating suspicious from verified tweets [29]. These lexicons include assertive verbs (assert a level of certainty to the complement cause), factive verbs (presuppose the truth of their complement cause), implicative verbs (implicate the truth or untruth of their complement), reportive verbs (also implicate the truth or untruth but preserve the truth under negation), hedges (introduce uncertainty about the proposition), and subjective words to indicate biased and subjective language. Further, to measure a writer's emotions, we used the Affective Norms for English Words (ANEW) [33]. This is a lexicon of 13,915 English lemmas with related valence, arousal, and dominance

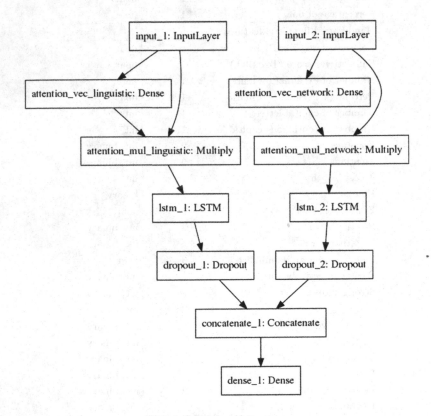

Fig. 2. Model architecture.

---

[9] http://norvig.com/spell-correct.html.

norms. Finally, we constructed two new lexicons with verbs of attribution and discourse connectives.[10]

4.4 Classification

We evaluated the discriminative power of both feature classes using a long short-term memory (LSTM) [10], which is a type of recurrent neural networks. It is well-known that RNNs can effectively capture the temporal dynamics of the spread of misinformation [20,21]. Additionally, we use an attention layer in between the input layer and the hidden LSTM layer to function as dynamic feature weighting technique [13]. Thus, unlike conventional attention mechanisms for RNNs, that compute weights for various time steps, this attention layer learns to weight features depending on the input vector. The advantages of using this technique is two-fold. First, it learns the feature importance by linking input values to the target value (misinformation or trusted information). This means that the feature importance is context dependent which results in different features being important for different misinformation articles. Secondly, it can give a deeper insight in which features are useful in general or for some specific cases of misinformation.

In order to combine both feature spaces (network and linguistic features) we rely on a technique called "late fusion". This method learns a combined representation from multiple input streams and has proved to be effective in various vision tasks [11]. In our case this means that we have an LSTM layer for each feature space separately and concatenate these latent feature spaces afterwards using a dense layer. This model was implemented using Keras [4] and is visualized in Fig. 2. The model has two input streams for the network and linguistic features, respectively. In case of evaluating one feature set the model uses only one input stream and discards the concatenation layer.

5 Experiments and Discussion

5.1 Experimental Settings

The various feature groups have resulted in five different models represent by the following acronyms: LSTM-N (network features), LSTM-H (handcrafted linguistic features), LSTM-T (tweet embeddings), LSTM-L (all linguistic features), and LSTM-ALL (combines LSTM-N and LSTM-L). For experimentation we divided the data set into a validation set (20%) and a train/test set (80%). The validation set was used for hyper-parameter optimization based on 10-fold cross-validation with a grid search. The optimal parameters for our models are shown in Table 2. To train the algorithm we applied stochastic gradient descent with the Adam update rule [12] and Dropout [28] was used for regularization. The number of epochs was set to 100 and early stopping was applied when the validation loss saturated for 10 epochs.

---

[10] The used lexicons can be found at https://github.com/lennartvandeguchte/Near-real-time-misinformation-detection.

Table 2. Model configurations obtained by doing a grid search.

	LSTM-N	LSTM-H	LSTM-T	LSTM-L	LSTM-ALL
Learning rate	0.01	0.001	0.001	0.001	0.001
Batch size	20	20	20	20	20
# LSTM cells	50	50	500	600	50 & 600
Dropout rate	0.1	0.1	0.1	0.1	0.1

To find out how different models perform with respect to early detection and the available temporal information we conducted different experiments. First we investigated if our models were able to learn from temporal information by using snapshots of a diffusion network. We did this by choosing two detection deadlines (15 min and 4 h) and varied the amount of snapshots for these time windows. Secondly, we used the optimal number of snapshots to perform the rest of our experiments with detection deadlines between 1 min and 10 days. For every configuration we applied a 10-fold cross validation on the 80% train/test data set and computed the average accuracy plus their standard deviation. A Wilcoxon signed-rank test was performed to measure significance and we reject the null hypothesis when the p-value is lower than 0.05.

5.2   Results

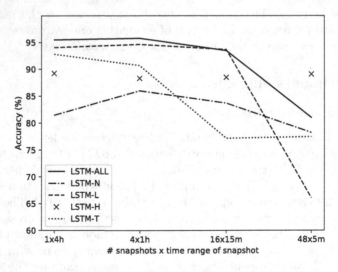

Fig. 3. Model accuracy for varying snapshots and a detection deadline of 4 h.

Snapshots. The performance of all models with a detection deadline of 4 h and varying amounts of snapshots is shown in Fig. 3. We observe that the accuracy of most models decreases with a larger number of snapshots except for LSTM-N. The network features can take advantage of the temporal information and show an increase in accuracy when the number of snapshots is 4 instead of 1, although not significant ($Z = 13.0, p = 0.138$). For higher amounts of snapshots the performance of all models degrades strongly. We repeated this experiment for a detection deadline of 15 min and found similar results, as shown in Table 3. Since no significant improvement was found when using multiple snapshots we performed the remaining experiments using only 1 snapshot.

Detection Deadlines. Figure 4 shows how the different models perform for ascending detection deadlines. We find that LSTM-ALL outperforms all other models for a detection deadline of 1 min ($Z = 3.0, p = 0.036$) indicating that a combination of network and linguistic features is optimal for near real-time detection. Furthermore we observe that each model improves for later detection deadlines. This makes sense because more social context becomes available. However, we see that network features take more advantage from later detection deadlines than linguistic features, a result also found in [30] and [15]. Interestingly, we find a decrease in accuracy between a detection deadline of 1 min and 5 min for some models. We assume that this is due to an increase in noise in the data when we average over multiple feature vectors in a snapshot.

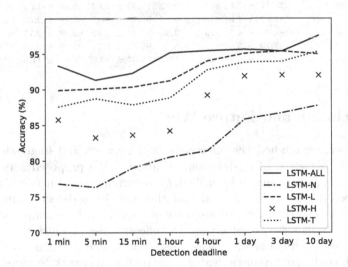

Fig. 4. Model accuracy using 1 snapshot and varying detection deadlines.

Model Comparison. The classification results of all experiments are presented in Table 3. We find that linguistic features (both handcrafted and tweet embeddings) outperform the network features for all detection deadlines. For the linguistic models we observe that the tweet embeddings are slightly better than the handcrafted features for a detection deadline of 1 min but no significant difference was found ($Z = 14.0, p = 0.169$). Between models LSTM-T and LSTM-L also no significant difference was found ($Z = 11.0$, $p = 0.171$). Finally, we find that the combination of linguistic and network features outperforms all other models for near real-time detection ($p < 0.05$). This model can classify articles as misinformation with an accuracy of 93.36% after 1 min.

Table 3. Misinformation detection accuracy and their standard deviation by doing 10-fold cross validation.

Detection deadline	# Snapshots	LSTM-N	LSTM-H	LSTM-T	LSTM-L	LSTM-ALL
1 min	1	76.83 ± 5.55	85.77 ± 4.40	87.59 ± 4.26	89.90 ± 4.35	93.36 ± 2.52
5 min	1	76.35 ± 4.79	83.27 ± 5.53	88.75 ± 2.95	90.10 ± 4.67	91.35 ± 3.65
15 min	1	79.04 ± 5.64	83.65 ± 4.32	87.88 ± 3.45	90.38 ± 3.57	92.31 ± 3.80
	3	81.35 ± 6.45	85.10 ± 3.95	88.17 ± 2.95	90.38 ± 6.94	94.04 ± 3.64
	15	81.63 ± 4.50	84.62 ± 3.01	86.92 ± 2.92	91.63 ± 4.26	93.27 ± 2.39
1 h	1	80.58 ± 3.79	84.23 ± 4.75	88.85 ± 3.45	91.25 ± 4.29	95.19 ± 2.47
4 h	1	81.44 ± 4.37	89.23 ± 3.18	92.79 ± 2.25	94.04 ± 3.07	95.48 ± 2.24
	4	85.96 ± 4.17	88.27 ± 3.35	90.67 ± 3.01	94.62 ± 3.14	95.77 ± 2.76
	16	83.65 ± 4.30	88.46 ± 4.39	77.12 ± 14.49	93.65 ± 3.47	93.46 ± 2.10
	48	78.17 ± 7.52	89.04 ± 3.92	77.40 ± 15.71	66.06 ± 13.31	80.96 ± 6.46
1 day	1	85.87 ± 4.87	91.92 ± 3.17	93.85 ± 3.47	95.10 ± 2.52	95.67 ± 2.29
3 days	1	86.73 ± 4.97	92.02 ± 3.50	93.94 ± 2.32	95.38 ± 2.75	95.38 ± 2.94
10 days	1	87.79 ± 5.64	92.02 ± 3.10	95.38 ± 1.71	95.00 ± 2.75	97.60 ± 1.44
	60	86.83 ± 4.15	81.15 ± 10.26	78.37 ± 13.95	69.62 ± 11.62	92.02 ± 5.57

6   Conclusion and Future Work

In this paper, we studied the effectiveness of network and linguistic features for the early detection of misinformation articles. We proposed a model that combines both feature spaces by utilizing a recurrent neural network for classification. Experiments demonstrated that this model can detect misinformation articles in near-real time with an accuracy of 93%. This, for example, could help fact-checkers to increase the efficiency and effectiveness in which they filter and verify the massive amount of articles posted on online social networks. Moreover, we showed that linguistic features outperform network features for early detection.

To substantiate the performance of our model we plan to perform experiments with different datasets and compare our model with other state-of-the-art detection methods. Furthermore, we have the following suggestions for future work:

- Design models that use dynamic detection deadlines so that a desired trade-off between accuracy and latency can be learned.
- Compare tweet volume-independent with volume-dependent detection models for near real-time detection.

References

1. Brena, G., Brambilla, M., Ceri, S., Di Giovanni, M., Pierri, F., Ramponi, G.: News sharing user behaviour on Twitter: a comprehensive data collection of news articles and social interactions. In: Proceedings of the International AAAI Conference on Web and Social Media, vol. 13, pp. 592–597 (2019)
2. Castillo, C., Mendoza, M., Poblete, B.: Information credibility on Twitter. In: Proceedings of the 20th International Conference on World Wide Web, pp. 675–684 (2011)
3. Chen, T., Li, X., Yin, H., Zhang, J.: Call attention to rumors: deep attention based recurrent neural networks for early rumor detection. In: Ganji, M., Rashidi, L., Fung, B.C.M., Wang, C. (eds.) PAKDD 2018. LNCS (LNAI), vol. 11154, pp. 40–52. Springer, Cham (2018). https://doi.org/10.1007/978-3-030-04503-6_4
4. Chollet, F., et al.: Keras (2015)
5. Davis, C.A., Varol, O., Ferrara, E., Flammini, A., Menczer, F.: BotOrNot: a system to evaluate social bots. In: Proceedings of the 25th International Conference Companion on World Wide Web, pp. 273–274 (2016)
6. Effrosynidis, D., Symeonidis, S., Arampatzis, A.: A comparison of pre-processing techniques for Twitter sentiment analysis. In: Kamps, J., Tsakonas, G., Manolopoulos, Y., Iliadis, L., Karydis, I. (eds.) TPDL 2017. LNCS, vol. 10450, pp. 394–406. Springer, Cham (2017). https://doi.org/10.1007/978-3-319-67008-9_31
7. Ferrara, E., Varol, O., Davis, C., Menczer, F., Flammini, A.: The rise of social bots. Commun. ACM 59(7), 96–104 (2016)
8. Godin, F., Vandersmissen, B., De Neve, W., Van de Walle, R.: Multimedia lab@ ACL WNUT NER shared task: named entity recognition for Twitter microposts using distributed word representations. In: Proceedings of the Workshop on Noisy User-Generated Text, pp. 146–153 (2015)
9. Guo, B., Ding, Y., Yao, L., Liang, Y., Yu, Z.: The future of misinformation detection: new perspectives and trends. arXiv preprint arXiv:1909.03654 (2019)
10. Hochreiter, S., Schmidhuber, J.: Long short-term memory. Neural Comput. 9(8), 1735–1780 (1997)
11. Karpathy, A., Toderici, G., Shetty, S., Leung, T., Sukthankar, R., Fei-Fei, L.: Large-scale video classification with convolutional neural networks. In: Proceedings of the IEEE Conference on Computer Vision and Pattern Recognition, pp. 1725–1732 (2014)
12. Kingma, D.P., Ba, J.: Adam: a method for stochastic optimization. arXiv preprint arXiv:1412.6980 (2014)
13. Kohita, R., Noji, H., Matsumoto, Y.: Dynamic feature selection with attention in incremental parsing. In: Proceedings of the 27th International Conference on Computational Linguistics, pp. 785–794 (2018)
14. Krishnan, S., Chen, M.: Identifying tweets with fake news. In: 2018 IEEE International Conference on Information Reuse and Integration (IRI), pp. 460–464. IEEE (2018)

15. Kwon, S., Cha, M., Jung, K.: Rumor detection over varying time windows. PloS One **12**(1), 1–19 (2017)
16. Kwon, S., Cha, M., Jung, K., Chen, W., Wang, Y.: Prominent features of rumor propagation in online social media. In: 2013 IEEE 13th International Conference on Data Mining, pp. 1103–1108. IEEE (2013)
17. Le, Q., Mikolov, T.: Distributed representations of sentences and documents. In: International Conference on Machine Learning, pp. 1188–1196 (2014)
18. Lewandowsky, S., Ecker, U.K., Cook, J.: Beyond misinformation: understanding and coping with the "post-truth" era. J. Appl. Res. Mem. Cogn. **6**(4), 353–369 (2017)
19. Lewandowsky, S., Ecker, U.K., Seifert, C.M., Schwarz, N., Cook, J.: Misinformation and its correction: continued influence and successful debiasing. Psychol. Sci. Public Interest **13**(3), 106–131 (2012)
20. Liu, Y., Wu, Y.F.B.: Early detection of fake news on social media through propagation path classification with recurrent and convolutional networks. In: Thirty-Second AAAI Conference on Artificial Intelligence (2018)
21. Ma, J., et al.: Detecting rumors from microblogs with recurrent neural networks (2016)
22. Mikolov, T., Chen, K., Corrado, G., Dean, J.: Efficient estimation of word representations in vector space. arXiv preprint arXiv:1301.3781 (2013)
23. Novak, P.K., Smailović, J., Sluban, B., Mozetič, I.: Sentiment of emojis. PloS One **10**(12), e0144296 (2015)
24. Pennycook, G., Rand, D.G.: Fighting misinformation on social media using crowd-sourced judgments of news source quality. Proc. Natl. Acad. Sci. **116**(7), 2521–2526 (2019)
25. Pierri, F., Ceri, S.: False news on social media: a data-driven survey. ACM SIGMOD Rec. **48**(2), 18–27 (2019)
26. Shao, C., Ciampaglia, G.L., Flammini, A., Menczer, F.: Hoaxy: a platform for tracking online misinformation. In: Proceedings of the 25th International Conference Companion on World Wide Web, pp. 745–750 (2016)
27. Shu, K., Sliva, A., Wang, S., Tang, J., Liu, H.: Fake news detection on social media: a data mining perspective. ACM SIGKDD Explor. Newslett. **19**(1), 22–36 (2017)
28. Srivastava, N., Hinton, G., Krizhevsky, A., Sutskever, I., Salakhutdinov, R.: Dropout: a simple way to prevent neural networks from overfitting. J. Mach. Learn. Res. **15**(1), 1929–1958 (2014)
29. Volkova, S., Shaffer, K., Jang, J.Y., Hodas, N.: Separating facts from fiction: linguistic models to classify suspicious and trusted news posts on Twitter. In: Proceedings of the 55th Annual Meeting of the Association for Computational Linguistics (Volume 2: Short Papers), pp. 647–653 (2017)
30. Vosoughi, S., Mohsenvand, M., Roy, D.: Rumor gauge: predicting the veracity of rumors on Twitter. ACM Trans. Knowl. Discov. Data (TKDD) **11**(4), 1–36 (2017)
31. Vosoughi, S., Roy, D., Aral, S.: The spread of true and false news online. Science **359**(6380), 1146–1151 (2018)
32. Wang, Y., et al.: EANN: event adversarial neural networks for multi-modal fake news detection. In: Proceedings of the 24th ACM SIGKDD International Conference on Knowledge Discovery & Data Mining, pp. 849–857 (2018)
33. Warriner, A.B., Kuperman, V., Brysbaert, M.: Norms of valence, arousal, and dominance for 13,915 English lemmas. Behav. Res. Methods **45**(4), 1191–1207 (2013). https://doi.org/10.3758/s13428-012-0314-x

Multi-modal Analysis of Misleading Political News

Anu Shrestha, Francesca Spezzano$^{(\boxtimes)}$, and Indhumathi Gurunathan

Computer Science Department, Boise State University, Boise, ID 83725, USA
{anushrestha,indhumathigurunathan}@u.boisestate.edu,
francescaspezzano@boisestate.edu

Abstract. The internet is a valuable resource to openly share information or opinions. Unfortunately, such internet openness has also made it increasingly easy to abuse these platforms through the dissemination of misinformation. As people are generally awash in information, they can sometimes have difficulty discerning misinformation propagated on these web platforms from truthful information. They may also lean too heavily on information providers or social media platforms to curate information even though such providers do not commonly validate sources. In this paper, we focus on political news and present an analysis of misleading news according to different modalities, including news content (headline, body, and associated image) and source bias. Our findings show that hyperpartisan news sources are more likely to spread misleading stories than other sources and that it is not necessary to read news body content to assess its validity, but considering other modalities such as headlines, visual content, and publisher bias can achieve better performances.

Keywords: Misinformation detection on the web · Multi-modal content analysis · Source bias

1 Introduction

The volume of misleading news present in current media has grown in popularity in recent years through social media and online news sources. In 2017, the Pew Research Center found that 67% of American adults (ages 18+) get news from social media, which was a 5% increase since 2016 [21]. An analysis of news leading up to the 2016 election conducted by BuzzFeed, found that there was more engagement with the leading misleading news stories than real news stories [24]. News is becoming more accessible and widespread than ever before. However, information proliferation has also contributed to the spread of misleading news, which has fostered the advancement of various methods to determine the validity of news. One such method is developed upon evaluating linguistic attributes such as features determining readability and lexical information [13,19,20]. These methods often mimic that of what would generally be considered the most effective of all: reading through the news with the purpose

© Springer Nature Switzerland AG 2020
M. van Duijn et al. (Eds.): MISDOOM 2020, LNCS 12259, pp. 261–276, 2020.
https://doi.org/10.1007/978-3-030-61841-4_18

of evaluating their accuracy. However, with the spread of misleading news, it is unlikely, if not impossible, for everyone to spend large quantities of time reading through multiple newspapers and sources. Of course, the news sharing process occurs rapidly, necessitating effective methods to recognize signals of misleading content. In fact, reading the news body content may be time-consuming, and often people are exposed to news through their snippet on social media, where only the news headline and images are shown.[1] This trend of showing only some flimsy cuts of news with catchy headline and visuals in social media news feeds has made people share such news frequently without having deep reading and monitoring. A recent study by Gabielkov et al. [10] found evidence that the number of news shares is an inaccurate measure of actual readership. Thus, people are immersed in information across social media, which is often shared without reading and validating the content, thus leading to possible consequences of its diffusion.

In this paper, we use machine learning and multi-modal content analysis to detect misleading political news. To the best of our knowledge, we present the *first* content-based study considering the headline, body content, visual, and source bias modalities together for misleading news detection. Because the news trends continuously evolve, we analyze news text (from body and headline) by focusing on linguistic style, text complexity, and psychological aspects of the text, rather than topic-dependent representations of documents (e.g., [7]). Moreover, we consider *new features* that have not been explored before such has to capture emotions in images and the political bias of the news publisher. Our analysis, conducted on two state-of-the-art political news datasets, namely FakeNewsNet [23] and BuzzFeedNews [20], reveals that:

- News headlines are more informative than news body content, suggesting that we can avoid to "read" the news excerpt and focus on other modalities to better detect misleading news.
- By comparing news headline and excerpt content, we observe that headline characteristics are more consistent than excerpt ones across datasets (e.g., punctuation features are the most important group of features in both datasets considered), and, in general, the headline focuses more on briefly drawing the attention of the reader, while a higher number of emotional/ psychological words is more a characteristic of an excerpt than the headline, for misleading news.
- Publisher bias is a strong predictor of news validity. In fact, by analyzing information collected from mediabiasfactcheck.com ("the most comprehensive media bias resource on the Internet"), we show that hyper-partisan news sources are more likely to spread misleading stories than other sources.
- Image features improve the automatic detection of misleading news with the most important features being the ones highlighting the expressions and emotions of depicted people.

---

[1] There are also some browser extensions that checks the source and further add the publisher bias to the news appearing in the social media feed [1].

- It is possible to detect misleading news from its snippet (news headline, image, and source bias) more accurately than looking into the body content: AUROC 0.91 vs. 0.78 on FakeNewsNet and 0.81 vs. 0.77 on BuzzFeedNews.

Overall, this paper contributes to determining effective and explicable multi-modal factors to recognize misleading news, that can be taught to people to recognize misleading news from its snippet and possibly decrease the unconscious spread of misinformation in social media [2].

2   Related Work

To detect misleading news, many works have considered news content (headline, body, image), the social network between the users and their social engagement (share, comment, and discuss given news), or a hybrid approach that considers both [22]. Regarding misleading news detection from news content (which is the focus of our paper), Potthast et al. [20] attempted to classify news as real or fake based on its style as being part of hyperpartisan news, mainstream news, or satire. This study used a dataset composed of 1,627 articles from a Buzzfeed dataset. Features such as n-grams, stop words, parts of speech, and readability were considered in this study. Although there was higher F1-measure in determining the hyperpartisan vs. mainstream articles (0.78 F1-measure based on stylistic features and 0.74 for topic) the research was limited in deciphering between fake and real news (0.46 F1-measure for style-based features).

Horne and Adali [13] considered both news body and headline for determining the validity of news. They included three datasets: a dataset created by Buzzfeed leading to the 2016 U.S. elections, one created by the researchers containing real, fake and satire sources, and a third dataset containing real and satire articles from a previous study. Based on textual features extracted from body and headline, they found out that the content of fake and real news is drastically different as they were able to obtain a 0.71 accuracy when considering the number of nouns, lexical redundancy (TTR), word count, and the number of quotes. Further, the study found that fake titles contain different sorts of words (stop words, extremely positive words, and slang, among others) than titles of real news articles resulting in a 0.78 accuracy. Pérez-Rosas et al. [19] collected two new datasets, the FakeNewsATM dataset covering seven different news domains (education, business, sport, politics, etc.) and the Celebrity dataset regarding news on celebrities. They analyzed the news body content only and achieved an F1-measure up to 0.76 in detecting misleading content. They also tested cross-domain classification obtaining poor performances by training in one dataset and testing in the other one, but better accuracies (ranging from 0.51 to 0.91) in training on all but the test domain in the FakeNewsATM dataset.

Images in news articles also play a role in misleading news detection [3,12,14, 25]. Fake images are used in news articles to provoke emotional responses from readers. Images are the most eye-catching type of content in the news; a reader can be convinced of a claim by just looking at the title of the news and the image

Table 1. Available datasets for misleading news detection.

Dataset	Size	Text	Images
BuzzFeedNews [20]	1,627	✓	
Horne and Adali DS1 [13]	71	✓	
Horne and Adali DS2 [13]	225	✓	
Pérez-Rosas et al. [19]	480	✓	
FakeNewsNet [23]	384	✓	✓

itself. So, it's crucial to include image analysis in fake news detection techniques. For instance, Jin et al. [15] showed that including visual and statistical features extracted from news images improves the results for microblogs news verification up to an F1-measure of 0.83 on a dataset collected from Sina Weibo on general news events and associated images. Wang et al. [27] proposed a deep-learning-based framework to extract features from both text and image of the tweets about news not related to specific events to detect misleading content. Results show an F1-measure ranging from 0.72 on Twitter to 0.83 on Sina Weibo.

In contrast with previous work, this paper provides a comprehensive study of four different content-based modalities to detect misleading political news. Other works have considered a single modality (e.g., either body content or images) or a subset of the modalities we considered (e.g., headline and body, or body, and image) but all these modalities together have not been investigated so far. Also, work involving image analysis [15,27] focused on micro-blog content rather than proper news content.

3 Datasets

In this section, we discuss the lack of a large scale misleading news dataset (especially in the political domain) and present the datasets we use in this paper, including a *new* dataset containing publisher bias and credibility we crawled from the MediaBias/FactCheck website.

Available Datasets and Limitations. There exist several datasets containing political news that have been used for fake news detection, as shown in Table 1. Horne and Adali used two datasets in their paper [13]. The first dataset, DS1, contains 36 real news stories and 35 fake news stories, while the second one, DS2, contains 75 real, misleading, and satire news (75 for each category). The main drawback of these two datasets is that labels are assigned according to the credibility of the news source, instead of via fact-checking. However, a news source can have mixed credibility and publish both factual and misleading information. Pérez-Rosas et al. [19] collected a dataset of 480 news where 240 are fact-checked real news belonging to six different domains (sports, business, politics, etc.) and 240 are fake news collected via crowdsourcing, i.e., they asked

AMT workers to write a fake news item based on one of their real news item and by mimic journalist style (hence these are unrealistic news articles). In this paper, we use two datasets (described later in the section) to conduct our analysis, namely FakeNewsNet [23] and BuzzFeedNews [20] (the largest available dataset). FakeNewsNet is the only state-of-the-art dataset containing information beyond the news content modality and in the political domain.

As Table 1 shows, there is generally limited availability of large scale benchmarks for fake news detection as collecting labels requires fact-checking, which is a time-consuming activity. As reported in [22], other datasets have been used for related tasks, but they are not suitable for our analysis as they do not contain proper news articles. For instance, LIAR [26] contains human-labeled short statements, while CREDBANK [16] contains news events, where each event is a collection of tweets. Finally, the MediaEval Verifying Multimedia Use benchmark dataset [6] used in [27] contains images and tweets instead of news articles.

FakeNewsNet Dataset. This dataset consists of details about the news content, publisher information, and social engagement information [23]. The ground truth labels are collected from journalist experts such as Buzzfeed and the fact-checking website Politifact. The dataset is divided into two networks, Buzzfeed and Politifact, and the news contents are collected from Facebook web links. We downloaded all the available images related to the news in this dataset. The publishers' bias is retrieved from the dataset described in the next section. We merged together the news from both Politifact and Buzzfeed to have a larger dataset to work with. After cleaning the dataset from missing news bodies or headlines, we obtained a total of 384 news, 175 misleading and 209 factual.

BuzzFeedNews Dataset. It contains news regarding the 2016 U.S. election published on Facebook by nine news agencies [20]. This dataset labels 356 news articles as left-leaning and 545 as right-leaning articles, while 1264 are mostly true, 212 are a mixture of true and false, and 87 are false.

MediaBias/FactCheck Dataset. To exploit the partisan information of the news source, we crawled the website mediabiasfactcheck.com, whose main goal is to educate the public on media bias and deceptive news practices. This website contains a comprehensive list of news sources, their bias, and their credibility of factual reporting scores. Here, the publisher's political bias is defined by using seven degrees of bias: *extreme-right, right, right-centered, neutral, left-centered, left, and extreme-left.* We collected the factual reporting score of all the news sources under five categories: *Left bias* (moderately to strongly biased toward liberal causes), *Left-center* (slight to moderate liberal bias), *Least* (minimal bias), *Right-Center* (slightly to moderately conservative in bias), and *Right bias* (moderately to strongly biased toward conservative causes). The credibility score of these publishers falls into three categories: *Very high* (which means the source is always factual), *High* (which means the source is almost always factual) and

Mixed (which means the source does not always use proper sourcing or sources to other biased/mixed sources). We also collected the publisher bias under the category *Questionable Sources*, which contains extremely biased publishers, mainly doing propaganda and/or writing misleading news. The number of publishers in each category considered is reported in Fig. 1. We retrieved a total of 1,783 publishers. The relationship between the source bias and its credibility is analyzed in Sect. 4.3.

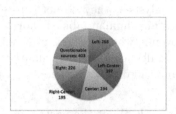 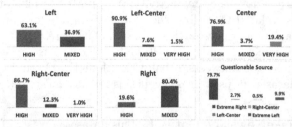

Fig. 1. Number of publishers per category in the MediaBias/FactCheck dataset.

Fig. 2. Publisher credibility per bias and bias distribution within questionable sources in the Media-Bias/FactCheck dataset.

4 Multi-modal Features

We now describe the set of features we used in the paper to analyze misleading political news. We consider four modalities, namely news content, and headline, images, and source bias.

4.1 Textual Features

Several approaches have been developed to extract features from text, from the widely used bag-of-words to the most recent BERT [7] deep learning-based approach. Although these approaches are popular in text analysis, they generate topic-dependent feature representation of documents that are not suitable for the dynamic environment of news where stories' topics change continuously. Therefore, in our analysis, we consider features that focus on linguistic style, text complexity, and psychological aspect to detect misleading news, such as Linguistic Inquiry and Word Count (LIWC) and text readability measures. Another approach is the Rhetorical Structure Theory (RST) which captures the writing style of documents [23]. However, as research has shown that the performance of LIWC is comparatively better than RST [23], we did not use RST in our analysis. Thus, to analyze the text of news body and headline, we consider the following groups of features (we also consider the number of stop words and upper case word count as additional features for news headline).

Linguistic Inquiry and Word Count (LIWC). LIWC is a transparent text analysis tool that counts words in psychologically meaningful categories. We use the LIWC 97 measures for analyzing the cognitive, affective, and grammatical processes in the text. To examine the difference between the factual and misleading news writing style, we divide the LIWC features into four categories [18]:

Linguistics features (28 features) refer to features that represent the functionality of text such as the average number of words per sentence and the rate of misspelling. This category of features also includes negations as well as part-of-speech (Adjective, Noun, Verb, Conjunction) frequencies.

Punctuation features (11 features) are used to dramatize or sensationalize a news story that can be analyzed through punctuation types used in the news such as Periods, Commas, Question, Exclamation, and Quotation marks, etc.

Similarly, *psychological features* (51 features) target emotional, social process, and cognitive processes. The affective processes (positive and negative emotions), social processes, cognitive processes, perceptual processes, biological processes, time orientations, relativity, personal concerns, and informal language (swear words, nonfluencies) can be used to scrutinize the emotional part of the news.

Summary features (7 features) define the frequency of words that reflect the thoughts, perspective, and honesty of the writer. It consists of Analytical thinking, Clout, Authenticity, Emotional tone, Words per sentence, Words more than six letters, and Dictionary words under this category.

Readability. Readability measures how easily the reader can read and understand a text. Text complexity is measured by using attributes such as word lengths, sentence lengths, and syllable counts. We use popular readability measures in our analysis: Flesh Reading Ease, Flesh Kincaid Grade Level, Coleman Liau Index, Gunning Fog Index, Simple Measure of Gobbledygook Index (SMOG), Automatic Readability Index (ARI), Lycee International Xavier Index (LIX), and Dale-chall Score. Higher scores of Flesch reading-ease indicate that the text is easier to read, and lower scores indicate difficult to read. Coleman Liau Index depends on characters of the word to measure the understandability of the text. The Gunning Fog Index, Automatic Readability Index, SMOG Index, Flesh Kincaid Grade Level are algorithmic heuristics used for estimating readability, that is, how many years of education is needed to understand the text. Dale-Chall readability test uses a list of words well-known for the fourth-grade students (easily readable words) to determine the difficulty of the text. We use this group of 9 readability features to measure news writing style complexity.

4.2 Image Features

To analyze the image associated with the news, we consider several tools, including (1) the ImageNet-VGG19 state-of-the-art deep-learning-based techniques to extract features from the images, (2) features describing face emotions, and (3) features referring to image quality such as noise and blur detection. Details regarding the features extracted to analyze images are reported in the following.

ImageNet-VGG19. We used a VGG19 pre-trained model from Keras for the visual feature extraction, which demonstrated a strong ability to generalize the images outside the ImageNet dataset via transfer learning [5]. We removed the classification layer of the VGG19 model and used the last fully connected layer of the neural network to generate a vector of latent features representing each input image. We used PCA to reduce the number of extracted features to 10.

Face Emotions. Images associated with factual news articles typically depict a figure speaking, whereas the misleading news articles contain more images of people with only expressions on their faces. Further, images in real news usually portray people with more positive expressions than people depicted in misleading news images. Thus, to capture face emotions in images, we used Microsoft Azure Cognitive Services API to detect faces in an image[2] which extracts several face attribute features. Among all the features extracted, we consider face emotion (anger, contempt, disgust, fear, happiness, neutral, sadness, and surprise) and smile features. Each of these features ranges in [0,1] and indicates the confidence of observing the feature in the image.

Image Quality. Misleading news images are more likely to have been manipulated (e.g., via photoshop) and have a lower quality than factual news images

Table 2. Feature ablation for FakeNewsNet (left) and BuzzFeedNews (right) datasets.

Features	AUROC	F1	Avg. Prec.
News Content			
Readability	0.622	0.520	0.530
Punctuation (LIWC)	0.744	0.625	0.662
Linguistic (LIWC)	0.732	0.599	0.642
Psychological (LIWC)	0.728	0.623	0.634
Summary (LIWC)	0.666	0.550	0.542
All LIWC	0.751	0.615	0.666
All (Feature reduction (30))	0.784	0.663	0.697
Headline			
Upper Case WC	0.630	0.536	0.525
Stop Word Count	0.640	0.577	0.514
Readability	0.680	0.589	0.579
Punctuation (LIWC)	0.716	0.570	0.639
Linguistic (LIWC)	0.679	0.544	0.561
Psychological (LIWC)	0.604	0.520	0.503
Summary (LIWC)	0.674	0.557	0.596
All LIWC	0.675	0.547	0.639
All (Feature reduction (30))	0.801	0.657	0.756
Bias	0.868	0.739	0.670
Image			
Face Emotions	0.559	0.415	0.431
ImageNet-VGG19	0.534	0.420	0.419
Image Quality	0.551	0.430	0.400
All (Feature reduction (10))	0.595	0.479	0.466

Features	AUROC	F1	Avg. Prec.
News Content			
Readability	0.638	0.355	0.306
Punctuation (LIWC)	0.735	0.453	0.342
Linguistic (LIWC)	0.706	0.416	0.332
Psychological (LIWC)	0.741	0.446	0.400
Summary (LIWC)	0.675	0.399	0.302
All LIWC	0.762	0.477	0.410
All (Feature reduction (30))	0.771	0.477	0.410
Headline			
Upper Case WC	0.700	0.454	0.316
Stop Word Count	0.668	0.408	0.293
Readability	0.672	0.388	0.319
Punctuation (LIWC)	0.686	0.403	0.348
Linguistic (LIWC)	0.639	0.367	0.276
Psychological (LIWC)	0.631	0.357	0.298
Summary (LIWC)	0.621	0.347	0.265
All LIWC	0.734	0.445	0.386
All(Feature reduction (30))	0.794	0.520	0.420
Bias	0.708	0.563	0.386

---

[2] https://docs.microsoft.com/en-us/azure/cognitive-services/face/quickstarts/csharp.

typically. Thus, to capture news image quality to some extent, we computed the amount of blur in an image by using the OpenCV blur detection tool[3] implementing a method based on the Laplacian Variance [17] along with noise level of face pixels provided by Microsoft Azure Cognitive Service API.

4.3 Source Bias

Several studies in the field of journalism have theorized a correlation between the political bias of a publisher and the trustworthiness of the news content it distributes [8,11]. To validate this assumption, we examine the relationship between the political bias of a news source and its credibility by analyzing the information about 1,785 publishers in the MediaBias/FactCheck dataset.

Figure 2 shows the distribution of the credibility score per political bias category (from Left to Right) and the bias distribution in the questionable sources. The plots show that when the news source is moderate to strongly biased (either conservative or liberal), then the source is more likely to publish misleading news than other news sources that are more moderate and declared as left-centered, right-centered, or neutral. Also, we see that *Extreme-right* (or strongly conservative) is the predominant bias among the questionable sources. Thus, we also use the news source bias as another modality in our analysis.

Table 3. Top-30 most important news body content features and their corresponding logistic regression coefficients for the FakeNewsNet (left) and BuzzFeedNews (right).

FakeNewsNet				BuzzFeedNews			
Factual		Misleading		Factual		Misleading	
-0.97	assent	1.77	death	-1.08	affect	0.97	posemo
-0.87	hear	1.02	discrep	-0.71	fleschkincaid	0.86	negemo
-0.86	interrog	0.85	sexual	-0.61	dalechallknown	0.77	smog
-0.84	risk	0.82	informal	-0.61	nonflu	0.62	ari
-0.83	sad	0.81	motion	-0.55	dalechallscore	0.48	bio
-0.83	Parenth	0.69	shehe	-0.46	Dash	0.46	male
-0.61	relativ	0.68	family	-0.44	percept	0.45	filler
-0.54	compare	0.68	swear	-0.43	SemiC	0.43	female
-0.54	gunningfog	0.67	bio	-0.43	body	0.36	see
-0.52	auxverb	0.65	QMark	-0.43	ingest	0.35	affiliation
-0.51	i	0.54	colon	-0.41	gunningfog	0.34	anx
-0.51	drives	0.53	they	-0.40	swear	0.33	relig
-0.50	cogproc	0.51	netspeak	-0.29	shehe	0.28	Colon
-0.45	social	0.51	tentat	-0.25	friend	0.26	adverb
-0.45	you	0.51	adj	-0.25	netspeak	0.26	assent

---

[3] https://www.pyimagesearch.com/2015/09/07/blur-detection-with-opencv/.

5   Multi-modal Analysis

We used each group of features described in the previous section in input to a logistic regression classifier with L2 regularization (with 5-fold cross-validation) to compute the performance of these features in classifying factual vs. misleading stories. We also tried other classifiers such as Support Vector Machine (SVM) and Random Forest, but Logistic Regression achieved the best results. Hence, we report in the paper Logistic Regression results only. We used class weighting to deal with class imbalance. The results for logistic regression are reported in Table 2 according to the area under the ROC curve (AUROC), F1-measure (F1), and average precision (AvgP) and discussed in the following.

News Body Content. The first modality we analyze is the news body content. Here, we see that the LIWC features are better than the readability features for both the datasets: 0.75 vs. 0.62 AUROC for FakeNewsNet and 0.76 vs. 0.64 for BuzzFeedNews. Also, performances are comparable for both the dataset, according to AUROC. One difference between the two datasets is the most important group of features within the LIWC features: punctuation features are the most important ones for FakeNewsNet (0.74 AUROC, 0.63 F1, 0.66 AvgP) whereas psychological features (0.69 AUROC, 0.40 F1, 0.35 AvgP) are the best predictors for the BuzzFeedNews dataset. As the latter has a higher class imbalance than FakeNewsNet (19% vs. 45% of misleading news), we obtain lower values of F1-measure and average precision.

Combining both readability and LIWC features (and by performing feature reduction to avoid overfitting) classification results improve with respect to each group of features individually: AUROC of 0.78 for FakeNewsNet and 0.77 for BuzzFeedNews. Feature reduction consists of the most informative features in the news body content computed by using the coefficients of a logistic regression model (30 features in total, 15 for factual news, and 15 for misleading ones). Table 3 shows these most important features for FakeNewsNet and BuzzFeedNews and the corresponding coefficients from the logistic regression model. We see that readability features appear within the most important features in both datasets. By comparing the readability of factual and misleading news, we observe

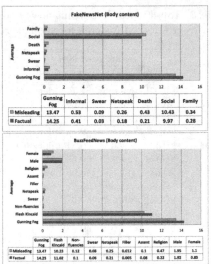

Fig. 3. Most important features for news body content with average values for factual and misleading news: FakeNewsNet (top) and BuzzFeedNews (bottom).

Table 4. Top-30 most important <u>headline</u> features and their corresponding logistic regression coefficients for FakeNewsNet (left) and BuzzFeedNews (right) datasets.

FakeNewsNet				BuzzFeedNews			
Factual		**Misleading**		**Factual**		**Misleading**	
-1.13	colemanliau	1.47	ari	-0.62	dalechallknown	0.35	# uppercase words
-1.12	Parenth	1.10	friend	-0.42	swear	0.22	ari
-1.10	affiliation	1.04	we	-0.39	nonflu	0.17	informal
-0.89	negate	0.67	Exclam	-0.36	# stopwords	0.17	fleshkincaid
-0.83	fleschkincaid	0.94	sexual	-0.32	assent	0.15	WPS
-0.76	# stopwords	0.79	motion	-0.22	netspeak	0.15	Exclam
-0.60	shehe	0.60	tentat	-0.20	dalechallscore	0.15	health
-0.48	relativ	0.57	family	-0.18	colemanliau	0.14	hear
-0.43	lix	0.55	space	-0.11	home	0.13	relig
-0.39	i	0.46	netspeak	-0.10	drives	0.13	female
-0.38	home	0.46	differ	-0.09	time	0.12	they
-0.33	male	0.45	they	-0.08	i	0.12	affiliation
-0.33	nonflu	0.45	reward	-0.08	WC	0.10	ingest
-0.32	bio	0.41	time	-0.08	Apostro	0.09	male
-0.30	Colon	0.37	body	-0.08	social	0.08	power

that factual news is harder to understand. We have, on average, higher values of readability scores in factual than misleading news, indicating higher text complexity (cf. Fig. 3). On the other hand, misleading news uses more informal language and tentative words evoking uncertainty than factual ones. As we see in Fig. 3, on average, misleading news has higher scores for these language features on both datasets: higher frequency of informal words (e.g., 'thnx', 'hmm', 'youknow'), swear words, and netspeak (words frequently used in social media and text messaging in FakeNewsNet, and higher frequencies of non-fluencies (e.g. 'er', 'umm', 'uh', 'uh-huh'), swear words, netspeak, filler words and assent words in BuzzFeedNews. The above analysis clearly shows that factual news in both datasets is written with complex constructions of texts, which is mostly seen in the field of journalism [4], unlike the misleading ones which are written informally showing non-professional character.

Also, misleading news in both datasets has higher frequencies of psychology related words such as personal concerns (death in FakeNewsNet and religion-related words in BuzzFeedNews) and social words (e.g., social and family-related words in FakeNewsNet and male and female related words in BuzzFeedNews).

News Headline. Among all the features we considered to analyze the news headline, we see in Table 2 that, LIWC punctuation features are the best group of features in both datasets achieving an AUROC of 0.72 (resp. 0.69), an F1-measure of 0.57 (resp. 0.40) and an average precision of 0.64 (resp. 0.35) on FakeNewsNet (resp. BuzzFeedNews) dataset. This shows that the headline's features are more consistent across datasets than news body content. Similarly to the news body content, by combining both readability and LIWC features (and by performing feature reduction to avoid overfitting as we did for excerpt features), classification results improve with respect to each group of features individually: AUROC of 0.80 for FakeNewsNet and 0.79 for BuzzFeedNews.

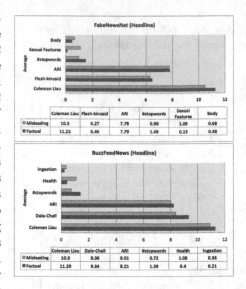

Fig. 4. Most important features for news headline with average values for factual and misleading news: FakeNewsNet (top) and BuzzFeedNews (bottom).

Table 4 shows the most important headline features in our datasets. Figure 4 shows the average values for factual vs. misleading news of the best features discussed in the following. Again, readability measures appear among the most important features in both datasets. Comparing the average values of readability features between factual and misleading news provides evidence that factual news headlines are written professionally than misleading ones. Also, factual news headlines of both datasets have a higher average value of stopwords count, while BuzzFeedNews misleading news headlines are written using more capital letters.

In addition, we see that the misleading news headlines have higher frequency of words related to biological processes (e.g., 'eat', 'blood', 'pain'), namely sex (e.g., 'love', 'incest', 'beauty') and body lexicon (e.g., 'cheek', 'hands', 'lips') in FakeNewsNet, and health related words (e.g., 'clinic', 'pill', 'ill') and ingestion (e.g., 'eat', 'dish') in BuzzFeedNews.

This analysis shows that the orientation towards the feelings, body, and health lexicon is a very strong characteristic of a misleading news headline. Observing such biological words occurring significantly more in misleading news than in factual ones indicates that the former is made more sensational along with more uppercase letters for exaggerations to catch the reader's attention.

News Source Bias. The news source bias is a strong predictor for news credibility in both the datasets considered, and it achieves AUROC of 0.87 (resp. 0.71), F1-measure of 0.74 (resp. 0.56), and average precision of 0.67 (resp. 0.39) in the FakeNewsNet (resp. BuzzFeedNews) dataset. This result further confirms the correlation between source bias and the credibility of the news it distributes. It is worth noting that the publisher's information is independent of the news labels as the former is collected from MediaBias/FactCheck, while the latter from Buzzfeed and Politifact.

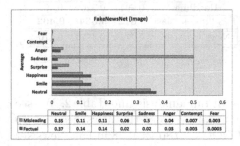

Fig. 5. Most important features for news image and average values for factual and misleading news.

Table 5. Top-10 most important image features and corresponding logistic regression coefficients for FakeNewsNet.

Factual		Misleading	
−0.16	Happiness	1.02	Surprise
−0.16	Smile	0.61	Sadness
−0.14	Noise	0.29	Anger
−0.07	Neutral	0.09	Contempt
−0.03	VGG19	0.08	Fear

News Image. Image features are not as good as other modalities in detecting misleading news in the FakeNewsNet dataset. However, when we use the image associated with the news to determine the news validity, we see that features describing face emotions achieve best results according to AUROC (0.56) and average precision (0.43), while image quality features are the best according to F1-measure. Moreover, by combining all the image features (and performing feature reduction by considering only the top-10 most important features according to the coefficients of the logistic regression), we improve the classification results up to 0.60 AUROC, 0.48 F1-measure, and 0.47 average precision. The top-10 most important image features are reported in Table 5. As expected, we see the face emotion-based features to be the most important ones. Figure 5 shows the average values for factual vs. misleading news of the best image features. Here, we see that, on average, images associated with factual news depict people with more neutral-positive emotions (neutral, smile, happiness) than images associated with misleading news. On the other hand, misleading news is paired with more provocative images showing people expressing, on average, more surprise, sadness, anger, contempt, and fear. Also, only one ImageNet-VGG19 feature appears in the top-10, where we find the noise level of face pixel feature as well.

5.1 Do We Need to "Read"?

Here, we address the question of whether we need to look at the news body content to detect misleading news, or we can achieve better results by using other modalities. Fairbanks et al. [9] posed and investigated this question for the first time and found that exploiting web links within news articles' bodies outperforms body text-based features for misleading news detection. To address the question

Table 6. Results comparing news snippet feature combination (headline, image, and source bias) with news body content for <u>FakeNewsNet</u> (left) and <u>BuzzFeedNews</u> (right).

Features	AUROC	F1	Avg. Prec.
Headline	0.801	0.657	0.756
Headline + Image	0.821	0.678	0.725
Headline + Image + Bias	**0.908**	**0.783**	**0.817**
News Content	0.784	0.663	0.697

Features	AUROC	F1	Avg. Prec.
Headline	0.794	0.520	0.420
Headline + Bias	**0.812**	**0.534**	**0.462**
News Content	0.771	0.477	0.410

in our case, we can refer to the first part of our analysis and Table 2. We see that, in both datasets, we get better information from the news headline to determine whether it is factual or not: AUROC of 0.80 vs. 0.78 in FakeNewsNet and 0.79 vs. 0.77 in BuzzFeedNews. This result confirms and generalizes by using larger datasets the finding of Horne and Adali [13] that the news title is more informative than the body content. Moreover, in the case of the FakeNewsNet dataset, considering the publisher bias achieves a better AUROC of 0.87.

5.2   Can We Detect Misleading News from Its Snippet?

Next, we address the question of whether combining headline, bias and image features, hence considering the news snippet and mimic how news is distributed on social networks, can further improve misleading news detection results. Table 6 report the combined results for FakeNewsNet (left) and BuzzFeedNews (right). For headline, image, and content, we consider the most important features previously computed via feature reduction (30, 10, 30 features, respectively). The first observation is that, even if the image features alone are not enough to differentiate between factual and misleading news (AUROC of 0.60 in the FakenewsNet, cf. Table 2), we see from Table 6 (left) that they help in improving classification results when combined with the headline features (2% improvement for AUROC and F1-measure). Moreover, adding the source bias further improves up to 0.91 AUROC, 0.78 F1-measure, and 0.82 average precision. In the case of the BuzzFeedNews dataset, we do not have image information, but Table 6 (right) shows that adding the bias to the headline features achieves 0.81 AUROC, 0.53 F1-measure, and average precision 0.46, which is better that only consider the news body content. It is worth noting that, as reported in Sect. 2, Potthast et al. [20] addressed the problem of automatically detecting misleading stories in the BuzzFeedNews dataset achieving an F1-measure of 0.46. They only analyzed news content with a different set of style-based features. However, their experimental setting was different from the one of this paper. Thus, for a fair comparison with the methods used in this paper, we reproduced their setting (considering only the left-wing articles and the right-wing articles of the corpus and balancing the dataset via oversampling) and computed classification results. We achieve an F1-measure of 0.58 with the news body content (best 30 features from readability and LIWC) and F1-measure of 0.61 when we consider the combination of the best 30 headline features and source bias. In both cases, we improve their proposed method.

Thus, our analysis reveals that looking at the news snippet by considering the headline characteristics from Table 4, checking the publisher bias and putting more attention on the associated images provides user-friendly tools that can be taught to people via media literacy to warn them about possible misleading news and can hopefully prevent people from massively spreading non-factual news through online social media.

6 Conclusion

We presented an analysis of the relative importance of different news modalities (body, headline, source bias, and visual content) in detecting misleading political news. In particular, our findings demonstrate a strong correlation between political bias and news credibility and the importance of image emotion features. Moreover, we showed that it is not necessary to analyze the news body to assess its validity, but comparable results can be achieved by looking at alternative modalities, including headline features, source bias, and visual content.

References

1. Mediabias/factcheck apps/extensions. https://mediabiasfactcheck.com/appsextensions/
2. Pen America: Faking news: Fraudulent news and the fight for truth (2018). https://pen.org/faking-news/
3. Antol, S., et al.: VQA: visual question answering. In: ICCV, pp. 2425–2433. IEEE (2015)
4. Barton, D.: Literacy: An Introduction to the Ecology of Written Language. Wiley, Hoboken (2017)
5. Chou, C.N., Shie, C.K., Chang, F.C., Chang, J., Chang, E.Y.: Representation learning on large and small data. arXiv:1707.09873 (2017)
6. Boididou, C., et al.: Verifying multimedia use at mediaeval 2015. In: MediaEval (2015)
7. Devlin, J., Chang, M., Lee, K., Toutanova, K.: BERT: pre-training of deep bidirectional transformers for language understanding. In: NAACL-HLT Volume 1 (Long and Short Papers), pp. 4171–4186 (2019)
8. Entman, R.M.: Framing bias: media in the distribution of power. J. Commun. **57**(1), 163–173 (2007)
9. Fairbanks, J.P., Knauf, N., Georgia, E.B.: Credibility assessment in the news: do we need to read? In: MIS2: Misinformation and Misbehavior Mining on the Web Workshop (2018)
10. Gabielkov, M., Ramachandran, A., Chaintreau, A., Legout, A.: Social clicks: what and who gets read on Twitter? ACM SIGMETRICS Perform. Eval. Rev. **44**(1), 179–192 (2016)
11. Gentzkow, M., Shapiro, J.M., Stone, D.F.: Media bias in the marketplace: theory. In: Handbook of Media Economics, vol. 1, pp. 623–645. Elsevier (2015)

12. Gupta, M., Zhao, P., Han, J.: Evaluating event credibility on Twitter. In: SDM, pp. 153–164. SIAM (2012)
13. Horne, B.D., Adali, S.: This just in: fake news packs a lot in title, uses simpler, repetitive content in text body, more similar to satire than real news. arXiv preprint arXiv:1703.09398 (2017)
14. Jin, Z., Cao, J., Guo, H., Zhang, Y., Luo, J.: Multimodal fusion with recurrent neural networks for rumor detection on microblogs. In: ACMMM, pp. 795–816 (2017)
15. Jin, Z., Cao, J., Zhang, Y., Zhou, J., Tian, Q.: Novel visual and statistical image features for microblogs news verification. IEEE Trans. Multimed. **19**(3), 598–608 (2017)
16. Mitra, T., Gilbert, E.: CREDBANK: a large-scale social media corpus with associated credibility annotations. In: ICWSM, pp. 258–267 (2015)
17. Pech-Pacheco, J.L., Cristóbal, G., Chamorro-Martinez, J., Fernández-Valdivia, J.: Diatom autofocusing in brightfield microscopy: a comparative study. In: ICPR, vol. 3, pp. 314–317. IEEE (2000)
18. Pennebaker, J.W., Boyd, R.L., Jordan, K., Blackburn, K.: The development and psychometric properties of LIWC2015. Technical report (2015)
19. Pérez-Rosas, V., Kleinberg, B., Lefevre, A., Mihalcea, R.: Automatic detection of fake news. In: ACL, pp. 3391–3401 (2018)
20. Potthast, M., Kiesel, J., Reinartz, K., Bevendorff, J., Stein, B.: A stylometric inquiry into hyperpartisan and fake news. In: ACL, pp. 231–240 (2018)
21. Shearer, E., Gottfried, J.: News use across social media platforms 2017 (2017)
22. Shu, K., Sliva, A., Wang, S., Tang, J., Liu, H.: Fake news detection on social media: a data mining perspective. ACM SIGKDD Explor. Newslett. **19**(1), 22–36 (2017)
23. Shu, K., Wang, S., Liu, H.: Beyond news contents: the role of social context for fake news detection. In: WSDM, pp. 312–320 (2019)
24. Silverman, C.: This analysis shows how viral fake election news stories outperformed real news on Facebook. BuzzFeed News **16** (2016)
25. Ping Tian, D., et al.: A review on image feature extraction and representation techniques. Int. J. Multimed. Ubiquit. Eng. **8**(4), 385–396 (2013)
26. Wang, W.Y.: "Liar, liar pants on fire": a new benchmark dataset for fake news detection. In: ACL, pp. 422–426 (2017)
27. Wang, Y., et al.: EANN: event adversarial neural networks for multi-modal fake news detection. In: SIGKDD, pp. 849–857. ACM (2018)

Correction to: Disinformation in Open Online Media

Max van Duijn [iD], Mike Preuss [iD], Viktoria Spaiser [iD],
Frank Takes [iD], and Suzan Verberne [iD]

Correction to:
M. van Duijn et al. (Eds.): *Disinformation in Open Online Media*,
LNCS 12259, https://doi.org/10.1007/978-3-030-61841-4

In the original online version of the chapter 5 was previously published non-open access. It was changed to open access retrospectively under a CC BY 4.0 license and, the presentation of Table 3 was different to that of Tables 2 and 4. This has been corrected. In addition, Tables 5 - 8 have been moved from the main text to Appendix B, at the request of the authors.

The original version of the chapter 11 contained an error in Table 2, which also affected Section 3.1 and the Conclusion. The original figure in Table 2 indicated that one community was retweeting from a smaller number of accounts than the other communities. A recalculation following publication showed that the community was retweeting from a pool of about the same number of accounts as the other communities. This has been updated.

The updated version of these chapters can be found at
https://doi.org/10.1007/978-3-030-61841-4_5
https://doi.org/10.1007/978-3-030-61841-4_11

M. van Duijn et al. (Eds.): MISDOOM 2020, LNCS 12259, p. C1, 2021.
https://doi.org/10.1007/978-3-030-61841-4_19

Author Index

Printed in the United States
By Bookmasters